OXFORD CONSTITUTIONAL THEORY

Series Editors:
Martin Loughlin, John P. McCormick, and Neil Walker

After Public Law

OXFORD CONSTITUTIONAL THEORY

Series editors:
Martin Loughlin, John P. McCormick, and Neil Walker

Oxford Constitutional Theory has rapidly established itself as the primary point of reference for theoretical reflections on the growing interest in constitutions and constitutional law in domestic, regional and global contexts. The majority of the works published in the series are monographs that advance new understandings of their subject. But the series aims to provide a forum for further innovation in the field by also including well-conceived edited collections that bring a variety of perspectives and disciplinary approaches to bear on specific themes in constitutional thought and by publishing English translations of leading monographs in constitutional theory that have originally been written in languages other than English.

ALSO AVAILABLE IN THE SERIES

The Twilight of Constitutionalism?
Edited by Petra Dobner and Martin Loughlin

Beyond Constitutionalism
The Pluralist Structure of Postnational Law
Nico Krisch

The Constitutional State
N W Barber

Sovereignty's Promise
The State as Fiduciary
Evan Fox-Decent

Constitutional Fragments
Societal Constitutionalism and Globalization
Gunther Teubner

Constitutional Referendums
The Theory and Practice of Republican Deliberation
Stephen Tierney

Constituting Economic and Social Rights
Katharine G. Young

The Global Model of Constitutional Rights
Kai Möller

The Three Branches
A Comparative Model of Separation of Powers
Christoph Möllers

The Cosmopolitan State
H Patrick Glenn

After Public Law

Edited by

Cormac Mac Amhlaigh
Claudio Michelon
and Neil Walker

OXFORD
UNIVERSITY PRESS

OXFORD

UNIVERSITY PRESS

Great Clarendon Street, Oxford, OX2 6DP,
United Kingdom

Oxford University Press is a department of the University of Oxford.
It furthers the University's objective of excellence in research, scholarship,
and education by publishing worldwide. Oxford is a registered trade mark of
Oxford University Press in the UK and in certain other countries

© The several contributors 2013

The moral rights of the authors have been asserted

First Edition published in 2013

Impression: 1

Crown copyright material is reproduced under Class Licence
Number C01P0000148 with the permission of OPSI
and the Queen's printer for Scotland

British Library Cataloguing in Publication Data

Data available

ISBN 978-0-19-966931-8

Printed in Great Britain by
CPI Group (UK) Ltd, Croydon, CR0 4YY

Preface

The origins of this book lie in a long series of conversations between the editors reflecting their overlapping interests in the overlapping preoccupations, methodologies, and evolutionary trajectories of public law and private law. These issues were discussed and debated in the more formal setting of a workshop held at Edinburgh University in 2011, where each of the contributors presented versions of the chapters which make up this volume. The workshop was generously sponsored by Edinburgh Law School, and warmly supported by its then Dean, Professor Douglas Brodie. His successor, Professor Lesley McAra continued that support and we are much indebted to both of them. The workshop itself was organized and run with consummate efficiency by Lorna Gallacher of the Law School without whose help and input we could not have managed. We also owe a debt of gratitude to those workshop participants who did not hesitate to accept our invitation to attend and comment on the papers; namely, Mike Wilkinson, Emilios Christodoulidis, Chris Himsworth, Chrisopther McCorkindale, and Jennifer Hendry.

The preparation of the manuscript for the current volume could not have proceeded without the sterling efforts help of Mark Boni, who copy-edited individual chapters, and the logistical support of Natasha Flemming and the in-house editors at Oxford University Press. We are grateful to them all. Finally, we would like to thank our families for putting up with so many project-related absences before, during, and after the workshop and in the course of editing the volume.

Cormac Mac Amhlaigh
Claudio Michelon
Neil Walker
Edinburgh, January 2013

Contents

PART III: THE EVOLUTION OF PUBLIC LAW?

List of Abbreviations

BVG	*Bundesverfassungsgericht*
CBD	Convention on Biodiversity
CJEU	Court of Justice of the European Union
DSB	Dispute Settlement Body
ECHR	European Convention on Human Rights
ECJ	European Court of Justice
ECtHR	European Court of Human Rights
EU	Euopean Union
FAO	Food and Agricultural Organisation
GAPP	Generally Accepted Practices and Principles
GATT	General Agreement on Tariffs and Trade
GMO	genetically modified organism
HRA	Human Rights Act
ICANN	Internet Corporation for Assigned Names and Numbers
ICC	International Criminal Court
IPR	intellectual property rights
MDB	multilateral development bank
NGO	non-governmental organization
OECD	Organisation for Economic Co-operation and Development
SPS	Sanitary and Phytosanitary Measures Agreement
TRIPS	Trade Related Aspects of Intellectual Property Rights Agreement
UNESCO	United Nations Educational, Scientific and Cultural Organisation
UNHCR	United High Commission for Refugees
WHO	World Health Organisation
WTO	World Trade Organisation

List of Contributors

Richard Bellamy is Professor of Political Science and Director of the European Institute at University College London.

Megan Donaldson is a J.S.D. candidate at the New York University School of Law.

Oliver Gerstenberg is Reader in Law and Director of the Centre for International Governance at the University of Leeds.

Benedict Kingsbury is Murry and Ida Becker Professor of Law and Director of the Institute for International Law and Justice at the New York University School of Law.

Martin Loughlin is Professor of Public Law at the London School of Economics.

William Lucy is Professor of Law at Durham University.

Cormac Mac Amhlaigh is Lecturer in Public Law at Edinburgh University.

Hector MacQueen is Professor of Private Law at Edinburgh University.

Claudio Michelon is Senior Lecturer in Law and Legal Theory at Edinburgh University.

Gianluigi Palombella is Professor of Legal Philosophy at the University of Parma.

Inger-Johanne Sand is Professor of Law at the University of Oslo.

Chris Thornhill is Professor of European Political Thought at the University of Glasgow.

Stephen Tierney is Professor of Constitutional Theory at Edinburgh University.

Neil Walker is Regius Professor of Public Law and the Law of Nature and Nations at Edinburgh University.

∞ 1 ∞

Introduction

Cormac Mac Amhlaigh, Claudio Michelon, and Neil Walker

The life of modern public law has been lived under siege. It first announced itself against pre-modern forms of political organization and it did so by pushing an agenda predicated upon ideas of political equality (as opposed to *status*-centred forms of political organization), sovereignty, state, nation, and constitution. As modern public law conceived of itself as the *legal* embodiment of such ideals and forms, and not merely a philosophically sophisticated account of politics, from the outset it had to assert itself against private law or what was then simply understood as 'the law'. The dynamics of this interaction also provoked lawyers to rethink the institutions of private law, and the reciprocal adjustments and accommodations between private law and public law drew contested and fragmented borderlines between the two realms.

But if the boundary with private law has been far from unproblematic, the relation between public law and government, and indeed the polity in general, has also been a perennial source of concern to public lawyers. The notion that, after the long ascendancy of collective planning, administrative centralism, and social welfarism, our political, social, and legal worlds are changing again due to the 'hollowing out of the state' and the growth of post-national governance, and that this poses challenges to our conventional understanding of these worlds, has become an important theme in contemporary legal and political scholarship. Awareness of such a rapidly transforming landscape calls into question the very conceptual and value structures upon which public law relies. If we understand public law as the 'part of the law that deals with the constitution and functions of the organs of central and local government, the relationship between individuals and the state, and relationship between individuals that are of direct concern to the state',[1] then any threat to the capacity and competence of our received institutions of public authority clearly creates vicarious challenges to the field of public law. What function and what future has a branch of law whose regulatory object is in decline? So prevalent are such concerns, indeed, that tracing transformation and discontinuity, and prognosticating the fate of the state and its cognate concepts and values has become the inarticulate premise of one prominent branch of contemporary public law scholarship.

---

[1] *A Dictionary of Law*, E. A. Martin and J. Law (eds) (Oxford: Oxford University Press, 2009).

With skirmishes on various fronts and a more fundamental challenge on the horizon, it is not surprising that public law has been conceived of in many different ways, sometimes overlapping and sometimes conflicting. One of the aims of this volume is to contribute to the literature on the various encounters of public law with its surrounding social and conceptual landscape. But there is also a more specific sense in which this book seeks to contribute to the debate. A common theme in the discussion of the many conceptual and political fault lines between public law and what lies beyond it (the private, post-state institutional legality, etc.), is that of loss. If these developments and transformations do result in 'losses',[2] particularly of the 'linchpin of all constitutional functions',[3] then one of the main objectives of this set of studies, which emerged from a workshop held at Edinburgh University in June 2011, is to assess carefully what, if anything, has been relinquished. The current volume, therefore, should be perceived as much as an occasion to take stock of the idea, concepts, and values of public law as it has flourished alongside the growth of the state in modernity, as an opportunity to examine what might be salvaged or offered as an alternative in the legal and governmental practices of globalized states and supra-state institutions. It is a project that can be seen to work in the spirit of Hegel's theory of philosophy; that is, as a search for deeper insight into a historical condition, in this case public law, just as it passes away or mutates into something significantly different.[4] The examination of public law in the shadow of Minerva's Owl, it is hoped, will reveal a particularly lucid picture of the forms through which it has dominated the legal, social, and political aspects of the world in modernity.

An ambiguity in the title indicates the variety of means employed to achieve the ambitions of the book. Perhaps most obviously, the volume, especially in its concluding section, seeks to explore what comes 'after public law' in a *chronological* sense; that is, if global transformations indicate the demise or degrading of public law along with the state, sovereignty, and democracy, then this section asks what can or will replace it. As such, the contributions of the final section of the book explore the possibilities and expressions of ideals and concepts of public law both within the globalized state and in the institutions of global governance. However, in keeping with the stock-taking approach prompted by the flight of Minerva's Owl, the volume is also 'after public law' in the *inquisitive* sense of attempting to capture, understand, or excavate the deeper essence of the field. Thus, both through theoretical reflection and analysis of the practice of public law, the book attempts to grasp the conceptual and axiological dimensions of public law as it has existed in the state context. The third sense of the title speaks to the *sequential* meaning of 'after', which in turn reflects a particular methodological approach to the object of study. A dominant conceit of public lawyers is

---

[2] D. Grimm, 'The Constitution in the Process of Denationalization' (2005) 13(4) Constellations, 447, 455.

[3] Grimm 'The Constitution in the Process of Denationalization', 455.

[4] 'When philosophy paints its grey in grey, then has a shape of life grown old. By philosophy's grey in grey it cannot be rejuvenated but only understood. The owl of Minerva spreads its wings only with the falling of the dusk'. G. W. F. Hegel, 1820 preface to the *Philosophy of Right*, T. M. Knox (trans.) (Oxford: Clarendon Press, 1971) 13.

that in any ordering of legal fields, public law necessarily comes first, given its foundational and constitutive nature, and its close relationship to sovereignty. With public law thus having granted itself top billing, the volume attempts to re-engage with what usually comes beneath public law in the list of credits; namely, *private law*. Yet, while the deep imbrication of the state and the field of public law in modernity has done much to promote the image of the derivative nature of private law and the private realm,[5] we must remind ourselves that this is not a disinterested 'view from nowhere'. In this third sense of 'after' public law, therefore, we wish to challenge this conceit of public lawyers—and their associated sense of the appropriate sequential logic in exploring the anatomy of law—by investigating what the vantage point of private law can tell us about public law. That re-interrogation of the relationship between public and private law may involve postulating the obverse of the position common in public law, that *public law is derivative of private law*. This position is suggested by the co-option by public law of private (particularly Roman) legal concepts, the foundational device of much of public law theory—the social *contract*—being a case in point. Alternatively, such a re-examination of the terms of mutual influence and engagement between public and private may reveal that both domains derive from or express a common institutional or ideational framework, as, for example, in the centrality of the language of rights to both domains, or their articulation of interlocking conceptions of freedom or autonomy. As such, part of our methodology in analysing the field of public law is to adopt the vantage point of its alter ego, thus gaining insights that would not be revealed through an exclusive reliance on the domain of the public as a point of departure.

The three sections of the volume, then, build on these objectives. The contributions in the first section offer a conceptual, philosophical, and historical understanding of the nature of public law, the nature of private law, and the relationship between the public, the private, and the concept of law. The second section focuses on the domains, values, and functions of public law in contemporary (state) legal practice as seen, in part, through its relationship with private domains, values, and functions. The third section engages with the new mainstream legal scholarship on global transformation. It analyses the changes in public law both at the national level, including the new forms of interpenetration of public and private in the market state, as well as exploring the ubiquitous use of public law values and concepts beyond the state.

The volume begins with a vigorous defence by Martin Loughlin of an older and often neglected understanding of public law as *droit publique*. This approach, which traces the secularization of natural law along a lengthy trajectory from Hobbes to Bodin and Rousseau, understands public law not as the positive law of government but as the pre-positive conceptual furniture of the state itself— understood as the embodiment of an autonomous political sphere. According to Loughlin, those who claim to see in the contemporary departure of governmental

---

[5] For example, Hobbes stipulated the power to create rules of private law as one of the rights of the sovereign. T. Hobbes, *Leviathan* [1651], R. Tuck (ed.) (Cambridge: Cambridge University Press, 1996) 125.

authority to private and supra-state sites either the demise or the rebirth of public law fail to appreciate the resilience or the significance of these deeper foundations. Some reduce public law to its positive state-centred manifestations, and so see only destabilization and loss, while others engage in an unanchored normativism which hypothesizes a new post-national legal world without attending to the need for a corresponding reimagining and re-embedding of the political domain similar to that which brought forth the juridical model of the modern state. For Loughlin, therefore, the new public law scholarship is prone either to misdirected pessimism or to ungrounded optimism.

Chris Thornhill's essay also excavates the deep conceptual and historical foundations of public law as a way of understanding its contemporary nature and potential, but in so doing draws quite different conclusions from Loughlin. Thornhill is critical of accounts which look to the political, and its constitutional coding, as occupying the symbolic centre of society and as reflecting a unifying substructure of behaviour and experience. Rather, he understands the concept of the political from the early modern period onwards as describing a discrete functional realm, as a way of dealing with those exchanges within an increasingly complex, differentiated society which possess a collective resonance not easily absorbed and contained within specific sectors. The political realm, for Thornhill, operates through a process of abstraction and inclusion, and public law, especially through the spread of the idea of rights, is best understood as the legal formula which gives effect to this process. In this view, far from being a categorical overextension, and so a denial or a parody of politics, the growth of public law forms beyond the state is seen as a way in which an ever more versatile menu of rights becomes vital to—even constitutive of—the practice of selectively inclusive forms of transnational politics.

William Lucy follows a quite different methodological track than either Loughlin or Thornhill in trying to divine the quality of publicness in law. He searches for definition at the boundary, seeking to illuminate the meaning of public law in and through its contrast with private law. That boundary, however, is quickly revealed as a complex one. There is no single, comprehensive, compelling, or doctrinally dispositive way to distinguish public and private juridical domains, just as there is no such clean distinction between public and private as general terms of reference. Lucy, however, also wants to insist that this does not render the distinction meaningless or without use. Rather, the many distinctions between public and private law map onto a series of more specific and sometimes cross-cutting oppositions to do with different types of actions, goods, interests, and institutional locations, and all such distinctions remain significant within legal theory and practice.

In his chapter, Claudio Michelon is also concerned with the public/private divide, but his emphasis is upon private law as a complementary rather than a contrasting project to that of public law. He looks beyond the easy distinction between private law as the sphere of individual choice and voluntary relations, and public law as the sphere of mutual necessity and the common good. He argues that the relational dimension of private law already implicates it in the kind of associative enterprise against which we understand and evaluate the legal order as a whole, including its public law parts. Michelon argues that in these terms, the contribution of private law is a shifting one, but that its tendency to objectify or reify the other in ways which conform to certain ideologies of privatism need not necessarily prevail over fuller and more respectful forms of mutual recognition.

The second part of the volume explores central aspects of the unfolding of public law and some of its traditional legal and social structures and explanatory categories in contemporary legal practice. Cormac Mac Amhlaigh's chapter connects the general discussion about the public/private distinction to the realm of legal practice. He is specifically concerned that the most prominent and familiar critiques of the divide tend to overlook its resilience as a central ordering component within our legal practices—a resilience that sustains the distinction in the face of transformations in positive law. Just because the division can be broken down into a number of more specific distinctions, or because it may reflect contingent ideological commitments, or because it may introduce harmful distinctions in certain legal sub-sectors, is no reason to consign the general legal categories of public and private to the conceptual scrapheap. In order to illustrate his argument, Mac Amhlaigh focuses on one key and contested area of our contemporary legal doctrine: namely, the state action provision in s. 6 of the Human Rights Act 1998 and its interpretation by the courts.

Richard Bellamy's contribution also departs from the identification of two salient features of public law. In his case its form and scope of application; namely, the regulation of the state and state functions, and its wider role in the justification and legitimization of public authority. Bellamy identifies a tendency to place constitutional rights at the core of the contemporary discourse of public law. This is a move that subjects the way public law constrains and regulates state power to a very particular account of the justificatory role of public law, that of fleshing out and protecting such rights. Bellamy considers this narrowing of the justificatory role to a constitutional rights discourse to be fundamentally misconceived. Instead, Bellamy puts forward an alternative conception of a public law discourse which is predicated on democracy which is legitimate in a way that, he argues, a constitutional rights account could never be.

Stephen Tierney's contribution looks at public law's current predicaments through the lens of what he identifies as its two basic functions; namely, facilitation of and restraint upon the exercise of political power. Tierney identifies a number of challenges which might affect public law's capacity to discharge those functions. In particular, he investigates the threat posed by the alleged demise of some of the central notions around which the modern juridical apparatus of public law was built: the state and the nation. He defends the resilience of those ideas against the overstated claim that contemporary trends towards globalization and privatization render them redundant. Indeed, Tierney argues that public law and its institutions not only remain relevant, but, as his discussion of referendums makes clear, become crucial instruments in helping polities to navigate their way in a globalized world in which nations continue to supply a vital point of reference and identity.

Hector MacQueen's chapter reflects on the relationship between private law and national identity, and on the related problem of the continuities and discontinuities between legal and political nationalism. Scotland provides Mac-Queen with an exceptionally fertile ground to investigate those connections, as the Scottish legal system survives as a relatively autonomous body of law more than three centuries after the disappearance of the Scottish state into the United Kingdom. The chapter traces the way in which the defenders of the distinctiveness of Scots law have conceived of its relationship with political nationalism on the one hand, and national identity in a more cultural register on the other. The lessons MacQueen draws from this discussion are broad in scope and are offered as a contribution to the debate on the role that even a relatively apolitical brand of law might play in the construction of national identities.

The final part of the volume focuses squarely on the chronologically 'after', addressing the problems posed to public law by the movement of competence and capacity beyond the state. Inger Johanne Sand's contribution traces the evolution of public law from its associations with a general will to a more complex and variegated contemporary phenomenon involving state and supra-state actors as well as public and private bodies. She identifies two dominant features of this development; namely, the interaction between law and other systems such as science and technology and the increased use of self-regulation as a regulatory mechanism. She illustrates these developments by reference to the hybridity of contemporary legal forms such as international economic law, transnational administrative law, internet regulation, and the regulation of biotechnology. She argues that, as new regulatory concepts and techniques develop in new and unexpected domain-specific ways, the resulting legal miscellany invites further study.

In his contribution, Oliver Gerstenberg identifies the widespread practice of judicial review of law and policy as a potential failure of public law, particularly on democratic grounds. The democratic problem is exacerbated in respect of supranational courts such as the European Court of Justice and European Court of Human Rights, given that they are not embedded in the polity or political community. However, Gerstenberg argues that a closer look at the practices of these courts and, more importantly, their relationship with domestic courts, reveals that supranational judicial review is not as unilateral or authoritarian as sceptics claim. Rather, the interaction between domestic and supranational courts opens up a recursively dialogical space in which national administrations are compelled to justify particular policy choices in response to supranational judicial decisions. In this way supranational courts force states to 'look again' at domestic policy choices, particularly in the interests of individuals or groups such as the elderly, transsexuals, or prisoners who may be disadvantaged or marginalized by these policy decisions or legislative interventions.

Focusing on the broadest themes of post-national law, Neil Walker considers two regulatory ideas—global public law and global constitutionalism—that are typically neither examined together frequently nor sufficiently clearly distinguished from one another. Both ideas reflect a preoccupation with the increasing density of post-state regulation and the influence of supra-state entities on national law and politics, yet differ in their emphasis upon the importance of input, throughput, and output legitimacy. Walker analyses four possible permutations and combinations of the role and relevance of both of these concepts beyond the state, from the double negative (no significant role for either post-state publicness or constitutionalism) to the double positive (a definite role for both), and positions in between. He concludes that whatever one's view of the possibilities of these concepts beyond the state, the problems and possibilities they frame remain an inescapable theme of our regulatory diagnoses, and even those who are 'doubly sceptical' about the export of publicness and constitutionalism beyond the state must reckon with this fact.

Megan Donaldson and Benedict Kingsbury pick up on the second of Walker's concerns—that of the notion of publicness beyond the state—through a focus on the public law regulatory techniques of institutions at the global level. They address this through an extended examination of one example of global level regulation—the *Handbook for Evaluating Infrastructure Regulatory Systems* of the World Bank. The chapter tracks Walker's twin concerns by offering the publicness of this type of regulation as a counterpoint to global constitutionalist discourses. The authors contend that the principles and standards of global regulation as illustrated in the *Handbook*, by tying together the managerial governance of the Bank with the ideals of the rule of (public) law, seek both to ensure the aims of good governance and to foster the legitimacy of the prescriptions and activities of the World Bank. As such, they argue, the broader regime of global administrative law and the exercise of international public authority, of which the *Handbook* is one instance, indicate a transformative trend in which global institutions such as the World Bank increasingly take on the role of the custodians of the future of public law.

Gianluigi Palombella's closing contribution also attends to a key duality of publicness—in his case 'political' and 'legal'—as it has evolved in the state context. He argues that, at least in the context of post-national law and organizations, the political dimension has received the greater attention, so inviting scepticism towards a post-state 'publicness' given the lack of indications of a social or political context within which such a public could emerge. By contrast, the *legal* dimension of publicness, which he dubs 'public through law', has been somewhat understated, yet offers a more promising starting point for consideration of publicness beyond the state. But even if law can forge a space for a post-national public sphere, it remains necessarily parasitic on thicker political contexts of publicness still domiciled in the state. The survival of publicness beyond the state depends, therefore, on whether a balance between different legal orders, global and domestic, can be achieved through dialogue, and in particular through post-national forms 'plugging in' to the normative power sources of extant nation-state political communities.

And so the collection ends as it begins, with a caution that the juridical successors to state-centred public law remain somehow, and somewhat paradoxically, dependent upon the legacy of the very forms and energies they seek to replace. Whatever comes after public law, we are reminded, can only be understood as emerging from and reacting to the presence or absence of public law, rather than as a tabula rasa on which we can set down an entirely new vision of legal and political ordering.

PART I

THE NATURE OF PUBLIC AND PRIVATE LAW

2

The Nature of Public Law

Martin Loughlin

I. INTRODUCTION

Jurists commonly draw a distinction between public law and private law, between the law regulating relations between institutions of government or between government and its subjects on the one hand, and the law regulating relations between subjects on the other. In this conception, public law is treated as a subset of positive law. The division provides the basis for organizing the standard categories of law: public law is assumed to have a distinctive anatomy and can be subdivided into constitutional law, administrative law, civil liberties law, criminal law, revenue law, EU law, and public international law. Working within this general framework, jurists regularly investigate the way public law is constituted as a set of authoritative institutions, principles, rules, and methods, with the more ambitious accounts also seeking to explain how these various rules and practices form a coherent whole.

Since the latter half of the 19th century, a huge amount of scholarly effort has been expended in providing a comprehensive exposition of public law as a set of rules that establish and regulate the workings of the institutions of government.[1] This endeavour seems now to be culminating in the aim of promoting harmonization across Europe of these rules and principles of public law.[2] But at this decisive moment the fundamentals of the subject are also being exposed to heightened levels of critical scrutiny. Many question whether the standard organizational categories (sovereignty, jurisdiction, ultra vires, etc.) continue to be authoritative, and some argue that the basic framework now needs to be reconceptualized.[3]

---

[1] Some insight is revealed in the monumental survey of German public law scholarship undertaken by Michael Stolleis: see M. Stolleis, *Public Law in Germany, 1800–1914* (New York: Berghahn Books, 2001); M. Stolleis, *A History of Public Law in Germany, 1914–1945* (Oxford: Oxford University Press, 2004). By comparison, the number of landmark texts in the development of British scholarship until, say, 1970 is remarkably small: we need not look much beyond the works of Dicey, Jennings, Robson, de Smith, Mitchell, and the Wades (ECS and HWR).

[2] See, eg, the work of Armin von Bogdandy and his Heidelberg colleagues to lay the foundations of a *ius publicum europaeum*: A. von Bogdandy et al. (eds), *Handbuch des Öffentlichen Rechts in Europa: Ius Publicum Europaeum*, 4 vols (Heidelberg: C.F. Müller Verlag, 2007–11); A. von Bogdandy and Jürgen Bast (eds), *Principles of European Constitutional Law*, 2nd edn (Oxford: Hart/Beck, 2009); A. von Bogdandy, 'Deutsche Rechtswissenschaft im europäische Rechtsraum' (2011) 66 Juristen Zeitung 1–6.

[3] Exemplary of those seeking to bring about what has been referred to as a 'paradigm shift' at domestic, European, and global levels (respectively) are: T. R. S. Allan, *Law, Liberty, and Justice: The Legal*

Presenting a direct challenge to the philosophy of legal positivism which has been so influential over the last 150 years, these critics now claim that rather than expressing a particular allocation of institutional competences, the architecture of public law is best understood as an edifice of abstract and value-laden principles of legality.[4] In these uncertain circumstances, in which the push for harmonization coincides with the claim of transformation, any sketch of the nature of the subject is likely to remain contested.

My argument will be that the nature of public law is unlikely to be revealed by focusing on such contemporary controversies. Although these debates have opened up many issues for consideration, there is a danger that symptoms will be mistaken for causes. If we are to specify the nature of the subject, we should begin by examining the conditions of its formation. And once this is done it becomes clear that the subject cannot be adequately grasped if it is treated as a subset of positive law. Scholars of the formative period of public law—the period prior to the last 150 years of legal positivist influence—were engaged in a more basic investigation. Rather than limiting their inquiries to the question of how the exercise of public authority is conducted through the forms of law, they were motivated to answer a foundational question: how can the constitution of public authority be justified in legal terms?

During the Middle Ages, this more basic issue had been addressed in the language of natural law, a type of law that was regarded as being in some sense 'higher' than—and prior to—ordinary (or positive) law. Ordinary law was made by the ruler and bound the subject whereas natural law—sometimes called 'fundamental law'—bound the ruler. With the formation of the modern world, born of 'the deepest ever fracture in history',[5] that hierarchically ordered world was radically reconstituted. The discourse of natural law was secularized, rationalized, and (in part) positivized as religiously framed understandings were overcome and scholarly thought was differentiated through the emergence of distinct modes of understanding human activity—economic, scientific, technical, historical, aesthetic, and political. These profound changes led to the establishment of new ways of conceiving collective ordering. The domain of the political was recognized to be a distinct mode of existence, founding its autonomy on the concept of sovereignty and on the institution of the state. The emergence of this distinctively political way of thinking had the effect of bringing about a radical

---

Foundations of British Constitutionalism (Oxford: Clarendon Press, 1993); Neil MacCormick, *Questioning Sovereignty: Law, State and Nation in the European Commonwealth* (Oxford: Oxford University Press, 1999); Mattias Kumm, 'The Cosmopolitan Turn in Constitutionalism: On the Relationship between Constitutionalism in and beyond the State' in Jeffrey L. Dunoff and Joel P. Trachtman (eds), *Ruling the World? Constitutionalism, International Law and Global Governance* (Cambridge: Cambridge University Press, 2009), 258–324.

[4] This seems to be the essential point underpinning the otherwise rather convoluted debates in the UK over ultra vires versus common law. See, eg, C. Forsyth (ed.), *Judicial Review and the Constitution* (Oxford: Hart, 2000) and over the broader issues debated by Allan and Craig: see T. R. S. Allan, 'Constitutional Dialogue and the Justification of Judicial Review' (2003) 23 OJLS 563–84; Paul Craig, 'The Common Law, Shared Power and Judicial Review' (2004) 24 OJLS 237–57.

[5] Marcel Gauchet, *The Disenchantment of the World: A Political History of Religion*, Oscar Burge (trans.) (Princeton NJ: Princeton University Press, 1997), 28.

reworking of medieval ideas of natural law.[6] This new anthropocentric 'science' of natural law in turn provided the basis for the creation of the concept of public law. Public law, it will be argued, was formed in the modern world as the jural coding of an autonomously conceived political domain, and the nature of public law is to be grasped only once this essential point is acknowledged.

2. NATURAL LAW TRANSFORMED

In this basic understanding of the subject, public law is concerned with the establishment and regulation of governing authority; it therefore addresses questions of 'right' (*droit*) relating to modern governmental ordering. Viewed in this light, the works of many leading political philosophers of the early modern period are best read as attempts to explicate the nature of public law. This undertaking flourished from the late sixteenth to the mid-nineteenth centuries, extending from the earlier work of Bodin, Althusius, Lipsius, Grotius, Hobbes, Spinoza, Locke, and Pufendorf to include the writings of Montesquieu, Rousseau, Kant, Fichte, Smith, and Hegel.

Consider, by way of illustration, the influential work of Samuel Pufendorf. In his magnum opus, *De jure naturae et gentium* (1672), Pufendorf eliminated all sense of a personal god from the workings of the world. Presenting an account of natural law not as the expression of the divine will of God but as 'the dictate of right reason', he set in place an anthropocentric conception of natural law. By reworking natural law in this way, Pufendorf was able to lay the grounding in natural law that established the authority of emerging nation-states. Following Grotius' views on man's natural sociability and Hobbes' on man's passion-directed nature, Pufendorf showed that although it is in man's rational interest to maintain the principle of sociability, his passions undermine this capacity for sociability. The only rational solution was to establish a sovereign power that could impose rules of sociability in the form of positive laws.

Pufendorf's analysis replaced medieval natural law theories that treated government as a form of moral ordering with a modern account in which the principles and precepts of natural law are formed immanently and within the evolving civil relationship. His account of the nature of 'modern' natural law provides the frame of the emerging idea of public law.

Pufendorf's jurisprudence held great sway across the continent of Europe. After the first university chair to profess natural law was established at Heidelberg in 1661—a chair that Pufendorf was first to occupy—the subject was quickly introduced throughout the German lands and thereafter across many other parts of Europe. This influential body of natural jurisprudence was placed at the service of specific political objectives, not least in challenging those Roman lawyers whose work bolstered the authority of the Holy Roman Empire, and replacing their claims with the foundational justification of the sovereign

[6] Richard Tuck, 'The "Modern" School of Natural Law' in Anthony Pagden (ed.), *The Languages of Political Theory in Early-Modern Europe* (Cambridge: Cambridge University Press, 1987), 99–122.

authority of territorial nation-states.[7] Natural jurisprudence laid the foundations of the modern concept of public law: public law as political jurisprudence.

This political jurisprudence operated according to its own internal dynamics. In order to establish the absolute authority of the sovereign—and thereby realize the autonomy of public law—the monarchical image of the sovereign ruler had first to be magnified and idealized. But idealization of the office of the sovereign was in reality the precondition for its institutionalization, and later its revolutionary transformation.[8] In Britain, the sovereign was from the early days a composite institution (the Crown-in-Council, later the Crown-in-Council-in-Parliament). In continental Europe, it took the form of the 'enlightened absolutism' of the sovereign ruler. In the latter case, which became a common European path, governmental modernization led to the establishment of comprehensive official machinery (by bringing the relatively autonomous—and feudal—institutions of local government into a hierarchical arrangement of government), the officialization of the judiciary (which had previously represented feudal interests), and the development of a separate jurisdiction to determine legal disputes of an official nature.[9] This trajectory led to the establishment of a formal division between private law and public law in continental Europe. It was an arrangement which the English did not follow,[10] but which—now that the UK has developed an extensive and formalized governmental network—has since been accommodated.[11]

From a European perspective, the UK pattern of public law development may be unusual, but it should not be assumed that it is altogether different. Such differences as exist are the product of a peculiar history of governmental development, and today they no longer seem to hold much sway. It might also be noted that whenever political conditions warranted, the British were content to work with the discrete concept of public law. Consider, for example, the circumstances leading in 1707 to the establishment of the first chair of public law in Britain at Edinburgh University. This chair, the Regius Chair of Public Law and the Law of Nature and Nations, was endowed by Queen Anne. It was endowed in accordance with a prospectus drafted (to all intents and purposes) by Pufendorf, and as a reward for the Scots agreeing to sign the Treaty of Union and acquiescing in the newly formed state of Great Britain. But it was no mere gift: its establishment served strategic objectives. Given the harmonizing public law mandate in Art. 18 of the Treaty, knowledge of 'the political Principles of all Laws; the Substantials of the Law of Nations; and of the Gothick Constitution'

---

[7] See K. Haakonssen, *Natural Law and Moral Philosophy: From Grotius to the Scottish Enlightenment* (Cambridge: Cambridge University Press, 1996), 135–45 (Prussia).

[8] See E. S. Morgan, *Inventing the People: The Rise of Popular Sovereignty in England and America* (New York: Norton, 1989).

[9] Peter Hans Reill, *The German Enlightenment and Rise of Historicism* (Berkeley: University of California Press, 1975); Steven Lestition, 'The Teaching and Practice of Jurisprudence in Eighteenth Century East Prussia: Konigsberg's First Chancellor, R. F. von Sahme (1682–1753)' (1989) 16 Ius Commune 27–80.

[10] See, eg, A. V. Dicey, *Introduction to the Study of the Law of the Constitution*, 8th edn (London: Macmillan, 1915), ch 12.

[11] See, eg, Harry Woolf, 'Droit Public—English Style' (1995) PL 57–72.

became an essential foundation for the study of Scots law.[12] Further, as John Cairns notes, 'natural-law theorizing could play a part in explaining the possibilities of the political communities of two sovereign entities each agreeing to dissolve to create a new sovereign polity'.[13] The study of 'how government should be conducted on the grounds of utility or public interest', he suggests, 'must have been made more pressing by the Union'.[14] The broader concept of public law, it would appear, was invoked by the British only when pressing 'reasons of state' required.

During the 18th century, this 'modern' notion of natural law provided the conceptual language through which the legitimacy of the emerging modern secular state could be debated.[15] Natural jurisprudence was useful in part because it formed a loosely structured discourse rather than a precisely formulated doctrine, and this aided its conversion into a type of political jurisprudence in which the exercise of sovereign authority over a defined territory and people was justified in the cause of promoting peace and sociability.[16] Public law was shaped in accordance with Pufendorf's tripartite scheme and which the Regius chair endowment expressed: (i) public law, in the sense of the (positive) rules concerning the establishment and regulation of the institutions of the state; (ii) the law of nature, in the sense of the 'new' natural jurisprudence—that is, political jurisprudence—which expressed the political precepts on which the authority of the institutions of state rested; and (iii) the law of nations, being the rules that were emerging to regulate the interactions of sovereign states in the international arena.

3. BODIN'S CONCEPT OF FUNDAMENTAL LAW

Pufendorf's work is of pivotal importance to the 18th-century debates, but the nature of this emerging concept of public law had already been specified in 1576 in Jean Bodin's *Les Six livres de la République*.[17] For understandable reasons, most scholars have focused on the first of the six books in which he argues that every viable state must possess a single, supreme centre of authority containing all governmental powers, this being the essence of the emerging phenomenon of

---

[12] Francis Grant (1715); cited in John W. Cairns 'The Origins of the Edinburgh Law School: the Union of 1707 and the Regius Chair' (2007) 11 Edinburgh Law Review 300–48, 314.

[13] Cairns, 'The Origins of the Edinburgh Law School', 235.

[14] Cairns 'The Origins of the Edinburgh Law School', 235.

[15] Tuck, above note 6; Quentin Skinner 'The State' in T. Ball, J. Farr, and R. L. Hanson (eds), *Political Innovation and Conceptual Change* (Cambridge: Cambridge University Press, 1989), 90–131 (Skinner refers to the school as 'natural law absolutism').

[16] That it was itself an intensely political exercise is illustrated by the language of Tooke's translation of Pufendorf's work into English (which, eg, failed to draw a distinction between sovereignty and government and substituted nation for state): see David Saunders and Ian Hunter, 'Bringing the State to England: Andrew Tooke's translation of Samuel Pufendorf's *De officio hominis et civis*' (2003) 24 History of Political Thought 218–34, esp. 229–30.

[17] Jean Bodin, *The Six Bookes of a Commonweale*, Richard Knolles (trans.) 1606, Kenneth Douglas McRae (ed.) (Cambridge, Mass: Harvard University Press, 1962).

sovereignty. But notwithstanding that book's originality, the remaining five books are neglected only at the price of distorting Bodin's overall aim. The objectives of the books that follow are to offer an analysis by way of comparisons drawn from history of the main forms of government, to specify the various factors that cause states to grow, flourish, and decline, and then to derive from these exercises certain prudential maxims that should enable rulers to maintain their state.

Treated as a whole, the *République* provides a systematic account of the 'fundamental laws' at work in the public realm: Book I specifies the constitutive rule and Books II-VI specify the regulative rules of public law. Drawing on historical illustrations, Bodin here sketches the 'political laws' of governmental development. Incorporated in his discussions are many claims that have become powerful tropes of modern political thought. These include: power corrupts;[18] the necessity of ensuring a separation of the legislative and executive power;[19] that relative equality in wealth distribution promotes the stability of the state;[20] that wars sustain democracies;[21] that most self-styled democracies are disguised aristocracies;[22] and that 'the less the power of the sovereignty is (the true marks of majesty thereunto still reserved), the more it is assured'.[23]

If the nature of public law is to be grasped, then these precepts of civil prudence constitute essential elements. But we also find important clues as to the nature of public law in the way Bodin re-specifies juristic method. First, rejecting the authority of Roman law, he argues that public law knowledge is not found through a scholastic method of exegesis, but is acquired through historical investigation: public law is a type of historico-political discourse. Secondly, we might note an important shift in orientation that the *République* brings about. Bodin begins his investigation not with an account of the *sovereign* but with the *commonwealth* (or the *state*). It is a study not of rulers but of a different object: the political constitution of a people (or nation). In its various sections, Bodin's objective is to show the importance of the ruler acquiring knowledge of the people. By taking as the focus of his inquiry the relation between the people and their institutions of government, Bodin relocates the power relationship at the core of the governing process from that of the highest power of command (Book I) to that generated by a field of forces (Book VI, harmonic proportion). Bodin shifts the

---

[18] Bodin, *Six Bookes*, 414: 'the power of command in sovereignty has this mischief in it, that often it makes a good man evil; a humble man proud; a merciful man a tyrant; a wise man a fool; and a valiant man a coward'.

[19] Bodin, *Six Bookes*, 277: 'them that give power of command unto a Senate . . . go about the destruction of the commonwealth, and utter ruin of the state'.

[20] Bodin, *Six Bookes*, 569: 'Among all the causes of sedition and changes of commonwealths there is not greater than the excessive wealth of some few subjects, and the extreme poverty of the greatest part'.

[21] Bodin, *Six Bookes*, 422: 'Whereby it is to be perceived, nothing to be more profitable for the preservation of a popular state, than to have wars'.

[22] Bodin, *Six Bookes*, 705: 'if we shall rip up all the popular states that ever were, we shall find that . . . they have been governed in show by the people; but in effect by some of the citizens, or by the wisest among them, who held the place of a prince and monarch'.

[23] Bodin, *Six Bookes*, 517.

focus of inquiry from positive law (the power of command) to public law (the precepts of political right). The subject is to be grasped, he is suggesting, only when our frame of reference is extended from the structure of official legal texts to include those informal understandings that condition the exercise of public authority. Public law concerns all those rules, principles, practices, and maxims that establish, sustain, and regulate the activity of governing the state.

4. ROUSSEAU'S CONCEPT OF POLITICAL RIGHT

If Bodin was the first to provide a systematic understanding of the autonomy (Book I) and method (Books II-VI) of public law, a deeper insight into its nature is acquired by scrolling forward almost 200 years to consider the work of Jean-Jacques Rousseau. Rousseau's political writings form an extended essay on the nature of state-building understood as a juristic exercise.

As is evident from its subtitle (*les principes du droit politique*), *Du Contrat Social* (*The Social Contract*) is directly concerned with the 'political laws, which constitute the form of Government'.[24] Rousseau argues that the principles of a just society derive not from precepts of natural right but from political reasoning; that is, only when natural law has been jettisoned is the space opened up for the emergence of an autonomous concept of 'political right'. Rousseau here builds on and radicalizes the work of Pufendorf, who had sought to de-theologize natural law by relieving it of transcendental moral claims. The immanent norms that Pufendorf had called natural laws are analogous to that which Rousseau labels 'principles of political right'.

Rousseau formulates the task right at the beginning: 'I want to inquire whether in the civil order there can be some legitimate and sure principle of government, taking men as they are, and laws as they can be'.[25] Is there some science of political right that yields the principles that make a governing order legitimate? Although this appears to be a purely philosophical exercise, the final clause of the opening sentence ('taking men as they are and laws as they can be') suggests it is not. This is not a purely speculative undertaking; it is an attempt to discover practical principles of good government. This practical feature distinguishes it as an attempt to specify the nature of public law.

Rousseau's solution is to posit a social contract in which (contrary to Hobbes' scheme) humans do not simply renounce their freedoms; instead, they exchange their natural freedom for a 'higher' political freedom. His point is that Hobbes had erred in treating the social contract as an exchange between being free and being governed. For Hobbes, the trade-off was between liberty (as the absence of constraint) and law (as the rule of the sovereign). Rousseau's argument is that liberty is not the mere absence of constraint: it entails self-government. Political freedom is acquired only in 'obedience to the law one has prescribed to oneself'.

---

[24] Jean-Jacques Rousseau, *The Social Contract* [1762] in *The Social Contract and other later political writings*, Victor Gourevitch (ed.) (Cambridge: Cambridge University Press, 1997), 39–152, at 81.

[25] Rousseau, *The Social Contract*, 41.

The question then is whether it is possible to reconcile liberty and law by establishing a state in which people live under the laws that they themselves have made. Rousseau's conception of the relationship between liberty and law makes the concept of political right (*droit politique*) the key to understanding governing order. The critical question is: how can *droit politique* operate to reconcile freedom and government?

The answer is given in stages. First, contrary to Hobbes, Rousseau argues that the sovereign cannot be a single person or a representative office: it must be the people themselves who, by this act of association, form a collective body. The sovereign is the public person formed by the union of all: it is the Nation or the Republic. This is the principle of solidarity. Secondly, Rousseau argues that, rather than substituting a *natural equality* for subjection to rule, the social contract replaces *natural inequality* with *political equality*. This is the principle of equality. Thirdly, this political equality is the precondition for the formation of a single will: each individual acquires the same rights over the others as is granted over himself. That is, all people must be acknowledged as equals and under such conditions all must work to promote the greatest good of all. This is the principle of equal liberty, otherwise known as the 'general will' or will of the sovereign. The general will is not a restriction on freedom. It is an expression of freedom: the principle of equal liberty in conditions of solidarity.

In Book I of *The Social Contract* Rousseau outlines the ideal elements of *droit politique*. The specification of its working practices is, however, much more challenging, and when we read beyond Book I, Rousseau's pessimism comes to the fore. Following Bodin in making a distinction between sovereignty and government, he argues that this distinction establishes a tension which will eventually corrupt and then destroy the (ideal) constitution. Sooner or later, 'the Prince ends up suppressing the Sovereign and breaking the Social treaty'.[26] We start with grand ideals, but they soon get corrupted. The best hope, he suggests, is with a type of law 'unknown to our political theorists', but one 'on which the success of all the other laws depends'.[27] It is the type of law that forms 'the State's genuine constitution'.[28] This is the living law which expresses the customs and beliefs of a people and which sustains the nation, a point that is similar to Bodin's on the importance of precepts of civil prudence.

Rousseau here brings out the ambivalent nature of public law. It might be regarded as some pure science of principle, as many legal and political theorists regard it today. This is a mistake: it cannot adequately be conceptualized without incorporating the basic practices of governing according to certain traditions of conduct.

This claim is reinforced once one recognizes that Rousseau offers us not one but two versions of the social contract. In addition to that presented in *The Social Contract*, we can read his account of the founding of government in his *Discourse*

---

[26] Rousseau, *The Social Contract*, 106.

[27] Rousseau, *The Social Contract*, 106.

[28] Rousseau, *The Social Contract*, 106.

on Inequality as a study of the manner in which this pact was actually framed in historical practice. Here, Rousseau argues that if we think of government as originating in a foundation, then the contract made was deceptive and fraudulent—it was drafted by the wealthy for the purpose of exploiting the poor. And in his *Discourse on Inequality*, he again finds hope only in custom.[29]

Rousseau understood the difficulties entailed in devising a science of public law. He suggested that putting the law above man is a problem in politics similar to that of squaring the circle in geometry. If this problem can be solved, good government results. If not, then wherever people believe that the rule of law prevails, they will be deceiving themselves: 'it will be men who will be ruling'.[30] Rousseau here reveals both the challenge and ambivalence of public law. It is easy to outline the normative scheme, the structure of principle expressing equal liberty: we can with relative ease elaborate a regime of basic principles, such as the necessity for institutional differentiation (separation of powers), recognition of basic rights of the citizen, and promotion of the structured exercise of governmental power (proportionality, subsidiarity, etc.), but this normative scheme does not explain public law as it is practised. For this understanding, we are obliged to take seriously the ambivalences in the character of the modern state, of which Rousseau's two versions of the social contract are but one expression. We are required openly to acknowledge the active character of the governing relationship, revealed in the tension between the sovereign and sovereignty (otherwise, 'the office of government' and 'the people'). And we must recognize that the practice of public law incorporates techniques of political reasoning that normative theorists invariably seek to suppress.

5. THE MODERN SCIENCE OF PUBLIC LAW

The ambiguities and tensions that permeate the field have given the concept of public law an uncertain meaning. The search for a 'science of political right' is driven by the conviction that there is some mode of right ordering of public life that free and equal individuals would rationally adopt. This is purely an exercise in imagination which experience has shown to be a journey without end: countless normative schemes have been postulated and all have foundered on the rocks of political necessity. In part, this is because political right must negotiate between norm and fact and this has left public law thought with a polarized consciousness.[31] But it is also because the modern state itself expresses 'an unresolved tension between the two irreconcilable dispositions', between the

---

[29] Rousseau, *Discourse on the Origin and Foundations of Inequality Among Men* [1755] in his *The Discourses and other early political writing*, Victor Gourevitch (ed.) (Cambridge: Cambridge University Press, 1997), 111–222.

[30] Rousseau, *Considerations on the Government of Poland and on its Projected Reformation* [1772] in his *The Social Contract and other later political writings*, Victor Gourevitch (ed.) (Cambridge: Cambridge University Press, 1997), 177–260, 179.

[31] See, eg, Jellinek's attempt to bring the German theory of *Staatsrecht* to culmination in his two-sided doctrine (*Zwei-Seiten Lehre*) of the state: Georg Jellinek, *Allgemeine Staatslehre*, 3rd edn (Berlin: Springer, 1921).

state as *societas* (a structure of rules of conduct), and the state as *universitas* (a corporation established in furtherance of designated purposes).[32]

Many contemporary scholars prefer the aesthetically pleasing symmetries of ideal formulations, but this leads only to a dead end—ultimately to one in which the exercise of power is equated with its abuse. Jurists who have sought to integrate the 'irreconcilable dispositions' into their frameworks bring us closest to grasping the nature of the subject. Such works include Mortati's constitutional analysis which moves beyond the formal framework of norms to embrace a 'material constitution' that amounts to an expression of the institutional arrangement of social forces,[33] Fraenkel's study of the Nazi dictatorship showing that, through law, the state divided into two coexisting orders of the normative state (*Normenstaat*, structured by statutes and court orders) and the prerogative state (*Maßnahmenstaat*, structured in accordance with the exigencies of party rule),[34] and Habermas' argument that the tension between the idealism of constitutional law and the materialism of administrative law is manifested by a drifting apart of philosophical and empirical approaches to the study of law.[35]

This fissure, which runs through the entire discipline, has profound significance for the attempt to grasp its nature. If the science of public law is not to amount either to an anatomical account of the rule structure of an existing regime or to a normative theory of how things ought to be, then it must aim to offer a positive account that reveals the postulates of the evolving practice.[36] The discontinuities that pervade the practice—between the universal and the local, the absolute and the conditional, the formal and the material—can be neither eliminated nor reconciled: these can only be negotiated. This means that the method of public law involves the exercise of prudential judgment. Public law remains a practical discourse which, although orientated to norms, must have regard to consequences; it recognizes 'abstract universals' but does not ignore 'necessary conditions'.[37] It is a reflexive discourse that negotiates the

---

[32] Michael Oakeshott, 'On the Character of a Modern European State' in his *On Human Conduct* (Oxford: Clarendon Press, 1975), 185–326, 200–201.

[33] Costantino Mortati, *La Costituzione in Senso Materiale* (Milan: Guiffrè, 1940). Mortati here follows in a German tradition that can be traced to the work of Ferdinand Lassalle: see Lassalle, 'Über Verfassungswesen' in his *Gesamtwerke*, Eric Blum (ed.) (Leipzig: Pfau, 1901), vol 1, 40–69, p 45: 'the actual power relationships which emerge in every society are the active determinants of all laws and constitutional orientations of the society'. Lineages are to be seen in John Griffith, 'The Political Constitution' (1979) 42 MLR 1–21.

[34] Ernst Fraenkel, *The Dual State: A Contribution to the Theory of Dictatorship*, E. A. Shils (trans.) (New York: Oxford University Press, 1941).

[35] Jürgen Habermas, *Between Facts and Norms: Contributions to a Discourse Theory of Law and Democracy*, William Rehg (trans.) (Cambridge: Polity Press, 1996), 38–41. In similar vein, I have tried to explain British public law thought as having evolved through tensions between normativist and functionalist styles: Martin Loughlin, *Public Law and Political Theory* (Oxford: Clarendon Press, 1992).

[36] Cf Hayek, who recognizes the importance of these polarities but seeks to resolve the tension by maintaining that one type of ordering (nomocratic) is correct and the other (teleocratic ordering) is a degenerate form: F. A. Hayek, *Law, Legislation and Liberty: Vol. 1 Rules and Orders* (London: Routledge Kegan Paul, 1973).

[37] G. W. F. Hegel, *Philosophy of Right* [1821], T.M. Knox (trans.) (Oxford: Clarendon Press, 1952), §§ 29–33. See Axel Honneth, *The Pathologies of Individual Freedom: Hegel's Social Theory* (Princeton: Princeton

evolving relation between instituted authority (the government/constituted power) and the people (the nation/constituent power). It expresses a special type of political reason. Public law is not, in essence, *voluntas*; it is *ratio*. But contrary to those who suggest that the tensions of public law can be overcome through an exercise of moral reason, it is a special type of reason: *ratio status*.

Public law is formed only with the establishment of the idea of the state as an autonomous public world, an autonomy that is clearly expressed in Rousseau's work. Rousseau rejects the Hobbesian idea that liberty stands outside the sphere of law; for Rousseau, concepts such as freedom and security must be understood to be products of the operation of law within this autonomous realm. But by law here, it must be emphasized, is not primarily meant positive law; it refers to *droit politique*, the code of this public world.

This point highlights the significance of the concept of *droit politique*. Operating under the prevailing influence of legal positivism, many today conceive law to be a set of posited rules enacted by the law-making institutions of the state. They tend to treat law as an entity that protects liberty by imposing limits on the exercise of power. But from the perspective of public law, law should not be conceived as a bridle on an otherwise unrestrained exercise of power: law (as *droit politique*) is itself a power-generating phenomenon. Like freedom, power is generated by the operations of *droit politique*. Political power is a special type of power created by the drawing together of 'the people' in an institutional frame. This type of symbolic power is founded on the 'consent' of the people, is rooted in trust, and is generated through the imposition of controls and checks on those who hold positions of authority. As Bodin was the first to explain, in this sphere, constraints on power generate power.

From the perspective of public law, modern constitutional structures do not impose limitations on the exercise of some pre-existing power; these structures are the means by which power is itself generated. It is through the workings of *droit politique* that this autonomously conceived public world maintains and enhances its power. From this perspective, sovereignty is an expression of that autonomously conceived public realm, and it cannot be overcome without jettisoning the entire modern practice of public law. Those who believe that sovereignty is compromised by, for example, supra-national governing arrangements, make the mistake of failing to maintain the distinction between sovereignty and government—a distinction that both Bodin and Rousseau recognized as being a constitutive feature of public law.

6. AFTER PUBLIC LAW?

In the light of this sketch of the nature of public law it might finally be asked: what can it mean to talk of 'after' public law? Those making this type of claim tend to have the foundational concept of sovereignty directly in their sights.

University Press, 2010), 15: 'here [in this section of *Philosophy of Right*] it becomes clear that the term *right* has the double meaning of a "necessary condition" and a "justifiable claim"'.

Their arguments follow one of two tracks: they maintain either that contemporary governmental developments now render the language of sovereignty anachronistic or that, as a consequence of globalizing trends, sovereignty must now be treated as a purely metaphorical notion, one that promises the eventual realization of the 'sovereignty of law'. I conclude by briefly addressing each of these claims.

The former contention suggests that as a result of developments in government we are now entering an era of 'post-sovereignty'. This argument possesses some force. After all, government today is ubiquitous and it functions mainly through an administrative modality. In these circumstances, it is not surprising to find scholars suggesting that modern constitutional assumptions, rooted in Enlightenment ideas of an arrangement of 'limited government' authorized by 'the people', no longer hold much sway. The difficulty with this claim is that, once the essential nature of public law is grasped, one can readily accept this empirical assessment while rejecting the sweeping conclusions that some seek to draw. Consider, for example, the question of sovereignty. Failing to recognize its juristic character, these critics conflate sovereignty with the ability of a nation-state fully to control the material conditions of its existence. It is not surprising that a state subjected to this test is found wanting: there has, after all, rarely ever existed in history any nation-state able to maintain such a high degree of power and autonomy. But this is to confuse sovereignty and government. As the early modern jurists fully appreciated, sovereignty and government are conceptually distinct: sovereignty is absolute, perpetual, and illimitable, whereas government is conditional, provisional, and limitable. Sovereignty is conceptual, government is empirical; sovereignty is juridical, government is sociological. Sovereignty cannot be divided, but government not only can but—for power-generating reasons—must be divided.

Once this distinction is acknowledged, it remains possible to accept the empirical assessment about the complexity of contemporary governing networks without it following that public law has lost its symbolic power. The modern discourse of public law seeks to manage such tensions between the conceptual and empirical: it aims not only to identify the formal right to rule but also to specify conditions that maintain the capacity to rule. Consequently, although the intricacy of contemporary governing arrangements undoubtedly imposes strains on the ability to manage these tensions, it is not evidently the case that this world of representation must now be treated as merely a façade that masks the realities of power networks operating in the world today. For those who do seek to draw this conclusion, the consequences are dramatic: they are obliged to argue either that we are now living in a post-jural world,[38] or they must do something that has not yet been undertaken, viz, to reconstitute 'public law' on some new conceptual foundation.[39] Most making this type of argument confuse the issues and avoid these radical consequences.

[38] This is the type of claim made by Foucault in his analysis of *gouvernementalité*: Michel Foucault, 'Governmentality' in his *Essential Works, vol. 3*, James D. Faubion (ed.) (London: Penguin, 2000), 201–22.

[39] For one such attempt see Edward L. Rubin, *Beyond Camelot: Rethinking Politics and Law for the Modern State* (Princeton: Princeton University Press, 2005).

If those who make the former type of argument invoke empirical arguments to undermine the normative arrangements of public law, those making the latter type of claim tend to accentuate the normative and neglect the empirical. This latter type of post-public law argument seems to be rooted ultimately in the claim that the basic principles of public law have now evolved beyond the nation-state form and should today be conceived as being based either on self-sustaining ideal principles of constitutionalism or on universal (that is, human) rights. These two claims—which might respectively be labelled 'hyper-constitutionalism' and 'rights-foundationalism'—are best viewed as variants on a common theme. They present a common challenge: whereas the post-sovereignty argument is that legality has become entirely instrumentalized and thereby lost its structural connection to legitimacy, the argument of hyper-constitutionalists and rights-foundationalists is that legality must now be fused with legitimacy.

Those making this latter type of claim are aided by the common contemporary assumption that modern constitutions—the written documents establishing and regulating the main institutions of government—are constitutive of the subject. Only once this assumption is accepted can the claim be made that constitutional principles now possess freestanding authority.[40] This exposes the normativism of the argument. Although modern constitutions are generally presented as establishing a scheme of 'fundamental' or 'higher-order' law, this status is conferred only within the frame of positive law. From the perspective of public law (that is, from public law as political jurisprudence), such constitutional rules are invariably regulative rather than constitutive. The basic relationships of public law—those establishing the political unity of 'the people' (or 'the state') and the governing relationship between state and government—are not constituted by modern constitutions; they evolve from more basic political circumstances concerning the ways in which governing authority is continually acknowledged.

Although this type of normativist manoeuvre is most clearly seen with respect to the assertion of a freestanding legitimacy of the principles of constitutionalism, a similar tactic is adopted by rights-foundationalists.[41] In the perspective of public law, rights do not found a political world: they are created within it. Persons acquire their status as equals only by virtue of the political pact. As equal citizens they become (in principle) the bearers of equal rights and duties, whose rights are recognized and protected by operation of law. But these civil, political, and constitutional rights possess only a provisional status: they are claims whose institutional recognition and enforcement is dependent on balancing against other rights claims or on their qualification in the public good. The rights-bearing citizen may be a central motif of contemporary public law, but this figure is both empowered and constrained by operation of law. Those who assert the

---

[40] See, eg, Kumm, see note 3.

[41] See, eg, Anne Peters, 'Humanity as the *A* and *Ω* of Sovereignty' (2009) 20 European Journal of International Law 513–44. Peters argues that principles of sovereignty must be made subject to the overarching principle that 'human rights, interests, needs, and security must be respected and promoted' and that sovereignty is not only limited by human rights but is 'from the outset determined and qualified by humanity'.

foundational character of universal rights are directly challenging the modern imagery of the political pact. And this claim can be sustained only by destroying the inclusionary–exclusionary distinction—the condition of solidarity—which forms its core.[42] As with the post-sovereignty claim, this claim—asserting the 'sovereignty of law'—requires a fundamental reconceptualization of the character of the political world. This is, of course, not inconceivable, although presently its normative assertions do not seem to connect in a meaningful way with existing political realities.

To conclude: the radical character of the claims made under the banner of 'after public law' can readily be grasped as innovative responses to evident uncertainties in contemporary political conditions. However, to the extent that they mark a retreat either to the empiricism of governmentalism or the normativism of constitutionalism, they cannot be accepted as offering viable solutions. The modern discourse of public law which has been sketched in this chapter may be murky and, in certain respects, aesthetically unappealing. But in its recognition of the autonomy of the political world—that is, the irreducibility of distinctions between political, economic, and moral claims—and in its acceptance of the tension between freedom and necessity within that political world, it continues to provide us with the apparatus by which we can best understand the juridical challenges posed by contemporary governmental developments.

---

[42] This point has been most directly addressed in various essays of Habermas: see Jürgen Habermas, *The Inclusion of the Other: Studies in Political Theory*, C. Cronin and P. de Greiff (trans.) (Cambridge: Polity Press, 1999); Habermas, *The Postnational Constellation*, M. Pensky (trans.) (Cambridge: Polity, 2001).

∞ 3 ∞

Public Law and the Emergence of the Political

Chris Thornhill

I. THE ELEMENTS OF PUBLIC LAW

The attempt to delineate a concept of the political has been the focus of much debate throughout the last century.[1] In particular, the construction of the political has gravitated around the assumption that *the political* is a category used to capture processes of deep conflict and resultant structural contest and refoundation in society, and that, in consequence, the concept of the political reflects a highly contested endeavour to imprint a clear and singular direction on societal order as a whole.[2] It is not possible here to elaborate even a tentative genealogy of the political as a social construction. It is noticeable, however, that this concept has been assimilated in an especially pervasive fashion in public law and constitutional law. Indeed, the concept of the political is widely associated with expressions of constituent power. In particular, the legitimating origin of public law is often traced to articulations of the ineradicable founding dimension of the political in society, and ideas of constitutional legitimacy commonly presuppose the existence of a clear and autonomous political will, antecedent to specific legal norms and specific political institutions.[3]

The account of public law offered in this chapter, however, stands outside this line of analysis. It rests on the claim that such emphatic and conflictually founded discussions of the political tend to imagine the political dimension of society by means of a rather simplified anthropological interpretation of societal form. Such approaches usually presume, somewhat counterfactually, that political institutions, because they assume positions of symbolic centrality in society, are refractions of experiences of conflict and disputed collective direction, which unite all members of society. These approaches thus derive their account of the political, in rather excessively intuitive style, from a conception of human society, which is

---

[1] This article reflects certain comments, both critical and affirmative, made in different contexts by Neil Walker, Martin Loughlin, Inger-Johanne Sand, and Johan van der Walt.

[2] For examples of this conflictual construction of politics, see at different junctures Max Weber, 'Parlament und Regierung im neugeordneten Deutschland', in Weber, *Gesammelte Politische Schriften* (Tübingen: J.C.B. Mohr, 1922) 306–43, esp. 340; Carl Schmitt, *Politische Theologie* (Berlin: Duncker und Humblot, 1922) 7; Chantal Mouffe, *On the Political* (London: Routledge, 2005) 9.

[3] See Carl Schmitt, *Verfassungslehre* (Berlin: Duncker und Humblot, 1928) 76–7; Bruce Ackermann, *We the People, I: Foundations* (Cambridge, Mass: Harvard University Press, 1991) 19; Martin Loughlin, *The Idea of Public Law* (Oxford: Oxford University Press, 2003) 43–4.

centred in anthropologically generalized human interests. Such approaches arrive at their concept of politics by imputing a simple yet unifying substructure of human behaviour and experience as the basis for all social exchange, and by construing *the political* as the primary expression of the basic elements of this substructure.

If viewed in a perspective that is less focused on the experiential dimension of society, and more attentive to the determinate sociological position of politics, however, the concept of the political might be employed, in more restricted fashion, to categorize a delineated set of societal functions. The concept of the political might be used simply to describe the construction of a distinct functional realm in a society, which enables this society to identify some of its exchanges as distinguished by high collective resonance, and as acquiring implications that cannot easily be absorbed within one sector or distinct set of practices in society, and to address such exchanges and their implications in adequately proportioned fashion. Following this account, a society can be seen to obtain a categorical political dimension if it develops a functional apparatus by means of which it can apply general reserves of power to resolve those problems emerging in the different domains of society (for example, in medicine, religion, art, science, economy, law, etc.) which cannot be addressed, autonomously, by the instruments internal and specific to these domains. Problems of this kind, accordingly, are likely to be problems that have a capacity to reach beyond the specific domain in which they originate, and to obtain unsettling *collective* implications across society in its entirety. A society evolves a political dimension, thus, if it acquires a regulatory intelligence, entailing the specific use of political power, that is able to identify, intercept, and proportionately to palliate problems that have disturbing consequences for all society. Exchanges in society become distinctively political, in turn, if they are perceptibly constructed as obtaining resonance beyond the limits of one distinct set of social functions, and if they require regulation in processes with complex and overreaching implications for all society. A sociological concept of the political, in consequence, simply defines and captures the facilities in society (procedures, norms, and institutions) for making decisions regarding exchanges perceived as political, which can be enforced in adequately general and inclusionary fashion across society. On this basis, what is generically political in a society need not be founded in conflict, and it need not contain or express defining constructions of society's total constitution. On the contrary, it is merely society's capacity for producing and utilizing political power as a specific and functionally proportioned phenomenon, which is abstracted against other social interactions and transmissible across all functional domains in society, and in the exercise of which functionally diverse social agents are implicated in approximately general and approximately equal fashion.

Following this definition, European societies began to acquire clearly political characteristics in the high medieval era.[4] The first emergence in modern European society of structures that we would recognize as categorically *political*

---

[4] Thomas N. Bisson, *The Crisis of the Twelfth Century. Power, Lordship, and the Origins of European Government* (Princeton, NJ: Princeton University Press, 2009) 484.

coincided with a process of geographical extension and functional specialization, which broadly determined the emergent forms of societal exchange at this time. In this process, notably, societies began to require and evolve patterns of extended and cohesive decision-making and normative integration that could not be extracted either from the highly personal modes of coercion or from the local/patrimonial conventions marking pre-modern social organization. Owing to this process, it became a feature of the more centralized European societies from the late 12th century onwards that they developed an extensive fabric of increasingly uniform *legal inclusion*. This meant, in simple terms, that they evolved a system of normative order, in which legal principles could be set out positively and could be reproduced to address phenomena separated by growing spatial and temporal differences. In addition, however, this meant that societies began to encounter the need for an increasing volume of legislation to regulate the diverse exchanges that they incorporated, and they constructed positive/legal forms for ascribing validity and consistency to such legislation, across widening geographical and temporal divides. To this end, societies began to use laws in the form of legal rulings that had a positively fixed and formally encoded distinction against highly local consuetudinal laws; that were relatively indifferent to private status and could override patrimonial indemnities and immunities; and that could be conserved in official written records and applied in a variety of contexts. Through this capacity, above all, societies began, very gradually, to presuppose autonomous sources of legal authorship, and to separate an autonomous political domain from the rest of society. This domain assumed responsibility for passing laws without deep reliance on private or sectoral authority, and for producing political decisions in increasingly rapid, independent fashion. Primarily, this domain assumed responsibility for constructing matters of functionally overarching or complex collective resonance, and for devising positive legal decisions to address such matters.

The formation of a set of functions classifiable as generically political was thus integrally tied to the positivization of law: that is, the authorization of law through principles internal to the law itself (legal self-reference), typically by means of decisions based in statutory or precedential norms. Most especially, the formation of the political in this sense was inseparable from the capacity of European societies for establishing legal systems organized around the creation of positive yet authoritative decisions: decisions formulated as *statutes*.[5] Societies progressively constructed themselves as possessing a political domain through the formal ascription of *ius statuendi* to their magistrates and regents. Indeed, the earliest emergence of specific political features in European society was tied to the evolution of written procedures for instituting, documenting, storing, and authoritatively reusing statutes.[6] Having once acquired these attributes, societies evolved a rudimentary political form; that is, they acquired facilities

---

[5] On this point, see Chris Thornhill, *A Sociology of Constitutions. Constitutions and State Legitimacy in Historical-Sociological Perspective* (Cambridge: Cambridge University Press, 2011) 49.

[6] Representing a mass of literature, see Hagen Keller, 'Rechtsgewohnheit, Satzungsrecht und Kodifikation in der Kommune Mailand vor der Errichtung der Signorie', in Hagen Keller and Jörg

for constructing and utilizing power as a distinctively *political* resource. Their possession of these features meant that societies were able to consolidate and reproduce increasingly complex institutional mechanisms that enabled them to generate and apply power as an inclusive and specifically authorized (political) phenomenon. Further, it enabled them to respond to their growing requirement for forms of decision-making that could be brought to bear in rapid and iterable manner in matters able to affect, in complex and unpredictable fashion, exchanges across all parts of society.

Contra more impassioned accounts of the political, therefore, it is proposed here, from a historical-functionalist viewpoint, that the abstraction of an independent political domain in society was to a large degree the outcome of the distillation of the law as a positive medium of exchange and temporal and geographical inclusion. This in itself was propelled by an underlying, more fundamental differentiation of society more widely. This functional nexus of law and the political, in particular, can be placed at the remote genesis of *public law*, defined as a series of higher-level norms explaining, conferring consistency on, and declaring at times *inviolable*, distinct procedures and legal forms for the collective distribution of power through society. The ability of European societies to produce, preserve, and consistently apply power as a political resource coincided with the first tentative construction of the basic elements of public law. The connection between the nascent political domain and reserves of positive law in fact of necessity began to isolate *public law* as a distinct social medium and vocabulary.

The claim that public law became functionally independent at such an early stage of societal construction may appear as a highly controversial statement. Indeed, the claim that a body of eminently *public* law existed prior to the late 18th or even the 19th century is by no means universally accepted. The rise of public law is usually associated with the late 18th century.[7] From Savigny to the present, moreover, it has been commonly presupposed that European legal formation in modern national societies began at the level of private law. Nonetheless, most centralized polities of medieval Europe elaborated legal texts, albeit often crudely constructed and uncertain in their formulae for differentiating private from public exchanges, which permitted them to delineate specific functions as determinately *public*, and to designate certain principles and procedures as definitively and incontrovertibly formative of institutions performing these functions.[8]

The first lineaments of public law in European society were integrally interlinked with the initial evolution of capacities for positive statutory legislation in different societal settings, and principles of public law were originally enunciated to give force to (that is, positively to organize, accompany, and confer legitimacy

---

W. Busch, (eds), *Statutencodices des 13. Jahrhunderts als Zeugen pragmatischer Schriftlichkeit. Die Handschriften von Como, Lodi, Novara, Pavia und Voghera* (Munich: Fink, 1991) 167–89.

[7] See Morton J. Horwitz, 'The History of the Public/Private Distinction', in University of Pennsylvania Law Review 130(6) (1982) 1423, 1426; Morton J. Horwitz, *The Transformation of American Law 1870–1960. The Crisis of Legal Orthodoxy* (Oxford: Oxford University Press, 1992) 11; Martin Loughlin, *Foundations of Public Law* (Oxford: Oxford University Press, 2010) 111.

[8] For discussion, see Christian Vogel, *Zur Rolle der Beherrschten in der mittelalterlichen Herrschaftslegitimation* (Düsseldorf: Düsseldorf University Press, 2011) 244, 255.

on) new laws: *statutes*. In fact, as already intimated, in most medieval societies the earliest forms of public law were themselves statutes, and the ability of these societies positively to organize their legal systems and so to promulgate new laws was inseparable from their ability autonomously to extract a public-legal political structure to account for their power. This can be observed in numerous contexts. A striking example of this can be found in the great Statutes of Westminster introduced by Edward I in England in 1275 and 1285. At one and the same time, these statutes acted to give positive statutory form to the common law and to set out consistent norms of public order to justify the introduction of new Acts of law by the English monarchy. This was most quintessentially the case, however, in the Italian city-states, probably the first examples of meaningfully *public* order in modern Europe. The Italian city-states consolidated themselves as public entities by means of formally drafted statutes which simultaneously prescribed positive written norms to replace (or, more commonly, to codify) existing customary laws and stipulated norms for the construction of municipalities as distinctly ordered polities; that is, as possessing an inner normative apparatus, which obtained consistency against private office holders and distinguished power privately applied from power publicly applied.[9] Subsequently, throughout later medieval and early modern Europe, statutes and constitutions were to a large degree synonymous.[10] The power of political actors to pass positive laws in a given society remained closely reliant on the existence of quasi-constitutional conventions for constructing a hierarchy of laws; that is, for setting certain principles of public order aside from private milieux and private associations and above the everyday functions of singular political actors.

In many cases, the first basic elements of European public law were borrowed from Roman law. Indeed, early European public law widely drew substance from a parasitic relation to the canon law. Canon law, as finally codified in Gratian's *Decretum*, acquired revolutionary significance in the development of medieval European society in that it gave a formal organizational structure to an institution (the church) that was sustained by a written legal order underscored both by implicit *supra-positive* norms (derived from divine law) and more fully evolved *positive* norms (based in Roman law). The aspect of supra-positivity in the canon law, in seeming paradox, generated a vital positivizing reference for ecclesiastical statutes, which meant the church could authorize and apply legal rulings at a high level of inner consistency and positive autonomy across great variations of time and place in expanding European societies. The church thus formed the

---

[9] For Padua, for example, it was stated that election to office of supreme magistrates (*podestà*) was not to be made *contra formam statuti* of the Padovan *commune*: Andrea Gloria (ed.), *Statuti del Comune di Padova dal secolo XII all'anno 1285* (Padua: Sacchetta, 1873) 6. For similar principles in Bologna, see Gina Fasoli and Pietro Sella (eds), *Statuti di Bologna dell'anno 1288*, in 2 vols (Vatican: Biblioteca Apostolica Vaticana, 1937) 5.

[10] Note that as late as 1610 in England the 'power to make constitutions' was still co-terminous with the power to make by-laws or local acts of legislation. See Elizabeth Read Foster (ed.), *Proceedings in Parliament 1610*, in 2 vols (New Haven: Yale University Press, 1966) I: 193. By the later seventeenth century, statutes and constitutions had been separated. For instance, the great Dutch jurist, Ulrich Huber, defined 'constitutiones' as fundamental laws [*leges fundamentales*] that give irrevocable foundation to the structure of the state: Ulrich Huber, *De Jure Civitatis*, in 3 vols (Franeker: J. Gyselaar, 1684) I: 125.

(somewhat paradoxical) locus in medieval European society, in which the leap, foundational for societal modernity, from *law-finding* to *law-making*, could be accomplished.[11] From this ecclesiastical source, the basic Roman law principles of canon law then rapidly migrated across the boundary between the sacred and the secular. In so doing, they informed the positivization of secular law, and they acted exponentially to intensify the ability of nascent modern societies to separate out a self-authorizing political domain from the rest of society, and to construct their legal and political functions at a high level of positive iterability (in categories which could be easily re-applied across society) and inner inclusionary regularity (in categories which could be spontaneously, yet repeatedly repro- duced from within the legal system itself). Principles of Roman law, inflected by ecclesiastical law, commonly established the primary foundations of public law, and they endowed emergent European societies with manifestly political qual- ities of differentiation and inclusion.

The first constructions of public law, in summary, can be identified as articu- lated responses to the structural requirement in medieval European societies for consolidating *the political* as a distinct functional realm. Early public law enabled societies both to isolate political agency and authority as a positive structure, and to distinguish matters of overarching resonance as requiring regulation by means of common positive statutes, which were increasingly applied by centralized and administratively concentrated political institutions. In fulfilling these functions, however, the statutory corpus of early public law contained several separate internal dimensions, and early public law evolved as an instrument for cementing and giving order to *three distinct elements* of public/political authority.

1.1 Public law and judicial power

The first element of public law emerging in response to these processes of abstraction can be observed in the judicial sphere. Through the initial process of inclusive legal/political formation of European societies, the judicial arena emerged as the primary dimension of political structure, and as the first set of differentiated societal functions that necessitated distinctively public-legal organ- ization.[12] In the more solid polities of medieval Europe, for instance, the first building blocks of modern statehood and modern public order arose from the commitment of regents (republican or monarchical) to provide for regular public justice (usually at a high price). Typically, this involved the imposition of ordered statutory law codes across broad territories, and it presupposed the preservation of basic thresholds of evidence and standards of punishment in penal cases. Most vitally, the growth of public justice was premised on the increasing exclusion of private judicial power (that is, manor courts, seigneurial courts, and feuding) and

---

[11] On the consequences of this principle, see Saïd Amir Arjomand, 'Constitutions and the Struggle for Political Order. A Study in the Modernization of political Traditions', in European Journal of Sociology, 32 (1992) 39.

[12] This sociological point is intuited in much classical political theory. See eg John Locke, *Two Treatises of Government* (Cambridge: Cambridge University Press, 1960 [1689]) 350; Adam Smith, *Lectures on Jurisprudence* (Oxford: Oxford University Press, 1978) 313.

the suppression of local law finding.[13] To exemplify this, the leading public officials in the earliest Italian city-states were bearers of specific judicial functions, and the coherence of Italian city-states as rudimentary public bodies depended vitally on the neutral provision of justice (usually administered by foreign officials, to ensure impartiality) and the detachment of the means of justice from private factions.[14] The judicial suppression of feuding, private violence, and private justice was at the heart of most emergent European states in the Middle Ages.[15] The construction of regular judicial power might in fact be viewed as the first essential moment in the construction of European society as political, or as *having politics*. This process gave elevated public standing to a realm of statutory norms, and it enabled these norms to be applied in inclusionary fashion, in indifference to simple personal actors, interests, and controversies, to exchanges assuming resonance beyond private and functionally specific spheres of social interaction. In this respect, public judicial authority translated power into a simply reusable form, and it imprinted on society a high degree of geographical and temporal consistency. Notably, the formation of public law, widely drawing on ecclesiastical legal norms, was of fundamental importance in this process, and the primary functions of the statutory apparatus of early public law were focused on articulating normatively acceptable principles and procedures to justify the administration and organization of justice. States possessing formal judicial authority were typically marked by *de facto* public-legal statutes to oversee access to judicial offices and to prescribe strict procedures for the administration of judicial power.

1.2 Public law and representation

From this judicial dimension of the political domain, the second dimension of public law gradually and necessarily evolved. Most societies connected by inclusive judicial functions and unified by shared judicial statutes witnessed the emergence of early forms of collective representation, and they rapidly acquired refined mechanisms for concerted political inclusion, habitually documented and controlled under carefully enunciated principles of public law. The first formation of a political domain capable of resonant yet abstracted judicial inclusion in fact immediately stimulated a broad intensification of the general political structure of society. This was tied in particular to the fact that the provision of justice augmented the number of exchanges in society directed towards the political

[13] For discussion of this in the English context, see George Burton Adams, *Council and Courts in Anglo-Norman England* (New Haven: Yale University Press, 1926) 185.

[14] The classic examples are the Florentine Ordinances of Justice of 1293 and similar documents in Bologna. However, the first rise of the city-states is traced to the construction of the office of the *podestà*, which was primarily a judicial office. On the rise of the *podestà*, see Andrea Zorzi, 'La giustizia imperiale nell'Italia comunale' in Pierre Toubert and Agostino Paravicini Bagliani (eds), *Federico II e le città italiane* (Palermo: Sellerio, 1994) 85.

[15] On this process in different context see Erich Klingelhöfer, *Die Reichsgesetze von 1220, 1231/32 und 1235. Ihr Werden und ihre Wirkung im deutschen Staat Friedrichs II* (Weimar: Hermann Böhlau, 1955) 221; Richard Kaeuper, *War, Justice, and Public Order. England and France in the later Middle Ages* (Oxford: Clarendon, 1988) 145; Alan Harding, *Medieval Law and the Foundations of the State* (Oxford: Oxford University Press, 2002) 69–108; John M. Najemy, *A History of Florence 1200–1575* (Oxford: Blackwell, 2006) 17–19.

domain. It induced a proliferation of demands for distinctively political decisions, and it gave rise to a rapid process of political institution-building in early European societies. The establishment of judicial order solidified the functions of related institutions, and it gave density to institutions of public order as a whole. Most notably, however, the rise of public justice (which, where it exceeded the powers of ambulatory royal courts, was very expensive) promoted a concomitant need for an increasing volume of revenue and for an institutional order for extracting public finance to fund the public application of law. The combination of these processes significantly contributed to the continued growth of statehood, and above all it created a requirement for institutions able to release finance from society in a fashion that did not destabilize the political domain as a whole. As a result, it also stimulated a growing need for bodies of acceded public law to organize the fiscal foundations of the political system.

In the later Middle Ages, in consequence, in most European societies institutions utilizing public power usually confronted (and engendered) a need to mobilize consent in order to produce reliable sources of public finance, to sustain professional judiciaries, and to obtain compliance for general statutes.[16] Societies normally addressed this by devising increasingly formalized representative institutions and increasingly settled bodies of public law to regulate representation.[17] In fact, the process of accelerated judicial organization and positive statutory extension characterizing many high medieval societies in Europe was widely reliant on the capacities of emergent states for mustering support and establishing veto chambers (parliaments) to test probable acceptance of statutes and the adequacy of judicial and fiscal arrangements. Arguably, those states that were most easily able to use and reproduce their power in the controlled and iterable form of statutes were those that consolidated the most far-reaching legal and political instruments for proclaiming consensus and for selectively co-opting potent social groups in the periphery of the state.[18] Early state institutions with strong judiciaries and strong representative assemblies usually possessed a high level of statutory power and a strongly abstracted political domain. In fact, in many cases the first introduction of statutes was authorized by representative assemblies.[19] The organization of the representative dimension of government under early public law was thus a second vital precondition for the rising autonomy of political power, and it facilitated the abstraction of political power as a resource that could be easily produced and positively circulated through society.

---

[16] Sometimes, in fact, consent was built into the judicial system. Note the functions of assizes, introduced by Henry II and acting as the 'headspring of English legislation': J. E. A. Jolliffe, *The Constitutional History of Medieval England: From the English Settlement to 1485* (London: Black, 1961) 239. Assizes made possible the positive changing of law, but they also presupposed a dimension of consent. See Ronald Butt, *A History of Parliament: The Middle Ages* (London: Constable, 1989) 81; J. R. Maddicott, *The Origins of the English Parliament, 924–1327* (Oxford: Oxford University Press, 2010) 75, 90.

[17] Early Italian statutes usually provided for procedures for representation. By 1300, the French monarchy had established a proto-parliamentary order. In England, parliaments were effectively protected under law by circa 1250.

[18] See Thornhill, *Sociology of Constitutions*, ch 1.

[19] The English Statutes of Westminster (1275 and 1285) are classic examples.

1.3 Public law and rights

The third element in the incipient construction of public law became evident more gradually, and its relation to the emergence of the political domain in European society was expressed in a rather more dialectical fashion. This element of public law was centred on the function and status of *rights*.

In earlier medieval European society, rights existed initially as potent societal counterweights both to the rise of the state as an autonomous political actor and to the formation of a corpus of manifestly *public* law. In medieval society, rights were usually enshrined as rights of private or patrimonial jurisdiction, and they originated as legal institutions reflecting immunities or indemnities granted to local authorities by more central political actors in order to maintain a residually diffuse structure of regulation across society. Early medieval governance relied on the general devolution or effective privatization in different localities of judicial and fiscal competence, and this devolution was refracted through the conferring of rights by regents in the form of immunities.[20] Rights, in consequence, were initially principles that were located both inside and outside the early corpus of public law: they placed private checks on state power, but they also formalized an array of private/public bargains between regents and potent local actors that made the restricted statutory transmission of power across society possible. In the course of the medieval period, however, such rights often became attached to particular persons, families, corporations, and towns, and they were widely transformed into honoured fiscal and jurisdictional rights and patrimonial privileges, typically preserving islands of private jurisdiction and authority outside the gradually tightening relations of vertical state authority. From the outset, therefore, there existed a tension between rights and public law. Although vital for the earliest expressions of European statehood, in the medieval era rights usually gave articulation to the intense centrifugal nature of medieval societies, and they typically pulled against the evenly inclusionary force of the nascent state. In some societies, this led to an endemic fragmentation of statehood.[21]

The first great leap forward in the construction of modern states occurred, however, because of a deep transformation in the societal status of rights, which began to eradicate the private, particular substance of rights, and to translate rights, unequivocally, into elements of public law. The first formation of a clear political domain in European society coincided with a reduction in the centrifugal quality of

---

[20] There is a substantial body of literature on immunities. Immunity is defined here as an institution that at once placed royal power as a private good in the hands of bearers of an immunity and allowed those holding immunities to 'isolate themselves from the state': Robert Boutruche, *Seigneurie et féodalité*, in 2 vols, vol. I: *Le premier age des liens d'homme à homme*, 2nd edn (Paris: Aubier, 1968) 132–3. It involved 'exemption from certain fiscal burdens' and delegation to the lord of 'certain judicial powers': Marc Bloch, *La société féodale*, vol. II: *Les classes et le gouvernement des hommes* (Paris: Albin Michel, 1949) 122. This captures the sense of the immunity as a legal principle that at once supported and gradually, through its patrimonial translation, fragmented centrally applied power. See also Arno Buschmann, 'Privilegien in der Verfassung des Heiligen Römischen Reiches im Hochmittelalter', in Barbara Dölemeyer and Heinz Mohnhaupt (eds), *Das Privileg im Europäischen Vergleich*, Volume II (Frankfurt am Main: Klostermann, 1999) 17–44.

[21] Chris Thornhill, *A Sociology of Constitutions*, 112–34.

rights. This was first reflected in the general establishment of *dualistic* state constitutions towards the end of the Middle Ages. These constitutions, which were usually formulated in documented treaties, assumed very different features across regional and cultural variations.[22] Yet, they generally provided instruments through which leading political actors (that is, regents, princes, magistrates, dynasties, etc.) were able to strengthen their judicial and fiscal supremacy by co-opting bearers of local/patrimonial jurisdiction and time-honoured feudal entitlement into the administrative margins of the emergent state. At the core of these constitutions was typically a compromise in which jurisdictional rights and privileges of private actors were confirmed, but in which the bearers of such privileges agreed, in recompense for the guarantee of rights, to cooperate in territorial consolidation, to renounce private violence, and to accept a certain degree of legal and statutory uniformity as a prerequisite of societal order. Building on the rise of the judicial and representative functions of the state, therefore, the fact that public actors began (initially in highly contested manner) to control the allocation of rights, and to ensure that rights were not gratuitously appropriated for the singular re-privatization of state authority and jurisdictional power formed a very powerful cornerstone in the emergence of the state as a public or distinctively *political* order. Notably, the dualistic constitutions of late medieval Europe functioned in a rather precarious equilibrium; they often consolidated state power by establishing highly diffuse balancing procedures to mediate between regal and local prerogatives, and their establishment of state power remained fragile, tentative, and easily reversible. Through the early move towards dualistic constitutionalism, however, rights were gradually and uncertainly, yet nonetheless perceptibly, transformed from semi-private specific institutions (exemptions), counteracting the absorptive power of the state, into formalized elements of essentially public legal and political inclusion. The granting of increasingly regular rights by state administrations eventually acted as a mechanism for consolidating the political sphere as an autonomous societal domain, for articulating conditions of legal compliance, for simplifying the societal acceptance of positive laws, and for heightening the reserves of statutory (political) power stored in the state.

The defining foundations of the modern political apparatus, or of the political domain *tout court*, can be briefly elucidated through this historical reconstruction of the *trifocal* functional origins of public law. The inclusionary consolidation of judicial power, the establishment of basic representative functions, and the increasingly compact administration of internally secured rights formed the original elements and preconditions of the political apparatus of modern society. Each of these elements acted to fulfill the basic functions of *the political* in society: to distinguish a structure of trans-functional collective inclusion, and to abstract and expand the reserves of effective and iterable power contained in society. Moreover, each of these elements was initially articulated in a rudimentary corpus of public law. Each of these elements was inseparable from public law,

---

[22] These constitutions were usually treaties between regents and estates regarding tax, representation, and jurisdiction. They existed, at varying levels of formality, in most European societies.

and each in fact came into being in conjunction with the first (albeit rudimentarily enunciated) principles of public law. Public law was the theoretical corpus that facilitated the first inclusionary abstraction of political power. It was in this primary functional respect, not for any deeply embedded volitional or anthropological reasons, that the rise of public law converged with the growing independence of a specifically political dimension in society.

If this trifocal constellation underpinned the first consolidation of the political, however, the construction of a pervasively inclusive and determinately positive political domain in society only approached completion in a second stage of rights formation. This process occurred at the threshold of modern statehood (between the 17th and the late 18th century, in the longer era of Enlightenment). In a number of cases (notably England in 1689, the USA in 1787–9, and France in 1789–91), this process culminated in a dynamic of revolutionary constitutional foundation, and it was expressed through a rapid growth in the formalization of public law. In this period, the dualistic and loosely fabricated constitutions arising in the later Middle Ages were supplanted by more institutionally specialized and functionally controlled legal-normative orders. Above all, at this time states acquired normative orders in which the ascription and distribution of rights were subject to stricter central oversight by actors attached to public institutions, and states progressively utilized rights as internal instruments, which permitted them to manage their power, to harden their social peripheries, and to govern inclusionary procedures for transmitting and gaining access to power. By the later 18th century, in fact, in most European societies political systems had begun to use quite strict models of public law to formalize clear rights structures. At this time, states habitually articulated concepts of legitimacy (under public law) to describe their power as proportioned to persons in society acting as *rights holders*: states imagined themselves as legitimate if they applied power to persons designated as *subjects endowed with rights*. Even in societies with an 'absolutistic' political structure, states increasingly explained their functions through reference to formal rights claimed by those subject to, and receiving power from, state institutions.

This construction of state legitimacy as derived, under public law, from the uniform recognition of rights acted exponentially to solidify the autonomous political domain in society, and it dramatically heightened the capacity of a society for the distilled and inclusive use of power. This was the case for a number of reasons. The reference to persons subject to power as rights holders meant that states could internally predefine those social exchanges in which political power became relevant and required. The reference to persons subject to power as rights holders meant that power could be transmitted through uniform procedures, and extreme variations in the application of power became unusual. The reference to persons subject to power as rights holders also meant that the ability of potent private actors to claim rights as patrimony or honoured entitlement was curtailed, and that the corporate landscape of variably pluralistic rights (that is, a social environment in which each locality, trade, or corporation had its own particular set of honoured rights) surviving from feudalism was flattened into a unified terrain for the simply reproducible use of power.[23] The reference to persons subject to power as rights holders meant, further, that the freedom of private actors to exempt themselves from state power or even to arrogate state power for their own private purposes was diminished.

By the 18th century, in consequence, rights had experienced a dramatic transformation. By this time, rights began to serve, not as particular or semi-private counterweights to the state, but as media of simplified public inclusion or even as *media of political abstraction* in the political systems of European societies, which enabled political systems to isolate themselves from exchanges and actors outside the political domain, and to presuppose consistent methods for the distilled use of power across society. To this degree, rights dramatically intensi-fied the *effective power* of emergent states. The formation of early modern society as marked by a relatively even rights fabric led to an exponential rise in the reserves of usable *political* power contained and made available in that society, and it allowed societies (and their primary political actors) easily to extend and to multiply the volume of political decisions that they were able to make.[24] At the centre of the expansion and generalization of political power in modern society was the fact that European states of later early modernity began to account for and internally to organize themselves as institutions based on rights, and they gradually learned to explain their legitimacy as obtained from the recognition of those persons subject to their power as citizens—as *uniform rights-entitled subjects.*

Throughout the long caesura between early modern and modern Europe (1640–1789), rights in fact contributed to the rising abstraction of political power in two quite distinct ways. First, the principle that states obtained legitimacy through recognition of their subjects as rights holders acted to heighten the abstracted inclusivity of the political system because, in identifying the primary classical rights of freedom in exchange, contract, opinion, confession, inquiry, expression, and so on, as inviolable against political control, it clearly ensured that the political system could delineate the boundaries of its power against other parts of society. In doing this, the formula of rights-based legitimacy enabled the political system quite strictly to identify and distinguish which parts of society were objects of eminent political inclusion and which were not, and it allowed the political system to position some exchanges and objects of inclusion as clearly external to its own administrative organs.[25] In the *external structure* of the state, in consequence, the construction of rights as a source of state legitimacy formalized

---

[23] The classic case of this was France where the decades before the revolution of 1789 saw the introduction of law to reduce the authority of collective rights bearers, such as corporations and guilds. This was clear in Turgot's edict to suppress corporations in 1776, which used Lockeian ideas of rights to eliminate collective privileges. See Anne-Robert-Jacques Turgot, 'Édit du Roi, portant suppression des jurandes', in Turgot, *Oeuvres*, edited in 2 vols by E. Daire and H. Dussard (Paris: Guillaumin, 1844), Volume II, 302–16.

[24] See Michael Th. Greven, *Die Politische Gesellschaft. Kontingenz und Dezision als Probleme des Regierens und der Demokratie* (Opladen: Leske + Budrich, 1999) 14.

[25] Here my argument has a background in Luhmann's theory of society. On Luhmann's approach to rights as cementing a functional conjuncture of political differentiation, see Niklas Luhmann, *Grundrechte als Institution* (Berlin: Duncker und Humblot, 1965) 135.

the presumption that actors throughout society only obtained relevance for the political system in a limited and highly predetermined set of functions. In this respect, rights brought the singular benefit that they enabled the political system gradually to arrange and distribute its power in a form that was largely indifferent to private status, and so to determine, positively and *from within itself*, which persons had access to power and in what ways different social agents should be included in the use of political power. Rights provided a pre-construction of citizens as only (highly) selectively participant in the political system: that is, they enabled the state to observe its addressees as constitutive for the political system as claimants, not over nebulously inherited patrimonial entitlements, but over freedoms prescribed and legally predefined by central legal/political actors. As a consequence, rights allowed states to stabilize the procedures in which they obtained support from citizens, and in which they applied power to citizens, so that states were able to incorporate citizens with minimal recognition of their particular status, their structural determinacy, or their private desires. In this, rights did much to solidify the external perimeters of the state, and they helped to create a rigid order of political inclusion which reduced the state's sensitivity to particular privilege and patrimonial diffusion, distinguished political power from other patterns of exchange, and it made it possible for the state to determine which exchanges needed to be reflected as intrinsically *political*. In this respect, rights objectified the structural boundaries of exchanges outside the state, and they ensured that such exchanges were only exceptionally subject to politicization; that is, this only occurred when they spilled out beyond their specific rights structure and rendered the general, differentiated rights fabric of society precarious. Rights heightened the autonomy of the political system as a domain focused only on matters of highly complex and functionally overarching resonance.

Secondly, the principle that rights formed the source of political legitimacy increased the autonomy and inclusivity of state power because it instilled in the *internal structure* of the political system a highly simplified legal image of the origins of its power. This formed a reference from which the political system was then able both to draw incessant inner legitimacy and to project a formalized construct of the persons in society to whom power was applied and of the exchanges requiring power for their conclusion. The modern political system's construction of itself (under public law) as *authorized by recognition of rights* enabled it—first—to incorporate within each of its legislative acts a legitimating reference to its constituent origin (the rights holder). In applying laws constructed by rights, the state could explain each law as endlessly articulating the grounds of its original legitimacy, and it was able to apply power to persons in society *as their own power*—as power in which they were internally implicated and to which they gave formal authority as rights holders. In defining itself as using power proportioned to rights, moreover, the political system was also able endlessly to pre-empt the conditions of power's transmission and recursively to apply power to its recipients in society, in reproducible fashion, without internal reflection of their social singularity or determinacy. In both respects, the concept of legitimacy as derived from the person as rights holder provided the invaluable service for emergent modern societies of permitting the political system to circulate political decisions through society in generalized, internally managed, and reproducibly authenticated fashion. It imprinted in the political system an inner self-definition through which it was able to use its power in easily reproducible fashion and in relatively constant and extensible procedures in a great variety of different temporal and functional societal contexts.

At the very inception of political modernity, in short, the construction of political power as rendered legitimate through rights made it possible for the political system at once to distinguish between those exchanges essentially constructed as political and those exchanges not essentially constructed as political. It also allowed the political system to use power in relation to exchanges as a resource that could be easily reproduced across the rapidly proliferating functional and temporal divisions of a society with an increasingly specialized and differentiated (modern) functional structure. Even more importantly, this construction made it possible for the political system to adapt to new and unpredictable objects for legislation and inclusion, and, *from within itself*, to establish legitimating principles and procedures that could be used to secure legislation in even the most rapidly changing environments of an increasingly complex modern society. In each respect, the basic functional autonomy of the political domain was reliant on the public-legal order of rights.

One structurally fundamental consequence of rights in the incremental abstraction of the functional realm of political power in European society was that rights enabled modern states to avail themselves of *increasingly democratic* procedures of inclusion in order to reinforce further and facilitate the inclusive transmission of their power. Indeed, in the first instance, the formalization of rights was often linked to the incipient growth of democracy as a principle of government and political legitimacy, and the circulation of power through society as proportioned to rights shaped the formation of political democracy as a pattern of coercive social inclusion. This occurred, at one level, because in using power as determined by rights, states reduced the degree to which power was embedded in intermediary bodies in society (corporations, guilds, courts, families, etc.), and instead applied power immediately to society in all its entirety. The modern political system, based on rights, thus effectively *presupposed* representative democracy as an even inclusive support for its circulation of power. Most importantly, however, the fact that it defined those persons subject to its power as rights holders meant that the developing modern state was able to utilize representative / democratic techniques to secure inclusivity and mobilize broad support and legitimacy for its power whilst guarding itself against endemic destabilization by the manifold demands of the persons that it claimed to represent. In accounting for itself as obtaining legitimacy through democratic representation of citizens *qua* rights holders, the modern state was in a position to explain its power as democratic power, or as *inclusive power*, which facilitated the relatively abstracted and iterable use of power across complex societal environments. Yet, the reference to rights also meant that the proclaimed author of the state's representative power (society as a whole, expressed through the popular / democratic constituent or sovereign body) was able only in very controlled fashion to become an integrated factual or originating element of the political system. The ability of the political system to proclaim its power as legitimate if derived from, and applied to, rights holders thus permitted emergent modern states to obtain the inclusive benefits of democracy (accelerated compliance for law, easier social control and mobilization, strong administrative apparatus). Yet, the legitimating power of rights allowed states to ensure that their power remained internally occluded against the manifold exercise of democratic agency by factually existing persons.[26]

In this respect, the principle of rights-based democracy established a uniquely expedient formula enabling the rising modern state to propose itself as a positively and internally *self-authorizing* political domain, able positively to delineate, and positively to legislate over, those exchanges registered as political. Above all, the principle of rights-based legitimacy permitted the emergent modern political system to presuppose the original source of its authority (its *pouvoir constituant*) as a constant and predefined element of its own inner structure, which it could articulate to accompany and support single acts of legislation. The assumption that power drawn from rights holders was automatically legitimate encapsulated the external presence of the *pouvoir constituant* as an incorporated dimension of the political system, so that each act of legislation determined by rights was able to refer to rights as a self-authorizing and perennially legitimating trace of constituent power. For this reason, the inner reference to rights within the political system made it possible for expanding European states to conduct processes of multiple and highly uncertain legal/political inclusion. The inner reference to rights established a normative order within the political system with the support of which states could internally pre-structure, pre-emptively legitimize, and extensively replicate their responses to highly contingent objects for legislation. At the same time, however, the inner reference to rights meant that states could pre-select how they recorded events as political, and they formed a matrix in which most social exchanges could be made exempt from politicization except under the most extreme and exceptional conditions – for example, under conditions in which different function systems exposed each other to intense and potentially volatile disruption.

Overall, rights played the most constitutive role in the creation of a political system adequate to the emergent pluralistic form of modern society. On the one hand, they enabled the political system at once to declare itself politically inclusive and able to register matters of overarching importance. On the other hand, they enabled it to manage its inclusivity, and to store a body of concepts to support and, internally, to dictate its reactions to highly fluid and emergent social conditions. Rights dramatically augmented the variety of resources and the capacities for flexible decision-making possessed by modern society, and they proved integral to the basic structure of political power.

2. RIGHTS AS A POLITICAL CODE

To sum up these points, public law can be defined as a trifocal normative apparatus, which, throughout its history, has consolidated a free-standing political

---

[26] This point appears repeatedly in Marcel Gauchet, *Révolution des pouvoirs. La souveraineté, le peuple et représentation 1789–1799* (Paris: Gallimard, 1995).

domain and has facilitated the statutory abstraction and decisive application of political power in differentiated societies. Public law in fact originally coincided with the rise of an abstracted political domain in society. It is usually suggested that public law establishes the political arena by expressing a set of a priori, defining norms to frame the use of power in society.[27] In our account, however, public law founds the political domain because the basic formulae of public law simplify the highly complex legal dynamics of political adaption, functional differentiation, and positive abstraction which are required for the use of power in societies reliant on large volumes of reflexively specialized political decisions.[28]

Seen from this functionalist perspective, above all, the capacity of public law for transforming rights from *private rights* (indemnities) against the state into *public rights* allocated by the state served as the final and most complex piece in the construction of the political as a generic domain, and it cemented the basic design of the modern state as an edifice of public/political order. The conclusive establishment of the modern state as an institution or set of institutions capable of acting politically—that is, of responding to matters of functionally overarching social resonance, of producing power at a high level of inner consistency and abstraction against local and private/personal variations, and of subjecting society to relatively even, iterable, and compliant inclusion in this power—is premised on the ability of states to articulate a *code of rights* able internally to secure, to underpin, and to accompany their power in the diverse settings of its application. Arguably, in fact, the originally formative dimensions of public law, which were focused on the uniform construction of judicial power and the stabilization of inclusionary/representative mechanisms, only became enduringly structured as a result of their coupling with laws of state providing for relatively uniform and internally defined rights. Notably, for example, in later early modernity the imputation of uniform rights to agents through society acted widely as a device for simplifying *judicial inclusion*, and for making sure that judicial offices did not erode or privatize the periphery of the state.[29] Moreover, as discussed, the construction of persons subject to power as holders of uniform rights served palpably to simplify and bring cohesion to the representative apparatus of the state, and rights permitted states to found their authority in open but internally

---

[27] Loughlin, *Foundations of Public Law* 12.

[28] For background, see the theory of power in Talcott Parsons, 'On the Concept of Political Power,' in *Proceedings of the American Philosophical Society*, 107 (3) (1963) 232–62; Niklas Luhmann, 'Soziologie des politischen Systems', in Niklas Luhmann (ed.) *Soziologische Aufklärung*, vol. I *Aufsätze zur Theorie sozialer Systeme* (Cologne: Westdeutscher Verlag, 1970) 154–77.

[29] Central to the theories of rights in the French Revolution was an attempt to reinforce state power by eradicating private holding of judicial office. This was reflected in the revolutionary assault on the *parlements*. The first report on the judiciary in the National Assembly denounced the patrimonial control of judicial rights and powers, and it reflected scathingly on the fact that in the *ancien régime* the judiciary had seen fit to emulate 'legislative power' and had 'disturbed the operations' of the administration: Jacques-Guillaume Thouret, *Discours. En ouvrant la discussion sur la nouvelle organisation du pouvoir judiciaire* (Paris: Imprimerie nationale, 1790) 2–3. Both early revolutionary constitutions in France (1791, 1793) contained articles to eradicate functional overreach on the part of judicial organs.

governed modes of *representative inclusion.*[30] In all these respects, at the decisive juncture between early modern and modern society, rights, normally framed in revolutionary constitutional documents, acted as internal filters that proportioned the inclusivity of the emergent political system and raised the abstraction of its power. Rights ensured that, in measured inclusion, the political system could avoid constant and unmanaged factual integration of those subject to power, and it could apply power across widening societies as an internally legitimated, functionally differentiated, and highly specialized—that is, political—resource.

These claims for the role of rights in giving rise to what we would now identify as the specifically political structures of society may appear counterintuitive if judged from conventional angles of inquiry. Both historically and in current literature, it is habitually argued that rights *check* political power, that they form an apolitical *limit* to the political constitution,[31] and even that they *reduce the amount of political power stored in society*. Amongst liberals, the argument that rights are institutions which provide 'protection' against the 'unilaterally imposed power' of the state remains almost universally commonplace.[32] Even the essential status of rights as elements of public law is often questioned, and rights, revealing their origins in indemnifying immunities, are classically observed as external or residually private principles that provide justiciable exemption from the encroachment of public authority.[33] Amongst (post-1900) conservatives, in reverse, the politics of a society is commonly imagined as an emphatically declared set of principles expressed with sovereign force across all social sectors, towards which rights act at most as static and often insufficiently mandated countervailing limits.[34] *Contra* such presuppositions at different points in the political spectrum, however, it can be quite clearly observed throughout the entire functional history of European societies that the progressive sanctioning of rights did not evolve as a block on the use of political power. On the contrary, the consolidation of rights as defining dimensions in the grammar of state legitimacy was the foundation for the constructive formation of the state as a repository of society's political power: as the centre of an autonomous political domain.

[30] Eg, during the period of state constitution writing in revolutionary America, the later, more stable state constitutions possessed longer and more restrictive catalogues of rights. This was at the heart of the second wave (post-1776) of constitution writing.

[31] This is the classical view, derived from Locke, but implicit in all liberal patterns of constitution writing. See Richard A. Primus, *The American Language of Rights* (Cambridge: Cambridge University Press, 1999) 12.

[32] For example, see Ulrich K. Preuss, 'Disconnecting Capitalism from Statehood: Is Global Constitutionalism a Viable Concept', in Petra Dobner and Martin Loughlin (eds), *The Twilight of Constitutionalism* (Oxford: Oxford University Press, 2010) 23–46, 23; Rodney Barker, *Political Legitimacy and the State* (Oxford: Clarendon Press, 1990) 199.

[33] For discussion of this tendency, see Cass R. Sunstein, 'Standing and the Privatization of Public Law', in Columbia Law Review 88 (1988) 1432–81, 1438.

[34] See this classical view of public law as expressing an incontrovertible founding grammar for all society in Schmitt, *Verfassungslehre*. Amongst recent literature heading in this direction, see Jeremy A. Rabkin, *Law without Nations? Why Constitutional Government requires Sovereign States* (Princeton, NJ: Princeton University Press, 2007) 70.

On these grounds, it can be appreciated that, although rights are perceived as originating in private relations, modern societies first elaborated rights as institutions acting in a fashion increasingly analogous to an *objective political code*. That is, European societies evolved rights to mark out the objective boundaries of the political system, to define those (private) exchanges that are not eminently constitutive of or relevant for political power, and to instil within political power a basic reference (an account of itself as obtaining power from an original constituent author) to support its inflationary public circulation through a pluralistic society.[35] The coding of power in relation to rights expressed the most essential moment in the construction of power as *specifically and irreducibly political*, and it is through the formalization of rights that public law has done most to extract from society a functional form for *the political*. The coding of political power through rights establishes rights as prerequisites of the statutory flexibility of society, and it enables society to generate multiple positive decisions to address its increasing inner plurality and complexity. Following this account of the political, clearly, it appears mistaken to define the political code as a society's emphatic or programmatic account of its defining form.[36] At one level, the coding of power in relation to rights dramatically raises the iterability and inclusionary force of political power, and, crucially, it endows society with capacities for pre-emptive adaption to future demands for comprehensive political inclusion. Yet, the coding of power in relation to rights produces political power as a highly abstracted and differentiated societal commodity, whose social universality is limited to collectively resonant but also quite circumscribed and deeply contingent processes of inclusion. The public-legal coding of power through rights, in summary, is the primary articulation of power adapted to a society needing to generate and preserve its political resources, not through large volitional declarations, but in highly unfounded and internally self-referential reproduction. The public-legal coding of power through rights is the code of *modern political power*.[37]

3. THE DECLINE OF PUBLIC LAW?

It has become widespread in recent years to observe a decline in the status of public law in modern society. Underlying this perspective is often the suggestion

---

[35] Note again the relation of these claims to Luhmann's theory of the political system. It appears to me that Luhmann was never fully certain how either the code or the medium of the political system should be defined. In particular, he intimated that although the medium of the political system is *power*, power is only transmissible through its second-coding as *law*. He argued that the second-coding of power by law leads to an 'immense expansion of the realm of application of political power' in a society: Niklas Luhmann, 'Verfassung als evolutionäre Errungenschaft', Rechtshistorisches Journal 9 (1991) 176–220, 201. See also Niklas Luhmann, *Macht*, 2nd edn (Stuttgart: Enke, 1988) 34. My contention, however, is that power is inevitably *second-coded*, not simply through law, but through legal rights. Luhmann himself came close to suggesting this by identifying second-coding with the formalization of power in the constitution.

[36] Note the rather critical relation of this analysis to Loughlin, *Foundations of Public Law*, 8.

[37] I remain fascinated by Jean Clam's work on the characteristics of modern power. See Jean Clam, 'What is modern power?', in Michael King and Chris Thornhill (eds), *Luhmann on Law and Politics. Critical Appraisals and Applications* (Oxford: Hart, 2006) 145–62.

that modern society is witness to a decline of *the political* more generally, such that the (perceived) dispersal of public law reflects the declining capacity of a society to provide a single definition of its essential form, able to provide collective orientation for all agents within society. This diagnosis is proposed from a number of different standpoints, and it is not possible here to survey all research on this question. The following approaches, however, have assumed salience in this body of reflection.

First, it is widely argued that public-legal allocation of competence within state institutions is no longer sustainable, such that public authority is now attributed, not under formal public law, but by various principles and procedures, which are not subject to uniformly centred constitutional regulation.[38] This view is often accompanied by the claim that modern societies have lost their ability to condense into strict principles the irreducibly political construction of their basic dispositions and their legitimacy. In particular, it is often suggested that the sources of public and constitutional law in contemporary society have become endemically pluralistic, so that no clearly or unequivocally extracted body of public-legal norms or principles can be identified to support and authorize the exercise of power. On the one hand, this argument observes that *de facto* constitutional force is assumed simultaneously by norms emanating from national and norms emanating from international sources, a fact which obstructs the imputation of an evident and categorical order of public law to any aggregate of political institutions. This perception may imply that public law is dissolved as national legislatures lose legislative sovereignty in their territories because of their obligation to show compliance with international norms. Similarly, this perception may imply that public law is eroded because of the increasing transplantation of public-legal norms from one transnational setting to another, or because of the rising power of international norms to set directives and obligations impacting on judiciaries and legislators with powers formerly defined under public law.[39] On the other hand, this argument indicates that *de facto* constitutional force is exercised simultaneously by norms emanating from traditionally public and norms emanating from traditionally private sources, so that private practices, disputes, conflicts, and actors generate norms possessing effective constitutional standing across both national and transnational societies.[40] This implies that the attribution (in Kelsen's sense of *Zurechnung*) of public-legal norms to original public acts or normatively extracted legitimating principles is no longer possible, and that the eminent public quality of constitutional norms, classically deriving from elected legislatures or constituent bodies, has evaporated. In each perspective, modern society is perceived as

---

[38] Nico Krisch, *Beyond Constitutionalism: The Pluralist Structure of Postnational Law* (Oxford: Oxford University Press, 2010) 17.

[39] See Vicki C. Jackson, *Constitutional Engagement in a Transnational Era* (Oxford: Oxford University Press, 2010) 20.

[40] Andreas Fischer-Lescano and Gunther Teubner, 'Regime-Collisions: The vain search for legal unity in the fragmentation of global law', in Michigan Journal of International Law 25(4) (2004) 999–1046, esp. 1015–16; Gunther Teubner, *Constitutional Fragments. Societal Constitutionalism and Globalization* (Oxford: Oxford University Press, 2012) 59–66; Gralf-Peter Calliess and Peer Zumbansen, *Rough Consensus and Running Code. A Theory of Transnational Private Law* (Oxford: Hart, 2010) 75, 166–8, 243.

possessing a *multi-normative* constitutional structure, in which gapless public-legal order is no longer conceivable and no self-evidently hierarchical position attaches to law generated by recognizably public bodies or acts.[41] In each perspective, the distinctively political quality of a society engendered by public law—that is, the ability of a society distinctively to set some norms above others, to provide reliable principles to justify this normative primacy, and to imagine itself as politically directed (or constituted) by public law—is also presumed to be diminished.[42]

Secondly, it is habitually asserted that, owing to the growing primacy of international law over the public law of single national states, the legal fabric of public institutional authority has experienced a dramatic displacement towards the judicial dimension. That is, it is widely observed that the increasing influence of an international legal arena has reconfigured the political domain by promoting a growth in the power of review and appeal courts (both national and supranational) as primary centres of public law and as primary authors of public-legal norms.[43] This claim implies first that the increasing power of courts has instituted a legal order in which a secure structure of national public law has been fractured at once by jurisdictional conflicts, by increasing patterns of lateral comity and synergy between distinct legal systems, and by the severing of judicial authority from publicly constituted actors.[44] More notably, this analysis tends to claim that, owing to the rising prominence of international obligations in respect of rights, judicial actors routinely acquire norm-building powers that outweigh institutions (national or international) mandated by constituent power. As a result, it is suggested that the normative force of the international rights-based legal arena circumvents classical principles of legitimacy (constituent power,

---

[41] Summarizing this, see Christoph Engel, 'Hybrid Governance across National Jurisdictions as a Challenge to Constitutional Law', in European Business Organization Law Review 2 (2001) 569–83, 583. More generally, see Neil Walker, 'Constitutionalism and Pluralism in Global Context', *RECON Online Working Paper 2010/03*; Neil Walker, 'Taking Constitutionalism beyond the State', in Political Studies 56 (2008) 519–43; Paul Schiff Berman, 'Global Legal Pluralism', in Southern California Law Review 80 (2007) 1155–238; Alec Stone Sweet, 'Constitutionalism, Legal Pluralism, and International Regimes', in Indiana Journal of Global Legal Studies 16 (2009) 621–45; Krisch, *Beyond Constitutionalism*, 31.

[42] Reflecting these anxieties quite generally, see Petra Dobner, 'More Law, Less Democracy: Democracy and Transnational Constitutionalism', in Martin Loughlin and Petra Dobner (eds), *The Twilight of Constitutionalism?* (Oxford: Oxford University Press, 2010) 141–61.

[43] This is seen both favourably and critically. For a favourable view, see Anne-Marie Slaughter, 'A Typology of Transjudicial Communication', in University of Richmond Law Review 29 (1995) 101; Anne-Marie Slaughter, 'A Global Community of Courts', in Harvard International Law Journal 44 (2003) 191–219. Supporting Slaughter's theory, see Christopher McCrudden, 'A Common Law of Human Rights? Transnational Judicial Conversations on Constitutional Rights', in Oxford Journal of Legal Studies 20(4) (2000) 499–532. Also favourable in its approach is Anne Peters, 'Compensatory Constitutionalism: The Function and Potential of Fundamental International Norms and Structures', in Leiden Journal of International Law 19 (2006) 579–610, esp. 583. For a critical alternative, see Ran Hirschl, 'The New Constitutionalism and the Judicialization of Pure Politics Worldwide', in Fordham Law Review 75 (2007) 721–53, esp. 723. More generally see, Ran Hirschl, *Towards Juristocracy. The Origins and the Consequences of the New Constitutionalism* (Cambridge, Mass.: Harvard University Press, 2004). See also John Ferejohn, 'Judicializing Politics, Politicizing Law', in Law and Contemporary Problems 65(3) (2002) 41–68, esp. 41, 44.

[44] See for example Andrew Le Sueur, 'The Conception of the UK's New Supreme Court', in Andrew Le Sueur (ed.), *Building the UK's New Supreme Court. National and Comparative Perspectives* (Oxford: Oxford University Press, 2004) 3–20, esp. 15.

representative consent, democratic legitimacy in legislation), and it renders void many classical prerogatives of national public law.[45] According to this account, typically, rights, in highly abstracted form, replace democratic power as the primary element of constitutional order, and the always-strained relation between rights and democracy is constitutionally resolved in favour of rights. This view indicates that rights, applied by powerful judicial actors, increasingly construct a transnational political system able to apply power at a high level of autonomy against the representative or constituent dimensions of public order. Even those processes and functions of polity building and constitutional design traditionally pertaining to constituent power are ceded to hyper-abstracted rights and institutions, often authorized by transnational norms, applying rights.[46] This is widely observed in the design of transnational polities, such as the EU and—to a lesser degree—the WTO.[47] Yet, it is increasingly perceived as characteristic of all constitutions that rights usurp legislative power, they constrain the integrity of political processes, and they transform classical models of public law into subsidiary dimensions of an overarching transnational (that is, trans-judicial) constitution, mediated through publicly affirmed rights.

Common to these reflections on the weakening of the basic constituent reserves of public law, in consequence, is the view that two of the primary historical foundations of public law (uniform judicial power, and mechanisms for generating inclusionary consent to ease the enforcement of power) have (at the least) entered a process of *heterarchical dispersal*. The contemporary fragmentation of public law is seen as coinciding both with the end of simple judicial regularity and with the end of representative patterns of political democracy as the dominant principles of institutional legitimacy. Indeed, as mentioned, it has even been contended that this process marks a decline or at least a dramatic refiguring of *the political* in more substantial terms.[48] Proceeding from the above reconstruction of public law as a trifocal system of functional abstraction and

---

[45] Standing in for much, see Frank Vibert, *The Rise of the Unelected. Democracy and the New Separation of Powers* (Cambridge: Cambridge University Press, 2007) 298.

[46] See especially Ran Hirschl, 'Israel's "Constitutional Revolution": The Legal Interpretation of Entrenched Civil Liberties in an Emerging Neo-Liberal Economic Order', in American Journal of Comparative Law 46 (1998) 427–52; Ran Hirschl, 'The Judicialization of Mega-Politics and the Rise of Political Courts', in Annual Review of Political Science 11 (2008) 93–118, esp. 106. For the concept of class underpinning this, see Ran Hirschl, 'The Political Origins of Judicial Empowerment through Constitutionalization: Lessons from Four Constitutional Revolutions', in Law and Social Inquiry (2000) 91–149, esp. 125.

[47] See the divergent perspectives in Hauke Brunkhorst, 'Europe in Crisis—An Evolutionary Genealogy', in Mikael Rask Madsen and Chris Thornhill (eds), *Law and the Formation of Modern Europe: Perspectives from the Historical Sociology of Law* (Cambridge: Cambridge University Press, forthcoming 2014); Sabine Frerichs, *Judicial Governance in der europäischen Rechtsgemeinschaft. Integration durch Recht jenseits des Staates* (Baden-Baden: Nomos, 2008) 67.

[48] See Andreas Fischer-Lescano, 'Luhmanns Staat und der transnationale Konstitutionalismus', in Marcelo Neves and Rüdiger Voigt (eds), *Die Staaten der Weltgesellschaft. Niklas Luhmanns Staatsverständnis* (Baden-Baden: Nomos, 2007) 99–1113, 109; Gunther Teubner, 'Verfassungen ohne Staat? Zur Konstitutionalisierung transnationaler Regimes', in Gret Haller, Klaus Günther, and Ulfrid Neumann (eds), *Menschenrechte und Volkssouveränität in Europa. Gerichte als Vormund der Demokratie?* (Frankfurt: Campus, 2011) 49–100, 72.

inclusion for the political system, however, we can observe that such analyses of the weakening of public law are premised, typically, on a somewhat simplified appreciation of public law in its classical form. Indeed, if the question of the fate of public law in modern society is examined from a functionalist perspective, a certain scepticism towards the common diagnosis of the decline of public law, its methodological basis, and the attendant reserves of societal political power, becomes almost inevitable.

From the functionalist standpoint proposed above, first, it is arguable that most approaches identifying a decline of public law, although seeking to comprehend sociologically unprecedented phenomena in the current transformation of public-legal order, adopt a static and rather sociologically under-reflected definition of public law, its functional origins, and its social status. Indeed, it is arguable that these approaches display a rather reductive or semantically pre-structured appreciation of the relation between public law and the political structure of society. That is to say, these approaches usually persevere in deploying excessively *literal* categories to analyse the relation between public law and politics, to examine the institutional arrangements supporting public law, and to elucidate the socio-political backgrounds in response to which societies have constructed their systems of public law. In opting for this literal approach to public law and the establishment of political institutions, second, these approaches fail to reflect on the emergence of the political as an adaptive sociological process, and they tend to retain a highly agency-centred or even anthropological account of political forma-tion. In particular, they commonly approach politics in the first instance as a primary volitional dimension of society, in which a society, through the medium of public law, spontaneously elects to nominate certain principles as defining its overarching form and thus as having primacy for all societal exchanges.[49] As a result of these tendencies, these approaches often lack a sociological perspective for examining the inner structure of the political as part of society's reflexivity, producing reserves of inclusivity and abstraction in response to resonant societal environments, and they struggle to account for changes in public law as reflecting socially variable requirements for normative political abstraction and inclusion. Perhaps most importantly, third, more conventional inquiries into the transform-ation of public law in contemporary society typically proceed from implicitly classical constructions of rights. In particular, they follow ingrained liberal prin-ciples to conceive of rights, at least residually, as elements of the political system countervailing the abstraction of the political domain, or withdrawing certain societal practices from the authority of public law. This establishes a perspective that accounts for the accentuation of judicial power and the proliferation of rights in the constitution of contemporary transnational society—habitually designated as a *sui generis* 'rights revolution' or even as a 'judicial review revolution'[50]—as a

---

[49] See Martin Loughlin, 'Constitutional Law: The Third Order of the Political', in Nicholas Bamforth and Peter Leyland (eds), *Public Law in a Multi-layered Constitution* (Oxford: Hart, 2003) 27–50, esp. 41–2, 50; Dieter Grimm, *Die Verfassung und die Politik. Einsprüche in Störfällen* (Munich: Beck, 2001) 249.

[50] Richard Münch, 'Constructing a European Society by Jurisdiction', in European Law Journal 14(5) (2008) 519–41; Thierry S. Renoux, 'Le Conseil constitutionnel et le pouvoir judiciaire en France dans le

process tending of necessity to weaken or to dismember and fragment the force of public law and ultimately to reduce the distinctively political content of society.[51] This approach, however, reflects an outlook that fails to show due sensitivity to the formative and inclusionary role of rights *qua political code*. It ignores, in part, ways in which rights direct and extend new structures of public law and reconfigure societally articulated processes of political inclusion. Indeed, the original idea of rights as entailing private *immunity from power* still imperceptibly informs common approaches to rights, and it undermines the capacity of theory for examining the status of rights-based legal norms in the contemporary political functions of public law.

The functionalist account of public law proposed in this article reacts against such (what we take to be) slightly simplifying interpretive approaches. If, from a functionally attuned perspective, public law is observed as a system of inclusion which abstracts a strict political arena in society, enabling the political system to adapt through the use of rights to varying and often deeply contingent demands for differentiated political inclusivity in modern societies, the suspicion that contemporary society reflects a weakening of public law is disputable, and the terms in which this suspicion is expressed appear (at least) somewhat simplistic.

4. THE FUNCTIONAL EXTENSION OF PUBLIC LAW

Against this background, the analyses following seek to examine how the emerging features of public law in contemporary transnational society, although showing prominent internal variations in relation to the classical corpus of public law, also disclose key continuities, at a more submerged functional level, with earlier patterns of public law. This is particularly the case in the status of public law in relation to the autonomy of the political domain. On one hand, in the contemporary inter- or transnational political system public law retains its original abstractive function: it is a defining feature of contemporary society that the role of public law in facilitating the iterable transmission of power is deeply accentuated. On the other hand, the late-modern system of public law relies to an increased degree on the quality of rights as institutions internally promoting the inclusionary abstraction of power, and the formation of a normative apparatus for applying power to matters of complex social resonance. Indeed, the great functional achievement of national public law in using rights to incorporate a construction of power's constituent source as recursively internal to power has become the vital dimension in the contemporary public-legal order of transnational society. Contemporary society, in consequence, is not marked by a decline in public law. Instead, tendencies already implied in classical public law, far from losing significance, have assumed greater refinement and functional prominence in the contemporary legal order.

---

modèle européen de contrôle de constitutionnalité des lois', in Revue internationale de droit comparé 46(3) (1994) 891–9, esp. 892.

[51] See notably Richard Bellamy, *Political Constitutionalism. A Republican Defence of the Constitutionality of Democracy* (Cambridge, Cambridge University Press, 2007), ch 3.

As discussed, for example, the first and most obvious feature of the emergent inter- or transnational political system, often viewed as reflecting a weakening of public law, is the consolidation of an increasingly autonomous arena of inter- or transnational law, capable of placing normative constraints, with effective constitutional force, on a variety of national and international political actors and institutions. This is evident in numerous facets of the contemporary legal arena. As noted, this is evident in the increasingly widespread phenomena of interjudicial comity and judicial transplantation (usually guided by the increasing uniformity of rights).[52] This is visible in the implicit expectation that international norms, applied by courts and other international actors authorized by international courts, will determine acts of constituent foundation and statutory legislation conducted in national settings.[53] Above all, this is reflected in the strong international presumptions in favour of abstract human rights, which mean that national legislatures (even those ideologically committed to legislative primacy) routinely subject statutes to scrutiny and review in light of an effectively international catalogue of rights.[54] As considered further on p. 52, this is also manifest in the sphere of international private law, especially in the fact that in some disputes private-legal controversies are easily able to generate normative rulings that transcend national boundaries and possess potentially constraining force for public actors.[55] In each of these cases, public law is either layered over or undercut (or both) by internationally constructed norms that fragment the consistency of legal order and have a provenance standing outside the classical sources of public law.

In each case, however, it is only if a highly literal perspective is deployed that these tendencies need to be seen as marking a categorical decline in public law. Instead, the formation of an autonomous inter- or transnational legal arena reflects a process in which the functions of inclusion and abstraction originally performed by public law are both preserved and intensified, and public law preserves its defining functions in reflexively demarcating an autonomous political domain in society. In particular, this process gives expression to a dynamic in

---

[52] See Christopher McCrudden, 'A Common Law of Human Rights? Transnational Judicial Conversations on Constitutional Rights', in Oxford Journal of Legal Studies 20(4) (2000) 499–532, esp. 501.

[53] For extreme cases, see Philipp Dann and Zaid Al-Ali, 'The Internationalized *Pouvoir Constituant*— Constitution-making under External Influence in Iraq, Sudan and East Timor', in *Max Planck Yearbook of United Nations Law* 10 (2006) 423–63. More generally, new states are now typically made, in part at least, by international organizations, and compliance with normative dictates of such organizations is a precondition of statehood. See on this José E. Alvarez, *International Organizations as Law-Makers* (Oxford: Oxford University Press, 2005) 128, 264; Alison Duxbury, *The Participation of States in International Organizations. The Role of Human Rights and Democracy* (Cambridge: Cambridge University Press, 2009) 104; Simon Chesterman, *You, the People. The United Nations, Transitional Administration, and State-building* (Oxford: Oxford University Press, 2004) 140.

[54] For this claim *in nuce*, see Alec Stone Sweet, 'The Constitutional Council and the Transformation of the Republic', in *Yale Law School Faculty Scholarship Series*. Paper 79: <http://digitalcommons.law.yale.edu/fss_papers/79/> 1–7, esp. 1.

[55] For diverse analysis of this in different contexts, see David Jacobson, 'New Border Customs: Migration and the changing Role of the State', in UCLA Journal of International Law and Foreign Affairs 3 (1999) 443–62, esp. 447; Karen J. Alter, 'Private Litigants and the New International Courts', in Comparative Political Studies 39 (2006) 22–49.

which the defining functional dimension of rights in public law is in certain key respects accentuated, and the constitutive capacity of rights for projecting normative premises for collective legal/political inclusion is dramatically augmented and refined. Notably, in the emergent inter- or transnational legal arena, rights project principles for the foundation of a normative structure for society, which is able to provide a cohesive premise for legal inclusion in extremely uncertain social terrains, and they institute a normative apparatus in which political power can be evenly applied to matters of complex, precariously contingent, and insecure resonance. Moreover, rights enable relatively stable processes of norm formation, even under circumstances where reference to an originating *voluntas* is highly restricted. Further, rights express implicit legitimating formulae for the legal system so that it can respond to an ever-increasing need for decisions and for iterable power in societal environments, in which the authorization of decisions by single volitional mandates is improbable.[56]

In each of these respects, the emerging transnational legal arena can be placed on a direct functional continuum with the elements of classical public law. The original structure of public law, formed to provide a reasonably stable, and internally extensible, system of normative inclusion for exchanges in society conducted at a rising level of complex collective resonance might even—in fact—be seen to *culminate* in the contemporary corpus of transnational law. Above all, in the emergent inter- or transnational legal order it is observable that rights continue to articulate and solidify an inner code for the political system. Rights are inscribed within the law as institutions which allow the rapid and contingent reproduction of political power, and they make possible the authorization of highly improbable, internally projected, yet also relatively reliable and extensible, systems of normative inclusion. The contemporary political system forms itself by transplanting power across society through, and as internally authorized by, rights, and it utilizes rights to secure processes of resonant legal and political inclusion against the highly precarious and uncertain realities to which they are applied. In this respect, rights remain, as ever, the code of the political, constructed in the evolving vocabulary of public law.

In addition, a second feature of the emergent inter- or transnational political system habitually taken to indicate a decline in the status of public law is the growing primacy of international judiciaries and national judiciaries bound by international norms, which means that courts themselves habitually function as constituent polity-building actors. The tendency towards polity construction through courts is manifest in a number of ways. It is evident—as already discussed—in the constraining of constituent acts in new or transitional polities, and in the expectation that spontaneous acts of constituent power will be proportioned to international rights-based expectations.[57] It is observable in the rising prominence of judicial actors, interpreting and enforcing international norms, as potent

---

[56] Richard Münch, *Das Projekt Europa. Zwischen Nationalstaat, regionaler Autonomie und Weltgesellschaft* (Frankfurt am Main: Suhrkamp, 1993) 134–5.

[57] For the most obvious recent case, see Heinz Klug, *Constituting Democracy. Law, Globalism and South Africa's Political Reconstruction* (Cambridge: Cambridge University Press, 2000) 1; John Dugard,

counterweights to established legislative organs within national states. It is also apparent in supranational political systems, in which courts create a normative structure that internally alters nation-state institutions, and removes certain questions a priori from effective nation-state-level jurisdiction. Salient in all of these respects, in particular, is the fact that rights are embodied in constitutions at a high level of international abstraction, and the original functions of political formation, institutional construction, and even legitimization once accorded to democratically authorized actors are now attributed to rights and institutions that apply rights. Across national divides, courts now habitually invoke rights *to stand in for* constituent power: in fact, courts often double up as constituent power and constituted power at the same time, and they implement a constitution which—paradoxically—they create *ex nihilo* through acts of simultaneously constituent and constituted interpretation.[58]

Clearly, at one level such tendencies appear to undermine most integral functions of public law, and they appear even to effect a return to the semi-pluralistic *gouvernement des juges* characteristic of some societies of early modernity: that is, before the politically unifying rights revolutions of the Enlightenment, where public law was still under-evolved.[59] At a different level, however, it needs to be seen that the growth in the power of international judicial functions does not as such stand in contradiction with the original functional substance of public law. Courts applying rights respond to the same functional requirements as classical public law, and the prominence of rights in the transnational growth of 'courtocracy' preserves and intensifies the classical function of public law in constructing an autonomous political domain and in facilitating the transmission of power through law, against a backdrop of escalating inclusionary demands, at a high level of insulation and inner consistency.[60] Indeed, underlying the current changes in transnational constitutional design is a process in which the original

---

'International Law and the South African Constitution', in European Journal of International Law 8 (1997) 77–97, esp. 78.

[58] Obvious examples can be found in court-led transitions to democracy (ie Poland and Hungary in the 1980s and 1990s). Another example might be the EU itself and the ECJ's doctrine of supremacy. In reference to this, one commentator has observed a process of constitutional integration *through rights*: Sionaidh Douglas-Scott, 'A Tale of Two Courts: Luxembourg, Strasbourg and the Growing European Human Rights Acquis', in Common Market Law Review 43 (2006) 619–65, esp, 645. In the EU, it is argued, there is 'no scope for creation *ex nihilo* of a distinctive constituent power': Neil Walker, 'Post-Constituent Constitutionalism? The Case of the European Union', in Martin Loughlin and Neil Walker (eds), *The Paradox of Constitutionalism. Constituent Power and Constitutional Form* (Oxford: Oxford University Press, 2007) 247–68, esp. 259. See additionally Neil Walker, 'Reframing EU Constitutionalism', in Jeffrey L. Dunoff and Joel P. Trachtman (eds), *Ruling the World? Constitutionalism, International Law, and Global* Governance (Cambridge: Cambridge University Press, 2009) 149–76, esp. 172. On the link between national and international courts as devices for stabilizing the constitutional order of the EU, see Andreas Voßkuhle, 'Multilevel Cooperation of the European Constitutional Courts: *Der Europäische Verfassungsgerichtsverbund*', in European Constitutional Law Review 6 (2010) 175–98; Ingolf Pernice, 'La Rete di Costituzionalità—Der Europäische Verfassungsverbund und die Netzwerktheorie', in Zeitschrift für ausländisches öffentliches Recht und Völkerrecht 70 (2010) 51–71, especially at 55.

[59] See Chris Thornhill, *A Sociology of Constitutions*, 178–81.

[60] Kim Lane Scheppele, 'Constitutional Negotiations. Political Contexts of Judicial Activism in Post-Soviet Europe', in International Sociology 18(1) (2003) 219–38, esp. at 222.

inclusionary and politically formative dimensions of public law are re-articulated, and a system of public-legal order is instituted which is specifically adapted to constructing a political arena able to absorb the most resonant exchanges in the ultra-interdependent functions of modern society. That is to say, a system of public law is presently emerging whose internal concentration on uniform subjective rights applied by courts enables it to produce and ascribe legitimacy to political power in a form requiring little external authorization, and capable of producing manifold decisions in highly iterable and recursive fashion. Such public law is internally responsive to the weak centralization of modern society, to the highly contingent environments to which the law needs to be applied, and to the uncontrollably proliferating requirement for decisions and statutory inclusion. Seen in these terms, the rising abstraction of rights and courts acting as custodians of rights appears as the defining dimension of a new model of public law, in which highly distilled rights construct a condition of transnationally extensible normativity, which is sustainable across intensely varied and unpredictable terrains. Far from marking the end of public law, however, this reconstructs and perpetuates the original functions of public law, and it intensifies the quality of public law in articulating the political functions of society. Once again, in fact, in the emergent judicial-democratic constitution of contemporary society rights can be identified as an internal coding of political power, which enables societies selectively to identify those exchanges relevant for and included in power, and to promote the inclusionary use of power across rapidly changing societal environments. In contemporary transnational society, rights act autonomously to produce political power, and the reference of social interactions to abstracted rights immediately stimulates the formation of effective political structures and the conduct of societal exchange in a distinctively political dimension.

A third component of the emergent inter- or transnational political system often viewed as reducing the force of public law is the growth of trans-judicial legal pluralism. As mentioned above, the increase in legal pluralism can be identified in and ascribed to many phenomena. To speak generally, however, rising legal pluralism can be attributed, on the one hand, to the fact that political actors are widely constrained by multiple overlapping national and international (and thus, *de facto, transnational*) norms. A particular consequence of this, clearly, is that the hierarchical order of classical public law dissolves, and ultimate points of normative regress become contestable and are often disputed between rival political and judicial actors. Moreover, rising legal pluralism can be attributed to the fact that the distinction between public and private law is increasingly unsettled. One consequence of this is that access to legislative power is distributed between apparently public and evidently private agents.[61] An additional consequence of

---

[61] Standing in for much, see the account of a new public law based in a 'dissolution of state sovereignty into function-oriented structures' and the 'accompanying decentralization of the production of law': Thomas Vesting, 'The Network Economy as a Challenge to Create New Public Law (Beyond the State)', in Karl-Heinz Ladeur (ed.), *Public Governance in the Age of Globalization* (Farnham: Ashgate, 2004) 247–88, esp. 286.

this is that private spheres of exchange generate both soft and hard legal structures outside the delineated jurisdiction of public law.[62]

In this respect, the argument that public law is in retreat, and that the emergence of new inter- or transnational legal forms obstructs typical functions of public law, appears at its most plausible. In support of this assumption, it is surely the case that in contemporary society even the most established national systems of public law demonstrate high porosity to norms of varying international provenance, and they are required to derive authorization from different sources in different spheres of jurisdiction.[63] Similarly, it is demonstrable that traditionally private agents (including, for example, NGOs, firms, law companies, standard-setting agencies, professional associations, and other bodies acting as private norm entrepreneurs) are able to assume roles with effective political substance, and their access to quasi-legislative power erodes the distinction and regularity of public-legal order.[64] In addition, it is equally apparent that formally private spheres of exchange currently generate norms with sufficient force to check and countervail the operations of political institutions: in many cases, legal norms now by-pass normative centres of public authority, and normative regulatory systems, capable of constraining the authority of embedded political actors, evolve without immediate political involvement and without reference to any founding public author.[65] In each respect, legal pluralism appears to contradict the basic pattern of public law, and it seems to reflect an emergent legal order *sui generis*, in which both the constitutional sources and the strict organization of classical public law are fragmented.

Nonetheless, to comprehend this emergent pluralistic legal order and to appreciate the connection between this order and classical models of public law, it is again vital to analyse the status of rights. In the formation of the present pluralistic constitution, rights once more play a highly prominent role. In this role, they can be seen as retaining traces of, and even as intensifying, the original functions first imputed to them as institutions of public law.

At one level, for example, the formation of law through the pluralistic intersection between national and international law is shaped decisively by rights. In fact, the pluralistic engendering of law along the lines of convergence between the national and the international domain relies structurally on rights, and rights, enforced by courts, form institutions that intermittently authorize the weakening of national law by transnational law. Rather than reflecting a decline in the status of public law, however, the abstract and inclusive functions of rights in classical public law are re-condensed in this process, and rights enable contemporary societies to

---

[62] See notes 38 and 40.

[63] Nicholas Bamforth, 'Courts in a Multi-layered Constitution', in Nicholas Bamforth and Peter Leyland (eds), *Public Law in a Multi-layered Constitution* (Oxford: Hart, 2003) 277–310, esp. 301–302.

[64] Peer Zumbansen, 'Transnational Legal Pluralism' in Transnational Legal Theory 1(2) (2010) 141-189, 152; Sigrid Quack, 'Legal Professionals and Transnational Law-Making: A Case of Distributed Agency' in Organization 14 (2007) 643–66, 645, 650, 655; Gralf-Peter Calliess and Moritz Renner, 'Between Law and Social Norms: The Evolution of Global Governance' in Ratio Juris 22(2) (2009) 260–80, 273.

[65] See notes 38 and 40.

adapt to their growing inner contingency and rapidly to construct relatively uniform modes of political inclusion across unstructured societal backgrounds. As discussed, the fact that rights assume intensifying importance as elements of legal formation allows transnational societies to adjust to the increasing precariousness of the environments and the increasing dislocation of the objects of legal inclusion. And law's internal reference to rights makes it possible for these societies to project foundations for, and then multiply political decisions across, society at an extreme level of contingency and extensibility. Rights implant in the law a formula which allows the law to replicate legal order across society without recourse to external norms or external support. As a result, legal order becomes positively and internally hyper-extensible: law dispenses with its original reliance on founding substructures such as representation or popular will formation, and it is able contingently to reach across and incorporate highly diverse social exchanges and to perform highly improbable acts of legal authorization and prohibition. In fact, as in classical public law, rights allow the law of contemporary transnational society to store an image of constituent power and, in the face of extreme societal uncertainty, invariably to supply this to accompany and facilitate its normative self-reproduction. In the contemporary transnational setting, rights abstract power where there is no clear authoritative origin for power: they become a final, virtual source of power's abstraction and inclusion. In this, however, they give intensified expression to their original functions at the genesis of modern society's functional structure.

Still more strikingly, rights play a similarly vital role in the creation of law by many actors and entities as it evolves at the interface between public and private legal domains. Most obviously, firstly, the widespread ascription of (originally) public powers of legislation to (originally) private actors (networks, NGOs, corporate bodies, etc.) depends typically on the ability of such actors to raise a claim to represent, enact, and show compliance with rights, regulated ultimately, at a national and at a transnational level, by courts.[66] This too, however, need not be viewed as a functional fragmentation of public law. In such cases, on the contrary, rights reinforce public law because they provide a rough constitutional system (that is, a bundle of legal and procedural norms) that makes it possible for political actors to assimilate bearers of private power (often for short periods of time) into the widened periphery of state authority and even to engender rapidly hybridized private/public sources of legislative and normative control.[67] In so doing, rights contribute in vitally spontaneous fashion to the extension of political power across society, and they serve as norms permitting the build-up of improvised political structures in the absence of strong, embedded institutions. In this respect, rights act autonomously to consolidate an informally extensible or networked political domain, sensitive to the weak, volitional structure of global society, and agents referring to rights are able locally to make rigid the cycles of normative political inclusion required by society.

---

[66] See Anne Peters, 'Compensatory Constitutionalism', esp. 583.

[67] Elsewhere, this is portrayed as 'partial de-constitutionalization': Engel, 'Hybrid Governance', 574.

In parallel, secondly, the fact that private-legal disputes are able to produce spontaneous but powerful norms across national divides also depends on law's internalization of rights as sources of its inner projective authority. The spontaneous force of private law in producing quasi-constitutional norms in contemporary society has been widely diagnosed in recent literature, and it is normally seen as a factor that restricts and disperses the authority of political actors and even reflects a 'de-centralization of the political' as a generic condition.[68] However, the opposite of this can be equally asserted. In the international setting, the reference to rights allows law, even law originally classified as *private*, to institute itself as *de facto* public law, and private law deploys rights to construct dimensions of an autonomous political domain, across national/geographical fault lines, in which resonant social objects are subject to inclusion through power.[69] The reference to transnational rights enables law to borrow a quantum of originally political power, and rights inscribe an image of constituent authority in law to solidify legal exchanges across otherwise normatively uncontrollable spaces and activities. In so doing, rights act *ex nihilo* to produce and make accessible political power for spheres of society generating highly contingent legal objects and requiring spontaneous normative order. In these respects, rights articulate a legal arena that is extra-political—or private. Yet rights also create a normative system with effectively political characteristics, able internally to overarch and capture informal and highly diffuse exchanges, to produce spontaneous grounds for quasi-legislative acts, and to authorize common normative structures in highly contingent fashion. Rights endlessly add a political dimension to the law, and they permit law, without specific constituent mandate, to construct *from within itself* a politically inclusionary apparatus for society, even where vertical patterns of jurisdiction are not sustainable. Even (or most particularly) in their extreme spontaneity and contingency, therefore, rights act as vital institutes for the abstraction and extension of specifically political power. Even (or most particularly) in such qualities, rights form a code for the political system, which sustains political inclusion and transmission in deeply counter-factual normative fashion. Indeed, the capacity of private exchanges to articulate themselves in relation to international rights norms means that these exchanges *become political*: that is, they provide a normative apparatus in which a society can positively address matters of deep uncertainty and high complex resonance, and these exchanges acquire an inner, highly iterable political structure through their coding as relevant for rights.[70]

---

[68] Fischer-Lescano, 'Luhmanns Staat und der transnationale Konstitutionalismus', 109. See also Peer Zumbansen, 'Piercing the Legal Veil: Commercial Arbitration and Transnational Law' in European Law Journal 8(3) (2002) 400–32, 432.

[69] On the quasi-constitutional status of rights in transnational private law see Peer Zumbansen, 'Transnational Law' in Jan Smits (ed.), *Encyclopedia of Comparative Law* (Cheltenham: Edward Elgar, 2006), 738–754, 747; Andreas Fischer-Lescano, 'Die Emergenz der Globalverfassung' in Zeitschrift für ausländisches öffentliches Recht und Völkerrecht 63 (2003) 717–60, 735, 751.

[70] Indeed, even the hyper-complex and spontaneous production of an international constitution of private law observed by Gunther Teubner is seen as structurally anchored in rights. See Gunther Teubner, 'Globale Zivilverfassungen: Alternativen zur staatszentrierten Verfassungstheorie', in Marcelo

5. CONCLUSION: RIGHTS AFTER PUBLIC LAW

As examined, the categorization of rights as aspects of public law is often subject to debate. However, rights are fundamentally integral to the functions of public law and to the construction of the political dimension of society. As discussed, rights are prerequisites for the abstraction of political power as a positively reproducible societal phenomenon, and they enable political power positively to reproduce itself as a source of consistent statutory force across highly variable legislative environments, and in relation to extremely precarious objects of inclusion and statutory outcomes. If public law is viewed as a formula of political abstraction and inclusion, rights are the vital and integral dimension of public law. Other dimensions of public law rely deeply on rights. In particular, rights accomplish their functions of abstraction and inclusion by allowing power to account for itself as authorized by a public constituent power which it internalizes within itself, and from which it projects its normative authority and performs acts of stable inclusion for exchanges of complex collective resonance at a high level of internally controlled, and often counter-factual, consistency. Notably, these public-legal functions of rights have assumed increasing importance as the environmental complexity of society has increased and its legislative processes and demands for legitimacy have become more uncertain, more transnationally interconnected, and less inherently manageable. Under these conditions, the ability of rights to provide an inner coding for power has become vital for the capacity of a modern, globally differentiated society to *have politics* and to respond to political objects at a level of selectively measured inclusivity. Rights endlessly consolidate the primary function of public law in tracing and preserving a distinct political arena in society.

On this basis, it appears that the suggestion that contemporary society is in some way marked by a decline in public law rests on a miscomprehension. The functionally dominant element of public-legal order—rights—has in fact become manifestly more pronounced in modern global society: this aspect of public law has been intensified whilst other (always latently less powerful) aspects have been diminished, or assimilated into rights. Above all, modern society avails itself to an increasing degree of the capacity of rights for constructing inclusionary norms without reference to external founding authors of power. This becomes the mainstay of political inclusion. Contemporary public law in fact gives final prominence to the functions of *virtual democratic inclusion* always implicit in public law. To facilitate this, however, the implicit coding of the political through rights is cemented and accentuated.[71] The fact that modern politics was always (albeit rather opaquely) coded as rights becomes acutely visible in contemporary transnational public law.

Neves and Rüdiger Voigt (eds), *Die Staaten der Weltgesellschaft. Niklas Luhmanns Staatsverständnis* (Baden-Baden: Nomos, 2007) 117–47, esp. 139.

[71] See David Jacobson and Galya Benarieh Ruffer, 'Courts across Borders: The Implications of Judicial Agency for Human Rights and Democracy', in Human Rights Quarterly 25(1) (2003) 74–92, esp. 83, 86, 90.

❧ 4 ❧

Private and Public: Some Banalities
About a Platitude

William Lucy[1]

I. THE PLATITUDE

Of all the platitudes with which we could begin, one is pre-eminently salient. It is not an everyday platitude, of which there are many, but an intellectual platitude, of which there are also many. It holds that there is no single, comprehensive, and compelling distinction between 'public' and 'private'. Like all platitudes, this requires only a little unpacking. 'Single', of course, means exactly what it says, but what of 'comprehensive' and 'compelling'? For present purposes, let us assume that a distinction is comprehensive if it fits almost all conceivable instances in which it might be appropriately used. Whenever a question about public and private arises, the same single version of the distinction must always be in play. For a distinction to be compelling, we will stipulate that the reasons supporting it are salient and weighty whenever it is in play. Thus the reasons for distinguishing between sheep and goats must have near-universal applicability, those reasons always being pertinent in all our interaction with and thought about sheep and goats. A final stipulation: assume that a compelling single version of the sheep/goat, public/private, or any other distinction must almost always generate a dispositive bivalent answer. Something must be either public or private, sheep or goat, and the claim that it is one or the other is always either true or false, right or wrong. There is no explicit middle ground.

The three features that the platitude denies—singularity, comprehensiveness, and 'dispositiveness'—might be regarded as impossibly demanding requirements for any version of any distinction, never mind 'the' public/private distinction. But our specification of these features is not absolute, by virtue of the qualifications '*almost* all', '*almost* always', and '*near* universal'. This mitigates their stringency to some degree. There is, however, an advantage in conceiving the three features in

---

[1] This essay extends some of the themes in my 'What's Private about Private Law?', ch 3 of A. Robertson and Tang Hang Wu (eds), *The Goals of Private Law* (Oxford: Hart Publishing, 2009) 47–75 and overlaps, in section 2, with W. Lucy and A. Williams, 'Private and Public: Neither Deep nor Meaningful?', ch. 2 of K. Barker and D. Jensen (eds), *Public and Private Law: Key Encounters* (Cambridge: Cambridge University Press 2013). I owe a debt of gratitude to Phil Handler, John Murphy, Robert Thomas, Adam Tucker, Alexander Williams, and participants at gatherings in Edinburgh and Brisbane for thoughts, comments, and corrections.

their most stringent form: any distinction that satisfies them will be maximally powerful, useful, and informative. It is also informative and interesting to see how far, and why, specific versions of particular distinctions fall short of satisfying the three features, stringently understood.

The platitude's three features can be stated in positive rather than negative terms. Taken as an affirmation, the platitude holds that 'the' public/private distinction is plural, limited, and tentative. This was presumably not always a platitudinous set of claims. The thought it expresses was once perhaps an original and interesting hunch, although it is now a well-embedded feature of our knowledge. The field of knowledge in which the platitude holds sway is the human sciences. Thus, many historians (economic, social, and cultural), anthropologists (cultural and social), sociologists, economists, and philosophers make one or more of the following claims, each of which serves either to echo or to support the platitude's three features.[2] In addition to holding that there is no single, uniquely salient way of distinguishing public from private, these scholars also note that various versions of the distinction not only overlap in some cases but pull in completely different directions in others. One version of the distinction can therefore place in one realm an institution, set of practices, rules, or expectations which, in another version of the distinction, is placed within the allegedly opposite realm. A third claim is this: the way in which any particular version of the distinction is drawn depends upon the purposes for which it is used, and the wider social, economic, and cultural context in which it is invoked. What is 'private' in some places and times is not so regarded in other places at other times. Fourth—and partly because of the issues illuminated in the third claim—it is maintained that particular versions of the distinction are almost always controversial and contested. A fifth claim, both common and well substantiated, is that many versions of the public/private distinction yield a genuine and explicit trichotomy—for example, 'public' (the state), 'private' (the market), and 'other' (civil society)—rather than a simple dichotomy. All versions presumably also yield an implicit trichotomy, simply because there lurks in the background of all ostensibly dichotomous distinctions a third, 'other', category. If the world contains more than just sheep and goats, and has dimensions beyond public and private, then this additional and rarely attended-to category is indispensible.

What inferences, if any, can lawyers and jurists draw from the platitude? There are three plausible inferences we are entitled to and probably should draw, although only two are discussed in what follows. Sections 2 and 3 elucidate them, the third inference having been examined elsewhere.[3] These three

---

[2] For a rich and varied range of examples, see S. Benn and G. Gaus (eds), *Public and Private in Social Life* (London: Croom Helm, 1983); J. Habermas, *The Structural Transformation of the Public Sphere* (Cambridge: Polity, 1989); J. Weintaub and K. Kumar (eds), *Public and Private in Thought and Practice* (Chicago: University of Chicago Press, 1997); M. P. d'Entreves and U. Vogel (eds), *Public and Private: Legal, Political and Philosophical Perspectives* (London: Routledge, 2000); R. Geuss, *Public Goods, Private Goods* (Princeton: Princeton University Press, 2001).

[3] The third inference holds that it is a mistake to expect any particular version of the public/private distinction to be dispositive in legal disputes. I discuss it at 70–74 of 'What's Private About Private Law?',

inferences are neither particularly obscure nor complex, nor can they be regarded as innovative and original. They deserve another label: they are banal. Sometimes, however, the obvious and banal needs be brought into focus since, although before our very eyes, we are so close as to be unable to see. As will become clear, the two inferences overlap to some extent and support one another. Taken in conjunction with the third, they generate a plausible, banal—but for lawyers at least, by no means commonplace—view of 'the' public/private distinction.

Can this view of 'the' public/private distinction aid our understanding of public and private *law*? Not directly. For while it throws some light on the dissatisfaction we lawyers often experience when grappling with that distinction, it tells us relatively little about how to conceive of public and private law, understood as the task of providing a theoretical framework for these disciplines. Each of the two conceptions of public law that inform this volume—the external conception, in which public law is essentially *droit publique*, and the internal conception, in which public law regulates the *inter se* relations between governing institutions and their relations with individuals[4]—resonates with a number of the distinctions between public and private examined herein. But neither conception of public law is made pre-eminently salient as a result. And that is exactly what we should expect, if the suggestion made in Section 3.2 is correct, namely, that 'the' public/private distinction is not as normatively deep as is often assumed. Most versions of the distinction are a consequence, and not a determinant, of prior and deeper normative commitments. Those commitments will surely determine the conception of public (or private) law we embrace, just as they seem to determine different versions of the public/private distinction.

2. BANALITY NO. I

The first banality holds that the platitude is as true of attempts to distinguish private and public in the juristic context as it is in many others. The issue tackled here is the legitimacy of that extrapolation. We cannot simply assume that the platitude applies within the legal context just as it does within others; this needs to be shown. How might this be done? One way is by noting both the longevity and multiplicity of juristic efforts to distinguish satisfactorily between public and private. Such efforts were made in the early Roman republic and beyond—for example, in table IX of the Twelve Tables (449 BC), or in the *Institutes* (circa

---

(see note 1), and in section 3 of W. Lucy and A. Williams, 'Public and Private: Neither Deep Nor Meaningful?', note 1. Not all lawyers succumb to the mistake: Peter Cane is a noteworthy exception. See his 'Accountability and the Public/Private Distinction', in N. Bamforth and P. Leyland (eds), *Public Law in a Multi-Layered Constitution* (Oxford: Hart Publishing, 2003) and 'Public Law and Private Law: A Study of the Analysis and Use of a Legal Concept' in J. Eekelaar and J. Bell (eds), *Oxford Essays in Jurisprudence, 3rd Series* (Oxford: Clarendon Press, 1987) 57–78.

[4] See Ch 1, pp 1–4 and Ch 2.

534 AD), book I, title I (4)—and they are still with us today.[5] Moreover, these various efforts to distinguish public and private range from the astonishingly simple, to the complex, multiple, and cross-cutting. The longevity and sheer variety of juristic efforts to distinguish public and private form an obvious parallel with efforts to distinguish the two in non-juristic contexts, thus lending plausibility to the extrapolation.

The extrapolation is plainly not a logically necessary inference. I suggest only that it is a plausible move because efforts to distinguish public and private in the juristic realm have a number of features in common with similar efforts in other realms, as the remainder of this chapter aims to show. The argument probably cannot be made more powerful than this without an assessment of all the reasons that might show the juristic realm to be exceptional or quite distinct from other realms. While that demanding task cannot be undertaken here, three tempting and not unrelated arguments about law's exceptional nature should be noted. The first takes this form: it could be insisted that the various versions of the public/private distinction espoused by non-lawyers cannot be relied upon when attempting to understand how that distinction operates *within* the law. The public/private distinction as drawn by lawyers is internal to the law—it is intended to operate within particular segments and sub-segments of legal doctrine as a solution to specific legal questions. By contrast, the multiple distinctions between public and private offered by historians, sociologists, and others can, at most, serve as organizing principles for legal doctrine as a whole, having no operative role within the law. That some versions of the public/private distinction are meaningfully 'internal' to law, while others are 'external' to it, is a significant point. But it is not, as we will see in the following section, sufficiently powerful to block the extrapolation.

The second attempt to block the extrapolation deserves attention because it highlights a familiar aspect of lawyerly experience. This aspect can be dubbed law's *stipulative sovereignty*, the idea being that contemporary legal systems are able to dictate the meaning of the terms and concepts they use. It is thus commonplace for lawyers to remind non-lawyers that legal usage and meaning is often very different indeed from non-legal usage and meaning. That the law does this is not just an expression of the standard stipulative power that all language users have.[6] Rather, it is thought necessary and appropriate in some

---

[5] In Roman discourse at least two understandings of the public sphere were available. One was the public sphere understood as *res publica* (the common property and concern of Roman citizens), while the other conceived the public domain as representing the range of imperial sovereignty or *imperium*. For discussion of a famous conflict between the former and one sense (self-interest) of 'the private', see Geuss, *Public Goods, Private Goods*, ch 3. It seems that medieval law did not regard public/private as marking a significant or interesting distinction or set of distinctions: W. Ullman, *The Medieval Idea of Law as Represented by Lucas de Penna* (London: Methuen, 1946) 58; C. Brooks, *Law, Politics and Society in Early Modern England* (Cambridge: Cambridge University Press, 2008) 352; and Habermas, note 2, at 7 ('[A] public sphere in the sense of a separate realm distinguished from the private sphere cannot be shown to have existed in the feudal society of the High Middle Ages'). For contemporary juristic discussions of the distinction, see notes 12 and 41.

[6] The classic exemplification of which was offered by Humpty Dumpty: see L. Carroll, *Through the Looking Glass, and What Alice Found There* (London: MacMillan, 1872) 72.

circumstances for the law to define words and concepts in a technical, non-standard way in order to accommodate particular legal goals or purposes. This supposedly general truth about law might be invoked in the current context to show that the platitude need not 'infect' the law. Law's stipulative sovereignty, it could be argued, insures it against variations in, and competition between, the sense and uses of concepts like public and private simply because law has the power to fix the meaning of its words and concepts.

Although not implausible, this argument falls short of blocking the extrapolation. While the law's stipulative sovereignty is undeniable, its range and power are constrained. For one thing, the law's language and concepts must be intelligible at some level to non-lawyers, if the law is to function as a means of subjecting human conduct to the governance of rules. One can only be guided by rules that one can understand. This is as true of non-lawyers wanting to live within the law and to deploy it, as it is of those non-experts charged with making legally significant decisions (such as jurors and lay magistrates). This very general constraint thus requires that the meaning of many legal words and concepts cannot be completely unintelligible to those to whom they apply. This requirement seems quite plausibly to inform another, namely, that the law's stipulative sovereignty be exercised sparingly. When words and concepts are given technical legal meanings, this is usually done explicitly and in order to achieve some or other specific legal goal. Moreover, it is done apologetically, with regret. But why? The tempting answer is because both lawyers and non-lawyers alike take seriously the general constraint just identified. And that, of course, is simply another way of saying that they value some elements of the rule of law ideal.[7] Finally, note that the argument from stipulative sovereignty just does not work in this particular context. Or, more accurately, it has not worked, since lawyers and jurists in most of the common law jurisdictions still find 'the' private/public distinction both problematic and contestable. We are therefore faced with either a domain into which law's stipulative sovereignty does not extend, or with one into which it has penetrated but without effect.

The point about law's stipulative sovereignty could be given a theoretically ambitious framework. That framework is systems theory and this is the third way in which the extrapolation might be blocked, for one of the key claims of systems theory is that different normative (and other) systems are marked by 'operative closure'. This means that they are not open to influence from other such systems except in the general sense that all systems are causally affected by their environment. Operative closure is a matter of one normative system policing its boundaries against other such systems, so that the concepts, ideas, and knowledge of one system maintain their integrity and autonomy as against those in other systems. Particular normative systems can, however, utilize concepts, ideas, and information from other such systems, but those concepts, ideas, and information become part of the accommodating normative system. Such concepts,

---

[7] For two near canonical statements, see L. L. Fuller, *The Morality of Law*, rev. edn (New Haven: Yale University Press, 1969) ch 2, and J. Raz, *The Authority of Law*, 2nd edn (Oxford: Clarendon Press, 2009) ch 11.

ideas, and information therefore cannot function, nor can they have the same meaning they once did, when part of their original normative system.[8] For some systems theorists, law is an operationally closed normative system par excellence, being particularly effective at policing its own boundaries and thus repelling 'interference' from other system domains. This general claim could clearly be invoked within the context of 'the' public/private distinction, holding that the understanding other bodies of thought and other possible normative systems have of that distinction will not influence the way in which the distinction is conceived and operates within law.

Systems theory's notion of operative closure, which asserts the relative impermeability of various systems to one another, is neither unintelligible nor radically implausible. Its problem, in the current context, is the intellectual price that needs to be paid to espouse it. That price is high: the wholesale adoption of systems theory itself, in one or other of its current versions and with all its attendant challenges and difficulties.[9] That is not a price that can be paid here, since a detailed engagement with systems theory is not part of our agenda. This potential block to the extrapolation must therefore remain a vague and brooding possibility hanging over all that follows. What immediately follows is an elucidation and evaluation of the second banality, save for one final point about the first.

If the platitude can be extended to the juristic realm, then its three features— plurality, limitedness, and tentativeness—apply there every bit as much as they apply elsewhere. The third feature, though, has special significance in the juristic context. This is because some lawyers apparently require that the distinction be doctrinally dispositive, that it should resolve actual cases. This is the fulcrum of the third inference that can be drawn from the platitude and, while undoubtedly interesting, it is not addressed here.[10]

3. BANALITY NO. 2

The second inferential banality that flows from the platitude has two principal components. The first holds that there is no single version of the public/private distinction operative in the law but a number of them. The second insists that some—but perhaps not all—versions of the distinction can be in play both practically (in particular cases) and juristically (in legal thought, teaching, and commentary). I attempt to substantiate both components by elucidating five general and two specific versions of the public/private distinction. These various versions of the distinction are worth separating out because, taken together, they accommodate many of our apparently contradictory intuitions about 'the' public/private distinction. These intuitions inform the sense many lawyers

---

[8] See N. Luhmann, *Law as a Social System* (Oxford: Clarendon Press, 2004) chs 2–4.

[9] The two principal versions on offer belong to Luhmann, *Law as a Social System* and G. Teubner (see his *Law as an Autopoietic System* (Blackwell: Oxford, 1993)). A fine critical overview of Luhmann's theory is M. King and C. Thornhill (eds), *Luhmann on Law and Politics: Critical Approaches and Applications* (Oxford: Hart Publishing, 2006).

[10] See note 3.

have, when grappling with questions of public and private, of hitting an impasse or falling into a quagmire. This sense disappears once we appreciate that our apparently conflicting intuitions can embody many or all of the following different distinctions between public and private.

Before examining the substance of these distinctions, we must note that they also differ in methodological terms. By this I mean that different versions of the distinction are constructed within different intellectual and cultural contexts and might therefore not only utilize different criteria of success and failure, but also be intended to perform different functions. In methodological terms, all of the substantively different versions of the public/private distinction examined here can usually be placed within one or other of two categories. On the one hand are general versions of the distinction. These are so named because they often have a life in the wider culture of particular societies, being part of ordinary discourse, and are usually given more precise expression, and certainly more sustained attention, by historians, sociologists, and other social scientists. It might be the case that versions of the public/private distinction at large in the culture of particular societies cannot be given more precise expression by social scientists because they are already as precise as they can be. But it is almost always true that social scientists, rather than minting a new version of the public/private distinction, purport to articulate and rediscover an already existing but insufficiently appreciated version of the distinction. That existing but insufficiently noticed version, while it might often exist in scholarly social scientific work, is also thought to have a life beyond that work, in some or other society or social context.

On the other hand are specific versions of the public/private distinction which, in contrast with general versions, are made only by lawyers about the law. This contrast can be extended a little, for specific distinctions are additionally *internal* to the law. This says more than that they are made only by lawyers and jurists, for the lawyers and jurists who espouse specific versions of the public/private distinction do so from the viewpoint of participants in, rather than external observers of, the legal system. This might be because some of these lawyers and jurists are indeed participants in the legal system in a limited sense: they are practitioners, such as judges, advocates, and legal advisers. Yet it is also because the participants' point of view is the default mode of all doctrinal and much jurisprudential scholarship.[11] Moreover, specific versions of the public/private distinction are usually intended by their proponents to operate *within* particular areas of legal doctrine (such as, for example, administrative law). These versions of the distinction therefore cannot often—if at all—be used as a means of organizing or structuring legal systems as a whole.

---

[11] I have made some effort to substantiate this claim elsewhere: *Philosophy of Private Law* (Oxford: Clarendon Press, 2007) 26–44; 'Method and Fit: Two Problems for Contemporary Philosophies of Tort Law' (2007) 52 McGill Law Journal 605; 'The Crises of Private Law', ch 7 of T. Wilhelmsson and S. Hurri, *From Dissonance to Sense: Welfare State-expectations, Privatization and Private Law* (London: Dartmouth, 1998) 177–218; and *Understanding and Explaining Adjudication* (Oxford: Clarendon Press, 1999) chs 2–3.

Many general versions of the distinction are used to do just that, being invoked as organizing principles under which many or all substantive legal doctrines are allegedly subsumable. General versions of the public/private distinction are also (i) rarely formulated from within the perspective of participants in the legal system, and (ii) almost never expected by their proponents to do legal doctrinal work. This is mainly because the methodological commitments of academic proponents of general versions of the distinction—they are, *inter alia*, historians, economists, and sociologists—entail that the participant's perspective is either suspect or not easily available. There is an interesting asymmetry here, though, which is that lawyers can make use of and recommend distinctions, ideas, and theories formulated outside the methodological perspective of their discipline. Furthermore, it is sometimes true that such distinctions, ideas, and theories resonate within the law, having a life therein, albeit in nascent or implicit form. That, at least, is what I argue about two of the general versions of the distinction between public and private. Two of the specific, allegedly purely legal versions of the public/private distinction are little more than echoes of one general version of the distinction, while the substance of another general version of the distinction resounds within a particular branch of the law of trusts. This is why, although seven versions of the distinction are in play, only five are discussed separately below. The remaining specific version of the distinction is not reducible to any more general version, but neither is it taken particularly seriously by jurists. This oddity is our starting point, but for one final preliminary observation.

The effort to classify versions of the public/private distinction as either general or specific is not exhaustive, nor do I claim that the various versions of the public/private distinction discussed here are the only versions of the distinction available. The first part of this observation highlights the fact that, in this context, the options 'general' and 'specific' need not exhaust the available logical space: there might be room for a hybrid category in which versions of the public/private distinction take on features of the other two. My claim is only that the versions of the public/private distinction considered here fit reasonably neatly into one or other category. That there are other conceivable versions of the distinction, which might fall between these two poles, is a possibility that none of the arguments following rule out. This possibility is, however, left unexplored. We have quite enough to grapple with.

3.1 Five ways of distinguishing public and private

(i). The first way of distinguishing public and private is a means of distinguishing only public and private *law*. It is, in the terminology used earlier, a specific version of the distinction, being deployed by lawyers from the perspective of lawyers. It is purely legal-doctrinal and, in English law at least, it seems both undeniable and unproblematic. The distinction consists of highlighting the various doctrinal and procedural differences between private and public law. For much of the common law's history in England the remedies for public law wrongs, the rules of standing, as well as the doctrinal requirements for establishing such wrongs and obtaining remedies, have been for the most part different from the wrongs, remedies, and doctrinal requirements embodied in private law.[12] There is now an administrative court in England, thus reinforcing a public law/private law divide.[13] This set of doctrinal, remedial, and procedural differences between public and private law is not, of course, the only possible set. Other jurisdictions draw the distinction in rather different ways,[14] but there can be no doubt that they add up to a significant distinction between the two domains.

The puzzle here is that some jurists find this way of distinguishing public and private law unsatisfying, without being perfectly clear as to why. They are content to note this legal-doctrinal distinction, yet then proceed as if it is in need of further explanation and justification.[15] What, then, is their worry? Perhaps that the legal-doctrinal distinction is insufficiently 'deep' or, what likely amounts to the same thing, is altogether too contingent. Thus, the distinction as currently embodied in English law might simply be an historical accident rather than a well-founded and valuable means of distinguishing private and public law. Espousing this view does not require great scepticism of the jurist or lawyer, but simply awareness that the law, either in the hands of judges, legislators, or both, can take wrong-turnings. These turnings can be wrong in legal, moral, or political terms. A statute, judicial decision, or line of decisions can inhibit desirable doctrinal development, or impact adversely on some aspect of commercial, social, or cultural life, as well as embodying morally and politically objectionable distinctions or suppositions.[16] This awareness inhibits the tendency to regard all legal-doctrinal development as always *prima facie* desirable and justified; it is part of the process of 'demystifying the law'.[17]

But there are at least two quite different responses to this aspect of law's fallibility. One response combines a perfectly proper critical awareness of law's normative (moral and political) fallibility with an equally proper awareness of law's normative (moral and political) contingency. The latter entails little more

---

[12] For an overview of administrative law remedies and related issues, see P. Craig, *Administrative Law*, 6th edn, (London: Thomson, 2008) part 3 and H. Wade and C. Forsyth, *Administrative Law*, 10th edn, (Oxford: Clarendon Press, 2009) part VII.

[13] From 1981 until 2000 the Crown Office List ensured that only judges with public law experience heard applications for judicial review; as a result of a Practice Direction of 20 July 2000 (Crown Office Practice Direction—The Administrative Court) the list was renamed 'The Administrative Court'.

[14] For a warning that the distinction as currently embodied in English law is a worrisome legal transplant, see J. Allison, *A Continental Distinction in the Common Law* (Oxford: Clarendon Press, 1996). A contemporary overview of the distinction in French and English law is provided by the essays in M. Freedland and J. -B. Auby (eds), *The Public Law/Private Law Divide: Une Entente assez Cordiale?* (Oxford: Hart Publishing, 2006).

[15] See Cane, 'Accountability and the Public/Private Distinction', 248–49 for some interesting observations on this issue.

[16] A common law list of shame usually includes *Lochner v New York* 198 US 45 (1905) and *Bartonshill Coal Co v Reid* (1858) 3 Macq 266.

[17] Possibly initiated or at least made prominent, in the Anglophone world, by Jeremy Bentham. See H. L. A. Hart, *Essays on Bentham* (Oxford: Clarendon Press, 1982) ch 1.

than a realization that some areas of law—taken to include not just chunks of substantive legal doctrine and their constitutive standards, but also procedural rules and broader aspects of institutional design such as the organization of the trial process—are morally and politically either over-, under-, or undetermined. The last possibility exists when some legal rule has no moral or political content, resonance, or analogue, the first when quite different substantive moral or political values actually determine the content of the same area of law. The second possibility is realized when various different substantive moral or political values are consistent with the same area of law.

Awareness of law's moral and political contingency and fallibility provides a fertile soil for this legal-doctrinal distinction between public and private. This version of the distinction is malleable, context-dependent, and unlikely to be dispositive in every legal dispute. Its contours have undeniably changed over time and, equally clearly, it has not been and is not now drawn in the same way as its legal-doctrinal equivalent in, for example, French law. Moreover, while the distinction is expected to bear some weight in particular cases, it seems rarely in and of itself dispositive. Judges and jurists usually provide a panoply of reasons to support their decisions in cases in which a public/private question arises and this version of the distinction is almost never itself conclusive.[18] This, of course, simply reinforces the overarching argumentative refrain of this chapter.

The mutability and context- (or jurisdictional) dependence of the legal-doctrinal version of the public/private distinction becomes morally and politically worrisome for some jurists in one or other of the following two scenarios. The first is simply that the distinction, as currently drawn, comes to be regarded as morally and politically mistaken. If that is so, then at some point it is likely that jurists will attempt to reformulate it and, as part and parcel of this process, will cast about for a moral and political blueprint that both explains the mistake and shows how it can be remedied. The other scenario is this: jurists and lawyers come to think that the law does and must embody a specific moral-cum-political blueprint and that this blueprint requires the public/private distinction be understood in a precise and exacting way. The current legal-doctrinal version of the distinction is objectionable if and when it departs from the ukases of the blueprint. The principal difference between these two scenarios is one of intellectual temper. In the first, the question as to what the normative basis of the public/private distinction might be is a genuinely open question; in the second, that question already has a compelling answer and the jurists' job is simply to implement it. There is a degree of normative certainty in the latter which is lacking in the former.

The latter scenario is, I think, the fulcrum of the second response to law's moral-cum-political fallibility. That the law can make moral and political mistakes is profoundly worrying on this view and jurists should aspire to minimize this possibility. One way of achieving this is by ensuring both that the law has a secure moral-cum-political basis and that this basis directly informs legal doctrine

---

[18] One example, from many, is *Aston Cantlow v Wallbank* [2004] 1 AC 546.

and legal-institutional design. This approach cannot take the legal-doctrinal version of the public/private distinction seriously without first determining its consonance with the law's moral-cum-political blueprint. If the law's moral fallibility looms large for proponents of this approach, then they are unlikely to take many of the distinctions and doctrines of existing legal systems particularly seriously.

This approach to law's fallibility and contingency informs some efforts to add normative weight to the legal-doctrinal version of the public/private distinction. One temptation here is to draw a bright and impermeable boundary between other, allegedly deep moral notions and use this as the foundation for the legal-doctrinal (or any other) version of the public/private distinction. Some jurists suggest that two pertinent and allegedly deep moral notions are those of distributive and corrective justice, although these are not the only plausible candidates. If it can be shown that (i) these two notions are absolutely incompatible, so they cannot coherently blend into one another or be meaningfully combined,[19] and (ii) that one of these notions animates public law while the other animates private law, then we might be close to generating a single, comprehensive, and compelling distinction. But the steps that need be taken for this argument to work look a great deal like unbridgeable chasms. One chasm comes to light with this question: what reasons are there to think that there is a bright and impermeable boundary between distributive and corrective justice, such that considerations of one kind cannot be coherently combined with considerations of the other? The fact that Aristotle thinks this is not enough because even if we love Aristotle, we should love truth more.[20] And the truth of the matter is that Aristotle's reasons for regarding corrective and distributive justice as separate notions that cannot be combined are weak.[21]

The second chasm concerns the *prima facie* lack of fit between existing systems of public and private law, on the one hand, and the allegedly utterly discrete notions of corrective and distributive justice, on the other. The point is that both corrective and distributive justice appear to be in play in existing systems of both private and public law. If this is not to be an embarrassment for proponents of this view, they must either explain this first impression as a mistake or conclude that this impression, while correct, serves only to indict existing systems of public and private law. Establishing the first possibility is tricky. It could involve a further specification of what corrective and distributive justice look like, the result being an improved view of their respective roles with regard to private and public law. It might also entail a closer look at these chunks of legal doctrine themselves, so as to correct the impression that corrective and distributive justice

---

[19] This seems to be Ernest Weinrib's view: *The Idea of Private Law* (Cambridge, Mass: Harvard University Press, 1995) 61 and 71–74. I have explored another possible normative basis for a distinction between public and private law in 'What's Private about Private Law?', at 58–69.

[20] I am mangling a phrase that was once thought to have been said by Aristotle of Plato; he said nothing of the kind (see *Nicomachean Ethics (NE)* in J. Barnes (ed.), *The Complete Works of Aristotle*, vol II (Princeton: Princeton University Press, 1984) at 1096a 16).

[21] See *NE* at 1131a, 10–1131b 21.

are in play in both. Both tasks are demanding and neither has as yet been discharged successfully.

The second possibility requires a heroic indifference to current law's moral and political status. This manifests itself in this judgment: the law's lack of fit with these two moral notions serves only to undermine its moral and political status and not, of course, the explanatory power of those notions. There is an unargued rule of explanatory priority at work here and it should be articulated—that law (and perhaps many other aspects of social life, institutions, and practices) must embody and fit these moral notions if it is to pass moral muster. But why start with the assumed priority of these notions, if our interest is in the moral and political and other normative value of the law itself? The question of what moral and political values do animate the law must surely be an open one that we, in part at least, answer by examining the law itself. Positing two or more pre-eminently salient moral or political notions and then indicting the law for not accommodating them either sufficiently, or in the right order, begs the question.

(ii). A second way of distinguishing public and private is by contrasting matters of general concern with matters of individual concern. This is a general version of the distinction, neither developed by lawyers nor used exclusively by them, although it is frequently articulated and refined by the courts in one context. It usually operates as a general structuring principle for whole legal systems and not only cuts across some specific versions of the public/private distinction, but also serves as a confusing background presence to their elaboration. This way of distinguishing public and private has a gravitational pull such as to cause dissatisfaction with some specific versions of the distinction.

The idea that issues of general, communal concern exist independently of those matters of concern to individuals *qua* individuals had a vivid life in the Roman republic. Matters of general communal concern and ownership were originally marked by the term *res publica* which, in one sense, was used to highlight the property and interests of the Roman army. That term came to be used in a more general sense, to include matters of concern to the community of Roman citizens in general, including their interest in public spaces constituted by various fora (religious, judicial, mercantile, etc.). Yet the term is seemingly always contrasted with those matters of concern only to individuals as individuals rather than individuals *qua* members of sub-groups within the community. The latter restriction is in need of justification, since the assumption that, when defining the realm of the private, 'individual concern' must mean 'single individual concern' (and not the concern of a collection of individuals) is just that: an assumption. This assumption makes it impossible for groups of individuals (incorporated or unincorporated, but smaller than everyone or the vast majority) to join together in their concern over some matter and remain private.[22]

---

[22] This seems to have been James Harrington's view: 'the people, taken apart, are but so many private interests, but if you take them together they are the public interest': J. Harrington and J. Toland, *The Oceana and Other Works of James Harrington* (London: A. Millar, 1700; [1st edn 1656]) 154–55. For Quentin Skinner, this is an expression of the neo-roman view that the will of the people is nothing more than 'the sum of the wills of each individual citizen': *Liberty Before Liberalism* (Cambridge: Cambridge University Press, 1998) at 28–29.

But there is no obvious and strong reason why we should not regard the interest a group of individuals has in some matter as private, provided this group is a sub-group of some larger group. The contrast between public and private in this context is therefore one between all, on the one hand, and many, some, or few, on the other. Where the group of individuals with some or other interest is identical with all the members of the only grouping in play, then it seems proper to characterize their interest not as private but as 'the' public interest. The absence of hard and fast rules of usage here also allows another twist: we might, quite properly, regard the interests of a group larger than a mere handful of people as representing the public interest in some circumstances. So, for example, it is not crazy to say that the public interest in some community would be served by the construction of a bridge across a river or a busy road, even when that community is small and when far fewer than all members will use the bridge. This scenario could also be justifiably characterized as an instance of private interest, where that means something more than 'single individual concern' but less than 'the concern of each and every member of the group'.

Bearing in mind the leeways of usage, a plausible interpretation of this version of the distinction between public and private can take alternative forms. The two terms could be used to contrast matters of relevance and interest to the whole or the vast majority of a community, on the one hand, with matters which are of relevance and interest to sub-groups of individuals (parents, occupants of a particular locale, etc.), on the other. The contrast here is between almost all (public) and some (private), rather than between many and one. Alternatively, the terms 'public' and 'private' could be used to characterize either the interests of all, or the interests of any but the very smallest group, on one hand, and the interests of individuals *qua* individuals, on the other. The contrast here is between many (public) and one or few (private).[23] Since usage licenses both characterizations, a case should be made for preferring one over the other. No such case made is presented here, however, since my argument requires only that these different uses be brought to light.

This variability of usage, and the way in which it permits lines to be drawn slightly differently in one and the same context, is evident in the deliberations of the English courts when determining the charitable status of a trust. One test that any trust must satisfy in order to be regarded as charitable in English law is that it be of public benefit.[24] The courts distinguish between sufficiently and insufficiently public groups for this purpose in ways that make use of each alternative formulation of this version of the public/private distinction. Thus it has been held that a trust can be of public benefit even if it benefits only a small number of people in a particular locality. The 'public' here is therefore envisaged as a very

[23] I do not claim that the quantifiers ('almost all', 'many', 'some', 'few') in these two formulations are ultimately logically robust; I hold only that they have some intuitive and serviceable 'everyday sense'.

[24] Charities Act 2006, ss. 2(1)(b) and 3. The case law on public benefit prior to the Act is still valid by virtue of s. 3(3) of the Act. The Charity Commission's guidance on the nature of public benefit has recently been found wanting: *The Independent Schools Council v The Charity Commission and others* [2011] UKUT 421.

small, small, or medium-sized group of individuals with an interest in common; it must, however, be more than just 'private individuals' or 'a fluctuating body of private individuals'.[25] Furthermore, even a very large number of individuals, such as 110,000 employees of a large multinational company, may not be enough to constitute the public.[26] What marks the line between a sufficiently and insufficiently 'public' group is thus not immediately obvious. It is something the courts struggle with and, viewed generously, is clearly a matter of judgment.

In the exercise of this judgment, the courts have concluded that trusts for the benefit of numerically very small groups, such as elderly Presbyterians or the occupants of a particular old-persons' home, benefit a sufficiently public group.[27] By contrast, it seems that a trust for the building and maintenance of a bridge open only to impecunious Methodists would not be of public benefit.[28] The former small groups are a segment of the public while the latter group, which could be numerically identical, is not: the distinction the courts are drawing here is therefore not one between the very many (public) and the very few (private). The courts have also accepted that trusts for the giving of public masses in a particular church and for the benefit of a specific synagogue are of public benefit, one reason being that both church and synagogue in question were open to the public at large.[29] A trust for the benefit of a Carmelite order was held to be non-charitable on the ground that, *inter alia*, the order's life had no public aspect, but was given over entirely to 'private' religious worship and meditation.[30] It seems that the only sure-fire blocks to charitable status, when the public benefit requirement is in play, is the fact that the group which stands to benefit is either much too small ('numerically negligible'),[31] or consists of members all or many of whom have a personal nexus with the benefactor(s).[32] While the courts will sometimes regard a numerically negligible group as private on grounds of its size, they will also usually regard a numerically very significant group as private if there is a personal nexus.[33]

The current version of the distinction, understood as marking a line either between almost all and some, on the one hand, or between many and few or one, on the other, is not only significant because instantiated in this area of law. The point is worth additional emphasis because it shows how a general version of the public/private distinction can resonate within the law. Neither the Charity Commission nor the lawyers and judges who grapple with the question of public

---

[25] *Verge v Summerville* [1924] AC 496 at 499 (Lord Wrenbury).

[26] See *Oppenheim v Tobacco Securities Trust Co Ltd* [1951] AC 297.

[27] See *Joseph Rowntree Memorial Trust Housing Association v Attorney General* [1983] ch 159 and *Re Neal* (1966) 110 SJ 549.

[28] *IRC v Baddeley* [1955] AC 527 at 592 (per Lord Simonds).

[29] See *Re Hetherington (Deceased)* [1990] ch 1 and *Neville Estates v Madden* [1962] ch 832.

[30] *Gilmour v Coats* [1949] AC 426.

[31] *Oppenheim*, see note 26, at 306 (per Lord Simonds).

[32] The personal nexus limit was thoroughly explored by the House of Lords in *Oppenheim*, note 26, at 306.

[33] See *Baddeley*, (note 28) (Methodists in West Ham and Leyton too small a group to be 'public').

benefit see themselves as striving to articulate non-legal common sense. Rather, they look almost exclusively to the previous cases and the body of doctrinal writing on the topic in order to reach decisions in particular cases. But, as should be obvious from the previous brief sketch of what the courts do, the issues they grapple with are exactly the same as those that animate any effort to utilize a general form of this version of the distinction.

Understood in its general form, the current version of the public/private distinction is significant for another reason. It presents a particularly vivid contrast with the fourth version of the distinction. The contrast concerns the state. While to the forefront of the fourth version of the distinction, the state is almost completely absent in the current version: it is not even a necessary condition of 'publicness' in the current version, while in the fourth version it assuredly is. However, since the state is such a prominent feature of contemporary societies, a version of the public/private distinction that does not register its presence risks being thought eccentric. That risk is nevertheless worth taking because the current version of the distinction provides both a salutary reminder about the state itself and warns of an egregious elision.

The reminder is that the state was not always with us. That is to say, humankind has not always lived with an agency of power and ostensibly legitimate authority separate from a collective body of people, on the one hand, and a powerful and presumably charismatic individual or collection of individuals, on the other hand. The state as we know it, and as it was 'invented' in modernity, is something different, in terms of its lifespan, deployment of power, and ostensible authority, from both kings and the multitude.[34] How this difference is to be conceived has been a staple of some strands of political philosophy since Thomas Hobbes posed the question and offered a distinctive and tremendously influential answer to it. One important point, for present purposes, is that we need a vocabulary to capture matters of public concern in those contexts, like the classical (not just Roman) world, in which the state as we know it did not exist.

The temptation is to read our modern notion of the state back into the historical record. Because we are familiar with this locus of power, distinct from personal and people power, we tend to assume that everyone, during every epoch, was. Once we start doing this, we are no distance at all from the egregious elision. It consists of blurring the distinction—or simply assuming it out of existence—between public concerns and interests that can be conceived independently of the state and those public concerns and interests that unavoidably involve the state. The elision usually involves assuming that the latter must subsume the former; that anything of public or collective interest must *ipso facto* involve the state or be of state interest. This assumption must be converted into an argument and that, surely, is unlikely to be categorical. It is simply very

---

[34] The argument belongs to Quentin Skinner: a lucid and magisterial presentation is ch 14 of his *Visions of Politics*, vol II (Cambridge: Cambridge University Press, 2002). A shorter version is 'The State' in T. Ball, J. Farr, and R. Hanson (eds), *Political Innovation and Conceptual Change* (Cambridge: Cambridge University Press, 1989).

difficult to imagine what reasons might show that *every* instance of the public interest, as conceived here, is also an instance of state interest or should involve the state.

If the state is not crucial to this version of the distinction, one might well wonder what relevance, if any, the distinction has for law. A rearrangement of legal doctrine around the two poles of this distinction can be attempted. The areas of law currently regarded as constituting private law might be conceived as involving matters of individual concern. The law of contract, torts, trusts, personal and real property certainly allow individuals *qua* individuals, or as members of corporate or unincorporated bodies, to give legal effect to their decisions. Private law not only provides protection for a number of interests individuals have (in their persons and holdings, for example), but also allows future planning through contracts and trusts. Public law might be regarded as entailing only matters of collective concern, being of relevance to all or the vast majority of the community. The community's constitution and rules for the deployment of force, for example, could be regarded in this light.

But there might be a problem with this attempt to inscribe the distinction into law. The distinction may not actually work as a general structuring principle for legal systems because it defines one of its poles out of existence. This worry arises once the examples mentioned in the previous paragraph are scrutinized. Think, again, of contract and tort, equity and trusts, personal and real property. While these areas of law surely protect various 'private' interests individuals have, and allow individuals to achieve various goals, is it not equally true that all members of the community have an interest in these areas of law functioning in those ways? If so, then private law, no less than public law, is a matter of public concern, an interest of, and of relevance to, each and every member of the community in which it exists. And, if all of a community's law is of interest and relevance to all members of that community, then all law is in one sense public (law).

Of course, the claim that a community's law is of interest and relevance to all members of that community is only plausible if understood as something other than an empirical truth. The claim normally contains an implicit 'ought' as well as another restriction, for it usually means: all *engaged* members of the group *ought* to interest themselves in their community's law. This 'ought' need not be a moral ought or in any sense other-directed; it can be purely prudential or self-interested. The weight carried by 'engaged' in this claim is considerable and it requires the support, at the very least, of an account of what group membership entails. In the context of the modern state, this usually becomes a discussion of citizenship and its limits.

Is it the case, then, that when deployed in the legal context this distinction actually defines one of its poles away? No. For, although the distinction generates a plausible and informative sense in which all law—public and private—is public, it also allows us to say in conjunction that some areas of law are more private than others. Some areas of law appear designed so as to facilitate and protect individuals in their pursuit of their own personal projects. This might seem like having one's cake and eating it, but only if we assume that a distinction between public and private must be unique, comprehensive, and dispositive. But this version of the distinction is clearly neither comprehensive nor dispositive, since it does not generate bivalent answers in every instance. It allows us, instead, to say that one and the same area of law is in some respects public and in other respects private. Some might regard that kind of judgment as sophisticated and informative, but it seems unlikely that all lawyers will agree.

Of all versions of the public/private distinction, the current one exercises strong gravitational force over at least two of the others. These are the two specific versions of the distinction that lawyers invoke within administrative law, which are examined in subsection (iv). For, however clear these specific versions are, almost all lawyers are uneasy about accepting them as comprehensive and deeply significant versions of the public/private distinction—they seem to miss too much about public and private. This sense is plausibly explained by the hold that the current version of the distinction has on us. All lawyers know (or feel they know) that all law is significantly public. The current version of the distinction accommodates and nurtures this view.

(iii). The third version of the distinction, like the previous version, warrants the judgment that there is an interesting and informative sense in which all law is public. The senses that 'public' and 'private' bear here are not, however, the same as the senses they have in the previous distinction. The distinction between public and private drawn here is altogether more technical and, while not as obvious in either law or the general culture as the second version, it nevertheless captures and conveys an important insight. The distinction has been drawn principally by economists and consists of distinguishing between public and private goods. Pure public goods, on this view, are non-excludable and non-rivalrous. A good is non-excludable if, once available, beneficiaries cannot be prevented from using it. The light from lighthouses has this property since, once lighthouses are functional, seafarers cannot be prevented from benefitting from their light: it is available for all to see. The light from lighthouses is also non-rivalrous, which means that its use by some does nothing to reduce its availability to others. This is clearly not true of many other goods, such as cake and apples, which are excludable and rivalrous. Such goods are quintessential private goods.

One key property of pure public goods—non-excludability—shows the difficulty in providing such goods. How might lighthouses and their attendant light be provided? An obvious path would be to seek contributions from all who stand to benefit from them. A consensual levy upon seafarers is a natural consequence. But purely self-interested seafarers have reason to avoid such a levy and to free-ride for, once light is provided, its non-excludability means that it is provided to all who stand to benefit from it whether or not they have contributed to its provision. An allegedly rational but purely self-interested individual seafarer will therefore conclude that it is better to benefit from the good without paying for it, rather than benefit from the good and pay for it. And so, too, will all other allegedly rational but purely self-interested seafarers. Yet, if this is so, the free-rider problem not only arises after provision of the good, as in our hypothetical; it will also prevent any pure public good being provided in the first place, if a sufficient number of potential beneficiaries asked for a contribution are rational and purely self-interested. They will conclude that it is better not to contribute and take the benefit if and when the good is provided by contributions from the rest. *All* economists and rational choice theorists accept that coercion is a standard solution to free-rider problems, particularly in the form of power to compel the beneficiaries of public goods to contribute towards their provision and upkeep. *Many* economists and rational choice theorists therefore conclude that the state, in the form of an organized monopoly of legitimate force, is the best or perhaps even the only way of ensuring the provision of public goods.[35]

While the argument just sketched takes as its example the light from light-houses, the view of some influential economists is that it works equally well with regard to law.[36] They think this despite the fact that law, unlike the light from lighthouses, is an impure public good at best and that much is often subsumed under the rubric 'law'. But if their claim is nevertheless that all law is a public good, this provokes a number of questions. First and foremost is this: *all* law? This question arises because 'law', when used in the claim that all law is a public good, includes not just the substantive law structured by traditional juristic divisions but also (i) the idea of the rule of law and its components, (ii) the fundamental constitutional compact that is the basis of any polity, and (iii) the notion of security (or lawfulness or stability) that supposedly flows from the presence of (i) and (ii).

One obvious worry is that these different aspects of law are not truly the same and might not therefore all be public goods. Some notions in play under the rubric 'law' seem more like 'indivisible lumps' than others: the idea of security appears, when conceived as characterizing a measurable property of community life, to be one from which some members cannot be excluded without wrong-doing.[37] So, for example, if a community has the institutions, practices, and personnel to ensure that its life is relatively free from crime and disorder, then it is hard to remove that benefit from some without subjecting them to victim-ization. Similarly, the benefits of the original constitutional compact, once entered into, appear difficult to ration in anything like a legitimate way. That the benefits and burdens of such a compact affect all who live under it is a fundamental component of its legitimacy. Any subsequent attempt to redistrib-ute those benefits and burdens seems unavoidably to undermine the power of the original compact.

While security and the original constitutional compact both look a great deal like indivisible lumps, and thus like public goods, private law does not. Not, at least, at first glance. Consider this hypothetical possibility about the private law (or laws) of contract. The merchants and consumers of one

---

[35] For an introduction to the alleged necessity of the state (and law) as a means of providing public goods see: D. Osterfeld, 'Anarchism and the Public Goods Issue: Law, Courts, and the Police' (1989) [IX/9] Journal of Libertarian Studies 47; T. Cowen, 'Law as a Public Good' (1992) 8 Economics and Philosophy 249, and the comment by D. Friedman in (1994) 10 Economics and Philosophy 319, and Cowen's rejoinder at 329–32.

[36] See J. Buchanan, *The Limits of Liberty* (Chicago: University of Chicago Press, 1975) chs 1–4 and 7.

[37] The term belongs to Osterfeld, 'Anarchism and the Public Goods Issue'; his principal argument is that security is not such an 'indivisible lump'.

geographical area use different standards to those in other areas, with merchants and consumers in different areas of economic activity doing likewise. While these different customary laws of contract could well be public goods for the various sub-groups in question, they are certainly not public goods for those outside these groups. The system of contract law used by bakers for bakers cannot be a public good for the candlestick makers who are excluded from it. This point—that it is conceivable that different laws of contract can emerge in different areas of one and the same polity—could be generalized across all aspects of private law. Thus, just as various groups might rely upon different rules for the creation or interpretation of contracts, so they might also use different rules to protect (*inter alia*) bodily integrity and physical holdings, or to distribute holdings on death.

The possibility of a plurality of systems of private law speaks against private law being a public good, at least at some originary hypothetical moment. Yet, the existence of a plurality of such systems within a single polity gives rise to externalities, the principal one being the costs involved to those participants who have to operate within more than one system.[38] A single private law system for all would reduce this particular cost and others besides. And such a system might therefore qualify as a public good for, once it is provided, its use is hard to limit on legitimate grounds. The doubt expressed by 'might' is appropriate, however, because even if it can be shown that the good a general system of private law would provide is non-excludable, there remains a question as to whether that good is indeed non-rivalrous. For, insofar as a court system and adjudication are adopted as the means of resolving private law and other legal disputes, the use of that system by some can in some circumstances prevent its use by others. One such circumstance is that in which the justice system is operating at or beyond the limits of its capacity.

This worry, and that about non-excluability, highlight the same general diffi-culty: is private law a pure public good? But the answer to that question, although interesting as a general matter, is not crucial in this context. For even if the argument in play here does not show that private law is a pure public good, it certainly shows that it has some features similar to such goods. And that is all that needs be shown to make the point that all law—private and public—is public, in the sense of being either a pure or impure public good.

(iv). The fourth distinction between public and private is often to the forefront of contemporary minds. It is, in effect, a distinction between the public conceived as the realm of the state, on the one hand, and the private understood as the realm beyond or free from the state, on the other. This version of the public/private distinction has different applications, including a role in relation to the provision of goods and services, where public (state) provision is contrasted with private (non-state) provision, and in relation to economic regulation, where public (state) regulation of the economy is compared with private (non-state) regulation. The 'public' pole of this version of the distinction can overlap with the public pole of

---

[38] The term 'externality' is almost as vague and mystifying as its close bedfellow 'transaction costs'. For guidance on both, a good starting point is C. Dahlman, 'The Problem of Externality' (1979) 22 Journal of Law and Economics 141.

the second distinction, particularly when we move (too) quickly from 'matter of interest to all or the vast majority' to 'matter of state interest'.

The principal difficulty with this version of the distinction is that it cannot always yield a bivalent answer to the question 'is this activity or conduct, practice, or institution public (or private)?' This is primarily because the domain of the state and that of the non-state are both malleable, subject to extension, contraction, and hybrid blurring. As to the latter, take the traditional state provision of some standard 'public' services, such as public transport, refuse collection, education, and health care as examples. It is not only in the UK that these services have recently been provided by private companies through a web of genuine and sometimes mock-contracts with a local or central government authority.[39] Indeed, this process of semi-privatization and 'contractualization' of public services is now a fairly common feature of many Western European democracies as well of many other nation states (such as Canada, Argentina, and the US). It is a process which, while undoubtedly public, is also significantly private. There are two quite different senses in which this process is public. First, it is public because the services provided are of interest and benefit to almost all members of the community; and, second, it is public in the sense that those services are funded, via various forms of taxation, by undeniable instruments of the 'state' (local and central government). It is also meaningfully private, this being most evident from the fact that the services in question are delivered by companies under a web of contracts which often link not only the funders and providers of services, but also the providers and consumers of services. These contracts include not just provisions relating to cost and quality but related requirements attempting to ensure responsiveness to consumers.

Is this type of service provision either public or private? Posing the question in this form shows its foolishness. It is clearly a hybrid that does not sit entirely comfortably under either description but can be accommodated by both. The most natural answer to the question, given the way in which the service provision process has just been sketched, is surely 'both'. There are, as we have seen, useful and intelligible senses in which that process can be described as both public and private. Once we understand that the question 'is X public or private?' can be answered in a more-or-less, matter-of-degree way, then our understanding of 'the' public/private distinction might improve. For if some activity or conduct, practice or institution might sensibly be both private and public in a number of ways, then it becomes plausible not just to chart those various ways, but also to consider the point of mapping the distinction in each of those various ways. We might then be able to offer judgments like this: for the purpose of constitutional oversight and accountability, activity A is public but, for purpose of applying the rules of contract law, it is private. The temptation to view such judgments as contradictory bespeaks simple-mindedness.

If this picture is accurate, then it in part explains why two specific versions of the distinction between public and private (or non-public) are far from

---

[39] There are many treatments of this process. One of the most interesting discussions of English developments is P. Vincent-Jones, *The New Public Contracting* (Oxford: Clarendon Press, 2006).

dispositive. In England and Wales, these two versions have been developed by public lawyers in an effort to distinguish between the state, conceived as the government, and its realm of activities, on the one hand, and civic society (or the non-state realm), on the other. Both are therefore specific, internal analogues to the general version of the distinction under consideration here. It also seems that both efforts to distinguish public from non-public are intended to do dispositive legal-doctrinal work, although as a matter of fact they rarely succeed in doing so. The two ostensibly different ways of formulating this version of the distinction are best labelled 'institutional' and 'functional'.[40] Elements of each appear when the courts are deciding whether or not some conduct or decision is subject to judicial review and/or covered by the Human Rights Act 1998 and/or falls within the ambit of EU law.[41] What, then, do these two approaches tell us?

The institutional approach to determining 'publicness', conceived as the domain of the state, is reducible to a disarmingly simple question: is the body or agent in question part of government? The functional approach is also reducible to a single, albeit slightly more complex question: is the process, conduct, or decision in question one typically discharged by government? The first approach is a matter of determining where, in the social-cum-political structure, the decision-making body or agent is located; the second involves determining what the decision-making body or agent actually does. Each approach has been refined to include additional, subsidiary questions and tests but, even in their most refined form, each is discernibly distinct in that they can generate quite different answers in one and the same case. Hence the Advertising Standards Authority and the Panel on Takeovers and Mergers could both quite comfortably be regarded as public bodies on the functional approach, whereas neither could be so regarded on the institutional approach.[42]

That each approach can yield different answers in the same case could be regarded as showing that both do dispositive doctrinal work in such cases. I do not believe that this is always or even often so, but that is not to say that these approaches, and the various subsidiary tests they have spawned, do no work at all. They undoubtedly carry some weight in the judicial decision-making process. Yet the crucial fact for current purposes is that the law *contains* these two quite different approaches for determining publicness. Why? As a matter of chronology, the institutional approach predated the functional approach. The latter was developed by judges simply as a result of dissatisfaction with the former, their primary concerns being that the development of the administrative state, on the one hand, and changes in the provision and management of what once were regarded as government activities and functions, on the other, set many activities and functions well beyond the sphere of judicial review. If this is correct, then it illustrates yet again that there is not one single public/private distinction in play

---

[40] I am following Cane, 'Accountability and the Public/Private Distinction', 249.

[41] For a helpful overview of the principal cases under each head, see C. Campbell, 'The Nature of Power as Public in English Judicial Review' (2009) 68 Cambridge Law Journal 90.

[42] *R v Datafin, ex p Panel on Takeovers and Mergers* [1987] QB 815; *R v Advertising Standards Authority Limited ex p The Insurance Service PLC* [1990] 2 Admin LR 77.

in the law. For even in this relatively limited segment of law—the component of administrative law concerned with judicial review—there is more than one version of the public/private distinction simply by virtue of there being available two different approaches to drawing that distinction. Although the two different approaches might generate the same answers in some cases, the fact that they can generate different answers in the one and the same case shows that there is more than one public/private distinction in play.

Finally, a point that has been lurking in the shadows of the discussion in this subsection should be brought to light. It is that the contrast yielded by the institutional and functional approaches to determining 'publicness' is probably not well understood as one between the public, on the one hand, and the private, on the other. Rather, the distinction generated seems to be between the public and the non-public, and the latter, of course, can include much more than just the realm of the private (however understood). Remember that public, in terms of this distinction, is a surrogate for 'state' and the realm of the non-state can surely include not just aspects of the paradigmatically private realm (what I choose for breakfast and what I do with my earnings), but also the public realm as understood in terms of the second distinction (*res publica*, etc.). This is important because it can explain the disquiet often felt with institutional and functional approaches when taken as a means of distinguishing public and private. For we suspect that not all that is meaningfully public is covered by these two approaches and that not all they relegate to the non-public realm is meaningfully private. This is the point of claiming, as I did above, that the second distinction exerts a gravitational pull over some specific versions of the distinction, such as to create a slight but insistent disquiet with them.

(v). The fifth version of the distinction between public and private is claimed to be implicit within many legal systems, operating as a general structuring principle that also informs legal doctrine. The distinction is that between the public realm of politics, law, and the market, on the one hand, and the private realm of family, the household, and intimacy, on the other. It is invoked as a critical tool, a means of illustrating the gender inequality embedded within the formal equality of modern legal systems.[43] On this critique, these legal systems have provided less protection for women who are subject to violence by men in domestic contexts, have valued the labour of women in the home less than the labour of men outside the home, and have been loath to enforce allegedly 'domestic' agreements between men and women in relationships. The rationale for the law's hesitancy to intervene in these and other areas is, in part, the thought that these realms are quintessentially private and therefore beyond the law's reach.

Few or no proponents of this gender critique of the law deny that there are some areas of social and individual life that should be beyond the law's reach. The difficulty critics highlight with this thought as currently or recently embodied in contemporary legal systems is that it serves to systematically devalue women, their work, and their interests. The question of where the limits

---

[43] A classic treatment of English law is K. O'Donovan, *Sexual Divisions in Law* (London: Weidenfeld and Nicolson, 1985).

upon the law's reach lie is one which should be posed and answered in a genuinely open way and not just on the basis of embedded social practices, assumptions, and stereotypes, particularly where these embody morally and politically questionable judgments. It might be thought that contemporary liberal polities already have an answer to this question and there is some truth in that. Most such polities do indeed have a conception of the limits of state power and influence which coexists with a commitment to equality under and before the law. A problem can, however, arise with the way in which such conceptions and their limits are instantiated within legal doctrine as well as with the way in which they inform policing and prosecutorial practice.

As to legal doctrine, consider Article 8 of the ECHR which holds, *inter alia*, that everyone has a right to respect for their private life. Such a right would be recognized by almost all liberal accounts of the limits of the state, yet the qualified guarantee it offers is by no means certain to accord the same value to the interests of men and women. For, if we set aside the actual case law on this article and consider how it *might* be interpreted, albeit unintentionally, in order to reach this end, our starting point is obvious and apparently innocuous.[44] A standard interpretative strategy for this and almost every other proposition of law, when they are either ambiguous or simply being applied to a particular legal dispute, involves construing them in light of the language, cultural context, and everyday common sense of the society in which they figure. The hope is that recourse to these factors will resolve the alleged ambiguity or guide interpreters as to the limits of the proposition or concept in play. This interpretative strategy is certainly not the only one the courts use. They must, for example, apply propositions of law and their constitutive concepts in light of existing law and that, almost always, necessitates consideration of other similar cases. But the contextual interpretative strategy is significant because it can constitute a Trojan horse by which common but morally and politically dubious judgments and assumptions enter into the law. This could happen with regard to Article 8 in this way. When provoked to deliberate upon the nature and range of 'private life', the courts could simply replicate the notion of private embodied in this version of the public/private distinction. For the view that private life—the domain of family life and intimate relationships—is a women's realm is not particularly uncommon in most societies with which we are familiar. If the courts follow this relatively widespread view of gender roles and the division of domestic labour, then they entrench it the law and, in so doing, immunize it against legal and political change. For if the division of domestic labour is unequal, and if women's work in and contribution towards family life is placed beyond the reach of law, then that inequality cannot be easily legally redressed. The difficulty, then, is not one of straightforward and explicit gender bias in either Article 8 itself or in the courts decisions. It is, rather, a problem of 'subtle distortions of prejudice and bias'[45] that

---

[44] For the actual case law, a good starting point is D. Harris, M. O'Boyle, E. Bates, and C. Buckley, *Harris, O'Boyle and Warbrick: The Law of the European Convention on Human Rights*, 2nd edn (Oxford: Clarendon Press, 2009) ch 9.

[45] J Rawls, *A Theory of Justice* (Cambridge, Mass: Harvard UP, 1971) 235.

enter into adjudication via some of the common assumptions and understandings of ordinary language. And, as our hypothetical tale about Article 8 suggests, and as some studies of private law have shown, these distortions of prejudice and bias can 'effectively discriminate against certain groups in the judicial process'.[46]

Exactly the same distortions of prejudice and bias can inform decision-making in policing and prosecution. The view that the domestic realm of the private is and should be beyond the law certainly seems to explain the hesitancy that police forces and prosecutors have traditionally displayed when dealing with domestic violence. Nowhere is this more obvious than in the once common view among police officers that violence in the home is 'just a domestic'.[47] This view automatically downgrades the alleged crime in question, suggesting it is not worthy of a proper police response. And that, of course, is simply to attach less weight to the interests of alleged victims of this kind of crime than to those who suffer exactly the same type and level of violence but in other contexts. Nor need this set of attitudes and assumptions be confined to the policing of domestic violence. There is evidence to suggest that they also inform—or have informed— the exercise of prosecutorial discretion.[48]

It is important to realize that propositions of law need not, as a matter of necessity, be informed by common understandings and assumptions that are morally and political dubious and which often serve to subvert the law's com-mitment to formal equality. For, while it is true that the law must be interpreted in light of the language, concepts, and understandings of the community of which it is part, by no means all aspects of that language and those concepts and understandings will be morally and politically dubious. Propositions of law must, first and foremost, be interpreted in such a way as to either embody or be consistent with the legal system's fundamental values and commitments. Only when that constraint is met should the law aim for broad consistency with ordinary language and common sense.

This version of the public/private distinction calls contemporary legal systems to account for various aspects of their practice in light of their fundamental values. There is no claim that either all law is public or all law is private or that all law is neither. Rather, the fundamental claim that proponents of this version of the distinction make is usually a warning and it counsels, at its broadest, something like this: that words, concepts, ideas, and distinctions have power in the world when embodied in conduct, practices, and institutions, and this power is not always benign. Taken more narrowly, the warning is that 'the' public/private distinction sometimes has just this kind of non-benign power and we must be aware of this and resist it. In practical terms, it warns us that the realm of

---

[46] Rawls, *A Theory of Justice*. The study of private law I have in mind is M. Moran, *Rethinking the Reasonable Person* (Oxford: Clarendon Press, 2003). Moran reminds us of the significance of Rawls's observation at 10 and in ch 5.

[47] See L. Richards, S. Letchford, and S. Stratton, *Policing Domestic Violence* (Oxford: Oxford University Press, 2008) 10.

[48] S. Edwards' now dated *Policing Domestic Violence: Women, Law and State* (London: Sage, 1989) was a pioneering discussion.

the private should not automatically be thought of as a law-free zone and, when it is, that the valuation such a judgment entails should always be made explicit.

3.2 *Bringing order into chaos*

It is now plain that more than one version of the public/private distinction can be in play in law and in our thinking about law. Equally plain is that it is a mistake to assume that all versions of the distinction do the same thing, or have the same purpose or aim. Some versions function as attempts to answer specific doctrinal questions—what is the nature of public power for the purposes of judicial review?—while others are means of organizing and sometimes rethinking swathes of legal doctrine. This point reminds us that three versions of the distinction are in play *within* the law—they are specific versions of the distinction, drawn and utilized by lawyers. The remaining distinctions can be used as general structuring principles for legal systems as a whole. They are general, not always offered by lawyers, yet sometimes resonate with specific versions of the distinction that lawyers draw. All versions of the distinction are salient for the law, though, in this sense: each is to some extent unsatisfactory from the perspective of one or more of the others, the consequence being that each version can be destabilized by the presence and power of the others. This instability need not be the product of explicit knowledge of all other versions of the distinction but, rather, a consequence of the intuitions that other versions embody. These intuitions explain the common thought among lawyers that talk and analysis of 'the' public/private distinction quickly becomes a swamp of confusion and frustration.

Another, but so far only implicit point merits mention. It is that the various versions of the public/private distinction are not in and of themselves deeply significant. Versions of the distinction are, rather, usually the sequelae of altogether more momentous commitments or values. Thus, for example, the fifth way of distinguishing public and private is a consequence of the attempt to highlight and challenge misogyny and sexism and patriarchy. The fourth version of the distinction is, of course, a consequence of a view of the range of a particular polity's constitutional commitments and of the role of legal accountability within those commitments. And attempts to give normative depth to the first way of distinguishing between public and private usually derive from liberal pre-commitments. In these instances, the distinction is cart, not horse; it is a result of prior normative commitments but not in and of itself deeply normatively significant. This is perhaps just an oblique way of saying that all versions of the distinction are only instrumentally valuable rather than being bearers of non-instrumental value.

This point, and the wider claims about the plural and limited nature of 'the' public/private distinction that inform it, might be regarded as a counsel of despair. Because the picture so far painted is somewhat untidy, it might provoke the thought that the responsible intellectual is duty-bound to impose order upon this near-Babel. The most tempting way in which order could be imposed, for contemporary jurists at least, is by invoking some or other moral or political blueprint as the anchor for one's preferred version of the public/private distinction (which, remember, is exactly the response adopted by those jurists who find the first version of the public/private distinction insufficiently 'deep'). Contemporary jurisprudential thought is marked by its hasty embrace of various substantive moral and political theories and the belief that the most important scholarship is that which explicitly invokes and applies such theories to law.[49] In this intellectual framework, legal scholarship is always required to have a theory of whatever area of law it focuses upon and 'theory' almost always means moral or political theory.[50]

We cannot know, a priori, that the enterprise of fixing one particular version of the public/private distinction within a more general moral or political theory will fail. But there is at least one reason to be sceptical about the prospects of success. It consists of the possibility, noted in the discussion of the first version of the public/private distinction, that areas of law (substantive, procedural, and other) might be morally and politically either over-, under-, or undetermined. Thus, there might well be more than one plausible and appealing substantive moral and political theory available to us as a normative anchor for the area of law in question; or all the available appealing substantive moral and political theories might be a bad justificatory fit with the area of law question, so that they provide either no or only limited normative support.[51] These three possibilities seem likely if it is the case that no one single moral or political theory is pre-eminently salient or obviously correct. Our situation does indeed appear to be one in which we are faced with a family of plausible yet different moral and political theories. On the assumption that each such theory has sufficient normative reach or determinacy to anchor a version of the public/private distinction, the possibility arises that each theory could anchor a different version of the public/private distinction. Babel, it seems, is hereby replaced with meta-normative Babel. Alternatively, if we assume that the moral and political theories available to us are indeterminate, failing to provide compelling normative support for some or other version of the distinction, then we must question the point of this normative detour. Babel, it seems, persists but is ignored for the sake of a possibly scenic but unhelpful normative journey.

Much work needs be done to actually show that one or other of these possibilities is indeed true of the effort to anchor a version of the public/private distinction. That task is not attempted here, for my aim has been simply to

---

[49] This picture of much contemporary legal and jurisprudential scholarship was originally and engagingly (and amusingly, hyperbolically, and archly) sketched in a series of essays by P. Schlag, a fine starting point being 'Normative and Nowhere to Go' (1990) 43 Stanford LR 167. Schlag's diagnosis still stands, it seems to me, despite being funny, and despite being part of an intellectual and political programme (second-wave American critical legal studies) that is now nowhere near as fashionable as it once was.

[50] For an amusingly pungent corrective to this thought see T. Weir, *An Introduction to Tort Law*, 2nd edn, (Oxford: Clarendon Press, 2006) ix.

[51] For further discussion of these possibilities, focusing on quite different juristic contexts, see my 'Method and Fit', 643–47, and 'Equality Under and Before the Law' (2011) LXI University of Toronto Law Journal 411 at 439–41.

problematize and thus slow down the almost automatic recourse to normative theory that is a hallmark of contemporary jurisprudential thought. The 'normative turn' should not be made without reflection, as if it were a guaranteed path to intellectual progress and enlightenment. Far from solving our problems, this 'turn' might compound them. Finally, note that what some might be tempted to regard as the principal vice of the argument of this essay could be taken as its main virtue. For rather than viewing the previous sketch of the varieties of public/private distinction as a chaotic Babel, it could instead be seen as a complex picture. One's ranking of the virtue of intellectual tidiness will in part determine which view one takes, but it needs be noted that intellectual tidiness is not in and of itself a supreme epistemic or methodological value. If our picture of the various public/private distinctions displays the other formal virtues of a good social-scientific explanation and understanding, then that should be enough to commend it. There is no a priori reason to believe that a tidy social-scientific explanation and understanding must always be preferred over an untidy one. Explanations and understandings need only be as tidy as the idea, practice, institution, or phenomenon in question allows.

4. CONCLUSION

As to 'the' public/private distinction, our conclusion must be this: there are many, not one. This is as true of the juristic context as it is of many others. Once we lawyers appreciate this, the search for that will o' the wisp—a single, comprehensive, compelling, and doctrinally dispositive distinction between public and private—can end. This should not be taken as an attempt to foreclose discussion of 'the' public/private distinction. It serves instead as an encouragement to discuss 'the' private/public distinction even more, but also better. For the platitude is surely an invitation to itemize, chart, and catalogue the various private/public *distinctions* in play about, within, and beyond the law. While this catalogue may seem fixed and immutable at particular historical junctures, it can surely always be added to (in principle, at least). If this invitation is accepted, then our knowledge of the multiplicity of ways of distinguishing between public and private will certainly increase. There is, however, no guarantee that this knowledge will contain a unifying thread.

The Public, the Private, and the Law

Claudio Michelon[1]

I. INTRODUCTION

One of the most central conceptual distinctions to be found in the deep structure of the modern imaginary is the distinction between two domains of *social action*, the public and the private. Its centrality is perhaps the reason why so much energy has been spent in the last century in debating the value and meaning of the public/private divide.[2] An interesting feature of this debate is that both critics and enthusiasts of the distinction seem to depart from assumptions (sometimes made explicit) that there is a direct relation between, on the one hand, the underlying social normative structures of each domain and, on the other hand, public and private law. Thus, for instance, Gunther Teubner talks critically of both the private domain and private law as inhabiting the space of an efficiency-driven economic rationality.[3] Similarly, many who would endorse private law and private enterprise, or public law and 'publicly interested' state policies, assume that the legal and non-legal dimensions of privateness and publicness respectively are coextensive.

My aim in this chapter is to challenge this perceived continuity between the underlying normativity of each domain and the normativity of public and private law. I will argue in what follows that the underlying normative assumptions of the utilization of law (in general) by the political community do not overlap significantly with the broader normative assumptions embedded in each domain. This would go a long way towards providing a framework within which the perceived (and often commended) movements towards a 'publicization of

[1] I am very thankful to the participants at the *After Public Law* workshop held at Edinburgh University in June 2011, in particular Michael Wilkinson for comments on an early draft of this paper. The paper also benefited from comments by Zenon Bankowski, Cormac Mac Ahmlaigh, Francisco Saffie, Felipe Oliveira de Souza, and especially, Neil Walker.

[2] The literature is too vast to summarize here. A sample of it will be discussed in more detail below, but a useful overview can be found at M. J. Horwitz, 'The History of the Public/Private Distinction' (1982) 130(6) University of Pennsylvania Law Review 1423.

[3] Eg in G. Teubner, 'State Policies in Private Law? A Comment on Hanoch Dagan' (2008) 56 American Journal of Comparative Law 835.

private law'[4] or, conversely, towards a 'privatization of public law'[5] could be understood.[6]

In order to present and defend this wider framework, I need to refine the claim made above about the centrality of the public/private divide in modernity, as its meaning and truth are far from obvious. In fact even in antiquity there are a number of socially relevant distinctions that map onto aspects of what we now might call the public/private divide.[7] Moreover, it is not likely that—either in antiquity or in modernity—there is only one conceptual distinction between the private and the public domains. Furthermore, those various distinctions do not necessarily overlap and, it has been suggested, they might even be unrelated.

So the claim that the distinction between a private domain and a public domain of social action is central to the modern social imaginary is already under pressure on many fronts. Diachronically, it does not seem to be all that distinctive of modernity; synchronically, there seems to be quite a few distinctions between the private and the public, and some of them might not be all that important to the self-understanding of the social agent in modernity. My first task is, therefore, to explain the particular way in which the public/private distinction is articulated in modernity both internally (what is the fundamental difference between the public and the private?) and externally (what role does the distinction play in the modern social and political imaginary?). That task is undertaken in Section 2 following.

The ideas of public and private, however, are not the only normative structures that provide a context of social legitimacy for modern institutions. The idea of legality, its meaning, value, and the roles it might play, also provide a context

---

[4] Discussion of the publicization of private law is not new. In 1929, Karl Renner's seminal *The Institutions of Private Law and their social function* (London: Routledge, 1949) concludes with a diagnosis of it (at 296–300). More recently, Hanoch Dagan has cautiously accepted this as a qualified good (among many other statements of his opinion, see H. Dagan, 'The Limited Autonomy of Private Law' (2008) 56 American Journal of Comparative Law 809 ff), while Ernest Weinrib, even more cautiously, accepts that 'public right' might generate exceptions to the logic of private law episodically, although in his own Kantian approach those interventions should not impair the conceptual integrity of private law (E. Weinrib, 'Private Law and Public Right' (2011) 61 University of Toronto Law Journal 191, *passim*, esp. 210).

[5] Thus, the phenomenon of government by private contract, with the outsourcing of some traditional state functions (including the running of police stations) has been widely discussed in the literature, often critically, as by A. C. L. Davies in her *The Public Law of Government Contracts* (Oxford: Oxford University Press, 2008) 63–82. See also M. R. Freedland, 'Government by contract and public law' (1994) Public Law 86.

[6] This is not the first attempt to provide one such framework. Günther Teubner's useful suggestion of polycontextuality—referring to the increasing diversity of forms and relations of legal ordering across national and transnational space of previously discrete domains of private and public normativity—as the touchstone of a new approach to the relation between the public and the private is one example of another attempt. However, it tells only part of the story, and, from the perspective of private and public law, not its most important part. See G. Teubner, 'Constitutionalizing Polycontextuality' (2011) 20 Social and Legal Studies 209.

[7] Hannah Arendt famously provided an account of the public and private domains in classical societies (Greek and Roman) which was predicated on a strict separation between, on the one hand, the Greek *oikos* and the Roman *domus* and, on the other, political life; H. Arendt, *The Human Condition*, 2nd edn (Chicago: University of Chicago Press, 1958) ch 2. Other accounts of forms of separation between public and private in antiquity, such as Raymond Geuss's, have defended not one, but many different ways in which what we call public and private in modernity would resonate with the self-understanding of people living in those societies; R. Geuss, *Public Goods, Private Goods* (Princeton: Princeton University Press, 2001).

for the social legitimacy of those institutions. In Section 3 I present an account of that legality that would be able to perform that role by expanding the idea of 'necessary mutual relevance' introduced in Section 2. This additional level of complexity will make problematic the apparently easy transition between the normativities of *the private domain of social action* and of the *legal domain of social action*. Section 4 tries to flesh out this tension, identifying both the 'puzzle of private law' and the stakes. In the same section I introduce a more complex conception of social action, and through it, a reworked conception of the private domain which can preserve the gains of 'elective relevance' (as also expounded in Section 2) while allowing for private law to play a role predicated upon necessary relevance. Section 5, in conclusion, outlines what this reworked conception of private law might look like, now liberated from its ties to elective relevance and to the conceptual and explanatory structures built by private law theory and doctrine around the idea of elective relevance. This outline will suggest that the organizing category of private law is recognition (rather than autonomy, free will, and the like), and that through the idea of recognition, we can find a better key not only to the evolution of private law since the mid-19th century, but also to the current predicaments we find in many areas of private law in Western legal systems.

2. SOCIAL IMAGINARIES OF PUBLIC AND PRIVATE

I have characterized the distinction between public and private as a distinction between *domains of social action*. Before moving on to identify the relevant differences, it might be worth pausing to consider what is meant by the phrase. A domain of social action is the social environment which lends meaning to that action. The action's meaning is given by a series of interpretative and evaluative structures that make up the action's context. This meaning is holistic, in the sense that it articulates both descriptive and evaluative elements, explanations, and justifications. Those domains are aspects of what Charles Taylor called 'social imaginaries', that is to say:

> [T]he ways in which they [people] imagine their social existence, how they fit together with others, how things go on between them and their fellows, the expectations which are normally met, and the deeper normative notions and images which underlie these expectations.[8]

So what we are looking for is a set of conceptual and evaluative indicia that constitute different domains of social action; that is to say, different structures of meaning attribution used by social agents to understand their actions.

The crucial conceptual distinction between private and public environments in modernity is between an environment in which my interest in the flourishing of others is constitutive of the meaning of my action, and an environment in which my action's meaning is given without reference to any interest I might have in the flourishing of other members of the social group. In other words, the public environment is predicated upon the existence of *necessary mutual relevance*

---

[8] C. Taylor, *A Secular Age* (Cambridge, Mass: Harvard University Press, 2007) 171.

between the social agents, while the private realm is predicated upon *elective relevance*. What is new in relation to the past is the idea of two domains of social action, in one of which it is perfectly unremarkable for all members of the political community to act on purely self-regarding reasons; the other in which action can only be understood as other-regarding. This does not mean that in the private domain all (or even most) people *act* for purely self-regarding motives all (or most of) the time and, conversely, that people were always acting on selfless reasons before the advent of modernity. It simply means that the ways in which we attribute social meaning to an agent's action within the private environment and, crucially, to the institutions that surround such action, belong to that realm in which the fulfilment of the interests of others is not a necessary component of our understanding of those actions and institutions. Thus structured, this distinction seems to map onto the distinctions between market and state, society and politics. It is a central part of my contention that this dichotomous way of trying to map the fundamental distinction between necessary mutual relevance and elective relevance onto those traditional distinctions hides the relevance of the former in the oversimplification of the latter. I will discuss that in more detail in Section 4.

What is typical of modernity is not only the sharpness of the distinction between the two domains of social action itself or its widespread social acceptance, but the way in which institutional structures became progressively more responsive to and embracing of both social imaginaries over the period between the 18th and the 19th centuries. That might at first sight seem surprising, for the distinction between necessary mutual relevance and elective relevance, as two radically different explanatory social imaginaries, carries with it the germ of competition between the two perspectives, and it is clear that, if not for the intervention of stabilizing mediating structures (both institutional and cultural), the competition would quickly escalate. More often than not those scaffoldings aimed at demonstrating how the *other* is not completely irrelevant in the private domain, but simply one step removed from the immediate action. Those constructions allowed conceptions of society to flourish in which private and public interests are not necessarily at odds with each other.

Invisible hand theories of the market (of which Adam Smith's is the best known)[9] produce an excellent illustration of such conceptual scaffoldings. The idea that the actions of purely self-regarding agents leads to collective advantage is a way to try and reconcile what would in pre-modern times involve the corruption of *pleonexia*—of unalloyed self-interest—with the common good.[10] Indeed, such conceptions of the relationship between private interest and public interest explain away the conflict in the realm of action by postulating *causal chains* that would have the pursuit of self-interest leading on to the furthering of

---

[9] Smith introduced the metaphor in the specific context of his discussion of the benefit of protecting the national industry in book IV, chapter II of the *Wealth of Nations*. More interesting for our purposes is Smith's defence of self-interest as a tool to better our condition, which he exemplifies with his famous line that '[i]t is not from the benevolence of the butcher, the brewer, or the baker, that we expect our dinner, but from their regard to their own interest.' See A. Smith, Adam *An inquiry into the Nature and the Causes of the Wealth of Nations* (Indianapolis: Liberty Fund 1982) 26–27.

[10] What Charles Taylor calls 'doctrines of the harmony of interests'. Taylor, *A Secular Age*, 229 ff.

the realization of everyone. 'Greed is good' is not a claim about what makes an agent improve herself morally, but a claim about the cunning of self-interest, whose pursuit, inadvertently to the agent, ends up benefitting all. The *other* regains relevance, but at the price of dissolving its identity into collective benefit. This connection between elective relevance and common interest had a significant influence in the rise, in the 19th century, of the 'autonomie de la volunté' as a central normative underpinning of private law.[11]

The flip side of that is the Rousseauian postulation of the coincidence between public interest and *true self-interest*, which inspired Robespierre's defence of 'public virtue'.[12] In this version of the harmonization between self-interest and public interest, the well-being of the nation takes precedence over any apparently conflicting self-interest by redefining self-interest as never being in conflict with the nation's interest. In both cases, the appearance of conflict is said to be misleading, as it conceals a deep harmony between the private and the public (that is, between elective relevance and necessary mutual relevance). Yet modernity produced another, very successful strategy to deal with the public/private tension, to wit, the postulation of a form of 'hermetic sealing' between the public and the private environments of meaning in such way that the same action would never have both a public and a private signification. The distinctive feature of this strategy is that it accepts that there is an irreconcilable difference between the public and the private realms, but introduces a strict boundary between those realms. Harmony is guaranteed by the policing of the borderline between the two environments of meaning. That is the original liberal insight, which is deeply rooted in liberal doctrines of religious toleration.[13]

What these different images of accommodation between public and private interest have in common is that they are all offered as answers to the puzzle generated by postulating the public and the private as two competing environments of meaning. If, in the private environment, the meaning of one's action is not connected with the realization of other members of the political community, and the public environment, by contrast, is one in which an action only finds meaning in the connectedness that is postulated between members of the political community, the problem of reconciliation of an action's meaning becomes urgent for anyone who wants to lead a coherent life. 'Invisible hand' strategies try to reconcile the two environments by postulating a causal connection between the pursuit of private interest and the public good in such a way that the pursuit of private interest would always have positive public meaning. 'General will' strategies, such as Rousseau's, try to reconcile the two environments by conceptual *fiat*—by redefining private interest. *True* private interest

---

[11]   See, for instance, Jacques Ghestin's account of the coming together of the will and utility in mid-19th-century law and legal doctrine (J. Ghestin, 'L'utile et le juste dans le droit des contrats', (1981) 26 Archives de Philosophie du Droit, 1981, 35, at 36). See also L. Reiser's classical 'Vertragsfunktion und Vertragsfreiheit'; I used the Italian translation: L. Reiser 'Funzione del Contratto e Libertà Contrattuale' in *Il Compito del Diritto Privato* (Milano: Giuffrè, 1990) 51–4.

[12]   Taylor, *A Secular Age*, 201–207.

[13]   A point made by John Rawls in *Political Liberalism* (New York: Columbia University Press, 1993) xxvi.

would always accord with public interest in such a way that what one particular individual believes to be in his private interest would only be the *appearance* of self-interest if in conflict with the public interest. The liberal accepts and celebrates the division as paving the path to liberty.

By contrast, I contend that accepting a separation between those two environments of meaning is a mistake on two accounts. It is a mistake, firstly, because this picture does not allow for a comprehensive explanation of agency in the private realm. It accepts too passively that the point of view of a particular (and idealized) private agent is the only possible source of an action's meaning. As a consequence, and secondly, it hides the interaction between the agent's psychological account of her action and the social structures that constrain it, in particular the social structures embedded in and by private law. What the dichotomous conception of the environment of social action cannot provide is the means to conceive of a more integrated environment of social meaning, one that takes into account not simple self-interest and public policy, but the mediating register of law itself.

In order to find the appropriate conceptual tools to present my argument for this more integrated conception of social meaning, I need to introduce further conceptual distinctions. Part of the problem is a pervasive tendency among theorists to identify notions of the public with notions such as the common good, which, in their original use by Aristotle and Aquinas referred to a form of communality that pervaded both the public and the private realms. Brian Tamanaha's discussion of the fall of the notion of common good in legal and political discourse offers a good example of just this conflation. What interests me here is not so much the wider argument that Tamanaha produces for his thesis, but the fact that, in building this historical evidence, Tamanaha uses 'common good' and the 'public good' interchangeably, thus relating Aristotle's notion of common good and Aquinas's *Bonum Commune* to Locke's thesis that political power is to be utilized 'for public purposes only'.[14] This is not merely a pedantic point about precision in the philosophical vocabulary but a claim about the loss of an important conceptual distinction. Both common good and the public good are defined negatively by contrast to what is for the benefit of particular groups (factions) within society. This is another way to say that the modern conception of the public environment of meaning is predicated on mutual relevance; that is, on a commonality established by each member of the political community's interest in the flourishing of every other member. The private realm is then cast out of the common good, thus setting up the agenda shared by Rousseau, Smith, and liberals at the centre of which is the question of how to bridge the gulf between necessary mutual relevance and elective relevance in the political community.

My contention is that, even though there might have been good historical reasons for the gap to have formed in the first place, and even though there might be some usefulness in ring-fencing part of the private realm from the imperatives of mutual relevance, mutual relevance is also an integral part of the private realm

---

[14] B. Tamanaha, *Law as a means to an End* (Cambridge: Cambridge University Press, 2006) 220.

and it would be impossible to understand the transformation endured by both the private realm and, more specifically, private law in the 20th century without attention to that particular feature of the private realm. The key to understanding (most of) the private realm as pervaded by the notion of necessary mutual relevance is to understand law's primary political purpose of mediation (which I discuss in Section 4) and to understand ways in which the other can be conceived as necessarily relevant to me.[15] In the next section I seek to provide an account of the ways in which the other might be legally relevant to me.

3. ALTERITY IN LAW AND POLITICS

In investigating how law relates to alterity, one would do well to start by investigating ways in which we can impinge on each other. There are multiple ways in which others encroach on the options available to me, but one of them has dominated the imagination of political and legal philosophers in recent times; namely, the subjection of one's options to the *will* of others. This section aims at showing other ways in which that encroachment might take place, ways that are crucial for my argument.

If, as said, the dominant way in which law is seen to relate to the recognition of alterity focuses on how the voluntary actions of others can impinge on the possibilities open to my own acting, what kind of anthropological assumptions are involved in this way of thinking? The other here is typically conceived as a potential disturbance to my options. This same focus is shared by republicans and liberals and covers much of the contemporary spectrum of legal and political theory. Take Nigel Simmonds's idea of freedom as independence, for instance. In his liberal outlook the value of freedom as independence is defined as the value of being relatively independent from the will of others, in the sense that others cannot unduly restrict one's options, as would occur, paradigmatically, in the case of slavery. As he stated:

> Freedom in this sense is not a matter of the number and diversity or value of options open to an individual: for we have seen that the slave may have more (and perhaps better) options available to him than the free man . . . The free man . . . may have few options available, but some at least of those options will be quite independent of the will of anyone else.[16]

As Simmonds sees it, the rule of law should, in turn, be conceived as a necessary condition to achieve the ideal of freedom as independence.[17] And while not every liberal would accept that a correct understanding of law depends on understanding its role in curbing the encroachment upon one's options by someone else's

---

[15] I am well aware that this comes dangerously close to what Teubner sees as the many 'vague assertions that private law is pervasively political' (Teubner, 'State Policies in Private Law? A Comment on Hanoch Dagan', 837). I hope my own account of private law's political nature, as put forward in Section 4, is more than a vague assertion.

[16] N. Simmonds, *Law as a Moral Idea* (Oxford: Oxford University Press, 2007) 141.

[17] Simmonds, *Law as a Moral Idea*, 141.

will, most liberals would accept that law has an important role to play in regulating those boundary disputes between my choices and the claims others might have in closing them down.

Liberals are not the only ones to connect law to the need to curb the encroachment of others upon my choices. Neo-republicans, for instance, are very worried about the threat posed by the will of others. Take, for instance, Pettit's conception of liberty as non-domination, which, although focusing more on *entitlement* to independence than on the actual enjoyment of independence, still holds as a central element of freedom that others do not have the capacity to intervene in one's affairs on an arbitrary basis.[18] Again, the problem Petit is dealing with is the intentional interference by someone else in my affairs and the institutional frameworks that might or might not entitle the other to exercise just such power.

There is much to be commended in seeking to investigate how someone else's will might encroach on my choices, but there are other ways in which others might limit my choices. Some are trivial (even though not politically irrelevant, as we will see), such as the fact that their mere physical existence might limit my choices. They might be sitting on my favourite bench in the park, thus creating transaction costs that might make it impossible (or highly costly) for me to do as I please. So there is a sense in which the other's mere existence, not his or her actions, is already able to encroach on my freedom.

The same occurs, I believe, in other situations which are more relevant from the political point of view. As we are surrounded by others, we are aware that it is good for each of us to achieve some kind of self-realization. We do not need to be overly prescriptive here. There are very different ways in which one (rightly or wrongly) might conceive of one's self-realization, but it remains a fact that the good of self-realization is still a constitutive feature of all of us in the political community.

Now suppose that each member of the political community has an interest in the self-realization of every other member of the political community. I shall try to argue for this supposition's plausibility in what follows, but let me first clarify the stakes here by drawing the consequences of this approach in relation to how others might encroach upon my choices. If I have an interest in the self-realization of others, the fact that they fail to achieve such realization is not only a tragedy for them, but a loss for me. I would have my own self-realization undermined by the other's failure. Now that would give me good reasons to try and achieve a situation in which we can enhance optimally the possibility of every member of the political community realizing themselves, at least up to a certain degree.

The way in which the other encroaches upon my choices here is much more subtle than the imposition of her will on me or even the mere physicality of her presence. The mere fact of belonging together in the one political community would change the reasons for my action, even if my primary goal is to achieve my own self-realization. As the other becomes an ineluctable political reality to me, my reasons for action, that is, the justification for my action, cannot remain the same.

---

[18] P. Petit, *Republicanism: A Theory of Freedom and Government* (Oxford: Oxford University Press, 1997) 51 ff.

There is a long tradition of arguing that the destinies of the members of the political community are intertwined not only as a result of factual necessity, but also as an ethical necessity. It would not be difficult to bring the likes of Aristotle, Aquinas, Rousseau, or Hegel in support of versions of what was introduced above as a hypothesis. Instead of going down that route, however, I would like to take the more direct approach of presenting my claim and mapping out some of its implications to lend some plausibility to it.

Let me start by briefly stating the claim: law and politics, different as they are as aspects of our social life, are both attempts at achieving a deeper understanding and realization of the meaning of communal life between beings whose self-realization is mutually important. In this context, 'the meaning of communal life' does not refer to one (or to a few) simple value(s) conceived in purely abstract terms, but to relatively complex articulations of a number of values in the several typical contexts of social interaction. The fact that this is the point of legal and political institutions is compatible with our current disagreement about both what constitutes self-realization for the kinds of beings we are and about what the relative weight of another's self-realization is in relation to one's commitment to one's own self-realization.

This, of course, is not meant as a descriptive statement of our political and legal institutions as they are. Many a time, political and legal institutions have disregarded the meaning of communal life and have been used to protect the interests of factions. In fact, for the epistemic and social reasons to be introduced shortly, that cannot but be the case. But this claim is not, by the same token, a purely normative claim about how institutions should behave. My suggestion is that there are clear traces in our political practices that show that the idea of a community of interest is embedded in our political institutions. That is the reason why a government which claimed explicitly to be protecting only one faction of the social group, without regard for any other part, would fit so awkwardly with most typical Western political institutions.

What is crucial is striving for the realization of the ultimate meaning of communal life is seen as the *arché*[19] of the practice embodied in our legal and political institutions. The *arché* of a social practice is a preliminary conception of what the people involved in that practice will have achieved if and when they achieve perfection in that practice. As such it is both an integral part of the practice and an incomplete conception of what the practice is really about.

In this conception of our political and legal institutions and practices, the connectedness, which we saw was a feature of the public environment of social meaning in modernity, is always constitutive of political life. But its complete articulation and the forms of its realization are not. In fact, part of the reason why we need a division of labour between law and politics is precisely the fact that there are powerful obstacles to the full realization of their common *arché*.

---

[19] My use of *arché* draws on Alisdair MacIntyre's as discussed both in ch 5 of *Whose Justice? Which Rationality?* (London: Duckworth, 1984) 80, and in *First Principles, Final Ends and Contemporary Philosophical Issues* (Milwaukee: Marquette University Press, 1990) 34–9.

Indeed, if law and politics have the same fundamental *arché*, the same cannot be said about their specific functions in the pursuit of that *arché*. Law and politics articulate with each other in a division of labour that allows for that pursuit. This division of labour is necessary precisely because a complete theory of the meaning of political life does not present itself in the form of clear and easy questions, let alone clear and easy answers. That difficulty is not simply epistemic, that is, it is not simply to do with the fact that people would be bound to disagree on those questions of meaning, nor is it a token of the fact that, *sub specie humanitatis*, no answer, even the one that commands absolute consensus for any given stretch of time, is immune to challenge. Certainty that we have got the meaning of communal life right cannot be but a measure of one's (or a group's) *confidence* that this is so. However, confidence is a mere psychological state and not something that can be predicated of any particular conception of the meaning of communal life itself. Such conceptions might be true or false, but not certain or uncertain.

The main reason why answers to the question of the meaning of collective life are so intractable runs deeper. The crucial point here is that politics must be conducted under conditions of alienation. As Fernando Atria has argued, the conceptual apparatus of politics only signifies imperfectly; that is to say, it can only convey approximations of the objects it describes.[20] It refers to what is known by the agents involved in the social practice only imperfectly, and this is due principally to the condition of alienation. This is a condition whose manifestations and effects can only be divined negatively, in the way in which our pervasive subjection to conflicting demands and structures reveals a deep instability in our social practices.

Such radical reflexivity of being together, conceived of as both the circumstance and the reinforced outcome of politics, is disabling. A firm grasp on the truth about the meaning of political life cannot be a precondition for social action. Social action has an urgency that is incompatible with waiting for that firm grasp. That urgency is at least a pragmatic imperative—a response to the palpable and pervasive turbulence of our collective social environment, even for those who are not impressed by the diagnosis of alienation. But it becomes politically essential if alienation is accepted as a structural condition that makes politics necessary. In that case, and given that alienation is socially constructed, the need for social action would not be simply pragmatic, but, more interestingly, it would be a necessary instrument to fight alienation by changing the social conditions under which alienation thrives. If this diagnosis is correct, action can only be made possible by means of introducing an order of practice that is not in desperate need of finding a sure footing for our collective commitments.

That order of practice is the law.

That is why law must be understood as a mediating institution, positioned between the struggle towards the *arché* of politics (which includes a raised consciousness of the ultimate meaning of political life), and the pressing need

---

[20]   F. Atria, 'Living under the Domain of Dead Ideas' in M. Del Mar and C. Michelon (eds), *The Anxiety of the Jurist* (Aldershot: Ashgate, 2013).

to act—to carry on in the absence of the fulfilment of that quest. This division of labour is what is paradigmatically expressed in Hobbes's oft-quoted statement that *auctoritas non veritas facit legem*. Law needs to insulate itself, at least partially, from the wider political struggle about the meaning of political life in order to be able to inform social decision-making. However, it can never insulate itself completely, as it would lose its point.[21] That mediating function is performed in different ways by different legal institutions within the scopes of both private and public law.

What is important for the argument presented here, however, is that, *in this conception, law is always a partial and incomplete version of the ultimate meaning of political life (or one aspect of it)*. At a philosophical level, the main opponents of such a claim would be, on the one hand, liberalism and, on the other, legal functionalism. The former would be wary of putting too much weight on conceiving law as a version of a substantive conception of the connectedness between members of the political community I am proposing. The latter would be suspicious of my claim that law and politics have a common vocation to investigate the meaning of communal life. I cannot discuss in detail here the advantages of 'law as mediation' over liberalism or functionalism, as that would demand a long detour from the more focused point of this chapter, although at least some of the shortcomings of both liberalism and functionalism will be made clear in the specific context of my account of the private domain of social action in Section 5 below. For now it is enough to present it as a plausible conception of law's intrinsic worth.[22]

4. THE PUZZLE OF PRIVATE LAW

Before we move forward, let me take stock of the argument so far. In Section 2 we identified the modern notion of two environments of meaning for social action; the public environment, which is predicated on what I called 'necessary mutual relevance', and the private environment which is predicated on what I called 'elective relevance'. We also saw that, in the modern imaginary, those environments are not simply different but initially opposed and then are more or less reconciled without loss of a sense of their basic ontological distinctiveness.

We embarked upon Section 3 trying to understand what mutual relevance means by placing it in the wider context of mutual encroachment. We distinguished different forms of encroachment, ranging from the subjection to someone else's will to the limitations on one's action caused by the mere physicality of

---

[21] This mediating function of law is crucial to answer the age-old problem of how the two aspects of particular justice (ie distributive and corrective justice) do not collapse into each other, a point I discuss in another work: C. Michelon, 'The Virtuous Circularity: positive law and particular justice' (2013) Ratio Juris (forthcoming).

[22] I sketched an argument for 'law as mediation' in C. Michelon, 'The Public Nature of Private Law?' in C. Michelon et al. (eds), *The Public in Law* (London: Ashgate, 2012). Other arguments which achieve similar conclusions by other routes are to be found in F. Atria, 'Living under the Domain of Dead Ideas' and L. F. O. Barzotto, 'Guardião da Constituição: elementos para uma epistemologia democrática' in Ives Gandra da Silva Martins (ed.), *Princípios Constitucionais Relevantes*, 1st edn, vol. 1 (São Paulo: Fischer 2, 2011) 13–34.

the other's presence, but we identified the form of encroachment that is most problematic in attempting to redraw the public/private distinction as the one caused by the moral relevance to ourselves of others *qua* beings that, like ourselves, aim at some form of self-realization.

Those steps allow me to restate the initial problem more clearly and in more detail. If all legal and political institutions are predicated on this latter form of encroachment, a difficulty arises for a theory of *private* law in particular. On the one hand, the private domain of social action is predicated on the idea of elective relevance. Social action in that realm is not to be conceived as being necessarily other-regarding. Rather, this is a realm of 'solitude', where the other has no claim on me. On the other hand, the social institutions that create and police the boundaries of the private realm, in particular private law, if we accept law's necessary implication in the imperfect project (and projection) of collective living, cannot but be conceived as other-regarding. So it would seem that the relationship between the private domain of social action and private law institutions might be more complex than both theorists of private law and doctrinal writers assume.

This seems to lead to a necessary choice between one of three alternatives: (a) to give up on the conception of the private realm as a space where agents are not obliged to take others into account (a realm of elective relevance), (b) to give up on my tentative conception of law as mediation, or (c) to give up the assumption that private law and the private realm share the same conceptual and normative presuppositions.

Alternative (a) comes at a cost, as both the elective relevance of the private domain of social action and the necessary mutual relevance of the public domain perform important tasks. The constitution of the private realm of action separated from the public realm is not a purposeless construct and elective relevance is part of the reason why it is in place. Among the many discernible, and only partially overlapping, purposes it fulfils, it allows for wealth to pass from hand to hand unchecked by politics and also for the construction of particular social identities, which are not tightly connected or derived from an overarching political structure. More generally, it creates a space in which the social agent can conceive of his decisions as primarily his own; that is, as decisions which do not bear the weight of having to take into consideration the realization of others.

Alternative (b) also comes at a cost. Although I did not provide a full defence of 'law as mediation' in the previous section, I hope to have made clear what is at stake in giving up on it. If that conception is correct, then the other-regardingness of law and its institutions would be an essential part of the justification for having such institutions in the first place.

Alternative (c) does not carry that sort of cost, although it generates the burden of having to explain in a more complex way what was assumed to be a straightforward and unproblematic relationship; that is, the one between the underlying normative presuppositions to the private realm and to private law. In what follows I provide a reworked conception of that relationship.

The key to understanding this reworked relationship is to avoid a (primarily) psychological conception of social action. A psychological explanation of social action gives pride of place to the agent's intention (conscious or, sometimes, unconscious) in performing an action. Thus, a psychological explanation of social action might qualify the act of giving money to a charity as an act of benevolence (or, perhaps, pride, if the agent is primarily seeking self-satisfaction). One of the most pervasive (and reductionist) kinds of psychological accounts of social action is the reduction of all action to preference satisfaction, a very common strategy in welfare economics.[23]

Not all social action can be appropriately understood solely (or even primarily) on the basis of the agent's own account of what she is doing. A more appropriate account of those actions would explain the action also in its relation to the institutions that shape it. Take voting, for instance. Its meaning cannot simply be thought to be an expression of preference or even an attempt to bring about a certain result (both explanations that give pride of place to the agent's psychological account of his own action). A vote would only count as a vote if it conforms to certain standards. An action practised by the same agent, with the same intention, but taken in a mock election (that the agent takes to be real), is not a vote.

The appropriate explanation of certain social actions, therefore, needs to take into account the institutions that regulate (and sometimes also constitute the possibility of) the action's performance. That more complex explanation of social action is what allows for a conception of the private sphere of social action as other-regarding. Elective relevance, the central feature of the modern conception of the private realm of social action, is preserved in the way we understand the motivational element of social action. But that action is also shaped by private legal institutions, which are, by contrast, constructed around the idea of necessary relevance. What private law does is to make the other present to me, despite my reluctance to see him as more than an object in the way of the satisfaction of my own desires. The social relationship mediated by private law (and the actions of the parties, if they abide by their legal duties) are other-regarding, even if the agent does that against the grain of his psychological lack of interest in the other.

There is an easy way to misunderstand the conception above: my claim might be taken as one in which private law is simply a limit to freely chosen actions by private agents. However, my claim is that private law has more than simply a limiting role on action; rather, it is constitutive of social action (together with other elements such as individual motivation).

That understanding of the respective roles of private law and psychological motivation in the private realm has a deep impact on the available narratives of, on the one hand, the development of private law and, on the other hand the relationship between private law and the private realm of social action. In the next section I try to provide just that narrative by constructing model conceptions of private law and the private sphere.

---

[23] A recent philosophical discussion of the role of preference satisfaction in Welfare Economics can be found in D. M. Hausman and M. S. McPherson, 'Preference satisfaction and Welfare Economics' (2009) 25 Economics and Philosophy 1–25.

5. PRIVATE LAW AND FORMS OF DISRESPECT

The dominant narrative of the unfolding of private law since the later half of the nineteenth century is one of public encroachment on an otherwise normatively and conceptually 'closed' system. The emergence of labour law, anti-trust law, consumer law, the rise of product liability, and good faith in contract law, the idea of abusing one's rights, are often seen as awkward insertions of the logic of the public domain into private law. Sometimes those encroachments are thought to be justified and sometimes they are thought to be spurious, but they are not normally seen as the natural unfolding of the normative and conceptual structures that constitute private law.

I believe that to be a mistake predicated on an oversimplified conception of private law and of its relation to private agents; that is, agents acting within the private domain of social action. In order to explain that mistake, I will not present an alternative narrative of private law's historical unfolding. Instead, I would like to put forward a conceptual scheme which will help explain the greater complexity of that unfolding (when compared to the 'standard account'). Although it does not provide a full narrative, the scheme I will sketch in what follows will help explain changes both in *positive private law* and *doctrinal accounts of private law* in many Western legal systems. This scheme is constructed around the relationship between private law and the different forms of disrespect that social agents might suffer. One of its advantages is that it incorporates an explanation of the mistake made by the traditional narrative of encroachment upon the private by the public.

The idea of disrespect is connected to a deficit or failure of recognition.[24] I would like to suggest that particular private law institutions and norms are better understood as attempts to tackle different forms of disrespect. Moreover, the way in which institutions of private law deal with a particular form of disrespect might generate the conditions for the emergence of another, more sophisticated, form of disrespect. In that sense, there is a conceptual progression between different forms of disrespect and a parallel progression of forms of social recognition.

Social agents display disrespect in three fundamentally different ways, each deriving from a particular sort of failure in recognizing the other. The first form of disrespect is failing to see the other as differentiated from the world. In that form of disrespect, the agent sees a qualitative difference between herself and the world in relation to need. The subject is in need in a way that the world is not; conversely, the world might be in a position of satisfy need in a way that the agent is not (hence the experience of need and not self-sufficiency). That form of disrespect we might call objectification.

A movement away from that form of disrespect is made when the agent perceives that there are in the world other entities that have needs. The agent does not perceive the specificity of the needs in each agent, only the existence of need. This has an equalizing effect and, in fact, the hallmark of that form of recognition that moves the agent away from objectifying the other is predicated

---

[24] For the related concepts of disrespect and recognition I am drawing here on Axel Honneth's work, in particular A. Honneth, *The Struggle for Recognition* (London: Polity Press, 1995).

on the equality of the entities (potentially or actually) experiencing need. *This is a movement achieved through law.*

However, the postulation of formal equality between the subjects, and their opposition to the world, that is, the entities which do not experience need, opens the possibility of another form of disrespect, to wit, the one caused by the opacity of the particular kinds of needs the other might have which are distinct from the agent's own needs. The form of recognition that can tackle this must be sensitive to the relative difference of need between subjects.

This division of disrespect and recognition into three different kinds resonates (although it is not fully identical) with Honneth's reconstruction of Hegel's early conception of the evolution of ethical life as a struggle for recognition. For Honneth, love, law (in a sense similar to the modern rational natural law), and the ethical life represent three forms of recognition respectively predicated on the perception of the other as having needs,[25] the perception of the other as formally equal,[26] and the perception of the other as valuable in the specificity of their needs.[27]

Although there is a conceptual progression between the forms of recognition (and disrespect), this progression does not map on to historically neatly separated phases of the development of legal and political institutions, nor should it be conceived as a historically necessary progression. Different forms of disrespect coexist in different aspects of the social relationship. In fact, if the analysis of the private domain put forward in Section 4 is correct, the combination of elective relevance (in the psychological aspect of agency) and necessary relevance (in its legal aspect), provides an example of how the same social relationship might be marked by both disrespect, as the psychological objectification of the other would be perfectly acceptable under the standards of elective relevance, and the relatively respectful recognition of formal equality (the law applicable to the instant case).

Those forms of recognition relate to private law in complex ways. First, they relate differently to, on the one hand, positive private law and, on the other, the explanatory constructions of private law that both doctrinal lawyers and legal theorists of private law produce.[28] Both positive private law and the narratives produced by doctrine are internally heterogeneous in their relation to forms of disrespect and to recognition. Certain aspects of positive private law could be reconstructed in different (sometimes opposing) ways. Moreover, different parts of positive law could be pulling in opposite directions in relation to recognition and disrespect. Furthermore, in relation to the doctrinal narratives of private law, although at certain junctures some narratives might become prevalent over rival narratives, that dominance is often only partial and certainly only temporary.

The explanatory scheme I am sketching in this section aims at being able to deal with this complexity. It is predicated on the existence of three models of the

---

[25] Honneth, *The Struggle for Recognition*, 95–107.

[26] Honneth, *The Struggle for Recognition*, 107–21.

[27] Honneth, *The Struggle for Recognition*, 121–30.

[28] Positive private law here refers to the authoritative legal sources that constitute the *explanandum* whose explanation is the job that both legal doctrine and legal theory do.

relationship between private law and each form of disrespect/recognition identified earlier. It would be useful to present each of those three models by reference to historical instantiations of those relationships.

The first model is well exemplified by the rise of the dogma of the will in 19th-century Europe. Much has been said about the *Willensdogma* and its grip on the imagination of 19th-century private lawyers.[29] The centrality of the will meant that traditional private law concepts were explained away, redefined, or relocated within the architecture of private law and it also meant that certain new concepts were introduced.

Take the *laesio enormis* as an example. In its original form it drew legal consequences from the fact that there was an imbalance between the mutual duties from party to party in a contract. That, of course, assumed the existence of a 'right price' for each good exchanged, but the rise of the will would make the standard measure of the price in a contract the will of the parties. Without an external comparator to the will of the parties, the doctrine was doomed to disappear, as it virtually did in European civil law systems in the 19th century.[30] Examples like that abound, but the most important changes, for my purposes here, relate to the progressively more abstract nature of some of the central private law concepts. Indeed, it has been remarked many times before that the 19th century, in particular in the civil law tradition, was marked by the decline of particularity and contextuality, and the gradual introduction of progressively more abstract concepts, such as the concept of 'legal act' (*Rechtgeschäft*, *negozio giuridico*), a genus within which one would find contracts, testaments, marriages, etc.[31]

The centrality of the will and the centrality of progressively more abstract concepts relate respectively to two different forms of disrespect. The centrality of the will (rather than, for instance, of the *relationship* between the parties) creates legal instruments centred on the agent and on the unfolding of his will in the world. The limits for the will are imagined primarily as stemming from the will itself, both as self-limitation and as a defect in the will formation. The latter is exemplified by the modern rise of the category of *vices du consentement*[32] and its centrality in the system of invalidity in Napoleon's *Code Civile*.

The centrality of the will places accounts of private law predicated on it squarely within the conception of the private domain as a realm of elective relevance. If that were the only possible story to be told about private law, my own reconstruction of the private domain as combining elective relevance as a

---

[29] Which is simply the highest point of a process that started centuries earlier. See A. Rieg, *Le rôle de la volonté dans l'acte juridique en droit civil français et allemand* (Paris: LGDJ, 1961).

[30] For a summarized and instructive account of the vissicitudes of *laesio enormis* in the last 200 years see R. Zimmerman, *The Law of Obligations: Roman Foundations of the Civilian Tradition* (Oxford: Oxford University Press, 1996) 264–70.

[31] On the pressure for a progressive abstraction of private law concepts during the nineteenth century (in particular in Germany and Italy), see, eg, E. Gabrielli, 'Appunti su Diritti soggettivi, interessi legitimi, interessi collettivi' (1984) XXXVIII(4) Rivista trimestrale di diritto e procedura civile 969.

[32] The theory of the *vices du consentement* attempts to systematize the kinds of defects in will-formation (mistake, duress, etc.) and the respective legal consequences in relation to the contract (eg voidability, obstacle to contract formation, modulation of legal effects).

psychological feature and the law that regulates the relationship as other-regarding would not be warranted. That conception of private law would go hand-in-hand with a conception of others as undifferentiated from the general environment that might potentially help satisfy (or frustrate) the agent's needs. The other might be hindering the satisfaction of my need in a way similar to the one in which a boulder which is blocking my way might hinder the satisfaction of possessing an object that lies behind it.

This conception of private law can only be understood as purely *instrumental*. The value of even the most basic rules of implying a degree of reciprocity, for example, the *pacta sunt servanda*, can only be seen as pursuant to my desire to satisfy my need for the object. That would be the case, for instance, if I believed people are going to be more likely to behave in the way I hope they behave in the presence of a particular rule. Hence, this conception of law as purely instrumental to the unfolding in the world of the arbitrary will of the private agent displays the first form of disrespect identified earlier; that is, *objectification*.

The centrality of progressively more abstract concepts relates to a second form of disrespect, which we might call *reification*. Reification, as conceived by Lukács (and developed by Honneth), is *not* a form of relationship to the other in which the other fails to be perceived apart from the world of objects. In reification, the disrespect stems from a lack of authenticity in the relationship one has with the other. In reification, the pathology is one of detachment from the living experience of the other. The reifying agent progressively becomes a 'contemplative' 'detached observer'.[33] As Honneth puts it:

> Here, the subject is no longer empathetically engaged in interaction with his surroundings, but is instead placed in the perspective of a neutral observer, psychically and existentially untouched by his surroundings.[34]

The progressive abstraction of private law concepts, whose heyday was the 19th century, but whose legacy remains present in contemporary Western legal systems, channelled precisely that detachment. Agents subject to private law (the legal subject) became progressively abstracted from the particular needs and idiosyncrasies of the individual who was assigned legal personality. Those developments in private law saw the subjects as equal, but as merely *formally* so. The indifference to particular vulnerabilities and needs of individuals (and sometimes whole classes of individuals) can be conceived in the scheme outlined above, as a second form of disrespect. The law that goes with it is *formal law*.[35]

The kind of recognition that moves beyond both objectification and reification is marked by the perception of the *concrete* other in her quest for self-realization.

---

[33] Expressions by Lukács, repeated by A. Honneth in *Reification: A New Look at an Old Idea* (Oxford: Oxford University Press, 2008) 24.

[34] Honneth, *Reification: A New Look at an Old Idea*, 24.

[35] Will theories as developed in the nineteenth century are of course not the only outlets for this way of conceiving private law and, in fact, one of the most sophisticated contemporary theories of private law, Weinrib's work on corrective justice, is a defence of formalism in private law; cf E. Weinrib, *The Idea of Private Law* (Cambridge, Mass: Harvard University Press, 1995).

Not recognizing the agent in this way, be it as a result of objectification or reification, is a type of disrespect which 'deprives a person of . . . the social approval of a form of self-realization that he or she had to discover . . .'.[36] Law's universalistic nature makes any attempt to generate that sort of recognition through law chimerical. However, many changes in contemporary private law can be better understood as attempts to battle objectification and reification, by making the law more attentive to the more particular needs of more particular social groups. One could point to the regulation of 'vulnerability' contracts (labour, consumer), the focus on the victim in product liability, among many other changes in contemporary private law as a result of that particular form of struggle.

The scheme I have sketched was presented here just in outline. In spite of its condensed presentation, however, it aims to offer a new interpretative pattern for studies on the foundation and development of private law institutions.

6. CONCLUSION

This chapter attempted to provide an alternative key for the interpretation of the private domain and private law. In that scheme, it was suggested that the private domain is not to be conceived as a domain of merely elective relevance, but instead as a domain in which law brings to the sphere of social action considerations of necessary relevance. That scheme would see private law's role as one of introducing into the social relationship elements of mutual recognition which makes agents behave in a respectful way. I also suggested that that social recognition is not a simple process and put forward two different ways in which agents could fail to recognize others, namely, objectification and reification. Each form of disrespect, that is, failure to recognize, relates to a particular way of conceiving of the role of private law. In objectification, the law can only be seen as an instrument; in reification, the law is marked by equality, but only by formal equality, which is not attentive to particular needs of individuals or social groups. The highest level of recognition does not correspond to a particular kind of private law. However, the aspiration to achieve that level of recognition has animated some of the most important recent developments in private law and it remains as the final horizon of aspiration for social action in the private domain.

---

[36] Honneth, *The Struggle for Recognition*, 134.

PART II

THE DOMAIN, VALUES, AND FUNCTIONS OF PUBLIC LAW

☙ 6 ❧

Defending the Domain of Public Law

Cormac Mac Amhlaigh*

I. INTRODUCTION—THE DOMAIN OF PUBLIC LAW

It is a commonplace that the public/private divide does not exist in any 'real' sense 'out there' to be 'discovered' through critical reflection.[1] In the words of one prominent commentator, '[t]here is no such thing as *the* public/private distinction, or, at any rate, it is a deep mistake to think that there is a single substantive distinction here that can be made do any real philosophical or political work'.[2] This commonplace has become an axiom of contemporary public law scholarship and has had a major influence on thinking about the public/private divide in the law.[3] For most public lawyers, the legal expression of the public/private divide is a malleable phenomenon which can be tailored to suit individual circumstances and aims, is necessarily political given its constructed and purposive nature, and can be dispensed with when it proves obstructive to particular aims. As such, three dominant theses regarding the public/private divide can be identified in contemporary public law scholarship; a 'local-ecologies' thesis, an ideological thesis, and a dispensability thesis. The local ecologies thesis assumes the non-immutability of the divide in the law by arguing that there is not, or should not be, any cross-fertilization between the various hermetic 'local ecologies' or 'micro-climates' of the divide scattered across the legal system. In these local ecologies the public/private divide is employed in a narrow and discrete way within a particular regulatory regime, such as a particular statute or under a series of rules of the common law. As such, the local ecologies thesis denies the existence of any broader or transcendental

* Thanks to all the participants at the *After Public Law* workshop held at Edinburgh University in June 2011 as well as Emilios Chistodoulidis, Francisco Saffie, Neil Walker, Claudio Michelon, Niamh Nic Shuibhne, and Mark Tushnet for helpful comments on previous drafts of this chapter.

[1] See Lucy's contribution, Ch 4.

[2] R. Guess, *Public Goods, Private Goods* (Princeton, NJ: Princeton University Press, 2001) 106.

[3] D. Kennedy, 'The Stages of the Decline of the Public/Private Distinction' (1982) 130 University of Pennsylvania Law Review 1349; K. Klare, 'The Public/Private Distinction in Labor Law' (1982) 130(6) University of Pennsylvania Law Review 1358; L. Seidman, 'Public Principle and Private Choice: The Uneasy Case for a Boundary Maintenance Theory of Constitutional Law' (1987) 96(5) Yale Law Journal 1006; C. Harlow, '"Public" and "Private": definition without distinction' (1983) 43 Modern Law Review 241; P. Cane, 'Public Law and Private Law: The Study of the Analysis and Use of a Legal Concept' in J. Eekelaar and J. Bell (eds), *Oxford Essays in Jurisprudence* 3rd series (USA: Oxford University Press, 1987).

notion of public and private beyond discrete regulatory regimes within a legal system.

The ideological thesis holds that the demarcation of the domain of the public is an inherently political act. If there is no 'real' public/private divide, 'out there', then its creation and application in the law is a necessarily subjective choice lending it an ideological quality. Moreover, it is ideology with a capital 'I', involving as it does perhaps the most political of questions; who are 'we' and what do we do in common? This contention is of particular relevance to questions of institutional design and competence in public law in that if the creation of the public/private divide is a political act, it is for democratically elected legislatures, and not courts, to decide where to draw the line.

The third thesis predicated on the axiom argues that in the light of the constructed nature of the divide in law, that it can be dispensed with or jettisoned. Indeed, on this view, a compelling case can be made for its jettisoning when it proves obstructive to the achievement of other values in the law. For example, feminist scholars have criticized the application of the divide in the criminal law in cases of domestic violence or marital rape, and human rights scholars have argued that its application in human rights law can inhibit the effective protection of human rights standards, particularly where these are violated by private, rather than public, actors.[4] From the human rights perspective in particular, the phenomena of globalization and privatization have led to calls for a rethink in human rights protection beyond traditional understandings of public and private, given that in a globalized world, private entities such as transnational corporations can and do wield considerable power, including the power to commit human rights violations.[5]

However, the axiom of the non-immutability of the public/private divide presents a paradox for public law as a field of study as well as an area of legal practice. Perhaps the most orthodox account of public law as a 'field', at least in the 'internal positivist'[6] sense, is that of an area or field of law which applies to the public realm, as institutionalized in the state. Thus, public law is the law which regulates the different branches of the state *inter se*, as well as the relationship between the state and the individual.[7] However, according to the axiom of the non-immutability of the divide, this orthodox account of the field of public law operates according to a dichotomy—public/private, state/non-state—that does not exist in any philosophically or conceptually satisfying way, nor is formulated to a satisfactory degree in legal doctrine (and is anyway an anachronism in an increasingly globalized world). As such, scholars working in the field of public

---

[4] See, eg, S. Boyd (ed.), *Challenging the Public/Private Divide: Feminism, Law, and Public Policy* (Toronto: University Toronto Press, 1997); A. Claphman, *Human Rights Obligations of non-state actors* (Oxford: Oxford University Press, 2006).

[5] For discussion see G. Teubner, 'The Anonymous Matrix: Human Rights Violations by "Private" Transnational Actors' (2006) 69(3) Modern Law Review 327.

[6] See N. Walker, 'On the Necessarily Public Character of Law' in C. McCorkindale, G. Clunie, H. Psarras, and C. Michelon, *The Public in Law* (Farnham: Ashgate, 2012) 11.

[7] See for example, H. Woolf, 'Public law—private law: why the divide?—a personal view' (1986) Public Law 220, 221.

law and judges faced with expressions of public and private in the law, must muddle through in a form of Orwellian 'doublethink', believing both that it exists but does not actually exist at the same time, or descend into a self-defeating Cartesian scepticism about legal domains, legal doctrine, and legal values.

This chapter will analyse this seeming paradox in the practice of public law. Focusing on one particular instance of the public/private divide in the law, it will argue that, even if we cannot claim a metaphysical truth about the public/private divide in law, that legal practice reveals a more deeply rooted and pervasive understanding of the public and the private than the axiom of the divide and its corresponding three theses in law suggest. It will argue that the notion of an overarching public/private divide has an indelible hold on our political and legal imagination which surfaces when considering the limits of the domain of the public in the law. As such, this deeper conceptual expression of the public and the private is not something which can be parsed for specific regulatory aims, dismissed as purely ideological, nor jettisoned at will. It represents a deeply rooted 'social imaginary'[8] in the contemporary legal world (even a post-metaphysical one), which is more than its expression in provisions of positive law and is not exhausted in this expression. This is something, the chapter concludes, that deserves more recognition in contemporary legal scholarship on the public/private divide.

In order to pursue this claim, the chapter will focus on one expression of the divide in the area of state action doctrines in constitutional law; more specifically on the state action provision in section 6 of the UK's Human Rights Act 1998 (HRA). This doctrine of constitutional law limits liability for breaches of consti-tutional rights to the subjects of public law, that is, bodies which have some sort of relationship with the state, and as such represents a particularly prominent example of a domain of public law through the public/private divide. The chapter will proceed as follows; section 2 will analyse s. 6 HRA and its interpretation by the courts in the UK. The ensuing sections will examine the various theses which flow from the axiom of the public/private divide. Section 3 will examine the extent to which the domain of public law can only ever exist as a series of 'local ecologies' in a legal system, as opposed to providing a foundational overarching structural ideal, arguing that the analysis of s. 6 HRA reveals that the nature of the 'public' in legal systems is more universal and trans-systemic than the fragmented picture of a series of 'local ecologies' would suggest.

Section 4 goes on to analyse the second thesis and its particular manifestation in critiques of judicial demarcation of the divide on ideological grounds. In analysing judicial reasoning in the s. 6 HRA cases, it argues that the phenomenon of the public/private divide in legal practice is more complex than this critique would have us believe, showing that the interpretation of s. 6 HRA can include purely conceptual considerations.

Section 5, furthermore, looks at the third thesis by examining calls for the jettisoning of the divide in certain areas of law, and particularly as a response to

---

[8] C. Taylor, *Modern Social Imaginaries* (Raleigh NC: Duke University Press, 2004). See Ch 5 in the current volume for further discussion on this point.

privatization and globalization. While acknowledging that shifts in politics and power pose challenges to the way the state has traditionally regulated and governed, it argues that attempts to jettison the divide in law are neither possible nor desirable, and can, in fact, be self-defeating, at least from the viewpoint of constitutional rights protection due to the fact that the apparatus of human rights law is necessarily predicated on a clear distinction between the public and the private in the law. The conclusion brings these threads together by proposing one way of conceptualizing this deeper sense of public and private in legal practice as a legal archetype.

2. A DOMAIN OF PUBLIC LAW: THE STATE ACTION DOCTRINE IN CONSTITUTIONAL LAW

Of the instances of the public/private divide in legal systems, one of the most prominent is the restriction of the application of fundamental rights norms to the public realm; that is, the state and its agents. This is partly to do with the legacy of the development of fundamental rights law in the revolutionary contexts of the French Declaration of the Rights of Man and the Citizen and the US Bill of Rights, which posited subjective rights enforceable exclusively against the state, then deemed the primary threat to individual liberty.[9] This restriction of the enforceability of rights against the state as the institutional expression of the public[10] is configured in different ways in different constitutional contexts.[11]

In the UK, section 6(1) HRA provides that 'it is unlawful for a public authority to act in a way which is incompatible with a Convention right'.[12] Section 6(3) states that '"public authority" includes (a) a court or tribunal, and (b) *any person certain of whose functions are functions of a public nature*, but does not include either House of Parliament or a person exercising functions in connection with proceedings in Parliament"'.[13] Section 6(5), moreover, states that '[i]n relation to a particular act, a person is not a public authority by virtue of subsection (3)(b) if the nature of the act is private'.

Thus, s. 6 HRA constitutes a form of state or 'public' action doctrine by limiting the effects of the rights protected by the Act to the public realm or the state, defined both substantively and functionally.

---

[9] See, eg, James Madison's speech to Congress on the inclusion of the Bill of Rights in the US Constitution: 'The prescriptions in favor of liberty ought to be levelled against that quarter where the danger lies, namely, that which possesses the highest prerogative of power...[which is] found...in the body of the people, operating by the majority against the minority'. J. Madison, 'Introduction to the Bill of Rights' in R. Ketcham (ed.), *Selected Writings of James Madison* (Indianapolis, IN: Hackett, 2006) 171.

[10] M. Loughlin, 'In Defense of Staatslehre' (2009) 48(1) Der Staat 1, 12.

[11] The limitation of fundamental rights law to the public realm exists on a spectrum from the strict 'vertical effect' of fundamental rights to public bodies and acts such as the state action doctrine in US constitutional law to the more open, indirect effect of human rights law beyond the public realm such as in German constitutional law to the complete horizontal effect of constitutional rights in Ireland and South Africa. See M. Hunt, 'The "Horizontal Effect" of the Human Rights Act' (1998) Public Law 423; S. Gardbaum, 'The "Horizontal Effect" of Constitutional Rights' (2003) 102(3) Michgan Law Review 387.

[12] s. 6(1) HRA.

[13] s. 6(3) HRA. Emphasis added.

As such, the state action doctrine and, in particular, its manifestation in s. 6 HRA, provides a particularly useful focus for consideration of the axiom of the public/private divide and the three theses which inform legal approaches to the divide. S. 6 HRA constitutes an instantiation of the dichotomy—public/private, state/non-state—which exists within a particular statutory regime with a particular purpose, that of the protection of particular rights contained in the European Convention on Human Rights (ECHR), and as such is a useful context within which to examine the local ecologies thesis. Thus, the extent to which there is or should be a measure of 'cross-fertilization' between the way the divide is applied under the Act and other areas of the legal system is crucial in assessing the viability of the thesis. Moreover, the state action doctrine in s. 6 HRA entails an area which has been the particular focus of critical scholars alleging the political nature of the divide and its interpretation and application by the judiciary.[14] The way in which the public and the private has been interpreted and applied has been a particular focus of the ideological charge, not least with respect to human rights protections where the refusal by courts to extend human rights protections by creating obligations for certain bodies can be interpreted as being motivated by ideology. Finally, as a limiting provision within a human rights protection law, s. 6 can be perceived as an obstacle to the remedying of human rights violations particularly by private actors through its limitation of rights claims to public authorities and has therefore been the catalyst for calls for the jettisoning of the divide in particular contexts.

The House of Lords[15] has had two opportunities to interpret and apply the public/private divide as contained in s. 6 HRA; in *Aston Cantlow Parochial Church Council v Wallbank*,[16] and *YL v Birmingham City Council*.[17]

2.1 Aston Cantlow v Wallbank

In *Aston Cantlow*, the House of Lords had to adjudicate upon a rather esoteric dispute about whether a Parochial Church council (PCC) in England could sue the respondents for the cost of repair to the local church on the grounds that the defendants were the owners of formerly rectorial land which allegedly entailed a common law obligation to repair the church. The respondents argued that such an action would constitute a form of indirect taxation, thereby interfering with their right to property protected under the HRA.[18] In order to succeed, then, the

---

[14] The Act itself does not provide any criteria for drawing the divide introduced in s. 6 HRA. The Government white paper on the Bill, *Bringing Rights Home*, did note that the definition of the 'public' under the Act was deliberately wide and would include 'central government (including executive agencies); local government; the police; immigration officers; prisons; courts and tribunals themselves; and to the extent that they are exercising public functions, companies responsible for areas of activity which were previously within the public sector, such as the privatized utilities', para 2.2.

[15] The Supreme Court has yet to consider the interpretation of s. 6 in detail.

[16] [2004] 1 AC 546; hereafter '*Aston*'.

[17] [2007] UKHL 27; hereafter '*YL*'.

[18] Protected in Art. 1, 1st Protocol ECHR and under the Human Rights Act in s. 1(1)(b) HRA.

respondents had to argue that the PCC either constituted a public authority under s. 6(1) HRA or exercised functions of a public nature under s. 6(3) HRA.

Considering these questions, the House of Lords found[19] that the PCC neither constituted a public authority under s. 6(1) nor discharged functions of a public nature under s. 6(3) and that therefore the human rights claim could not succeed.

Analysing the public/private divide contained within s. 6 HRA, the court found that the provision distinguished between 'core' and 'hybrid' public bodies and a distinction was to be drawn between those persons who are 'governmental organisations' and those who are 'non-governmental organisations'.[20] A body which fell under s. 6(1) is required to act 'compatibly with Convention rights in everything it does'[21] and is a public authority 'through and through'.[22] As such, they cannot themselves enjoy Convention rights. Hybrid bodies on the other hand, are not absolutely barred from enjoying Convention rights. They may enjoy Convention rights or be subject to Convention obligations depending on the function being discharged.[23] Thus, according to the court, the public/private divide as contained in s. 6 HRA, can be drawn in two ways in relation to 'core' public authorities under s. 6(1), and in relation to 'hybrid' bodies to which s. 6(3) and s. 6(5) apply.[24]

On the substantive approach to the public, that is, the question of whether Aston Cantlow PCC or the Church of England more generally constituted a 'core public authority' for the purposes of s. 6(1), Lord Nicholls noted that the term 'public authority' related to a body whose nature is 'governmental in a broad sense',[25] and would include 'government departments, local authorities, the police and the armed forces'.[26] The factors which lead to this classification would include the 'possession of special powers, democratic accountability, public funding in whole or in part, and obligation to act only in the public interests, and a statutory constitution'.[27] In the instant case, Lord Nicholls found that neither the PCC nor the Church of England qualified as a 'core' public authority for the purposes of s. 6(1),[28] relying on the 'constitution and functions'[29] of the Council and the Church of England as well as whether it would qualify for 'victim' status under Art. 34 ECHR. Reviewing the form and nature and functions of the Church of England in particular, notwithstanding the privileged relationship between the Church, its 'special links with central government',[30] and the fact that it discharged functions which could be considered governmental such as the execution of marriages and the provision of education, he found that it did not constitute a public authority due to the fact that the Church was 'essentially a

---

[19] Lord Scott dissenting.   [20] Lord Hope, para 47.

[21] Lord Nicholls, para 7.

[22] Lord Hope, para 35.   [23] Lord Nicholls, para 11.

[24] See Oliver, 'The Frontiers of the State: Public Authorities and Public Functions under the Human Rights Act' (2000) Public Law 476.

[25] *Aston*, para 7.   [26] *Aston*, para 7.   [27] *Aston*, para 7.

[28] *Aston*, para 7.   [29] *Aston*, para 14.   [30] *Aston*, para 13.

religious organisation'.[31] With regard to the PCC, he emphasized the functions of the council as the promotion of 'the mission of the Church' and the undertaking of financial responsibilities, functions which were 'far removed' from a body which would engage state responsibility under the ECHR.[32]

Lord Hope dwelt upon the question of whether the Church of England or the PCC could claim 'victim' status under Art. 34 ECHR (and incorporated into the HRA in s. 7(7)) which he argued was central to the question at hand. Summarizing the Strasbourg case law on the issue, and particularly cases involving established churches or churches with a special connection with the state such as in Sweden and Greece, for Hope, the central question related to the constitution of the body in question and in particular whether it was a governmental organization 'established for public administration purposes'.[33] Thus, the central question to be asked in the light of the Strasbourg case law was whether the body was established 'with a view to public administration as part of the process of government'.[34] On this analysis, considering the constitution and the functions both of the Church of England and PCC, the extent of public funding as well as their statutory powers and regulatory functions, Lord Hope concluded that neither the PCC nor the Church of England more generally could be considered a 'core' public authority in the sense of s. 6(1) HRA.[35]

Lord Hobhouse considered both the functions and constitution of PCCs under the relevant measures establishing PCCs[36] by the Church of England. Relying particularly on the functions of the PCC, as well as the fact that it did not act in the public interest, he concluded that it did not constitute a 'core' public authority for the purposes of the HRA.[37]

Lord Rodger reached a similar conclusion through a focus on the constitution of the authorities in question as well as looking at the functions undertaken by the PCC.[38] Notwithstanding its constitution as a body corporate, Lord Rodger argued that the functions of the body militated against the Council being considered a public authority for s. 6(1) purposes.[39] He found that a purposive construction of s. 6 indicated that the 'essential characteristic of a public authority is that it carries out a *function of government*'[40] which would engage state responsibility under the ECHR regime. As such, he found that 'what matters is that the PCC's general function is to carry out the religious mission of the Church in the parish, rather than to exercise any government power'.[41]

A minority considered the question of 'hybrid' bodies in the case. On this particular question, Lord Nicholls found that:[42]

---

[31] *Aston*, para 13.   [32] *Aston*, para 14.

[33] Citing the ECtHR in *Holy Monasteries v Greece* (1995) 20 EHRR 1.

[34] *Aston*, para 50.   [35] *Aston*, paras 56–62.

[36] Namely the Parochial Church Councils (Powers) Measure 1921 and the Parochial Church Council (Powers) Measure 1956.

[37] *Aston*, para 86.   [38] *Aston*, see particularly paras 155–156, 163.

[39] *Aston*, para 166.   [40] *Aston*, para 160. Emphasis added.   [41] *Aston*, para 166.

[42] *Aston*, para 16. Which was approved by Lord Hobhouse, para 85.

[I]t is not necessary to analyse each of the functions of a parochial church council and see if any of them is a public function. What matters is whether the particular act done by the plaintiff council of which complaint is made is a private act as contrasted with the discharge of a public function.

As such, the question of the repair of the chancel was only very tangentially a public function in the sense that the 'state of repair of the church building may be said to affect rights of the public'.[43]

Lord Hope considered crucial the question of whether the Council, in attempting to enforce a civil debt, rather that repair of the chancel, was discharging functions which were owed to the public by the state.[44] As such, for Lord Hope, the question of the enforcement of a civil debt came within the definition in s. 6(5) of the HRA, and the PCC therefore could not be considered to be exercising a public function for the purposes of s. 6. On the question of function, Lord Rodger argued that, even if some of the functions of the Council could be understood to be acting in the public interest 'in a general sense',[45] and particularly, for example, when it was involved in marriage ceremonies, the enforcement of a common law obligation was insufficient to bring it into the classification of a public authority, even under the s. 6(3)(b) functional test.[46]

Lord Scott, dissenting on this point, found that the church in question was a public building, that the PCC discharged functions of a charitable nature, and that the decision to enforce chancel repair was a liability taken in the interests of the parishioners as a whole, not in any private interest and that the provisions have an 'unmistakable public law flavour to them'.[47] As such, Scott concluded that the PCC was discharging a public function for the purposes of s. 6 HRA.[48]

2.2 *YL v Birmingham City Council*

Continuing on the question of 'hybrid' bodies under the Act, the House of Lords revisited the issue in *YL v Birmingham City Council*.[49] This case involved a privately owned and run company, part of whose business was carried out pursuant to a contract with a public authority, that is, a local government body, which was under a statutory duty to discharge particular functions. As such, it was the latest in a series of cases of contracting out, frequently involving the right to home and family life,[50] where the question at stake was not whether the entity itself was a 'core' public authority for s. 6(1) HRA purposes, but rather whether it constituted a hybrid body which could be said to discharge 'public functions' in providing, for example, housing or care for the elderly for the purposes of s. 6(3) HRA.

---

[43] *Aston*, para 16.

[44] *Aston*, para 64. Lord Hobhouse similarly considered that the function in question was the 'enforcement of a civil liability', para 89.

[45] *Aston*, para 170.   [46] *Aston*, para 171.   [47] *Aston*, paras 130, 131.

[48] *Aston*, para 131.   [49] [2007] UKHL 27.

[50] See *Poplar Housing v Donoghue* [2001] EWCA (Civ) 595; [2002] Q.B. 48; *R (Heather) v Leonard Cheshire Foundation* [2002] EWCA (Civ) 366; [2002] 2 All ER 936. For an overview see Joint Committee on Human Rights, *The Meaning of Public Authority Under the Human Rights Act*, (2003–4) HL 39, HC 382.

The action was taken in response to the attempted eviction of an elderly resident of the home suffering from Alzheimer's disease. She was resident in the care home under an agreement between the home and the local authority who was under a statutory duty to make arrangements for elderly residents within their remit under the National Assistance Act 1948. The individual in question was subsidized by the local authority pursuant to this statutory obligation. The applicant challenged her eviction from the home through the termination of her contract on the grounds that it would breach her right to home and family life protected by the HRA.

Given the nature of the entity in question, a private commercial operator running a care home, albeit that it had contracts with a public authority for the care of particular persons, it was common ground that the entity itself did not qualify as a 'core' public body for s. 6(1) purposes. Thus, the question before the court, was whether the private entity, in caring for elderly residents in a private care home pursuant to a contract with the public authority who was under a statutory duty to provide such care, was undertaking a 'public function' within the meaning of s. 6(3), in order for the human rights claim to succeed.

For the majority, Lord Scott found that the private company did not exercise public functions due to the fact that it received no public funding, had no statutory powers, was under no obligation to accept resident tenants, and set its own pricing policy. It was therefore a commercial operator in a commercial market.[51] The situation would have been different, Scott argued, if the company had enjoyed special statutory powers over the residents such as the power to restrain or discipline them in some way,[52] a function which involved the 'exercise of the regulatory or coercive powers of the state',[53] as Lady Hale put it.[54] For Lord Scott, this was central to the definition of public function as there was nothing inherently public in *any* particular function.[55] He argued that many functions could be undertaken by private actors which are undertaken by local authorities and thus nothing inheres in, for example, the provision of care services qualifying them as essentially public functions. Thus, the ultimate test for determining whether something was 'public' or not was the source of the exercise of the function; that is, whether they were statutory or stemmed from a private contract as part of a commercial venture.[56]

Reviewing the Strasbourg case law on the issue, Lord Mance found that factors determinative of the 'public' realm would include the exercise of 'state power' or duties, public funding, or a 'non-delegable state function'.[57] Lord Mance, in particular, was swayed by the case law on which bodies were subject to judicial review, finding that there was such as thing as an inexorably public function that even if not undertaken by the state, the state could be said to have delegated. In

---

[51] YL, para 26. This was supported by the fact that the company received no public funds or subsidy but was party to a contract with a public authority. This did not alter its private nature. Otherwise, Scott argued, a contract to provide cleaning or catering services with a public authority would fall under the state action definition which for Scott was patently absurd, para 27.

[52] YL, para 28.   [53] YL, para 63.   [54] See also judgment of Lord Neuberger, YL, para 166.

[55] YL, para 29.   [56] YL, para 31.   [57] YL, para 99.

such cases, the state would not be absolved from its responsibilities, including respect for fundamental rights. He cited with approval the notion of 'governmental functions' and 'functions of government' adopted in *Aston* which, he argued, included 'powers conferred and duties imposed or undertaken in the general public interest'.[58] Thus, the test of publicness included, following the majority in *Aston*, democratic accountability, an obligation to act in the public interest, and the provision of public funding.[59] However, while holding out the possibility that there is such a thing as an 'inherently governmental function',[60] he found that the provision of care and accommodation for the elderly was not one of them.

Both Lady Hale and Lord Bingham dissented. For Lady Hale, the crux of state action in terms of public function was whether the state had assumed responsibility for a particular function at public expense if need be and in the public interest.[61] For Lady Hale, each of these criteria was satisfied with respect to care of the elderly. Thus, the provision of care of the elderly was public given the public interest aspect of the function regardless of whether it could also be provided privately.[62] She also considered public funding as an important factor for s. 6 purposes.[63]

Lord Bingham found that there were core and peripheral state functions, and that the existence and extent of statutory powers in relation to the function would be relevant for the purposes of the notion of a public function under s. 6(3) HRA.[64] Another important factor for state action purposes in Lord Bingham's view was the extent to which the 'state' regulates or supervises the execution of the function, including the imposition of criminal penalties where the body falls below publicly promulgated standards.[65] This in turn is evidence of the state's recognition of the importance of the function in question.[66] A third factor identified by Bingham was the question of whether public funds were involved in the discharge of the particular function.

In considering the question of elderly care in particular, Lord Bingham found that the statutory duty to provide care on local authorities as well as the fact that regulation and supervision of such provision was taken on by the legislation, militated in favour of the provision of elderly care constituting a public function for the purposes of s. 6(3). Furthermore, the fact that public funds could be implicated in the provision of the service, based on a means test, supported this conclusion.[67]

The majority on the evidence rejected the contention that the private company which ran elderly care homes in agreement with a local authority was exercising

---

[58] *YL*, para 103. Similarly Lord Neuberger emphasized the approach of the House in *Aston* in terms of the notion of 'public administration as part of the process of government' and the notion of 'exercising governmental power', para 159.

[59] *YL*, para 105.   [60] *YL*, para 115.   [61] *YL*, para 65.

[62] *YL*, para 67.   [63] *YL*, para 68.   [64] *YL*, para 8.

[65] *YL*, para 9. Something to which the majority disagreed. 'As a matter of ordinary language and concepts, the mere fact that the public interest requires a service to be closely regulated and supervised pursuant to statutory rules cannot mean that the provision of the service, as opposed to its regulation and supervision, is a function of a public nature'. Lord Neuberger, para 134.

[66] *YL*, para 9.   [67] *YL*, para 17.

a public function for the purposes of s. 6(3) HRA, and dismissed the appeal. A distinction was to be made between the statutory duty to provide care on the local authority and the provision of care pursuant to the statutory duty by a private operator under contract with the local authority. Such provision of care was not intrinsically a public function. The upshot was that the private corporation was not 'public' for the purposes of s. 6(3) and therefore the applicant could not rely on Convention rights against the care home under the HRA, and in particular the protection of her right to privacy, home, and family life under Art. 8 of the Convention.

To summarize the approach taken by the court in these cases on the demarcation of the public domain under the HRA regime, for the purposes of the ensuing argument, the factors taken into account by the court in *Aston* as to whether a body is a 'public authority' in a substantive sense, then, included the nature of the body itself in terms of its constitution as a 'government body', the nature of the function undertaken by the body, the extent to which a body enjoys statutory powers, the extent of state supervision of the activities of the body, the extent to which the body is subsidized by the state, the extent to which liability would be incurred under the ECHR regime, and the extent of democratic oversight or public accountability of the body. In terms of the question of function of a public nature, in *YL* on the purely functional analysis, in deciding that the company in question was not undertaking public functions for the purposes of s. 6(3) HRA, the factors taken into consideration (by both the majority and minority) in order to answer this question included the nature of the function itself, the traditional role of the state in discharging the function, the presence or absence of a statutory duty to provide the function, the enjoyment of statutory powers, the extent of state supervision of the discharge of the function, the extent to which public funds were available to provide for the function, and the extent to which the entity charged with undertaking the function was subsidized for this purpose, the extent to which the function was in the public interest, the possibility of judicial review of bodies discharging the function, the degree of democratic accountability over the body, and the extent to which the state was under positive obligations to prevent Convention violations.

The ensuing sections of this chapter will use this experience of the public/ private divide in the law as a basis to show how a deeper sense of the public and private necessarily insinuates itself into legal and judicial consideration of the divide which has important implications for the three theses common in approaches to the divide in legal scholarship; namely, the local-ecologies thesis, the ideological thesis, and the dispensability thesis.

3. THE LOCAL-ECOLOGIES THESIS

The first implication stemming from the axiom regarding the nature of the public and private realms, that there is no such thing as 'a' single public/private divide, that our institutional practices do not allow for the conclusion that there is *one overarching public/private divide* providing a superstructure for the entire legal system. Rather, in law, the public/private divide appears as a series of 'local ecologies' or 'micro-climates' scattered across the legal system, bearing little or no relation to each other in terms of their definition or understanding of 'publicness'. Moreover, given this state of affairs, the local ecologies thesis maintains that there should be no 'cross-fertilization' of meanings of public and private between different local ecologies. It was clearly influential in the *Aston Cantlow* and *YL* decisions, where the court explicitly considered (and ultimately rejected) the issue of the cross-fertilization of conceptions of publicness between s. 6 HRA and other local ecologies in the UK legal system. In particular, in these cases the court explicitly considered the extent to which other areas of law with a public/private divide such as judicial review[68] or particular statutory frameworks such as Race Relations Act 1976 and the Freedom of Information Act 2000[69] could provide guidance as to how it should be demarcated under the HRA's regime, whether under s. 6(1) or s. 6(3). However, the court's opinion was overwhelmingly against any such cross-fertilization between the different areas in the law.[70]

This thesis was particularly evident in the court's emphasis in both *Aston* and *YL*, that the European Court of Human Rights' (ECtHR) interpretation of the 'victim' requirement under Art. 34 of the Convention in order to determine publicness was of paramount relevance for s. 6 HRA. This purposive approach to s. 6 HRA reflects the local-ecologies thesis in that the linking of 'publicness' to the ability to hold Convention rights or not under Art. 34,[71] is itself an intimation of the particularity, even *sui generis* nature, of the public/private divide under s. 6 HRA, distinguishing it from other 'local ecologies' of the divide in the legal system. In a robust statement of the 'local ecologies' thesis, Hobhouse argued that, 'the relevant underlying principles [in interpreting s. 6 HRA] are to be found in human rights law not in Community law nor in the administrative law of England and Wales'.[72] Lord Roger also advanced the thesis in commenting that '[a] purposive construction of [public authority in the HRA] accordingly indicates that the essential characteristic of a public authority is that it carries out a function of government which would engage the responsibility of the United Kingdom before the Strasbourg organs'.[73] Lord Hope explicitly criticized the Court of Appeal for ignoring this factor in its analysis.[74]

Dawn Oliver has supported this 'local ecologies' approach in considering the concept of publicness under the HRA.[75] On considering the extent to which the

---

[68] For example, *R v Panel on Takeovers and Mergers, ex p. Datafin* [1987] QB 815.

[69] See Lord Mance in *YL*, para 106.

[70] With the exception of Lord Mance's consideration of administrative law and judicial review in *YL* (see paras 101–102).

[71] See, eg, Lord Nicholls in *Aston*, para 8.   [72] Lord Hobhouse, *YL*, para 87.

[73] *Aston*, para 160.   [74] *Aston*, para 51.

[75] Oliver, 'The Frontiers of the State: Public Authorities and Public Functions under the Human Rights Act'.

understanding of the public/private divide in other areas of law can aid the understanding of the divide under the HRA, Oliver has argued against cross-fertilization particularly with reference to the areas of the regime of the Freedom of Information Act 2000 which define 'public authority',[76] the applicability of EU law in relation to 'emanations of the state',[77] judicial review in administrative law with its notions of 'public element' and 'public function',[78] the common law doctrine of common callings where an undertaking can be regarded as 'affected with a public interest',[79] and the notion of 'services of general interest' under the EU treaties.[80]

For Oliver, the concept of the public is 'elusive in [the] law',[81] and she argues for a version of the 'local-ecologies' thesis to the divide under the HRA, on the grounds that the 'public' in each area is defined for specific purposes which are not transferrable to other areas.[82] In particular, cross-fertilization from other local-ecologies to that of the HRA is potentially dangerous, she argues. It could run the risk of an overly broad application of human rights obligations, putting onerous obligations on private parties,[83] and more significantly, leading to a number of bodies potentially losing their Convention rights due to the fact that they would not fall within the 'victim' requirements of Art. 34 ECHR.[84] Indeed, the court in *Aston* implicitly heeded Oliver's counsel by including this reasoning as part of the finding that the applicant in question fell on the private side of the divide for s. 6 HRA purposes.[85]

Whereas this purposive approach is understandable from the viewpoint of local systemic and doctrinal coherence, it is not clear that it is possible to maintain a *cordon sanitarie* around each of the various local ecologies of the public/private divide scattered across the legal system, as the 'local ecologies' thesis maintains. Even if the public/private divide is being invoked for different purposes—the application of international human rights obligations, the protection of liberty, the propriety of administrative decision making, the accountability of public officials, the effectiveness of supranational law, or considerations of justice more broadly—there is a sense in which each demarcation of the divide is working from a common template of publicness, reflecting a deeper structural

---

[76] Section 1(1) and Schedule 1 to the FoIA 2000.

[77] Case C-188/89 *Foster v British Gas (plc)* [1990] ECR I-3313; [1991] 2 AC 306; [1990] 3 All ER 897.

[78] *Datafin*, p. 847-E.

[79] See N. Arterburn, 'The origin and first test of public callings' (1926–27) 75 University of Pennsylvania Law Review 411 cited by Oliver, 'The Frontiers of the State: Public Authorities and Public Functions under the Human Rights Act', 488.

[80] Now contained in Art. 14 Treaty on the Functioning of the European Union. Oliver, 'The Frontiers of the State: Public Authorities and Public Functions under the Human Rights Act', 489.

[81] Oliver 'The Frontiers of the State' 345.

[82] Oliver 'The Frontiers of the State' *passim*.

[83] Oliver 'The Frontiers of the State' 485.

[84] Oliver 'The Frontiers of the State' 490.

[85] See particularly, Lord Hope in *Aston*, para 47.

public/private divide in the law which traverses individual local ecologies. The existence of this deeper sense of the public going beyond its immediate expression in a particular statutory provision such as s. 6 HRA is evident in two issues which emerge from the Court's adjudication of s. 6 HRA.

First of all, a degree of confusion between taking a substantive or functional approach to 'publicness' under s. 6 HRA is apparent in the Court's reasoning. With respect to the criteria of publicness under s. 6 HRA, as noted above the court drew a distinction between s. 6(1) HRA 'publicness' involving 'core' public bodies, and s. 6(3)(b) 'publicness' which involved 'hybrid' bodies which could be considered 'public' if it could be said that they were exercising a public function, and emphasized the importance of drawing a clear distinction between the two forms of 'publicness' in s. 6 HRA. However, a brief examination of the criteria, rationale, and justification for the determination of a public authority or public function in these cases reveals that the question of whether something was a public authority or a public function used the *same criteria of publicness* for the supposedly distinct heads of s. 6(1) and s. 6(3)(b) HRA.

For example, in *Aston Cantlow*, the interpretation of 'public authority' under s. 6(1) HRA, that is a substantive, institutional analysis of 'core public authority', included liberal references to 'governmental *functions*'.[86] Moreover, the application of s. 6(1) HRA to the Church of England and PCC resulted in much discussion of the *functions* of these bodies in order to determine whether they constituted 'core', that is, institutional, public authorities.[87] More specifically, on considering the Strasbourg case law on the question, Lord Hope emphasized that the test of publicness for s. 6(1) HRA related to whether a body was established for 'public administration purposes',[88] another way of saying that the *function* of the body must in some way be related to public administration. Similarly, in *YL*, consideration of the publicness of a *function* under s. 6(3)(b) HRA included much discussion of the *substantive make up or constitution* of these bodies exercising those functions. Thus, the court took into consideration whether a body exercising a particular function was under a statutory duty to exercise it,[89] whether the body enjoyed statutory powers,[90] the extent of state supervision of the body in discharging the function,[91] the extent to which public funds were available to the body to discharge the function and the extent to which the body charged with undertaking the function was subsidized for this purpose,[92] and the degree of democratic accountability over the body.[93]

Oliver has noted and critiqued this confused conflation of institutional and functional factors by the courts in determining the 'publicness' of authorities and

---

[86] *Aston*, para 9.

[87] *Aston*, para 14. Similarly Lord Hope, on considering the nature of the Church of England *qua* public authority gave consideration to its 'regulatory functions', as compared with the 'functions of government', para 61.

[88] *Aston*, para 50.   [89] See, *Aston Cantlow* and *YL*, *passim*.

[90] *Aston Cantlow* and *YL*, *passim*   [91] *Aston Cantlow* and *YL*, *passim*.

[92] *Aston Cantlow* and *YL*, *passim*.   [93] See in particular Lord Mance in *YL* para. 105 on this point.

functions under s. 6 HRA in other cases.[94] For example, in the decision in the earlier case of *Poplar Housing*, the Court of Appeal found that a housing association was exercising a public function under s. 6(3)(b), relying primarily on *substantive* factors relating to the constitutional make-up of the association; in particular, its relationship to the local authority which established it.[95] In finding that the function of the provision of housing by the housing association constituted a public function for s. 6(3) purposes, Lord Woolf noted that 'the role of the [housing association] is so closely assimilated to that of the [local authority] that it was performing public and not private functions'.[96] Thus, as Oliver notes in this case, 'not all of the considerations and criteria identified by Lord Woolf [in the Court of Appeal] relate to the nature of the functions or acts in question . . . but are institutional . . . and relational'.[97]

The solution to this sloppiness of analysis under the two heads of s. 6 HRA, argues Oliver, is to dispense with the terminology of 'hybrid' or 'functional' public authorities under s. 6(3) altogether, as it necessarily implicates an analysis of the nature of the body rather than the nature of the functions.[98] Rather, she argues that on the functional analysis under s. 6(3) the focus should be on the 'intrinsic nature of an act, activity or function, rather than who performs it',[99] given that '[e]ither a function is of a public nature or not'[100] regardless of who performs it. Admitting that it is not easy to determine what makes a function public or private, Oliver offers her own criteria in order to resolve the issue; that 'public function' should include 'only those activities which involve the exercise by private bodies of specifically legally authorized coercion or authority over others which it would normally be unlawful for a private body to exercise'.[101] This is indeed one of the criteria of publicness discussed by the courts in *Aston* and *YL*, However, the problem with this proposed definition is that it loops back into the question of the nature of the body itself which Oliver is specifically attempting to avoid. An analysis of whether a body involves legal powers of coercion or authority in order to exercise certain functions necessarily involves an analysis of the body itself. The fact that a body, even a body far removed from central government such as a semi-state commercial enterprise, enjoys powers of

---

[94] D. Oliver, 'Functions of a Public Nature under the Human Rights Act' (2004) Public Law 329, 337.

[95] *Popular Housing*, para 9.

[96] *Poplar Housing*, para 66.

[97] Oliver 'Functions of a Public Nature under the Human Rights Act', 331. This was also the case in the *Hammer Trout Farm* decision where the consideration on whether a not-for-profit company was exercising public functions for s. 6(3) purposes (the court held that it was) was largely influenced by the company's relationship with a local authority; it had been created by the local authority in order to undertake several of its functions. Again the conflation of substance and function is instructive in this case. *R (on the application of Beer (trading as Hammer Trout Farm)) v Hampshire Farmers Market Ltd and another* [2003] EWCA Civ 1056.

[98] Oliver 'Functions of a Public Nature under the Human Rights Act', 331.

[99] Oliver 'Functions of a Public Nature' 337.

[100] Oliver 'Functions of a Public Nature' 339.

[101] Oliver 'Functions of a Public Nature' 329.

legal compulsion, coercion, or authority for the purposes of its publicness is a question of its substantive nature or institutional make-up and not one of the functions it exercises.

Moreover, there is a circularity in justifications for a narrow interpretation of 'publicness' under s. 6 HRA. As Oliver has noted, and the court concurred, an overly broad understanding of the 'public' under s. 6 HRA could result in 'absurd'[102] and problematic outcomes, placing undue burdens on certain entities such as hoteliers or taxi-drivers,[103] or depriving certain institutions such as universities of the freedom of expression given that public bodies do not enjoy human rights under the Convention under Art. 34.[104] This was clearly put by a Court of Appeal decision in *Poplar Housing*:[105]

> The fact that a body performs an activity which otherwise a public body would be under a duty to perform cannot mean that such a performance is necessarily a public function... If this were to be the assumption, then when a small hotel provides bed and breakfast accommodation as a temporary measure, at the request of a housing authority that is under a duty to provide that accommodation, the small hotel would be performing public functions and required to comply with the Human Rights Act 1998.

Providing a stipulative definition of public and private by claiming that, for example, hoteliers or taxi drivers are not public bodies is simply to beg the question. These positions bring a pre-existing *a priori* understanding of public and private to bear on the question of what is public and what is private which itself eludes justification. The result is a definition of publicness by fiat.

It is submitted that the conflation of substantive and functional factors as well as the circularity in attempting to limit the extent of the public under s. 6 stems from the fact that in applying s. 6 HRA in these cases, the court is drawing on broader, more extensive understandings of publicness beyond the strict confines of s. 6 HRA and ECtHR case law. As can be seen from the rationale for limiting the reach of s. 6 HRA in these cases, it necessarily engages with a pre-existing template or an *a priori* intuitive theoretical framework of the public and the private which influences the consideration of publicness within the law such as under the HRA. It is precisely this theoretical framework, it is argued, which causes the conflation of institutional and functional factors as well as inform the arguments that certain bodies and functions could not be saddled with human rights obligations under the HRA because there are somehow self-evidently not public.

This, in turn, speaks to a broader understanding of the public/private divide which informs the determination of 'publicness' in *any* legal context. This broader conceptual understanding involves two different ways of thinking about the public in terms of both substance and function.[106]

As such, the notion of 'publicness' is necessarily broader than its regulation by statute or the common law. Thus, the picture of the public/private divide as a series

---

[102] *YL*, para 27 per Lord Scott.   [103] See Oliver, 'The Frontiers of the State', 485.

[104] *Aston*, para 47 per Lord Hope.   [105] Per Lord Woolf, 67.   [106] See Section 4.

of hermetically sealed pockets scattered across the legal system with little or no cross-fertilization as the local-ecologies thesis promotes, belies this broader, deeper understanding of public and private which impacts upon and influences consideration of individual instances of the divide such as that entailed in s. 6 HRA.

4. THE IDEOLOGICAL THESIS

The second implication predicated on the axiom of the non-immutability of the public/private divide, is that the way in which the domain is drawn is *political*. That is, if there is no single overarching public/private divide, then any demarcation of the public and the private, including in law, is necessarily subjective, lending it a contested, political quality.

Within legal contexts, the political nature of the divide leads to questions of institutional design and particularly the question of which body should have the final say on how the domain is drawn, courts or legislatures; the implication being that political questions should be decided by political, that is democratically elected, bodies. As such, this second implication of the axiom of the domain of public law is a species of the argument common in constitutional rights adjudication as to the impropriety of strong judicial review of legislative measures on fundamental rights grounds given that the nature and meaning of fundamental rights, like that of the domain of public law, is a contested issue.[107] Indeed, this second implication of the axiom of the domain of public law is, perhaps, most clearly evident in a notorious case in US constitutional law involving precisely the question of judicial review of legislation. In the *Lochner v New York*[108] decision, the US Supreme Court struck down a New York state labour law limiting the working hours of bakers as a violation of the freedom of contract. The court implicitly created a public/private divide in the due process clause of the constitution based on the rationale that the public sphere ends where it encroaches upon individual liberty, and in particular, the personal liberty to 'sell labor'[109] as one wished. The judgment elicited a scathing critique by the nascent legal realist movement as an example of the intensely political nature of judicial decision-making.[110]

The bad faith on the part of the judiciary alleged in the realist critique related to the ostensible neutrality of the public/private in the US constitution as somehow reflecting an objective, non-partisan 'truth' about the world, thereby masking what was in reality a particular tendentious ideology by the majority in the case. Indeed, the critique was made most forcefully by the dissenting voice on the bench in the case itself, that of Oliver Wendell Holmes, who argued that the court had wrongly interpolated its own tendentious political reading of the constitution in the place of a democratically elected legislature.[111]

---

[107] See J. Waldron, 'The Core of the Case Against Judicial Review' (2006) 115 Yale Law Journal 1346.

[108] 198 US 45 (1905).   [109] See Peckham, J.

[110] See R. Pound, 'Liberty of Contract' (1909) 18(7) Yale Law Journal 454.

[111] 'This case is decided upon an economic theory which a large part of the country does not entertain. If it were a question whether I agreed with that theory, I should desire to study it further and long before making up my mind. But I do not conceive that to be my duty, because I strongly believe that my

This ideological critique has also emerged in the UK context in the series of cases involving the 'contracting out' of services by public authorities to commercial operators under the HRA culminating in the *YL* decision, cited earlier.[112] In this context, the courts have been criticized for refusing to extend public law protections to vulnerable individuals by extending human rights obligations to the contractees in these cases. The circumstances in *YL* are exemplary in this regard, where the elderly resident with Alzheimer's was legally ejected from the care home without being able to vindicate her right to home and family life against the care-home operator. Whereas the circumstances and criticism in this context are less dramatic than in the context of *Lochner*, at least part of this critique stemming from the *YL* decision relates to the support (as opposed to the creation) of an ideological agenda through their refusal to extend human rights protections to commercial actors leaving vulnerable individuals at risk.[113] The legislative intervention in the aftermath of the *YL* decision could be seen as the vindication of the ideological charge levelled against the judiciary.[114]

The ideological critique can be seen as a direct descendent of the non-immutability axiom of the public/private divide in that if the divide is not immutable or objective but fallible and subjective, then wherever and whenever the divide is drawn can be interpreted as a political act.

However, there is a sense in which this critique is self-defeating, at least in respect of the HRA context. This is because the ideological critique, in relation to the HRA, must rely on the notion that the courts have got it wrong; that, for example, a commercial operator providing elderly care services pursuant to a contract with a local authority which is under a statutory duty to provide such services is, in fact, discharging a public function. However, this is to presuppose a 'right' answer to the drawing of the public/private divide which the ideological critique implicitly repudiates.

Therefore, the ideological critique must challenge the agent delimiting the divide rather than the substantive outcome of the case; that is, that it is not that the divide has been drawn in the 'wrong way'—for there is no 'right way' if the divide is a

agreement or disagreement has nothing to do with the right of a majority to embody their opinions in law ... a constitution is not intended to embody a particular economic theory, whether of paternalism and the organic relation of the citizen to the State or of laissez faire. It is made for people of fundamentally differing views, and the accident of our finding certain opinions natural and familiar or novel and even shocking ought not to conclude our judgment upon the question whether statutes embodying them conflict with the Constitution of the United States', 75–76.

[112] See P. Craig, 'Contracting Out, the Human Rights Act and the scope of judicial review' (2002) 118(4) Law Quarterly Review 551; S. Palmer, 'Public Functions and Private Services: A gap in human rights protection' (2008) 6(3–4) International Journal of Constitutional Law 585. See also the Joint Committee of Human Rights, *The Meaning of Public Authority Under the Human Rights Act*, (2003–4).

[113] See Palmer 'Public Functions and Private Services: A gap in human rights protection', 602.

[114] s. 145 of the Health and Social Care Act 2008, was amended in the aftermath of the *YL* decision to include contractees in a position similar to the company in *YL* within the definition of 'functions of a public nature' under s. 6 HRA. See Ministry of Justice, *The Human Rights Act 1998: The Definition of 'Public Authority'*, set superscript format as closing quates. Government Response to the Joint Committee on Human Rights' Ninth Report of Session 2006–7, October 2009, para 44.

necessarily political phenomenon—but rather, that it should be for legislatures, and not the judiciary to take such political decisions.[115] The problem *here* is, of course, that the legislature can and does leave such interpretations up to the judiciary and arguably cannot cover all the potential interpretive issues surrounding the divide; the HRA's protection of the right to privacy being a case in point.[116]

However, we need not accept the pessimistic conclusion of the ideological critique regarding the illegitimacy of adjudication as an alternative representation of judicial demarcation of the divide such as under s. 6 HRA is available, which takes some of the sting out of the ideological critique. This involves looking more closely at precisely what is at stake in circumstances such as that in *Aston Cantlow* and *YL*.

As illustrated by the cases involving s. 6 HRA, the various opinions in this case drew upon rival understandings of the essence of 'publicness' in order to determine whether or not the entities involved betrayed the qualities of 'publicness' in order to come within the obligations under s. 6 HRA. In particular, the question whether something came under the rubric of 'public' for s. 6 HRA purposes, was determined by reference to a combination of two factors; the nature of the body (for example, publicly funded, enjoyment of statutory powers, etc.),[117] and the nature of the function (security, defence, welfare, etc.), and this was the case when the court was undertaking both a substantive/institutional *and* functional analysis under s. 6(1) and s. 6(3)(b) HRA. In these cases, the weight and nature of each of the factors differed within the different opinions. Some found the enjoyment or exercise of statutory powers to be a decisive indicator of the public nature of a body or function,[118] whereas for others, certain bodies and functions were 'inherently public' which necessarily brought them within the realm of the public.[119]

What this instance of adjudication of publicness reveals is that there is something more to the deeper sense of the public and private outlined in the previous section than a purely political decision. The determination of publicness involves good faith disagreement about the essence of the public in the abstract, and not simply whether an entity is or should be subject to human rights standards or subject to particular privileges or duties under the law. As such, disagreement on the essence of 'publicness' is conceptual and not purely ideological. What the

---

[115] See Griffith 'The Political Constitution' (1979) 41(1) Modern Law Review 1.

[116] The interpretative difficulties surrounding a definition of privacy have been repeatedly emphasized by the European Court of Human Rights. See *Peck v UK* 2003-I; 36 EHRR 719.

[117] Whereas the public subsidy question was treated as a separate factor from form, it is, in reality, based on substantive/institutional factors. The relationship between finance and the state can be traced back to its coercive powers. Thus, what differentiates the state (or its agents) from other commercial enterprises when it engages in commercial activities from an economic viewpoint are its advantages in terms of being able to raise revenue through coercive taxation. This view was present in *Aston* where Lord Scott defined taxation as 'not a voluntary payment or donation but an enforced contribution, exacted pursuant to legislative authority', para 133.

[118] For example, see Bingham, Foscotte, Hale, and Mance in *YL*.

[119] This was put forward most strongly by Lord Mance in *YL*, see paras, 99, 103, 105, and 115.

example of the HRA illustrates, is that conceptually, publicness as institutionalized in the state, can be defined according to *ends,* and *means,* and each of these approaches has a respectable philosophical pedigree.

The ends-oriented conception of publicness entails the notion that the public, can be identified or defined according to its *ends.* On this view, it is the *ends* of the state which distinguish it from other forms of human association. This ends conception of the state is present in early modern political theory such as Hobbes's theory of sovereignty. Loughlin identifies four main categories of the tasks of government in Hobbes, four types of public function in modern terms; to maintain defence, to preserve internal peace, to enable the citizen to acquire wealth, and to promote full enjoyment of citizen's liberty.[120]

Another, more contemporary, example of this tendency is the *Staatsaufgaben-lehre* in late 19th-century German constitutional theory which attempted to create an exhaustive and definitive list of the core functions and responsibilities of the state.[121] In the event, no such *Staatsaufgabenlehre* was ever produced.[122] Nonetheless, even without a definitive list of essential functions of the state, this way of thinking about defining publicness through its institutionalization in the state is still influential and can be seen in contemporary judicial decisions such as the various court judgments under s. 6 HRA considered above.[123]

The second conception of publicness is the definition of the state according to the *means* through which it achieves its objectives. It was, perhaps, most famously articulated by Max Weber in his 1918 lecture 'Politics as Vocation'.[124] Considering the questions raised by the *Staatsaufgabenlehre,* Weber found this an unsatisfactory exercise. Given that the modern state was engaged in an increasing number of activities, and that the early state and its predecessors could not be said to have had any one specific or particular purpose, it was more appropriate to define the state in terms of its *means,* 'namely the use of physical force'.[125] Noting that the

---

[120] Loughlin, *The Idea of Public Law* (Oxford: Oxford University Press, 2003) 8 drawing upon T. Hobbes, *On the Citizen* (R. Tuck and M. Silverthorne eds.), (Cambridge: Cambridge University Press, 1998), xxii.6.

[121] C. Mollers, *Staat Als Argument* (Mohr Siebeck, 2011).

[122] Although Halberstam and Mollers note that, Hans Peter Bull, *Die Staatsaufgaben Nach Dem Grundgesetz,* 2nd edn (Athenaum Verlag, Kronberg, 1977) is perhaps the closest that anyone has ever come to providing such a list, see D. Halberstam and C. Mollers, 'The German Constitutional Court says "Ja zu Deutschland"' (2009) 10 German Law Journal 1241.

[123] See in particular Lord Mance's opinion in *YL* were he referred to 'non-delegable' state functions, para 103, as well as 'inherently public functions', para 105. In Particular Lords Nicholls, Hope, Hobhouse, and Roger in *Aston* placed reliance on an objective conception of functions associated with 'government', paras 7, 9, 13, 50, and 58. In *YL,* Lords Nicholls and Mance took a similar view as to the possibilities of a clear conception of the functions of government, paras 6, 7, 12, and 102. The theory was also resurrected by the German Federal Constitutional Court in its decision on the constitutionality of German ratification of the Lisbon Treaty. It identified five core areas which characterize a state and which therefore cannot be alienated: substantive and procedural criminal law, the waging of war and the making of peace, public expenditure, welfare, and culture and religion. Halberstam and Mollers, 'The German Constitutional Court says "Ja zu Deutschland"' 1250.

[124] H. Gerth and C. Wright Mills (eds), *From Max Weber: Essays in Sociology* (London: Routledge, 2001) ch IV.

[125] Gerth and Wright Mills, *From Max Weber,* 83.

relationship between the state and violence was an 'especially intimate one', he went on to provide his influential definition of the state as 'a human community that (successfully) claims the *monopoly of the legitimate use of physical force* within a given territory'.[126] Thus, what distinguished the state from other forms of human association was this monopoly of legitimate violence through its connection with the public realm.

As such, the disagreement as to publicness which emerged in consideration of s. 6 HRA, reveals that disagreement about publicness can stem from the fact that it is an essentially contested concept, and not simply a smokescreen to advance the interests of a particular sectors of society as the ideological critique maintains.

Jeremy Waldron has argued that this notion of an essentially contested concept introduced originally by William Gallie in a paper to the Aristotelian Society in 1955 has 'run wild',[127] having drifted from its original meaning of concepts which are *essentially* contested and applied to any concept which is 'very hotly contested, with no resolution in sight'.[128] In his seminal paper, Gallie was very specific that essential contestability does not relate to the use of concepts which are simply confused or mistaken;[129] that is, that the contestation, disagreement, and indeterminacy surrounding essentially contestable concepts relate to the *essence* of the concept itself, not different concepts which are related or share the same name, nor disagreement about the application of the concept in different contexts. Waldron argues that a useful way of thinking about *essential* contestability relates to the *location* of the disagreement or indeterminacy.[130] Essential contestability relates to 'contestation at the core, not just at the borderlines or penumbra of a concept'.[131]

As such the essential contestability surrounding publicness does not cease on disclosure of the variety of meanings to which the concept is put (as would be the case, for example, with simple confusion). Even after full disclosure of the meanings put forward in disagreement, 'each party continues to defend its case with what it claims to be convincing arguments, evidence and other forms of justification'.[132] As such, an essentially contested concept lacks a 'general method or principle for deciding between the claims made',[133] regarding the uses of the concept. That the notion of the public can be characterized as an essentially contested concept is clear from the parallel analyses by the Court in *Aston Cantlow* and *YL*.

---

[126] Gerth and Wright Mills, *From Max Weber*, 78.

[127] J. Waldron, 'Is the Rule of Law an Essentially Contested Concept (In Florida)?' (2002) 21 Law and Philosophy 137.

[128] Waldron 'Is the Rule of Law an Essentially Contested Concept (In Florida)?' 149.

[129] W. B. Gallie, 'Essentially Contested Concepts' (1955–1956) 56 Proceedings of the Aristotelian Society 167, 175.

[130] Waldron, 'Is the Rule of Law an Essentially Contested Concept (In Florida)?', 149.

[131] Waldron ' Is the Rule of Law an Essentially Contested Concept'(2002) 149.

[132] Gallie, 'Essentially Contested Concepts', 168.

[133] Gallie 'Essentially Contested Concepts', 178.

Approaching 'publicness' from the viewpoint of essential contestability has a particular relevance for the ideological critique of judicial demarcation of the domain(s) of public law. As an essentially contestable concept, then, we can appreciate how the method of defining the public in terms of means, and the resulting finding that a commercial company providing elderly care services pursuant to a contract with a local authority was not a public function—that is, it was within the private domain—is not only 'logically permissible'[134] but also 'humanly likely'.[135] Therefore, the disagreement between the judiciary in these cases can be characterized, not in terms of the crude ideology of individual judges, but as *conceptual* disagreement about the nature of the public. This conceptual disagreement reflected in the House of Lords decisions, is part of the structure of the *a priori* sense of the public which influences its expression and adjudication in the law.

Gallie, himself, was quite clear about the utility of thinking about certain concepts as essentially contested ones arguing that:

> Recognition of a given concept as essentially contested implies recognition of rival uses of it (such as oneself repudiates) as not only logically permissible and humanly 'likely', but as of *permanent potential critical value to one's own use or interpretation of the concept in question* . . . One very desirable consequence of the required recognition in any proper instance of essential contentedness might therefore be expected to be a marked raising of the level of quality of arguments in the disputes of the contested parties.[136]

As such, the contestation 'deepens and enriches all sides' understanding of the area of value that the contested concept marks out'.[137] The characterization of publicness as an essentially contestable concept therefore can serve to deepen our understanding of what's at stake in considering the public/private divide beyond mere ideology which avoids the pessimistic conclusion regarding judicial activity in this area. Moreover, it gives further shape to the deeper sense of the public and private which is immanent in the legal system.

5. THE DISPENSABILITY THESIS

The third implication of the non-immutability axiom of the public/private divide is that the public/private divide, as a human construction, is a dispensable tool. As such this dispensability thesis has been applied in certain legal contexts to argue for its dissolution where it proves unnecessary or unhelpful. Feminist legal scholars have argued that the public/private divide can be harmful in certain cases such as the traditional treatment by the criminal law of domestic violence or marital rape.[138] However, perhaps the most prominent example of the dispensability

---

[134] Gallie, 'Essentially Contested Concepts', 193.

[135] Gallie, 'Essentially Contested Concepts', 193.

[136] Gallie 'Essentially Contested Concepts', 193.

[137] Waldron, 'Is the Rule of Law an Essentially Contested Concept (In Florida)?', 152.

[138] Boyd, *Challenging the Public/Private Divide: Feminism, Law, and Public Policy*.

thesis is in the area of human rights law which is evident in reactions to the judicial approaches to the divide in s. 6 HRA outlined earlier.

A contemporary trend in human rights scholarship highlights the problematic nature of the public/private divide in an era of privatization and 'contracting out'. In particular, the human rights critique of the public/private divide is, in part, based on the concern that the increase in the privatization and 'contracting out' programmes of successive governments creates a emerging 'gap' in human rights protection;[139] that is, that the shrinking of the public domain through privatization results in a concomitant shrinking of human rights protection.[140] The circumstances in *YL*, where the carrying out of a function hitherto undertaken by the state, the care of the elderly, was 'contracted out' to a private entity, is an example of this development. Where the state no longer executes a function, then certain acts which would have given rise to a human rights-based claim no longer do so, given that the claim cannot be made against private parties. As Craig summarizes, in such cases:[141]

> [T]here will often be no viable claim to be made against the [public body]. The type of rights-based claim that would have been pursued against the local authority, if the activity had been undertaken in house, is no longer available against it when the activity is contracted out.

Palmer argues that the solution to the gaps in human rights protection under the HRA regime is for 'human rights values [to] traverse the public-private divide'.[142] With regard to the *YL* decision in particular, she argues that the majority's conclusion on the contracting of services in *YL* as not constituting a public function is to dramatically limit the effects of human rights protection given that states, and the British state in particular, engage in a wide range of contracts in the discharge of their duties. Moreover, the 'artificial distinction' between public funding and paying for a service fails to appreciate the realties of modern government which employ a series of private mechanisms to deliver their functions.[143] These critiques of contracting out adopt a more pluralistic approach to the threats to human rights values beyond the power exercised by states. On this view, private actors, and particularly the economic power of private corporations are as much, if not in some cases more, of a threat to human rights values in society and beyond.

Oliver's seminal work on the public/private divide[144] advances a robust defence of the dispensability thesis adopting this power-pluralist approach. She analyses typologies of power in society[145] to argue that both public and private bodies

---

[139] For a clear statement of this argument, see P. Verkuil, *Outsourcing Sovereignty: Why Privatization of Government Functions Threatens Democracy and What We Can Do About It* (New York and Cambridge: Cambridge University Press, 2007).

[140] Palmer, 'Public Functions and Private Services: A gap in human rights protection'; Craig 'Contracting Out, the Human Rights Act and the Scope of Judicial Review'.

[141] Craig, 'Contracting Out, the Human Rights Act and the Scope of Judicial Review' 554.

[142] Palmer, 'Public Functions and Private Services: A gap in human rights protection', 604.

[143] Palmer, 'Public Functions and Private Services' 602.

[144] D. Oliver, *Common Values and the Public/Private Divide* (Butterworths, 2000).

[145] More specifically Galbraith's condign power, compensatory power, and conditional power, and Daintith's analysis of public power in terms of 'imperium' and 'dominum', D. Oliver, *Common Values and the Public/Private Divide* 34–36.

exercise these different forms of power.[146] For Oliver, the role and function of law is to set limits and restraints on the exercise of power, whatever its provenance or form. Notwithstanding their different *modus operandi*, different legal fields in both private and public law are all aimed at preserving the fundamental values of dignity, autonomy, respect, status, and security,[147] which are protected through the restraint of power which is the role of law in contemporary society. As such, the maintenance of a strict divide between public law and private law should not be maintained. Rather an 'integrated approach' to the mechanisms of public and private law should be adopted,[148] which emphasizes the protection of fundamental values over a clear-cut distinction between public and private in the law.[149]

This power-pluralist approach has been particularly prevalent in globalization discourses where the state's diminishing purchase on trans-border movements of people, goods, capital, technology, and information leads to the empowerment of private actors, such as transnational corporations, at the expense of political institutions and the public sphere.[150] In the light of these realities, the traditional legal approaches to the public/private divide fail to capture the realities of power in contemporary society, particularly the very real power of private actors. As such, an insistence on a rigid distinction between public and private fails to protect vulnerable groups, a goal to which the law, and human rights law in particular, aspires.[151]

Against this backdrop, Clapham has argued for a 'progressive change' in the application of human rights to private actors in the pursuit of human well-being given the changing circumstances and configurations of power in society.[152] He argues for a new approach to human rights to deal with the new global realities of power pluralism, where traditional conceptions of rights limiting public or political power are increasingly antiquated and run the risk of undermining the objectives and ideals of the human rights movement more generally, rooted in the Universal Declaration of 1948.[153]

The common conclusion of these disparate views on the nature of power, role of human rights law, and the privatized and/or globalized state is that the divide should be *jettisoned* to allow for the penetration of the private sphere by human rights norms or the spreading of 'common values' to protect vulnerable individuals against abuses of power whether public or private. Given that the

---

[146] Oliver, *Common Values* 36.

[147] Oliver, *Common Values* 60.

[148] Oliver, *Common Values* 248.

[149] Oliver, *Common Values* 249.

[150] See Verkuikl, *Outsourcing Sovereignty* (Cambridge: Cambridge University Press, 2007) and Ch 10 in the current volume.

[151] See particularly Oliver, *Common Values and the Public/Private Divide*, ch 3.

[152] Clapham, *Human Rights Obligations of Non-State Actors*, 54. See also, P. Alston (ed.), *Non-state Actors and Human Rights* (Oxford: Oxford University Press, 2000).

[153] Clapham, *Human Rights Obligations of Non-State Actors*, 56.

public/private divide is dispensable, in cases where it inhibits the achievement of other values or can be detrimental to particular groups, then it should be jettisoned.

There are a number of questions which emerge from this third implication for the domain of public law and its conclusion that the divide should be jettisoned. For example, it is not clear that jettisoning the divide to allow for the application of human rights norms to private actors would actually enhance human rights protection itself. This is due to the substantive values which are immanent in the phenomenon of the public and the private. As Habermas argues, the values of the public and the private are not hierarchical but 'co-original'.[154] What this means in practical terms is that '[o]ne is not possible without the other, but neither sets limits on the other . . . *private and public autonomy require each other*'.[155]

The implications of this are that the private sphere and private values, not least the private values which underpin many human rights norms (particularly those at issue in the *YL* and *Aston Cantlow*, rights to private property and home and family life), need a public sphere in order to be identified, defined, and most importantly, *protected*. The absence of a public sphere, which would result in dispensing the notion of public and private in the law, means that the private values of autonomy and dignity, which human rights law aims to protect, would be without clear definition or significance. In a world without a 'public', privacy makes no sense.

Moreover, the absence of a public sphere creates particular problems for courts involved in human rights litigation. If human rights norms penetrate the private sphere, then a court faced with a dispute such as that in the *YL* case, would have to resolve competing claims to autonomy and dignity. A commercial enterprise, such as that operating the care home in *YL*, could *also* draw on individualist human rights-inspired values to support its claims,[156] alleging a violation of its right to property as contained in Protocol 1 to the ECHR, competing with the right to home and family life of the care-home resident.

A court faced with such a dispute would simply be 'balancing' one human rights norm against another, which would deprive them of their status as 'trumps'.[157] Therefore, courts would lack a framework for adjudicating such

---

[154] J. Habermas, 'Constitutional Democracy: A Paradoxical Union of Contradictory Principles?' (2001) 29 Political Theory 766.

[155] Habermas, 'Constitutional Democracy' 767. Emphasis added.

[156] This explains the logic of defining the public by reference to the question of the ability to hold fundamental rights under Art. 34.

[157] R. Dworkin, 'Rights as Trumps' in J. Waldron (ed.) *Theories of Rights* (Oxford: Oxford University Press, 1984). The question of balancing in constitutional rights adjudication is an increasingly common aspect of much constitutional rights scholarship. See for example, K. Moller, 'Balancing and the structure of constitutional rights' (2007) 5(3) International Journal of Constitutional Law 453 and G. Webber, 'Proportionality, Balancing and the Cult of Constitutional Rights Scholarship' (2010) XXIII(1) Canadian Journal of Law and Jurisprudence 179. The point here is not to evaluate the inevitability, propriety, or desirability of balancing as a strategy for adjudicating constitutional rights claims. It is, rather, to point out the potentially problematic result of jettisoning the divide made by human rights advocates for the feasibility of the human rights project more generally. If balancing is considered problematic between rights and public policy, then this is exacerbated with respect to balancing competing rights claims, which potentially undermines the role and status of human rights norms as special cases or 'trumps' promoted by the human rights project.

disputes given the pre-emptive nature of both claims, heightening the risk of arbitrary judicial decision-making by forcing a court to decide whether a right to property is 'worth' more than a right to privacy. This, in turn, exposes the judiciary to the charge of ideology, using personal subjective political preference to plump for one right over another; an ironic twist for an argument which is, at least in part, predicated on avoiding judicial preference in remedying human rights violations.

Again, it is submitted that these problems reveal the deeply rooted nature of the public/private divide in law and gives shape to different areas of law. Human rights law relies on this deeper structure, meaning that attempts to jettison part of this structure could result in the undermining of the aims and purposes of human rights law itself.

6. CONCLUSION: POSITIVE LAW AND THE PUBLIC AND PRIVATE REALM

This chapter attempted to outline problems with three particular common approaches, or theses, prevalent in legal scholarship on the public/private divide which are based on the axiom of the non-immutability of the divide. It illustrated that the expression of the domain of public law, through a focus on s. 6 HRA, necessarily draws on more theoretical dimensions of the problem beyond the provisions of positive law. Once this Rubicon is crossed, we intuitively rely on quasi-metaphysical notions of a self-evidently public and private realm which is more immutable and less flexible than the theses and the axiom contend. The failure to recognize and appreciate the role of this intuitive theoretical expression of the public/private divide in legal approaches leads to circularity, an unwarranted belief in the purely ideological nature of the divide that can be 'contained' by positive law (such that courts simply mechanically 'apply' the—ideological—will of the legislature with respect to this question), or self-defeating arguments about the jettisoning of the divide to achieve particular values, when those very values require the public/private divide to given them definition.

The relationship between this deeper theoretical understanding of the public and the private and positive law can be understood in terms of a 'legal archetype';[158] a phenomenon of a legal system which has a significance beyond its particular expression in rules of positive law.[159] A legal archetype operates in a way that 'expresses or epitomizes the spirit of a whole structured area of doctrine, and does so vividly, effectively, and publicly, establishing the significance of that area for the entire legal enterprise'.[160]

As a legal archetype, then, the public/private divide makes clear to us the *a priori* conceptual frameworks through which we understand the practice of

---

[158] J. Waldron, 'Torture and Positive Law: Jurisprudence for the White House' (2005) 105 Columbia Law Review 1723.

[159] Waldron, 'Torture and Positive Law'.

[160] Waldron, 'Torture and Positive Law', 1723.

(public) law, the nature of the values which inform the legal system, and the ordering of those values within the system. The public/private divide resonates through the law and appears as specific instances of the divide created by positive law. However, the framework of the divide is not contingent upon positive law itself. Rather the role of provisions of positive law such as s. 6 HRA *vis-à-vis* the legal archetype of the public and the private is that of *representation*. In representing the divide, positive law makes concrete the public and the private in particular ways. Moreover, what this signifies is that there is more to the public and the private 'than that which a concrete order of positive law has actualized or could actualize'.[161] As such, the phenomenon of the public and private is necessarily broader than its expression or representation in positive law. Positive law does not exhaust its possibilities nor embody either realm completely.

In performing this representational role with respect to the public and the private, positive law can be understood as a *parergon,* a frame or boundary for the public and the private. However, it is a member of neither; the law is neither inside the public nor inside the private, yet is the condition of possibility of both.[162]

This representative, parergonal role of positive law with regard to the phenomenon of the public and the private is similar to Arendt's account of the law of the ancients with regard to the public and private realms. According to Arendt, for the ancients, the law:[163]

> originally was identified with [a] boundary line which in ancient times was still actually a space, a kind of *no man's land* between the private and the public, sheltering and protecting both realms while, at the same time, separating them from each other.

As such it is beyond the gift of positive law to fundamentally change the legal archetype of the public and the private realms. They are always already part of the conceptual and phenomenological universe within which law operates. This remains the case in a globalized and privatized world and is something which deserves more attention in public law scholarship.

---

[161] H. Lindahl, 'Acquiring a Community: The Acquis and the Institution of European Legal Order' (2003) 9(4) European Law Journal 433, 448.

[162] For discussion in the context of sovereignty see J. Bartelson, *A Genealogy of Sovereignty* (Cambridge: Cambridge University Press, 1995) 51.

[163] H. Arendt, *The Human Condition* (Chicago: University of Chicago Press, 1998) 63.

❦ 7 ❦

Public Law as Democracy: The Case of Constitutional Rights

Richard Bellamy

I. INTRODUCTION

The distinctive domain and character of public law have become—and in certain respects always were—unclear and, to a degree, contested.[1] As a result, any definition is likely to be to some extent stipulative. For my purposes, I want to refer to public law in two broad and related senses—as applying to a certain kind of body and its functions, and as requiring a certain kind of justification. The first sense refers to the actions of the state and its administration. Of course, it will be pointed out that these are increasingly performed by private bodies and often involve legal activities that have been associated with private parties and doctrines, such as procurement and contract.[2] Nevertheless, government and the administrative apparatus more generally can still be considered as possessing distinctively broad, authoritative, and coercive powers which in various ways make their subjection to the law both problematic and pressing: problematic in that they play a central role in the making and enforcement of the law, pressing in that this role renders them more powerful than other bodies. The second sense enters here. For the justification of state power has come to rest on its serving the public ends of the ruled rather than the private ends of the rulers, and certain public qualities of law have been thought to oblige those who wield state power to do so in a publically justified and justifiable way. Ruling through laws has been viewed as different from rule by wilful, ad hoc commands because laws have certain characteristics that render them capable of coordinating and shaping public behaviour in consistent and coherent ways over time, while ruling under the law likewise forces rulers to adopt public processes and offers an additional incentive to devise laws that treat rulers and ruled equitably.[3] Again, these matters are far from straightforward. How far laws need to, or even can, always possess the requisite qualities and the degree to which these do constrain

---

[1] N. Walker, 'On the Necessarily Public Character of Law', 'The Public Nature of Private Law?' in C. Michelon et al. (eds), *The Public in Law* (London: Ashgate, 2012), 9.

[2] Walker 'On the Necessarily Public Character of Law' 10–12.

[3] L. Fuller *The Morality of Law* (New Haven: Yale University Press, 1969), 33–38.

power holders are matters of dispute.[4] Yet, that all law has to have some public qualities—for example, that it be promulgated and capable of being followed in ways that make it publicly recognized as law—and that these features formalize power to a degree, is reasonably undisputed. Increasingly, though, and even more controversially, many jurists have wanted to suggest that legality also involves certain substantive qualities of a public kind—that laws must appeal to public reasons that all subject to them can accept as reflecting, or being compatible with certain basic interests or values that are equally shared by all. Such arguments have come to be identified with rights and in particular constitutional rights, which are deemed to set the terms of how and to what purpose political power may be legally exercised.[5] In this way the two senses of public law come together. Constitutional rights define and mark the limits of public power in ways that can be publicly justified, and thereby ensure it serves public ends.[6] They thereby serve what Martin Loughlin[7] calls the 'basic tasks of public law'; namely, 'the constitution, maintenance and regulation of governmental authority'.

In what follows, I want to explore a paradox in this account. What is missing in this view is the public as actors themselves. They are the supposed beneficiaries of public law, whose interests it exists to protect and promote in the activities of those political authorities that act on their behalf. Yet, the public reason of the law does not actively involve the reasoning of the public themselves. The rule of persons comes under the rule of law through being entrusted to putatively non-political actors—courts and legal officers—and guided by legal norms that are held logically to prefigure the public political authorities they constitute, maintain, and regulate. Indeed, in a certain sense this view conceives public law as bringing into being the public itself, as a society of individuals politically united to secure and enjoy their pre-existing rights.[8] Against this account, I want to present a democratic view of public law as the rule of the public. In this view, democratic mechanisms offer the means for the public not just to authorize and control those who rule, be it through elections or via their representatives in the legislature, but also to generate and justify law and policies that reflect the reasons of the public. Democracy satisfies both senses of public law outlined above; it offers oversight of the public authorities and their functions, and does so in conformity to public processes and norms. However, in each case, it is the public itself that does so, through their actions and reasons rather than via legal intermediaries. In this way, democracy undertakes 'the basic tasks of public law' by providing the process whereby the public constitutes, maintains, and regulates government

[4] J. Raz, 'The Rule of Law and its Virtue' in his *The Authority of Law* (Oxford: Clarendon Press, 1979); J. Waldron *Law and Disagreement* (Oxford: Oxford University Press, 1999); R. Bellamy, *Political Constitutionalism: A Republican Defence of the Constitutionality of Democracy* (Cambridge: Cambridge University Press, 2007) 57–66.

[5] R. Dworkin, 'Political Judges and the Rule of Law' in *A Matter of Principle* (Oxford: Clarendon Press, 1985) 11–12; J. Rawls *Political Liberalism* (New York: Columbia University Press, 1993), 212–54.

[6] Rawls, *Political Liberalism*, 232.

[7] M. Loughlin, *The Idea of Public Law* (Oxford: Oxford University Press, 2003) 1.

[8] Dworkin, 'Political Judges and the Rule of Law' 32.

authority by setting the terms and conditions under which power can be legitimately held and exercised over them. It will be objected that this process itself will need to be constituted, maintained, and regulated and some of its decisions be constrained to protect some sections of the public oppressing or neglecting the concerns of other sections of the public, and that these are the tasks that public law—especially in the form of constitutional rights—performs.[9] However, I wish to dispute this very claim and argue that for such rights to be justified and have validity as law that can apply to and serve the interests of the public, then such rights need to be themselves constituted through, maintained by, and regulated via a democratic process. Naturally, constitutional rights do not exhaust the field of public law. However, they now lie at its heart, with their relationship to democracy forming a key issue in modern conceptions of public law.[10] If they can be shown to lie within democracy, therefore, then an important part of the argument for conceiving public law as democracy will have been achieved. That does not mean there is no role for courts or for laws that pertain to public bodies; merely that the legitimacy of courts rests on their being servants of the public and responsible for administering law that ultimately has the public as its source.[11]

I proceed to this conclusion in three main steps. First, I argue that for rights to be justified as principles of public reason that treat all with equal concern and respect, they must meet with democratic endorsement. Second, I contend that rights so conceived can still perform the key role that is often attributed to them as ways of constraining the exercise of government authority. I suggest that the extra- and counter-democratic view of rights, on the one hand, and the democratic view of rights, on the other, can be linked to liberal and republican views of freedom as non-interference and as non-domination respectively. When freedom is understood in the more holistic terms of the latter, then rights can be seen as public goods and democracy as the only legitimate heuristic for their identification and promotion in a non-dominating manner. Finally, I argue that the democratic process need not be regarded as being itself constituted through rights and regulated by constitutional courts. However, it may generate its own public laws, which provide a basis for some members of the public to use the courts to contest the degree to which other members of the public uphold the public standards they have authored together. In certain respects the Human Rights Act 1998 can be conceived in these terms, as a form of weak review that leaves the last word with democracy while allowing it may constitute, maintain, and regulate itself through the laws it enacts.[12]

---

[9] Dworkin 'Political Judges and the Rule of Law' 27–8.

[10] Loughlin, *The Idea of Public Law*, 114–15, 128–30.

[11] J. Waldron, 'Can There Be a Democratic Jurisprudence?' (2008–9) 58 Emory Law Journal 675.

[12] R. Bellamy, 'Political Constitutionalism and the Human Rights Act' (2011) 9 (1) International Journal of Constitutional Law 86.

2. RIGHTS, POLITICAL EQUALITY, AND DEMOCRACY

Rights theorists working within the mainstream liberal tradition typically distinguish human and natural from institutional rights on the grounds that the former are in some sense prior to politics.[13] That is to say, they are either moral entitlements that human beings could and ought to be granted even in a putative state of nature, such as freedom from physical assault, or—more demandingly— they encompass those basic interests of human beings that all political communities should seek to secure not just for their members but also for non-members. In other words, such rights should either exist outside of any polity, or be realized within and upheld by all polities. As such, they define the boundaries, foundations, and, to some extent, the goals of politics.[14]

So conceived, rights readily appear as constraints on democracy. Rights can be viewed as 'trumping' those political decisions that curtail or fail to promote them. Yet, their apparent status as somehow prior to and above politics proves hard to sustain. Rights are sometimes presented as a two-term relationship, whereby X has a right to some Y. That gives rights a somewhat peremptory sounding character. However, rights are always a three-term relationship, whereby X asks some Z to recognize and respect his or her claim to Y, with attendant costs and benefits to Z, who will wish X to likewise recognize either his or her similar claim to Y, or to some other good such as Y. That is true even of a Hohfeldian 'liberty-right', whereby all that is being asked of others is that they have 'no right' to prevent its exercise.[15] For such forbearance may itself be controversial, as in certain instances of someone exercising a liberty-right to do what might be commonly regarded as wrong.[16] Therefore, X and Z need to agree on rights and their respective correlative duties, or lack of them, in given situations. It is this need for a collective agreement on which rights we possess, when, and where, what their implications may be in a given case, how they interact with other rights, and which policies and procedures might be most suited to realizing them, that places rights within what Albert Weale and Jeremy Waldron have called the 'circumstances of politics'.[17] For, these are all matters on which we may reasonably disagree yet require a common decision, producing the need for a political mechanism of some kind to resolve our disputes.

Theorists of natural and human rights have tended to assume away such disagreements. They have sought to ground their case for at least a set of basic rights on their 'self-evident' character as dictates of reason, divine law, or essential elements of human well-being.[18] Yet, self-evidence 'is not a very

---

[13] P. Jones, *Rights* (Houndmills: Macmillan, 1994) 72–3, Loughlin, *The Idea of Public Law*, ch 7.

[14] Jones, *Rights*, 75–81.

[15] See Jones *Rights* 12–14, 17–22 for a discussion of Hohfeld's classification of rights and of liberty rights in particular.

[16] J. Waldron, 'A Right to do Wrong' (1981) XCII Ethics 21.

[17] A. Weale, *Democracy*, 2nd edn (Basingstoke: Palgrave, 2007), 12–18; J. Waldron, *Law and Disagreement* (Oxford: Oxford University Press, 1999) 107–13.

[18] Jones, *Rights*, 96–7.

promising foundation for rights'.[19] What leads us to identify specific features of human beings or human sociability as 'natural', 'basic', or 'divinely ordained', depends ultimately on the moral theories we hold for which the specified capacities prove important. The upshot is that appeals to human nature and other supposedly 'objective' and 'universal' foundations of rights reflect rival ontological claims for which no generally agreed epistemology exists with the capacity to mediate between them. Even where there is agreement on the rather abstract set of general rights found in international human rights conventions or domestic bills of rights, there can be disagreement about what they involve in practice with regard to a given case.[20] These disagreements need not reflect self-interest or bad faith—although on occasion they clearly do so, as in the case of regimes whose reluctance to recognize rights results from their oppression of their subject populations. Rather, disagreements—such as one finds in most democratic countries—may simply issue from what Rawls has called 'the burdens of judgement . . . the many hazards involved in the correct (and conscientious) exercise of our powers of reason and judgement in the ordinary course of political life'.[21] In Rawls's account, these burdens range from the different life experiences people bring to the assessment of a situation, to the multiple normative considerations likely to be involved, and the difficulties of relating them to the often complex empirical evidence. Although he believed these 'burdens' only applied to conceptions of the good, they clearly also produce different understandings of the right. People may reasonably hold differing views of not only the sources and substance of rights, but also their subjects and scope, and how they might best be secured.[22] Thus, Nozickian libertarians, Ricardian socialists, Rawlsean social democrats, and Burkean conservatives all offer different accounts of the origins and extent of property rights and their relationship to other rights, which are expressed to different degrees, albeit usually in a less abstruse or sophisticated manner, in the everyday political debates of all mature democracies. At the level of principle, these disputes have not proved any more resolvable in the seminar rooms of philosophy departments than they have among policy makers and citizens.

As I remarked, such reasonable, good faith, ontological, and epistemological disagreements about the nature of rights mean that the determination of which rights we have and how they should be upheld requires a political process. However, not any kind of process will do if it is to be consistent with both the very idea of rights, as something possessed and claimable by all, and the reasonableness of these disagreements about them. The argument that best fits these two criteria would appear to be something like the fairness argument for democracy. According to this view, if the interests of individuals are equally affected by the overall decisions of the community to which they belong, and we

---

[19] Jones, *Rights* 97.   [20] Jones, *Rights* 224–5.

[21] Rawls, *Political Liberalism*, 55–6.

[22] R. Bellamy, 'Constitutive Citizenship vs. Constitutional Rights: Republican Reflections on the EU Charter and the Human Rights Act' in T. Campbell, K. D. Ewing, and A. Tomkins (eds), *Sceptical Essays on Human Rights* (Oxford: Oxford University Press, 2001) 15–39.

follow J. S. Mill in regarding each individual as the best guardian of his or her own interest, then fairness dictates that they should all be able to play an equal part in the political process that makes those decisions.[23] On the one hand, decisions about rights are ones in which those affected will have an equal stake over the long term and taking into account the full range of decisions. So we need a process that will treat all as political equals in reaching mutually acceptable agreements such as a system of majority decision-making on the basis of equal votes offers. On the other hand, majority voting per se is not tied to any of the arguments; voters can vote for any position and for any reason. As such, it delivers a fair and neutral process for deciding which position can claim the most public support as being in the collective interest.[24]

So conceived, the choice of democracy is not purely pragmatic. It follows from the very idea of rights and certain structural features of any claim to a right and the disagreements that will surround it. First, although there are many different arguments for human rights, it is an intrinsic feature of all of them that since rights attach to human beings as such, they apply equally to all. Second, and related to the first, although rights connect to individuals, we have seen how they also have a collective dimension. A right is not claimed solely for the individual in question but as a right that can be held and upheld equally by all other individuals, hence the need for a process to collectively agree on the right. Moreover, for the right to be collectively held and upheld requires not just each individual doing his or her bit according to some commonly agreed norm, but also common, publicly provided, structures; at a minimum a legal system, and the means for law enforcement, such as a police force, courts, and prisons. So secured, rights function in many ways similarly to that which Raz has called an inherent public good;[25] that is, they promote common benefits that we must collectively produce through our attitudes to others and in which we can all equally share, a point to which I return below. Finally, we have noted how rights also operate as claims against those in authority. They imply that certain things should not be done or should not be denied to any individual.

These three aspects of rights point towards a core claim that underpins all rights claims; namely, the claim by each individual to be treated as a political equal who owes and deserves equal concern and respect to and from every other individual in the shared arrangements that frame their social life, a claim that must also be acknowledged by the authorities charged with administering these arrangements. The intimate link between democracy and rights arises from this core claim. For democracy offers the only forum where different rights claims can be made, and the collective structures necessary for their realization can be provided, in a way that is consistent with rights claimants recognizing their fellow citizens, with their potentially rival claims, as deserving of equal concern and respect, and ensuring that the public authorities are responsive to their collective

---

[23] Jones, *Rights*, 180.

[24] K. May, 'A Set of Independent, Necessary and Sufficient Conditions for Simple Majority Decision' (1952) 10 *Econometrica* 680.

[25] J. Raz, *The Morality of Freedom* (Oxford: Clarendon Press, 1986) 198–9.

disagreements and deliberations about rights. Democracy offers a means for making decisions in which all meet as political equals to make reciprocal claims on each other when framing common policies, and can hold governments to account when they fail to reflect their preferences. In this way, the democratic process grants what Hannah Arendt termed the 'right to have rights'.[26] I am not thereby implying that all rights are intrinsic to democracy. Clearly, not all rights relate to the democratic process. What I am arguing is that all rights involve a democratic form of justification; they imply a spirit of political equality to be accorded equal concern and respect that can only be achieved through a democratic process.

3. RIGHTS AND INDIVIDUAL LIBERTY: LIBERAL AND REPUBLICAN PERSPECTIVES

Seeing rights as somehow intrinsically democratic might be thought to subvert their 'traditional political purpose'; that of telling 'those who wield political power what they may and may not do'.[27] For the chief advantage of rights in this respect has been held to lie in their having a basis outside of politics: they can perform the 'basic tasks' of public law precisely because their foundations are distinct from the government authority that they are supposed to constitute, maintain, and regulate.[28] However, that perception arises from aligning that 'traditional' understanding of the function of rights with the liberal conception of liberty as non-interference. By contrast, when that purpose is linked to the republican conception of liberty as non-domination—a view that more accurately accords with the nature of rights claims as delineated above—then democracy emerges as a necessary, even if not always sufficient, condition for its realization.

3.1 Liberalism, rights, and freedom as non-interference

The liberal notion of freedom as non-interference seems to capture what many see as the central aspect of rights; namely, that there are certain things nobody should be allowed to do to another individual, such as torture, or prevent them from doing, such as exercising their freedom of speech. Given such rights only require the forbearance of others, they ought to be compossible—able to be held by all others—by their very nature, and so be non-negotiable because they do not require negotiation. Not all rights may be of this kind, but those that are offer some of the most important safeguards for individuals. On this account, there is no role for democracy to play in their formulation or maintenance; as noted above, they may even need to be exercised against democratic decisions.

Rights to non-interference seem the best candidates for being in some sense pre- and possibly anti-political. Indeed, all law becomes inimical to rights in being

---

[26] H. Arendt *The Origins of Totalitarianism*, new edn (Orlando, FL: Harcourt Brace, 1958) 296.

[27] Jones, *Rights*, 222.

[28] Loughlin, *The Idea of Public Law*, 1, 115.

a form of interference, albeit potentially necessary to render them secure. This approach offers the paradigm of the view of rights as trumps that are held by individuals against the collective. Such rights seek to drive a wedge between the right and any notion of the common good, offering preconditions for each and every individual to pursue his or her own good in his or her own way. Yet, even rights of this form cannot be isolated from the 'circumstances of politics', for they will not be immune from disputes as to their definition, from conflicts between the uses of these rights by different people as well as with other rights, or from the need for the intervention of public laws and collective structures to realize them. All these issues prove political in the broad sense noted above. This is because they require a collective decision over the content and scope of these rights that will rest on value judgments concerning their purpose and nature— the public good or goods they serve—that allow for reasonable disagreement.

Thus, there may be agreement that no-one should be tortured and all authorities and individuals should simply refrain from acts of torture, but interpretative disputes nevertheless exist as to whether certain punishments shade into torture or not. Think of the arguments in the United States over whether the death penalty is per se 'cruel and unusual' or only certain methods for delivering it. It might be countered that although the practical meaning and implementation of this right are political, the right itself is not—it is a moral right that attaches to individuals as something one simply should not do to any person—hence the aforementioned agreement that torture is wrong. As I noted earlier, though, the moral force of even the most basic human rights does not follow from our humanity per se but the moral theory we hold, and people can and do have different views about the morality of torture, not all of which are rights-based. These differences will always prove relevant because the circumstances in which even a right such as this arises are always political to the extent that the claim is made against other persons and requires institutions or at least an agreement to be reliably enforced among them. There is no right of the individual as such, but only of the social individual within a political and legal context.[29] Indeed, the historical origins of a right not to be tortured lie not in an absolutist view that this right ought to be upheld whatever the consequences, but because it was regarded as ineffective as a means for extracting evidence and corrupting of those who employed it. It was the general utility of torture as a means for upholding the rights of the public, rather than the right of an individual regardless of its impact on the public, that led to its abolition.[30] A political agreement on the public meaning and the good served by this right, as well as the best means to uphold it, is neither additional to or potentially at odds with the nature of such a right. It is essential to its definition and justification.

Similar debates arise in the case of free speech and whether incitement or libel count as speech. Here, though, there is the additional issue of how a right the

---

[29] R. Bellamy, 'Dirty Hands and White Gloves: Liberal Ideals and Real Politics' (2010) 9 European Journal of Political Theory 412, 416–20.

[30] C. Beccaria, *On Crimes and Punishments* [1764], R. Bellamy (ed.) (Cambridge: Cambridge University Press, 1995).

exercise of which appears to simply involve forbearance can nonetheless clash with its similar exercise by others. We regard rights as important not simply for a single individual but for all individuals. If a right to free speech is to be collectively exercised we will need rules of order so we do not always all speak at once so that nobody can be heard above the cacophony, and there may be uses of that right that subvert other rights of individuals, as is the case with slander, hate speech, or the leaking of official secrets. Finally, such conflicts also mean that although many rights may appear simply to depend on an absence of interference, making them available to all will require intervention by public authorities to facilitate their use and guard against their abuse or subversion. It might be argued that we should simply seek to interfere as little as possible with the right in question so as to maximize its availability to all. Yet, what counts as interference is normatively laden,[31] as are the choices of what arrangements might enhance a right maximally in given circumstances. Some will regard certain omissions as well as acts as forms of interference, for example, or see threats and intimidation as potentially as inhibiting as physical force; others will not. Likewise, some might see an equal right as requiring no more than an equal chance to exercise it, such as might be achieved by a lottery, others that it be exercisable to an equal extent, with both views proving highly contestable even in their own terms, especially when it comes to establishing them in practice.

In collectively evaluating the nature and limits of rights and providing common means for their realization, the right comes to fall within, rather being separate from and potentially opposed to and 'trumping', the common or public good. For the rights that will be viewed as commanding the equal concern and respect of all citizens will be those that correspond to their commonly avowable interests and that therefore provide an equal benefit to all. Indeed, not to align rights with the public good in this way has the perverse effect of making rights seem like the privileges of particular individuals rather than the universal entitlements of all citizens; an aristocratic rather than a democratic view. As Raz has noted with regard to free speech,[32] issues such as libel and slander make it implausible to see free speech as the right of each and every individual to say whatever he or she wants regardless of its more general effects on the rights of others. It also seems odd to suggest that we have an interest in this right for our own personal use as individuals in order to vent our frustrations in monologues delivered in front of the bathroom mirror, satisfying though this may be on occasion. It is also the case that few of us are likely to be opinion-formers or whistle-blowers either. So we do not necessarily have a personal interest in exercising this right ourselves. Rather, we all have an equal interest in the benefits of free debate and criticism of public policy by the comparatively small group of people with the time and expertise to do so—politicians, journalists, those with specialist knowledge in a given area, and so on—and in the possibility to join that group being equally open to all, including ourselves,

[31] O. O'Neill, 'The Most Extensive Liberty' (1979–80) 80 Proceedings of the Aristotelian Society 45.

[32] J. Raz, *Ethics in the Public Domain* (Oxford: Clarendon Press, 1994) 54.

should we feel motivated to do so. An equal right to free speech is thus instrumental to securing a public good rather than being distinct from any such good. Hence, the common rules and structures that we favour for regulating free speech are those that we believe best serve that public purpose, for these are the rights all should and could have. Once such structures are in place, their role is to provide an equal and common benefit for all rather than a privilege for an individual to indiscriminately berate his or her neighbours or business rivals out of spite or for personal profit.

3.2 Republicanism, rights, and freedom as non-domination

Rights, then, cannot be removed from politics. Instead, we need a form of politics that is consistent with their character. As we saw at the end of the first section, rights involve a core claim to be treated with equal concern and respect, both by one's fellow citizens in the shared arrangements that coordinate social life, and by the public authorities empowered to oversee them. Consequently, a political process for collectively claiming and deciding on rights will need to possess three key features. First, it must show equal respect for the different views of individuals as rights bearers. Second, it should also demonstrate equal concern for their capacity to employ their rights on the same terms as others. As such, it will need to be doubly collective, a process that involves all the public on an equal basis and promotes those rights and conceptions of rights that best reflect commonly avowed interests. Third, it will have to answer to the 'traditional purpose' of rights as means for holding power to account and marking its limits.

Unlike the classic liberal view of freedom as non-interference, the republican notion of non-domination captures this core claim underlying rights by offering a normative basis for these three requirements of a justified rights-generating political process. On this account, freedom and rights belong not to an asocial agent outside all social and institutional arrangements and able to do what he or she wants because of the lack of interference with or by others, but rather is a civic achievement of socially situated individuals whose relations are regulated by law. What gives these legal arrangements their liberty-preserving quality lies in them being formulated by free and equal citizens who are not bound to any master, but who rather negotiate their collective arrangements together as political equals in order to arrive at policies that serve the common good rather than the partial and potentially dominating interests of particular powerful individuals or factions. The rights that arise from these arrangements still reflect the ways in which citizens tell those in power what they may or may not do. Yet, citizens achieve that 'traditional purpose' through claiming their rights through laws that apply equally to all—including their rulers—and which they ultimately control through a democratic process that shows each of them equal concern and respect as autonomous individuals.

Freedom as non-domination is not inimical to politics and law in the same way as freedom as non-interference.[33] Its aim is to achieve freedom from the arbitrary

---

[33] P. Pettit, *Republicanism: A Theory of Freedom and Government* (Oxford: Oxford University Press, 1997) ch 2.

rule of a master rather than freedom from any rule. Rights play a part in that achievement, but they are the rights of citizens, not the natural rights of human beings that could be held either outside of any society, or as members of any society. Rather, they result from the laws that citizens give themselves as equal members of a given polity.

The view of rights as existing outside and potentially against politics, and hence able to trump a democratic process, overlooks how rights are claims made by citizens on fellow citizens within a social and political setting. Two key errors flow from this oversight. First, it ignores the fact, explored above, that the rights claims of one individual impact on those of other individuals. As we have seen, rights do not attach to human beings as such within a putative state of nature. They belong to and reflect a given social context and the public goods it provides for those who exist within and support it. An individual claiming a right is not the only person possessing trumps. All those he or she is claiming against possess trumps too. The trumping metaphor ceases to be useful in this context. At best, one can argue that there are some especially weighty claims that individuals may have that need to be weighed in the balance with the similarly weighty claims of other individuals. Second, these trumps have already been played in the democratic process where we decide what rights the legal system should enshrine within the relevant legislation.[34] Legislators and, indirectly, those who have elected them can all express their views on rights in framing legislation, and seek to have their most basic interests and core views protected. All effectively play their trumps, but only on the same terms as everyone else. Therefore, in making a claim against a democratic decision, the rights claimer is illegitimately attempting to play his or her cards again, and in the process is failing to treat his or her fellow citizens with the equal concern and respect rights demand.

What, though, do we do in the case of those who do not have access to any or to the relevant democratic institutions—who either live in non-democratic states or outside a given democratic state, be it as a stateless person or as a citizen of a different state—yet have a claim against the democratic decisions of a state that has adversely affected them? Surely, human rights claims often arise in their most powerful and urgent forms precisely in such situations, where either no democratic redress is available or democratic processes have ignored the interests of those excluded from them. Indeed, many established democratic systems have excluded certain members of the political community in the past—women, those without property, ethnic minorities, among other groups—and many continue to do so. All of this is undeniable. And yet, the claims such groups make can be seen primarily as claims for inclusion within the democratic community, to be treated as political equals.

Far from overlooking the claims of the excluded, the republican account has decisive advantages over the liberal in this regard, because the liberal view can be used by the privileged to mandate such exclusions to prevent unjustified

---

[34] Waldron, *Law and Disagreement* 12.

interferences with their entitlements, be it the property rights of the rich or the sovereignty of wealthy states. By contrast, the republican view mandates inclusion as a political equal within the decision-making processes of those powerful bodies capable of exercising domination over our lives. These may be public bodies—the state or its agencies—or private bodies, such as large corporations or financial institutions. The liberal language of human or natural rights leaves the unprivileged outside the city walls, as mere petitioners for redress by the privileged within, who may deploy these same rights to deny any civic responsibility for these others. The republican approach brings all rights-claimants within the city walls, giving them access to the political mechanisms required to offer them redress. Yet, inclusion in the polity brings the obligations as well as the privileges of citizenship, not least the duty to take the rights claims of others as seriously as one takes one's own. Unsurprisingly, the evidence shows that rights will only be reliably upheld where the democratic mechanisms exist for them to be claimed in this way, and that rights are just as reliably ignored and infringed where such mechanisms are absent.[35] It is to the specific virtues of actually existing democracy that we now turn.

4. RIGHTS AND DEMOCRACY: REAL AND IDEAL

A number of theorists have acknowledged the democratic character of rights in framing their accounts in terms of an idealized democratic process, be it the rights that must be presupposed by free and equal dialogue or discourse with another, or that would be agreed to, or could not be reasonably rejected, in circumstances where all participants are equally situated with regard to each other and none has power over another. This democratic argument for rights has been most explicitly stated by Jürgen Habermas.[36] Yet a parallel argument also informs John Rawls's *Political Liberalism,* where he characterizes his first principle of justice as reflecting an agreement between idealized citizens of a liberal democratic state as the necessary conditions for them to coexist as political equals.[37] However, this idealized democratic argument for the foundations of rights does not necessarily entail a practical commitment to use real democratic systems to uphold them. First, both Habermas and Rawls seek to distinguish constitutional from normal politics, regarding the more general and public debate they associate with the one as legitimately constraining and providing the norms underlying the other.[38] Second, both see constitutional courts as exemplifying a more ideal form of democratic discourse than real democratic processes. Habermas argues that courts can review democratic decisions on procedural grounds to ensure they

---

[35] T. Christiano, 'An Instrumental Argument for a Human Right to Democracy' (2011) 39(2) Philosophy and Public Affairs 142.

[36] Eg J. Habermas, *The Inclusion of the Other* (Cambridge: Polity Press, 1998) ch 10.

[37] Rawls, *Political Liberalism,* 3.

[38] J. Habermas, *Between Facts and Norms,* W. Rehg (trans.) (Cambridge: Polity Press, 1996) 304, 486; Rawls, *Political Liberalism,* 232–33—for a critique, see Bellamy, *Political Constitutionalism: A Republican Defence of the Constitutionality of Democracy,* ch 3.

have issued from a duly democratic process,[39] while Rawls maintains they may review them on substantive grounds as well to ensure that certain non-democratic rights have not been infringed, thereby removing certain rights from politics altogether.[40] Finally, and as a corollary of this last point, both see litigation as a form of democratic participation.

This section challenges and qualifies all three of these arguments. I shall argue that idealized, court-based democracy is no substitute for real democracy. If political equality is necessary for all to be treated with equal concern and respect as both the claimers and the duty bearers of rights within the circumstances of politics, then no purely ideal account of democracy can substitute for real democratic practices and participation. Such ideal theories risk being entirely circular, so construing the democratic process that it favours their preferred view of rights. Nor can any abstract theory be so specific as to incorporate all the features that figure within actual contexts, not least the very diverse life experiences and concerns of those involved.

I shall start by outlining the constitutional qualities of normal democratic politics. The superiority of real democratic systems over courts lies in their providing a mechanism for identifying the legislative embodiment of rights most likely to track the commonly avowed interests of citizens by treating them with equal concern and respect. It achieves that result through providing a means for citizens to reach agreements in conditions of political equality. On this account, so-called normal politics is constitutional politics, for it allows the ongoing legislative enactment of rights in the democratic terms required to justify and legitimately realize rights claims. I then turn to an examination of courts and argue that far from offering a more ideal version of this process, courts lack the fundamental democratic quality of allowing an equal input from all affected citizens—their 'right' to author their rights. Nor can their interpretation of a constitutional document that may at some stage have had democratic legitimation in a referendum be regarded as offering a democratic basis for their judgments, isolated as these are from the democratic views of current citizens. Meanwhile, the distinction between procedural and substantive review proves hard to sustain. Not only are the rights inherent in a democratic process as contentious as those that lie outside it, with the latter (as I noted) often more basic and important than the former, but also judgments on what counts as a due process turn to a considerable degree on views of the nature of an appropriate outcome. However, if the courts cannot provide a forum for what Pettit terms 'authorial' democracy,[41] they can provide a venue for what he calls 'editorial' or contestatory democracy for those groups that may not have had voice in the democratic determination of the right. Litigation can play a democratic role here. However, such 'editorial' democracy is necessarily weaker than, and subordinate

---

[39] Habermas, *Between Facts and Norms*, 263, 278–9.

[40] Rawls, *Political Liberalism*, 157, 161.

[41] P. Pettit, 'Democracy: Electoral and Contestatory' in I. Shapiro and S. Macedo (eds), *Designing Democratic Institutions* (New York: New York University Press, 2000).

to, 'authorial' democracy; it offers the basis for a weak form of judicial review that can be overridden by the legislature.

4.1 The Authorial Merits of Real Democracy

Democratic systems have undeniable defects, and although they can be improved must always be expected to fall short of the ideal. However, much the same can be said of any human institution, including courts. So, in advocating courts as correctives for the mistakes of democratically elected and accountable executives and legislatures it is necessary to bear in mind the mistakes that courts will also make. The key question has to be whether courts possess practical and normative qualities that render them more likely to uphold rights and to do so in more justified ways than democratic systems might do. In posing this question, I do not wish to deny that courts and democratic mechanisms have various complementary qualities, with each being best supplemented by the other—a point I return to later. However, their complementarity per se is not at issue here. Rather, the central point is which should have constitutional supremacy in defining whether rights have been upheld or not. Political systems, such as the United States, which have strong rights-based judicial review, hand over that decision to a supreme or constitutional court which can disapply laws they believe infringe rights. But many other systems—such as the UK and Nordic countries like Finland and Norway—have traditionally had far weaker forms of judicial review and give more power on these matters to legislatures and special parliamentary committees. In what follows, I shall argue that the use of these legislative as opposed to judicial mechanisms for rights protection can be justified not just on pragmatic grounds but also for normative reasons to do with the democratic character of rights, for these normative arguments can never be embodied as fully in judicial practices as they are in legislative ones.

As I have argued elsewhere,[42] the key constitutional quality of actually existing democratic systems arises from their combining majority rule with a dynamic form of the balance of power that results from electoral competition between parties. This combination allows such systems to meet the requirement for political equality demanded of a republican notion of freedom as non-domination, thereby allowing rights to be considered in ways consistent with equal concern and respect, on the one side, and the blocking of arbitrary uses of power by those in government, on the other. Majority rule offers a fair decision procedure for resolving disagreements that give all involved an equal voice, thereby satisfying the need for equal respect. Electoral competition in societies typified by cross-cutting cleavages, and where the main policy differences can be plotted on a left–right continuum, obliges voters indirectly and politicians vying for power directly to 'hear the other side', thereby meeting the requirement for equal concern. To build a majority, parties—or coalitions of parties—must bring together the preferences of as many different groupings among the electorate as

---

[42] Bellamy, *Political Constitutionalism: A Republican Defence of the Constitutionality of Democracy*, ch 6.

possible. The result is that the rival party blocks tend to converge on the median voter, which usually represents the Condorcet winner on a pair-wise comparison of the various policy preferences of the electorate as a whole.[43] As research on the relationship of party manifestos to government policies has shown,[44] within democracies that have these characteristics there is a reasonably high correlation between the electoral campaign and the legislative programme of the successful parties. Moreover, governments in such systems inevitably operate under the shadow of the forthcoming election, and so remain accountable to shifts in electoral opinion. They have an ever-present incentive to formulate polices that are non-arbitrary because they track public interests—those that will coincide with respecting the views of most citizens and addressing their common concerns as far as possible.

In this scenario, the prospects of any tyranny of the majority are low.[45] Those who lose consistently will be groups at the extremes of the political spectrum, who have failed to modify their views sufficiently to be able to link up with other sections of the electorate. It is not that their rights have been denied, for they have had the right to express their views on which rights ought to be available and in what ways.[46] Their opinions about rights and the interests that lie behind them have been treated on an equal basis to everyone else's. However, they have not managed to convince their fellow citizens that their view of rights would treat all those affected by its implementation with equal concern and respect, and that failure largely results from not heeding the equally important rights claims of a sufficient number of their fellow citizens, so that the costs and benefits of any collective policy on rights can be shown to be fairly shared by all.

This argument will not satisfy a rights theorist who holds that rights attach to individuals outside any social or political arrangements and should be respected regardless of their costs to others. However, the previous section showed this position to be self-defeating, since it involves a violation of rights itself. The justification of any rights claim needs to be on the grounds that it offers an equal recognition of the mutual rights claims of those others who will have the correlative duty to uphold it. Given disagreement about rights, the best available way of mediating between rival claims is via a fair process in which each person's views are treated on a par with everyone else's, and there is encouragement for all to accommodate the preferences of everyone else as far as they can. As we saw, such a process can be regarded as reflecting the democratic spirit that lies at the heart of any reasonable rights claim. It also provides a means for realizing

---

[43] P. C. Ordeshook, *Game Theory and Political Theory* (Cambridge: Cambridge University Press, 1986) 245–57.

[44] H.-D. Klingermann, R. I. Hofferbert, and I. Budge, *Parties, Policies and Democracy* (Oxford: Westview Press, 1994).

[45] A. J. McGann, 'The Tyranny of the Supermajority: How Majority Rule Protects Minorities' (2004) 16 Journal of Theoretical Politics 53.

[46] M. Tushnet, *Taking the Constitution Away from the Courts* (Princeton: Princeton University Press, 1999) 159.

freedom as non-domination, for it attempts to allow only those interferences that track common avowable interests; that is, those interests that can be avowed politically as showing those involved in a shared social scheme equal concern and respect through functioning as a public good in the sense discussed earlier. What I have now argued is that actual democratic systems offer a realistic approximation to such a rights-promoting process.

4.2 Courts as unreal democracy

Nevertheless, there will certainly be occasions when democratic mechanisms, either inadvertently or otherwise, do not treat all interests equitably or accommodate certain key concerns sufficiently. Certain persons affected by collective decisions may be excluded from the decision-making process altogether, or be ignored by others due to prejudice, or because they are too small and dispersed a group to have any hope of being able to organize themselves so as to be electorally significant. Electorates may also act myopically or be misinformed. In any democratic system there is also the possibility that certain constituencies may prove to have disproportionate influence or others none at all, with the result that electoral decisions may register false positives or false negatives. In these situations, many have thought courts might offer a legitimate safeguard against democratic failures, not least because their processes can claim a certain democratic legitimacy of their own.

Two related claims are made in this regard. First, it is claimed that courts, especially constitutional courts, employ a form of public reasoning and deliberation that is more truly democratic than a standard electoral process. Judges are not only trained to interpret the law impartially, so that it applies equally to all, but also are bound to justify their arguments in terms of constitutional rights norms that themselves reflect the upshot of an ideal democratic process— roughly speaking, the main liberal civil, political, and even certain socio-economic rights—that anyone who accepted democracy would regard as necessary to secure participation as an equal within the public sphere broadly construed. The judiciary's independence from electoral pressures means it is less swayed by the need to pander to popular prejudices. Instead, it can ask whether legislation could be regarded as consistent with a publically justified reading of these rights. As I noted, this argument may be interpreted in either a substantive manner, as relating to the outcome of democratic decisions,[47] or in a procedural manner, with regard to the processes by which democratic decisions are made.[48] Second, it is held that litigation is itself a form of participation. In particular, it allows legislation to be contested on the basis that it fails to meet the standards of equity and fairness inherent in democracy by giving those unable to get

---

[47] Rawls, *Political Liberalism*, 212–54; R. Dworkin, *Freedom's Law: The Moral Reading of the American Constitution* (Oxford: Oxford University Press, 1996) Introduction.

[48] J. H. Ely, *Democracy and Distrust: A Theory of judicial Review* (Cambridge, Mass: Harvard University Press, 1980); Habermas, *Between Facts and Norms*, ch 6.

an adequate hearing in the regular political process a chance to voice their concerns.[49]

Both these claims for courts to offer a better and more ideal democratic forum for the authorship of rights than real democracy can be challenged. For a start, we have seen that constitutional rights norms can be subject to reasonable disagreements, especially when applied to particular cases. Given that the decisions of multi-member courts are often made on the basis of a majority vote, the judiciary can clearly disagree as much as the rest of the population. Yet, their disagreements need not be representative of, or responsive to, the electorate as a whole. That might be no bad thing if we had grounds for regarding their disagreements as somehow resulting from more 'rights-responsive' reasons to those of the general public. But it is not obvious why that should be the case. The fact that they refer to rights in their reasoning does not of itself necessarily mean that their views of them are especially conscientious, better informed, or less biased than other people's. In fact, they may well be less so than politicians who, precisely because they need to engage with the views of the electorate, have to be aware of the impact of a particular way of interpreting and implementing rights on the lives and interests of those they represent. Each citizen's views may be partial, but the nature of the electoral contest makes politicians views rather less so as they have to appeal across the board. By contrast, the danger is that the views of the judiciary are simply arbitrary from the public's perspective; they are merely the views of those individuals on the bench.

It will be objected that judicial reasoning is constrained by precedent and law. However, neither of these constraints per se can be regarded as necessarily producing a more objectively correct view of rights. If there were a clear methodology for arriving at the right answer on moral questions, then there would no longer be such disagreement about these issues, but no agreed method exists. At best, we have rival methods, each of which tends to exist in a circular relation to the view it wishes to promote. Meanwhile, not only is precedent a notoriously weak constraint—especially when dealing with hard or novel cases of the kinds that typically give rise to judicial review—but it may also, insofar as it does apply, provide inappropriate constraints. If courts are tied by precedent, then that implies a *status quo* bias that hinders those cases that might rightly challenge previous decisions. Likewise, the only parties and considerations a court can consider are those that have legal standing in the case at hand. But when deciding public policy it is often necessary to consider the knock-on effects for a wide range of seemingly unrelated policies. Moreover, not all the relevant moral issues involved need be best articulated in terms of rights. Indeed, exclusive focus on the way a right has been legally defined may subvert a full discussion of the question at hand. Think of the distorting effect of arguments about the right to free speech that focus on whether a given form of expression can be characterized as 'speech' as defined by constitutional law and precedent or not.

---

[49] A. Kavanagh, 'Participation and Judicial Review: A Reply to Jeremy Waldron' (2003) 22 Law and Philosophy 451.

Some theorists have argued that these difficulties can be overcome by a procedural approach to judicial review.[50] As Habermas puts it, 'a constitutional court guided by a proceduralist understanding of the constitution does not have to draw on its legitimation credit'; it can leave the substance of rights to a democratic process and confine its views to simply adjudicating on whether democratic decisions respect the 'logic of argumentation'.[51] Yet, he defines valid procedures in terms of 'the communicative presuppositions that allow the better arguments to come into play in various forms of deliberation'.[52] A 'consistent proceduralist understanding of the constitution relies on the intrinsically rational character of a democratic process that grounds the presumption of rational outcomes'.[53] In other words, the test for judging the rationality and appropriateness of a given democratic procedure rests on whether it produces rational outcomes. This argument simply undermines the procedural-substantive distinction. As with other rights, rights related to the democratic process need to be claimed and reformed within existing, normal democratic politics. For example, it is through such mechanisms that workers and women gained the right to vote in the United Kingdom, that forms of proportional representation were introduced in New Zealand and in the UK for regional and European elections, and so on. Compare these dramatic and progressive changes to the blocking of similar measures in the United States by successive judgments of the Supreme Court.[54]

What about the alleged potential of litigation as an additional forum for democratic participation and contestation? This argument also fails, in part for reasons related to those presented earlier. Litigation will only be possible for those parties that the court views as having a case in law. So it is a restricted forum, the terms of which are controlled by the court. As we saw, these controls may be such as to hinder rather than facilitate new or hitherto excluded voices getting heard. Then there are the resource problems of going to court. Access to justice is costly and time-consuming, and cases can take years to be heard. This can often favour those with deep pockets. Given that all citizens start with an equal vote, there is the danger that courts enable illegitimate double counting, with those who cannot muster sufficient popular support to win in politics shopping in an alternative forum that is less open and hence more favourable to the position of privileged minorities or sectional interests.

As a result of these defects, courts, like legislatures, can register false negatives and positives as well as legislatures.[55] But this practical weakness is not entirely symmetrical to that found in political processes. Although those who go to court

---

[50] Ely, *Democracy and Distrust: A Theory of Judicial Review.*

[51] Habermas, *Between Facts and Norms,* 279.

[52] Habermas *Between Facts and Norms,* 278–9.

[53] Habermas *Between Facts and Norms,* 285.

[54] Bellamy, *Political Constitutionalism: A Republican Defence of the Constitutionality of Democracy,* 107–29.

[55] R. Bellamy, 'The Republic of Reasons: Public Reasoning, Depoliticisation and Non-Domination' in S. Besson and J.-L. Marti (eds), *Legal Republicanism: National and International Perspectives* (Oxford: Oxford University Press, 2009) 102–20.

may be treated equally with regard to the law, in contrast to the political system they cannot claim their rights to equal concern and respect on their own terms as political equals. The terms whereby they get access to the law are always the law's, and in these sorts of cases the tribunal they must address is not one of their peers but the judiciary who are set above them as those who determine the state of the law on the case in question. The difficulty is that the very constraints needed to give individuals a fair trial under the law by impartial judges can make courts inappropriate forums for considering the public good aspects of rights and ensuring that they show equal concern and respect to all those not represented within them. The insistence on legality, on the one side, and independence from extraneous influences, on the other, aim to ensure judges make decisions as far as possible free from personal bias, financial inducements, or fear of reprisals from those sympathetic to one or other of the parties. Yet, the common good aspects of rights may involve considerations beyond the law in question and require a responsiveness to the consequences for the public at large. Courts engaged in rights-based review typically deal with such questions under the heading of 'proportionality'. Yet, unlike legislatures they lack the feedback mechanisms likely to ensure such judgments are well-informed. Governments have to respond to the votes of millions of citizens and their assorted needs by presenting them with a programme of government and have both the opposition and several hundred representatives seeking re-election from their diverse constituencies to remind them of that fact. For good reasons, courts are isolated from such pressures.

4.3 Courts and editorial democracy

It will be pointed out that not all litigants in human rights cases are tobacco companies contesting restrictions on advertising in the name of free speech, or film stars protecting their ability to sell their wedding photos to the highest bidder in the name of privacy. There are also asylum seekers, prisoners, the mentally ill, immigrants, and other unpopular or isolated minority groups, with limited if any access to the democratic sphere. Even if not all deserving cases get to court and not all those that do are decided well, there is at least the prospect that some of those individuals whose rights will go unregarded otherwise will get a hearing. For these cases, courts can offer a legitimate avenue of contestatory democracy. While the constraints typical of courts make them a poor authorial forum, they prove well suited as supports for an editorial forum. Courts seek in their own proceedings to ensure that litigants are treated impartially with regard to the settled norms of the law. In doing so, they apply notions of equity and procedural fairness. As a result, they are highly attuned to adjudicating on the issue of whether a given party to a dispute has been given an adequate hearing, or if the norms governing a case have been interpreted even-handedly to all parties. In cases where a litigant, such as an asylum seeker or a prisoner, could show that his or her position had failed to be treated equitably in either of these ways, then contestation of the authorial decision seems legitimate with the courts the appropriate forum. The issue then becomes how strong can such contestation be before it merges into a less legitimate form of authorial democracy?

Some accounts of editorial democracy, such as Pettit's—at least in some formulations—see a written constitution and bill of rights as offering the authorial basis for such editorial contestation.[56] However, that overlooks the fact that the electoral branch may have claimed to offer these as much attention as the judicial, and sought to legitimately reinterpret them so that they accorded more truly with the current views and interests of people with regard to certain issues. If a court is allowed, as under strong contestatory review, to strike down legislation or to read into it its own reading of its fit with constitutional norms, then it is in effect usurping the authorial function of electoral democracy. By contrast, a weak form of contestation allows courts merely to question the compatibility on the fairness grounds outlined above and to force a reconsideration by the legislature. In many respects, the British Human Rights Act can be read in such terms as a form of 'weak' contestatory judicial review.[57] Under this scheme, the rights enumerated under the Act remain an ordinary piece of legislation that the electoral branch can alter if it deems that necessary. However, in the meantime, it seeks to ensure its current legislation is compatible with such rights norms and to mark when it seeks, for reasons it deems legitimate, to depart from them. Yet, courts can dispute whether it has done this sufficiently thoroughly and ask the legislature to reconsider, although how and when remains the prerogative of the authorial branch of democracy. Here democracy—real democracy—remains the authorial foundation for rights, with the courts offering a supplementary function as an editorial alarm bell.

5. CONCLUSION

I have argued that rights involve an implicit appeal to democratic forms of public reasoning. Nevertheless, this view can still capture 'the traditional political purpose of natural or human or fundamental rights', which accords with the 'basic tasks' of public law; that of constraining those wielding political power. This purpose and these tasks are best conceived in terms of the republican view of liberty as non-domination rather than the liberal view of liberty as non-interference. On this account, the state pursues public purposes that accord with rights to the extent it is under the ultimate control of the public by way of democratic mechanisms that show them equal concern and respect. It follows that constitutional rights cannot offer a higher public law that defines and circumscribes the public realm, its officials, and ultimately the public themselves, with public reason not the reasoning of the public but that of courts applying norms that lie outside of politics.

---

[56] P. Pettit, 'Republican Freedom and Contestatory Democratization' in I. Shapiro and C. Haker-Cordón (eds), *Democracy's Value* (Cambridge: Cambridge University Press, 1999); Pettit, 'Democracy: Electoral and Contestatory'.

[57] Bellamy, 'Political Constitutionalism and the Human Rights Act'.

The justifiable authorial foundation of rights must be some form of ongoing democratic decision-making that allows rights to be claimed under conditions of political equality. At best, courts provide the basis for a weak form of contestatory or 'editorial' democracy that draws attention to neglected or otherwise unheard voices among the public. However, the only legitimate final say on rights rests with the people, among whom the benefits and burdens of rights must equally fall as commonly avowed goods that serve their shared interests. In summary, rights and law in general will only be truly public to the extent that they are law and rights that the members of the public give to themselves.

∽ 8 ∽

The Nation as 'The Public': The Resilient Functionalism of Public Law

Stephen Tierney

I. INTRODUCTION

The notion that the age of public law is somehow passing recalls persistent claims that the age of the nation state and the nation itself is also drawing to a close. I have elsewhere argued that these latter claims are overstated,[1] and in this chapter I will also challenge the notion that the role for public law is likewise being undermined. In doing so I will draw parallels between both sets of claims and in turn will suggest that the resilience of both the nation and public law is, through the functional role the latter serves, in fact relational.

I will address the resilience of the concept of public law in the context of privatization on the one hand and globalization on the other. The former, for our purposes, has involved the hollowing out of the public sphere and the concomitant diminution of the role of the state in regulating areas of private activity, particularly in the economic arena; the latter is an increasingly indeterminate term, but again for the legal theorist it refers to those new transnational normative structures which challenge, and in some ways already supplant, the state's authority from the outside. National identity and its relationship to public law can be situated in the context of each of these processes of change, but the highly particular relationship between the nation and the state which emerged with the modern, classical form of public law must be presented as in many ways a discrete concern, not unaffected by privatization or globalization, and yet also sufficiently robust and distinctive to raise specific issues for how we understand public law and its continuing relevance and resilience today. My concern in this chapter is to re-emphasize the extent to which ties of identification and loyalty between a people—and in some cases a number of peoples—and the constitutional order and public law system of a particular polity remain strong, as in many respects do the states themselves which host these ties, and that 'classical' systems of public law therefore remain central in managing these polities. Although the relationship between a people and its polity is inevitably affected by changing dynamics beyond the state, and by the arguably diminishing public space within it, there is also and perhaps paradoxically considerable evidence

---

[1] S. Tierney, *Constitutional Law and National Pluralism* (Oxford: Oxford University Press, 2004).

pointing to the resilience of national identities and the power of states, dynamics which challenge the early 21st-century prognosis that we have entered a post-national era.

This argument for the resilience of the nation-state nexus leads me to situate the chapter within 'the domain of public law'.[2] The introductory chapter to this collection adopts this term in calling for reflection on the worth of the ethical and political project that public law embodies. And here my primary focus will be upon the functionalism, or what I will call the 'resilient functionalism', of public law in continuing to support the important relationship between nations and states. I will begin by outlining what I understand by the functionalism of public law in its broadest sense, tracing very briefly its historical development as a discrete subject. Secondly, I will explore further how public law's primary function in the modern era has been to facilitate the relationship between national identity and the state. Thirdly, I will offer empirical evidence to defend the 'resilience thesis' and the ongoing importance of public law as facilitator of the continuing, albeit changing, relationship between nation, national identity, and state.

2. NATION-STATE: THE FUNCTIONALISM OF PUBLIC LAW

The resourcefulness of public law is to be found in its functional role as a form of practice per Loughlin's 'broad conception of public law as one that encompasses all the rules, principles, habits and practices that sustain the autonomy of the world of the political'.[3] Public law in this sense is the husbanding of public power, but it is not a process that does or can insulate public power from political forces. This political functionalism of public law leads us to two important implications for the purposes of this book. The first is that as a form of practice, public law is a product of lived, historical experience. It is in this sense bound up with the political reality of power. Where public power exists in whatever form, then a system of public law will invariably emerge to facilitate and regulate it, and so public law as a form of management of public power has ancient origins. Although the modernist functionalism of public law as we understand it today is bound up with the birth of the nation-state, the management of public power itself long pre-dates this. With the development of social organization beyond the tribe there has been some conceptualization of a public that is abstracted from the bonds of kinship; the sphere—however articulated—that transcends private relations. And indeed a notion of the public, albeit very different from our modern conception, has thus been identified in the ancient world.[4] With this abstraction has come the need for a society to manage the power exercised

---

[2] See Ch 6.

[3] M. Loughlin, 'Towards a Republican Revival?' (2006) 26 Oxford Journal of Legal Studies 425, 436.

[4] A. Lanni and A. Vermeule, 'Constitutional Design in the Ancient World' (2012) 64 (4) Stanford Law Review 907–49; R. C. Van Caenegem, *An Historical Introduction to Western Constitutional Law* (Cambridge, Cambridge University Press, 1995), Introduction.

therein; in short we might say, so long as there is a public sphere, there will be public law.

The second implication is that public law adapts to the particular functions it needs to perform. Public power manifests itself in different ways and so too does public law from time to time and place to place. I use the term 'managing' public power because this connotes two separate but related functions which, acting symbiotically but also in tension with one another, continue to define the role of public law: facilitation and restraint. This dual and at times Janus-faced functionalism of public law has provided the environment for the prudent exercise of public power, while also controlling excesses committed in its name;[5] in other words, public law offers us a vision of public power as both a promise and a threat, varying in form by these markers from system to system.[6]

Understood then as a tool of management, other things flow, in particular the institutional structure for power management, and here through our modernist lens we locate the state, emerging in the late Middle Ages and maturing in the 19th century. The state is both itself the pre-eminent institutional form embodying the higher-order legal norm that somehow sustains its own sovereignty,[7] and at the same time the receptacle for governmental institutions which generate second-order norms. And with the establishment of institutions of government suitable for managing a large polity has come the delineation of the myriad ancillary functions that need to be performed by the state: representation, legislation, government, responsibility, adjudication, etc. Accordingly, so too have been developed doctrines that manage relations among those institutions—separation of powers, checks and balances, rule of law, the legal concept of citizenship to establish the boundaries and qualification for individual membership and non-membership in the polity, and the establishment of a concept of hierarchy of laws from the ordinary to the constitutional to provide an internal circle of authority establishing legal rule, finality but also adaptability.

Therefore, the modernist or classical model of public law with which we deal today has been tailored to suit the social conditions which themselves brought about the state: the imperial accretion of territory and the consolidation of the membership, identity, and loyalty of disparate peoples brought together by this process. In a more economically determinist take, Laski argued constitutional law is only meaningful when understood as the expression of an economic system of which it was designed to serve as a rampart.[8] But, crucially for this book, it is the insight that we can only understand public law by the *political* function it performs that also inspires the idea that our age is somehow 'after public law'

[5] C. Harlow and R. Rawlings, 'Red and Green Light Theories', in *Law and Administration*, 3rd edn (Cambridge: Cambridge University Press, 2009), 1–48.

[6] One of the fascinating while frustrating features of our discipline is its propensity to throw paradoxes at us; the imperfect world of public law as political praxis leaves us with loose ends that are only avoidable in the ideal world of normative political theory. In many ways this is a premise, and implied by the title, of a recent important collection: M. Loughlin and N. Walker (eds), *The Paradox of Constitutionalism* (Oxford: Oxford University Press, 2007).

[7] J. Elster, 'Constitutional bootstrapping in Paris and Philadelphia' (1992–93) 14 Cardozo Law Journal 549.

[8] H. Laski, *A Grammar of Politics* (London: Allen and Unwin, 1925) 578.

or approaching such a condition. As the legal competence of the state as unitary and omnipotent receptacle of sovereignty is constricted by new competences beyond the state and the diminishing capacity of state-based public institutions in the face of lateral privatization, then the function of public law as tool of state management is, it seems, diminishing. There is no doubt that the state, at least in much of Europe, has lost and continues to lose much of its formerly exclusive normative purchase as public functions move to supra-state institutions where they must be managed in concert with others. We must not lose sight of the point that while public law is, given the nature of its function, in a sense timeless, its instantiation and the specific purposes it serves have varied from time to time and place to place. It is its inherently political dynamic that now leads me in the next section to extrapolate the link between state and nation in the modernist manifestation of public law, and in due course to an account of public law's resilient functionalism in the face of a seemingly linear trend to a post-state and post-public law world.

3. A FUNCTION OF MODERN PUBLIC LAW: THE NATION AND ITS IDENTITY

The state has emerged to govern large numbers of people and the normative resource it has called upon to facilitate this is the politico-legal hybrid, sovereignty. But it is one thing to assert sovereignty; a particular task of the state has been to foster bonds of loyalty among its members both to the state and to its governmental institutions, without which sovereignty would be considerably harder to sustain. A key device in producing these bonds has been the somewhat inchoate notion of national identity. At one level, sovereignty can be viewed as the monopoly over the control and application of public power. But sovereignty is misconceived if it is presented only as overwhelming *authority by the state over the people* in the Hobbesian sense.

Here Kalyvas reminds us that we should think of sovereignty as legitimizer as well as sovereignty as power in his distinction between 'command sovereignty' and 'constituent sovereignty'.[9] The former is the classical model of the final word, central to modernist accounts of the legal system as *Rechtsstaat*. Within the Westphalian tradition of state-building, as conceptualized by Kelsen and Hart, it is considered that any legal order must have an absolute and final arbiter, and hence the sovereign is characterized, for example by de Spinoza, as he who 'has the sovereign right of imposing any commands he pleases'.[10] Constituent sovereignty, however, is for Kalyvas a neglected model which is concerned not with 'coercive power' but rather 'constituting power': 'Thus, contrary to the paradigm of the sovereign command that invites personification and can better be exercised by an individual who represents and embodies the unity of authority—from the ancient *imperatore* to the king to the modern executive—the constituent power

---

[9] A. Kalyvas 'Popular Sovereignty, Democracy and Constituent Power' (2005) 12 Constellations 223, 224.

[10] B. de Spinoza, *A Theologico-Political Treatise*, R. H. M. Elwes (trans.) (New York: Dover, 1951) 207.

points at the collective, intersubjective, and impersonal attributes of sovereignty, at its co-operative, public dimension'.[11] This involves seeing the sovereign as 'constituent subject', as the one who shapes not only the governmental structure of a community but also its juridical and political identity;[12] in other words, as the source of the constitution and of its authority.

This mirrors the two-dimensional aspect of public law as both facilitator of and limitation to the exercise of public power. Sovereignty as the ultimate source of authority for public law facilitates its voluntary, popular feature alongside its coercive dynamic. It is not simply something to be borne out of sufferance, coercion being the unfortunate side-effect of the benefits accruing from the modern state. It is also the life-blood of the polity which gives it its popular impetus and which makes the life lived as a public actor and citizen rewarding and enhancing. The state can be a *res publicae*—genuinely a thing of the public— within which the public has the power to create, and indeed constantly recreate, the state in its own image.

Thus, the key feature upon which the modern functionalism of public law has come to rely is legitimacy, and this notion has been shaped by a growing association between the modern state, on the one hand, and democracy, defined as popular government and even popular sovereignty, on the other. Sovereignty in the modern era has come to rest upon consent; *the rule of the people over the state* mirroring *authority by the state over the people*. And it is in the context of democracy's emergence as the dominant ideology of state legitimacy that we need to situate also the link between public law and national identity, which is crucial to appreciating how modernist sovereignty has developed its double-sided character.

Since a vital task of the modern state has been to legitimize its claim to a monopoly in the management of public power, and since in doing so by any means short of absolute dictatorship it has needed to find a way to harness the identity and loyalty of its subjects, the resource adapted to this task more than any other is the concept of the nation.[13] This idea is vast in its complexity as recent decades of intense academic interest have illustrated. At the first-order level, what is the nation? Is it simply a synonym for the people of a particular state, as we see it constructed within classical French constitutionalism? Or must we disentangle the concept of nation from the state and consider it to manifest itself in more organic sociological terms, at some level of detachment from the institutional construc-tion of the polity? But when we move beyond the perfect mapping of state to nation, looking for a meaning of the latter in sociological terms, it is clear that consensus on what constitutes a nation is impossible to find, as seen, for example, in international law's failure to define the term 'national minority'.[14]

---

[11] Kalyvas, 'Popular Sovereignty' 235–36.

[12] Kalyvas, 'Popular Sovereignty' 226.

[13] E. J. Weber, *Peasants into Frenchmen: The modernization of rural France, 1870–1914* (London: Chatto and Windus, 1977).

[14] No international legal instrument, even those which expressly address minority rights, attempts such a definition.

Among sociologists, the key debate takes place within the spectrum of instrumentalism, with the nation considered to be more or less the instrumental outcome of other social phenomena. At one end of this spectrum, the nation is the functional creation of the state. This is a form of modernist thinking which we find, for example, among Marxist thinkers like Hobsbawm.[15] The nation as a vehicle for collective identity has little or no self-generated life of its own. It is contingent upon the functioning of the polity which it supports, and just as it was manufactured to support the modern capitalist state, so too would it disappear as it ceased to serve any useful function, supplanted, as many Marxists supposed, by the triumph of a particular internationalized social class. At the other extreme are what we might call the ethno-essentialists who consider the nation to be deep-rooted in largely immutable social attachments built up through shared experiences over centuries and founded at least in part upon inherent markers of ethnic particularity; in other words, political institutions emerged to serve rather than to shape the nation, and could not of themselves either create or transform the structure of the nation in any meaningful way.

Much of the literature within nationalism studies since the 1960s has tended to try and make sense of some middle ground, offering a variety of alternative accounts[16] that seek to grasp the modernism, instrumentalism, and contingency of nationalism which has made it a particularly useful ideological vehicle for the large-scale state, while recognizing also that individual states constructed nations upon sites of identity which did in many cases pre-date the state; in other words, the modern state appropriated more or less these older attachments together with the languages and cultures that had developed within nascent national communities, adapting and consolidating these identities to suit an emerging constitutional identity for the large-scale polity. The nation was instrumentally useful and in some cases had indeed been 'forged',[17] but it has also relied upon cultural and ethnic markers that pre-dated the state it was adapted to serve. Particular nations therefore can be situated on a scale moving from the more manufactured or 'imagined',[18] to those which built more upon pre-existing identity patterns. But this scale is more or less not either/or; each nation to differing extents and in differing ways combine attributes that on the one hand pre-date the nation-building dynamic of modernism, and on the other have been shaped by the institutional structures and ideologies this dynamic brought with it.

Therefore, the important work that has formed our contemporary understanding of the complexity of the nation is that which, particularly in the ground-breaking

---

[15] E. J. Hobsbawm, *The Age of Revolution: Europe 1789–1848* (London: Abacus, 1962); *Nations and Nationalism Since 1780: programme, myth, reality* (Cambridge: Cambridge University Press, 1991).

[16] M. Billig, *Banal Nationalism* (London: Sage, 1995); J. Breuilly, *Nationalism and the State*, 2nd edn, (Manchester: Manchester University Press, 1993); R. Brubaker, *Nationalism Reframed: Nationhood and the National Question in the New Europe* (Cambridge: Cambridge University Press, 1996); E. Gellner, *Nations and Nationalism* (Oxford: Blackwell, 1983); T. Nairn, *Faces of Nationalism: Janus revisited* (London: Verso, 1997); and A. D. Smith, *Nations and Nationalism in a Global Era* (Cambridge: Polity Press, 1995).

[17] L. Colley, *Britons: Forging the Nation 1707–1837* (New Haven and London: Yale University Press, 1992).

[18] B. Anderson, *Imagined Communities: Reflections on the Origin and Spread of Nationalism* (London: Verso, 1991).

efforts of Anthony Smith, offers a nuanced and complex account (calling into question any essentialist vision of the nation as inherently ethnic and eternal), but also questions crude assumptions that it is simply an invented construct of the modernist state, which might serve a function for a time before being self-consciously ditched in favour of a more suitable construction for a post-state era. This presents a challenge for notions that we are moving beyond public law. If the nation is not just constructed, does it merely serve the state? Or does to some extent the state also serve the nation, providing a set of institutions which allows it to set its own priorities, and represent its own identity? If the latter, mixed account is more accurate, then we need to think about how the contemporary functionalism of public law comes to facilitate a still important, albeit in some ways and in some cases changing, relationship between state and nation, a relationship which we should not be too hasty to assume has run its course.

4. THE CHANGING FUNCTIONALISM OF STATE-BASED PUBLIC LAW

National identity is generally agreed, at least by all but the most extreme ethno-nationalists, to be partly functional. In today's condition of global normative flux therefore, we need to take stock in order to ask what role it has played, and how might this role be changing as we see the functions of public law within the state also develop. In the remainder of the chapter, I will consider empirical evidence which seems to suggest that both the nation and the state, in mutually supportive ways, retain considerable resilience today.

4.1 *The resilience of the nation*

The 20th-century expectation that the nation as a focus for people's public identities would wane was in large part the consequence of eliding an 'ought' with an 'is'. It was hoped the nation would diminish, and in part, expectations were built upon this. A very understandable reason for this aspiration was the loss of moral capital the nation suffered particularly in the early part of that century through its association with the much corrupted currency of national-ism.[19] Indeed, the sense that the nation, and in particular nationalism as an ideology, or more accurately as a mode of structuring public identities, was increasingly revanchist and outmoded was one of the few commitments shared by both models of cosmopolitanism—liberal and Marxist—during the Cold War, albeit each informed by very different ideological presuppositions.

But this has not proven to be the case. We can point to several pieces of evidence that suggest national attachments have not disappeared and indeed remain strong, even in Europe. If it is the case that the state is losing much of its

---

[19] A common assumption left by the bitter ethnic hatreds of the last century posits nationalism and liberalism as inherently incompatible. F. A. Hayek, *The Constitution of Liberty* (London: Routledge & Kegan Paul, 1960) 14–15; H. Arendt, *On Revolution* (London: Penguin, 1963) 163; D. Miller, *On Nationality* (New York: Oxford University Press, 1995); M. Ignatieff, *The Warrior's Honour: Ethnic War and the Modern Conscience* (New York: Metropolitan Books, 1998); T. Franck, *The Empowered Self: Law and Society in the Age of Individualism* (Oxford: Oxford University Press, 1999).

purchase as the exclusive site for normative control (and I will return to and in some respects contest this point later), it is a curious trend that the nation remains strong as the primary site of identity and loyalty for citizens, and that in some respects it seems to be enjoying something of a renaissance. Many have expected European integration to lead inevitably to a redrawing of popular attachments with the prospect of a newly emerging polity that promises to replace the divisive, polarizing, and historically contingent nations of the continent. But it is clear national attachments have not dissipated, even in 'EUrope'.

Another factor has been the emergence of national identity as a key player in the collapse of the USSR and the Socialist Federal Republic of Yugoslavia. There were of course complex political dynamics at work as these states dissolved, including popular revolt against oppressive governments, but the strength of national feeling expressed in so many republics and reiterated in overwhelming referendum turnout and votes for independence cannot be denied.[20] This also extended to national reawakening in the Soviet satellite states of Eastern Europe. We continue to see situations where subordinate peoples have retained an attachment to their own national community and an aspiration for self-determination, even in the face of overwhelming oppression. This is evident in the recent moves towards independence by Montenegro and Kosovo,[21] recent and ongoing acts of decolonization in East Timor and New Caledonia respectively, the emergence of Eritrea and Southern Sudan as states, and the struggles of the Palestinian people and the Sahrawis of Western Sahara for statehood.

While again, as in the post-communist era, it might be argued that these developments have more to do with resisting oppression than nationalism, another and for many a perplexing phenomenon, has been the resilience and indeed strengthening of national identities among sub-state regions within relatively prosperous and harmonious states such as the UK, Canada, Belgium, and Spain. Although this phenomenon has led to strong autonomy regimes for sub-state nations, perhaps paradoxically this institutional accommodation has in some cases at least not quelled the political and constitutional aspirations for greater accommodation and has perhaps re-energized political nationalism within certain territories.[22]

We also see on the international plane a proliferation of instruments designed to protect minorities, minority languages, etc. The national identities of sub-state peoples who have no realistic opportunity or desire for statehood or for territorial transfer to a kin state remains strong, and the accommodation of these identities remains an issue for international law both at general[23] and regional

---

[20] S. Tierney, *Constitutional Referendums: The Theory and Practice of Republican Deliberation* (Oxford, Oxford University Press, 2012) 67–73.

[21] S. Tierney, 'The Long Intervention in Kosovo: a Self-Determination Imperative?' in James Summers (ed.), *Kosovo and International Law* (Leiden: Martinus Nijhoff, 2011) 249–78.

[22] The respective levels of sub-state national identity and its connection to aspirations for independence are uneven from one territory to another; eg, the sovereignty movement in Quebec is currently weak, whereas in Scotland it has strengthened in recent years.

[23] United Nations Declaration on the Rights of Persons Belonging to National or Ethnic, Religious and Linguistic Minorities; UN Declaration on the Rights of Indigenous Peoples (adopted 14 September 2007).

levels.[24] These regimes are at an early stage of development and remain weak. But time will tell if they help foster nationalist claims in the developing world where sub-state national groups are now beginning to advance claims to territorial accommodation similar to those in Canada and Western Europe.[25]

Another phenomenon we have seen is the spread of direct democracy as a means of settling major constitutional issues including sovereignty matters, which has provided a real instantiation of the connection between sovereignty as power and sovereignty as democratic legitimacy. The rise of the referendum within the modern democratic state has many causes and offers many implications for the functioning of representative government, but one consequence which is particularly relevant for this chapter is the way in which the referendum provides colonized, subordinate, and minority nations with a vehicle to voice their discrete national identities and aspirations. We see this in the key role the referendum has played in leading to independent statehood in Eastern Europe, in East Timor, Eritrea, and in Southern Sudan, and in constitution-building in Iraq and elsewhere. It is also notable how the international community has fostered the referendum to facilitate expressions of national self-determination in recent years, and in a way that was not deployed in the earlier self-determination processes of 1919 and the 1950s and 1960s. This is partly through the hands-on engagement in particular peace-making or constitution-building processes (Eritrea 1993, Iraq 2005, Montenegro 2006, and South Sudan 2011), and partly through more general processes of norm creation through the issuing of guidelines; for example, by the Council of Europe's Commission for Democracy Through Law (Venice Commission).[26] Referendums have also been used in moves towards national autonomy in Spain and the UK, and it is no surprise that nationalists in these territories and in Quebec have attempted or are now attempting to stage their own referendums on independence, sovereignty, etc.

There is also evidence that these referendums can be nation-affirming if not directly nation-building; in other words, the direct manifestation of a people in an act of collective self-determination is not only a constitutional moment, it is a national moment. National identity, if it means anything, constitutes the ongoing imagined collective consciousness of a nation's members. It is the lived attachment of a group of people in the same polity specifically to one another, and it is consolidated not only through the 'everyday plebiscite' of a shared and lived political experience, but also and increasingly by 'every so often plebiscites'; that is, real acts of collective, popular deliberation concluded at the ballot box. One

---

[24] Council of Europe Framework Convention for the Protection of National Minorities; European Charter for Regional or Minority Languages; OSCE Copenhagen Document of 1990.

[25] W. Kymlicka and M. Opalski (eds), *Can Liberal Pluralism be Exported? Western Political Theory and Ethnic Relations in Eastern Europe* (Oxford: Oxford University Press, 2002); B. Berman, D. Eyoh, and W. Kymlicka (eds), *Ethnicity and Democracy in Africa*, (Oxford: James Currey Publishers and Ohio University Press, 2004); W. Kymlicka and B. He (eds), *Multiculturalism in Asia* (Oxford: Oxford University Press, 2005); J. Castellino and E. Dominguez Redondo, *Minority Rights in Asia* (Oxford: Oxford University Press, 2006).

[26] European Commission for Democracy Through Law (Venice Commission) Code of Good Practice on Referendums, CDL-AD (2007) 008 rev, Council of Europe Strasbourg, 20 January 2009.

paradox here is the use of referendums on EU integration, which perhaps threaten to have the opposite of the effect intended.[27] Citizens from discrete nations come together in an act of popular sovereignty, but the issue at stake is the transfer of that sovereignty to a supranational body. What we see from these processes is that not only does the nexus between state and popular legitimacy remain strong, but so too do national attachments in Europe. To take Ireland as an example, referendums have been used for all of the significant treaty processes, and it has been a bumpy ride, with evidence that over time, Euroscepticism has steadily been growing.[28] This can be seen in the rise of the No vote: 17 per cent on accession in 1972; 30 per cent in 1987 (Single European Act); 31 per cent in 1992 on the Treaty of European Union; 38 per cent in 1998 on the Amsterdam Treaty; and finally, rejection of the Treaty of Nice in 2001. Following a minor concession by way of the Seville Declaration recognizing Ireland's policy of military neutrality, a second referendum was held and the Nice Treaty was eventually accepted by Irish voters in 2002. But the more dramatic rejection was that of the Treaty of Lisbon in 2008, intensifying as it did the shockwaves still reverberating from the failure of the draft Constitutional Treaty. Once again the Irish government negotiated minor compromises and Lisbon was eventually accepted by the Irish people in 2009. The popular rebellions against both the Constitutional Treaty and the Lisbon Treaty in states where referendums were held seem to bear this out.[29]

There remains the question, however, whether the opprobrium heaped upon nationalism is not having an effect. The image of nationalism we were left with after the age of Fascism and National Socialism should surely have diminished nationalism and national identity in an age when liberalism with its cosmopolitan aspirations holds sway.[30] But in fact what we have seen is that the revival of national identity in the past few decades has brought with it a new turn in scholarship which calls into question the 20th-century stereotype of the nation as backward and outdated. This new work across a range of disciplines questions the caricature of the nation and national identity as undemocratic, dangerous, and unfit for purpose in an age of state transformation.

---

[27] M. Shu, 'Referendums and the Political Constitutionalisation of the EU' (2008) 14 European Law Journal 423.

[28] J. O'Brennan, 'Ireland says No (again): the 12 June 2008 Referendum on the Lisbon Treaty' (2009) 62 (2) Parliamentary Affairs 258–77, 274.

[29] Qvortrup on the first Irish Lisbon referendum concluded that 'the voters, while not opposed to the EU as such, were unhappy with further integration or transfer of sovereignty': M. Qvortrup, 'Rebels without a Cause? The Irish Referendum on the Lisbon Treaty', (2009) 80 Political Quarterly 59, 65. Schuck and De Vreese are among those who consider Euroscepticism among the Dutch electorate to be a more significant factor behind the No vote on the Reform Treaty than domestic, second-order issues: A. Schuck and C. De Vreese, 'The Dutch No to the EU Constitution: Assessing the Role of EU Skepticism and the Campaign', (2008) 18 Journal of Elections, Public Opinion & Parties 101, 120; R. Sinnott, 'Attitudes and Behaviour of the Irish Electorate in the Referendum on the Treaty of Nice' (2003) University of College Dublin Working Papers <http://www.ucd.ie/dempart/workingpapers/nice2.pdf> (accessed 10 October 2011).

[30] Franck, The Empowered Self.

We saw the first challenge to the stereotype in the work of sociologists who have since the 1960s demonstrated the resilience of national identity and, surprisingly, the strengthening of it particularly at the sub-state level within democratic, liberal, tolerant states. Sociologists have found national identities to be resilient, but they have also found them not to be particularly thick, with markers of membership based decreasingly on ethnic markers and more on civic models of belonging.[31] They have also found that national identity remains strong even as cultural distinctions within multinational states and around the world seem to diminish in an era of cosmopolitanism.[32]

Secondly, political scientists have addressed the constitutional aspirations of this new nationalism and found, contrary to many expectations, that political actors adopting the nationalist mantle are for the most part not backward-looking or reactionary, but espouse values wholly consistent with the plurality of opinion in modern Western societies, for example on issues such as social welfare, citizenship, and human rights.[33] Furthermore, they have advanced political programmes that run largely with the grain of changing state power, supra-state integration, and internationalization of previously monopolistic state functions; nationalists in Scotland, Catalonia, and Quebec situate themselves within the context of their respective integrating continents in ways similar to state nationalists, and in some ways are in fact more pro-integrationist.[34] In other words, the new nationalism was found to fit wholly consistently within the 'progressive' trend of modern politics, weakening the negative stereotype with which nationalism has been tarnished.

Thirdly, we find in political theory, including perhaps surprisingly liberal political theory, a subtle turn that has served to question the notion that nationalism and liberalism are inherently incompatible. Political philosophers, most comprehensively Will Kymlicka, have found the aspirations of these national groups to be wholly consistent with liberalism and have in fact argued that liberalism has a duty to accommodate these political and constitutional aspirations if it is to be true to its own values of liberty and equality.[35] It is only in the context of individual people's societal culture that they can advance

---

[31] D. McCrone, *Understanding Scotland: The sociology of a nation*, 2nd edn (London: Routledge, 2001).

[32] The ever closer alignment of values among nations within plurinational states at the same time as nationalist sentiment within these nations grows has been called 'de Tocqueville's paradox' by Stephane Dion. S. Dion, 'Le nationalisme dans la convergence culturelle: le Québec contemporain et le paradoxe de Tocqueville', in R. Hudon and R. Pelletier, (eds), *L'engagement intellectuel: Mélange en l'honneur de Léon Dion* (Québec: Presses de l'Université Laval, 1991), 291–338.

[33] M. Keating, *Nations Against the State—The New Politics of Nationalism in Quebec, Catalonia and Scotland*, 2nd edn (London: Palgrave, 2001); A.-G. Gagnon and J. Tully (eds), *Multinational Democracies* (Cambridge: Cambridge University Press, 2001).

[34] M. Keating, *Plurinational Democracy: stateless nations in a post-sovereignty era* (Oxford: Oxford University Press, 2001).

[35] W. Kymlicka, *Multicultural Citizenship: A Liberal Theory of Minority Rights* (Oxford: Oxford University Press, 1995); M. Moore, 'Normative Justifications for Liberal Nationalism: justice, democracy and national identity', (2001) 7 Nations and Nationalism 1; F. Requejo (ed.), *Democracy and National Pluralism* (London: Routledge, 2001).

their own life goals in a fulfilled way, achieving the liberal goals of equality and liberty.[36]

Therefore, just as in empirical terms national identity has shown itself to remain strong, within the social sciences there is considerable evidence that it is also adaptable, and can remain fit for purpose in an internationalizing world. If it is the case that national identities remain resilient, with people finding primary identity in their societal cultures, while open to the opportunities this increasingly cosmopolitan environment has to offer, what of the state?

4.2 The resilience of the state

Here again, rumours of the state's demise seem to be overstated. The resilience of the nation and national identity cannot be detached from the ongoing functional role of the state, and 'public law of the state' is still required to service this nexus.

We do of course need to observe that the normative order in which states exist has changed greatly; the state is no longer the exclusive resource through which public power is facilitated and restrained. In Europe, with its particularly sophisticated supranational apparatus, there is no doubt that the particular manifestation of European public law, to facilitate the monopolistic public power of the sovereign state, is changing. But, from a European perspective, it is easy to develop a skewed outlook and miss how strong the state is in other parts of the world. The state has not disappeared; arguably it remains strong even in Europe. More broadly, its function within the international legal environment remains crucial and pre-eminent.

4.3 Supranationalism and its diffusion

There are a number of ways in which we can re-emphasize the ongoing importance of the state. One is to observe that the proliferation of normative sites beyond the state in some ways, and perhaps paradoxically, reinforces the state's importance. Both the international community and the state in its dealings with it have become more porous, open to new actors, developing more accessible and, in some ways, more transparent processes, and developing in turn new horizontal (state to state and non-state actor to non-state actor) and vertical (state to supranational institution and non-state actor to supranational institution) dynamics. Given this connection between the emergence of institutions which seem in some light to form the origins of a proto-global governance matrix, we cannot conceive of these communities of states and the communities of non-state actors as somehow separable, particularly since individuals, non-governmental organizations (NGOs), and political movements within this 'supranational civil society' are increasingly able to access, and are

---

[36] W. Kymlicka, *Politics in the Vernacular* (Oxford: Oxford University Press, 2001); S. Tierney, 'The Search for a New Normativity: Thomas Franck, Post-Modern Neo-Tribalism and the Law of Self-Determination' (2002) 13 (4) European Journal of International Law 941.

structured in order best to influence, the communities of states and supranational institutions.

However, it may also be observed that this increasingly diverse set of relations makes the idea of a unified, central system of global government a less rather than a more realistic prospect. With the multiplication of institutions, agents, and processes comes a wider diversification of sites of authority and a less clear hierarchical structure among actors within these sites and across normative sites themselves, giving the impression of 'governance without government'.[37] Recent normative clashes in cases such as *Kadi*[38] hint at a possible 'chaos theory'. In particular, it is not clear how, if at all, the increasing interaction of and competition among international organizations and treaty bodies affects the simple architecture of the UN and its commitment to the equality of sovereign states.

Even the most advanced model of supranationalism, the EU, presents a very mixed picture of the prospects for macro-constitutional architecture beyond the state.[39] Certainly it seems to offer at least the beginnings of some type of transnational community of individuals, or even a proto-form of state itself. But if this is the ultimate goal, there remain considerable political and constitutional obstacles facing such supranational state-building projects which did not confront the first modernist wave of nation-building in the late 18th–19th centuries.

4.4 The end of coercive nation-building

It should not be overlooked that the Westphalian order was built largely by coercion. Nation-building in the 18th and 19th centuries, as well as post-colonial societal construction, was often imposed from the top with no democratic political traditions in place to generate resistance. State-building elites had a much freer hand in overriding the niceties of pluralism, respect for national minorities, linguistic diversity, and the like than governments today, which are generally dependent upon popular consent. It is difficult to see how new normative orders can deploy such an aggressive approach, at least directly. There are attempts of course, such as the refusal to take no for an answer in the empire-building referendums of the EU. But on the other hand, the recent referendums in Ireland, France, and the Netherlands show that the political and at some level consensual road to integration will only allow such a top-down approach to proceed so far, and with the referendum a stronger part of many constitutions, the future road to further integration looks potentially rocky. Another possible avenue is economic dependence. We have seen how the recent economic crisis in

---

[37] K. E. Jorgensen and B. Rosamund, 'Europe: a regional laboratory for a global polity?' in R. Higgott and M. Ougaard (eds), *Towards a Global Polity* (London: Routledge, 2000) 189–206.

[38] Joined Cases C-402/05 P and C-415/05 *Yassin Abdullah Kadi and Al Barakaat International Foundation v Council of the European Union and Commission of the European Communities* [2008] ECR I-6351.

[39] J. H. H. Weiler and M. Wind, *European Constitutionalism Beyond the State* (Cambridge: Cambridge University Press, 2003).

Greece and the danger this poses to the Euro has led powerful actors within the EU to move for further political integration as a way of exerting further economic control throughout the Eurozone.

Also the new nation-states of the post-Enlightenment period often replaced antiquated, undemocratic relics of feudalism, and so the normative argument for the new, proto-democratic state was more easily made (even where it had to be) in cases of imposition. Also, other new nations were born from popular revolutions and grew a new national identity from this fertile soil. But today the supra-nation or supra-state entities seek a place alongside or in place of often well-established and reasonably contented national democracies, so the attractiveness of supra-state centralization is often less than self-evident from a democratic perspective.[40] Although earlier periods of nation-building were often taken to be politically progressive, and as such they attracted political support across the political spectrum, this is not always the case with globalization or further integration in Europe, each of which faces popular opposition at the vernacular and even cosmopolitan levels, from left and right. A recent example again is the left-wing backlash against the economic austerity imposed upon Greece by the European Union.

Finally, in the 18th and 19th centuries, warfare played a huge part in uniting disparate communities within the state in order to resist external threats. There was no shortage of regional enemies who provided a ready-made source for a new patriotism; the development of militaristic Prussian nationalism as a vital resource in forging 19th-century German identity is a good example. We wait to see whether attempts to construct elaborate supranational governmental structures such as a more integrated EU will, in time, seek to harness a defensive mentality in relation to other countries or to external aggression, and the instillation of an 'us' and 'them' mentality. This has not been particularly evident hitherto, although the hardening of a Western, liberal, civic European identity in the face of Islamic extremism or even internal dissent may provide one analogous, and unfortunate, context for the development of a nascent European supranational identity.[41]

4.5 *International law and the pre-eminence of the state*

Moving beyond the EU arena, one of the consequences of a EUro-centric perspective is that we can overlook the fact that under international law the state still retains unrivalled privileges, and that a number of sub-state peoples

---

[40] It is also notable that post-war decolonization movements when they sought to centralize power were often unsuccessful. Many secessionist movements quickly developed resulting in bloody civil wars, and almost every post-colonial federation constructed in Asia, Africa, and the Caribbean before independence collapsed into their constituent ex-colonial parts soon afterwards. As Jackson notes: 'Societas Europe and not federalist America was the wave of the future almost everywhere in the world after 1945'. R. Jackson, *The Global Covenant: Human Conduct in a World of States* (Oxford: Oxford University Press, 2003) 346. It is certainly ironic that the one exception to this has been Europe itself.

[41] S. Tierney, 'Rights versus Democracy? The Bill of Rights in Plurinational States', in C. Harvey and A. Schwartz, (eds), *Bills of Rights in Divided Societies* (Oxford: Hart Publishing, 2012) 11–32.

aspire to join the club of states. Certainly the number of states is increasing, as we see in recent times with the emergence of Montenegro and the other recently established states mentioned earlier. It also seems to be getting easier to become a new state. Kosovo's apparently inevitable move to statehood may well set a precedent that was not anticipated by the tight rules on decolonization or by the *uti possidetis* rule as applied by the EC Guidelines on Recognition for the former Yugoslavia.[42] It remains to be seen how other territories will try to apply the Kosovo case in the making of sovereignty claims.

At the level of privileges we should not overlook the resilience of the external dimension of state sovereignty. States retain a monopoly of control on the law-making process within international law, and crucially, a monopoly also over the rules of membership. Very few new members of the club emerge without prior international authorization. New states have tended to have their access mediated through well-regulated channels of recognition, external oversight, etc. Even Kosovo enjoys authorization of sorts, by virtue of the delay in determining final status under Security Council Resolution 1244 which, by being overtaken by events on the ground, led in the end to a *fait accompli*, and one which the great powers could be said to have facilitated indirectly by their ambiguous attitude to Kosovan statehood since the draft Rambouillet Accord in 1999.

Another privilege is that states retain very high levels of autonomy in treaty-making. Much is made of the roles of new actors in law-making processes, but in fact states enjoy an overwhelming monopoly in these processes with the access of NGOs to such processes limited and highly attenuated.[43] Even when offered the highest levels of involvement—for example, within the drafting council that led to the Statute of the International Criminal Court (ICC)—NGOs still lacked any voting power. Even the EU treaty process largely follows the international principle of the sovereign equality of states. Also, non-state entities do not in general have personality before international tribunals, etc., and the state remains the only viable institution to which to ascribe responsibility; in other words, it is to the state and the state alone that actors must turn for the enforcement of international obligations.

It is also notable that the sovereignty of a particular state cannot be terminated. Its functional use may decline or elements of it be surrendered as they have in the EU, but the state's lawful competence cannot be forcibly removed. We see this when we reflect that although many new states have been created since 1945, very few have disappeared. Another way in which state existence is guaranteed is through prohibition of the use of force. It is very difficult for states to use force against other states without facing international opprobrium. Even when they seek to secure UN Security Council authorization this is difficult, as we saw ahead of the invasion of Iraq, and the level of criticism faced by the USA and UK over this conflict must surely act as a deterrent. Ironically it would seem that the Security Council has been strengthened through its refusal to endorse this action,

---

[42] J. Summers (ed.), *Kosovo and International Law* (Leiden: Martinus Nijhoff, 2011).

[43] A. Boyle and C. Chinkin, *The Making of International Law* (Oxford: Oxford University Press, 2007) 62–77, 93–97.

even though it went ahead anyway. This is another aspect of the growth of democratization. Just as it is more difficult to forge a nation internally by coercion, so too is it more difficult to forge internationalism of empire externally by conquest.

It should also be noted that although the government of Iraq was overthrown, Iraq itself has not disappeared. A term that has entered the international relations vocabulary in recent times is 'failed state'. But this is a misnomer; states do not fail, governments and institutions do. Indeed it is testimony to state resilience that pathological political situations in recent years that have overtaken Rwanda, Cote D'Ivoire, Liberia, etc., have not led to state collapse.

It is therefore important to restate that international law still massively prioritizes the state–nation nexus, and although individual human rights is expanding, the enforcement of these rights is highly variable from region to region, and in many respects still depends upon the filter of state consent.[44] We should also note how weakly international law protects minority rights both within Art 27 ICCPR which offers so many concessions to state power, and to the very general and non-prescriptive terms of specific instruments on minority rights. International law may become a greater focus for disgruntled minorities in the coming decades in attempts to go behind the veil of statehood, but for now the state and its dominant nation are the key players in the international arena. Indeed the lesson for minorities seems to be, become a state if you want international status, do not wait for either the end of statehood or international recognition of regional government.[45]

5. THE CHANGING FUNCTIONALISM OF THE NATION

The state is still with us and so is the nation, and it seems that each continues to feed on the vitality of the other. But this is also a complex, symbiotic, and mutually reinforcing relationship. Public law in its modernist functionalism as the resource that has managed and sustained this relationship is therefore more than alive. Insofar as the state's role is changing, and in some cases that role is diminishing as it is in Europe, public law is changing its environment. In other words, it is exercising the function of managing public power in new and diverse ways across multiple sites. In this sense it is analogous to energy in the natural world; it can change its state but does not disappear.

The bigger story is that we can be distracted by the tale of globalization and even of privatization. The state too is adapting to change as it always has. We are reminded of Carr's comment: 'We nod approvingly today when someone tells us that, whereas the State used to be merely policeman, judge, and protector, it has now become schoolmaster, doctor, house-builder, road-maker, town-planner, public utility supplier, and all the rest of it'.[46] Some of these functions change, but

---

[44] K. McCall Smith, 'Reservations to Human Rights Treaties', PhD thesis, University of Edinburgh, 2011.

[45] It is often noted for example that the weakness of EU Committee of the Regions leads sub-state nations to conclude there is no substitute for full membership which can only come with statehood.

[46] C. Carr, *Concerning English Administrative Law* (Oxford: Oxford University Press, 1941) 10–11.

the state today, even in Europe, retains functions considerably stronger than those exercised 100 years ago, including additional regulatory functions it did not exercise even in Carr's time. Some states are getting stronger; there is a renewed vitality in large states in particular.[47] So it should perhaps be no surprise that sub-state national groups recognize the inherent privileges states possess. Indeed, there is perhaps no stronger indication of the state's strength than the appetite among sub-state peoples to create new ones and the fact that once-created states rarely disappear.

In this sense, resilient too is the nation. National attachments remain strong. The past forty years has seen the re-emergence of nascent national identities and their consolidation, even as cultural markers of distinction seem to diminish. The key seems to be legitimacy, and in particular the democratic imperative which is also spreading at the same time as the world becomes more integrated. Economic forces may undermine some functions of the state, but it does remain the only vehicle that hosts popular government, and it is in this function, offering vernacular legitimacy for government, that the state retains its strength. Public law, which has been developed in such subtle ways over the past century, crafting institutions that both facilitate and restrain the popular will of the people, remains central to our understanding of the public space. The function of modern constitutionalism is to serve the democratic relationship between the state and the nation, and while both are with us as they assuredly still are, so too will be public law.

---

[47] '[O]ne expects an Asia-dominated international law to emphasize traditional concerns of sovereignty, non-interference, and mutual cooperation rather than the constitutionalist vision of supranational institutions reaching deep into the way states govern themselves and treat their own populations'. T. Ginsburg, 'Eastphalia as a Return to Westphalia' (2010) 17 Indiana Journal of Global Legal Studies 1.

9

Public Law, Private Law, and National Identity

Hector MacQueen*

As the conference whose proceedings are published in this volume took place in mid-June 2011 in the elegant rooms of Edinburgh University's Old College, outside an unseemly political spat had broken out over an alleged threat posed to the Scottish legal system by the Supreme Court of the United Kingdom, with leading figures in the newly re-elected Scottish Nationalist Party Government whipping up something of a media frenzy on the subject.

An important piece of context is that prior to devolution in 1999 there was no appeal in criminal matters in Scotland beyond the High Court of Justiciary sitting in Edinburgh as the Court of Criminal Appeal. That position had been substantially transformed by two things: first, the requirement placed by the Scotland Act 1998 upon the Scottish (then) Executive, including the Lord Advocate as the head of the criminal prosecution service,[1] to act in compliance with the European Convention on Human Rights; and, second, the conferral upon first the Privy Council and the House of Lords, then from October 2009 the Supreme Court, of the status of the final court of appeal in such 'devolution issues'.[2] The story immediately behind the June 2011 controversy, however, went back primarily to the Supreme Court's decision in the *Cadder* case, handed down on 26 October 2010,[3] that the Scottish legislation which allowed the prosecution to rely on confessions made by a suspect without access to legal advice during police interviews was contrary to that individual's right to a fair trial under Article 6 of the ECHR as authoritatively defined by the European Court on Human Rights in *Salduz v Turkey*.[4] In direct consequence of the Supreme Court decision, a significant legislative reform of Scots criminal procedure in the form of the Criminal Procedure (Legal Assistance, Detention and Appeals) (Scotland) Bill was instantly put through the Scottish

* The views expressed in this paper are entirely personal to the author and not to be attributed in any way to the Scottish Law Commission. He is grateful to John Cairns who, as ever, responded readily and kindly to an importunate request to read over and comment upon an earlier draft. The usual caveats however apply. Website references last checked at 28 February 2012 unless otherwise stated.

[1] Scotland Act 1998, ss. 44 and 57(3).

[2] Constitutional Reform Act 2005 s. 40, amending Scotland Act 1998 s. 98 and Schedule 6.

[3] *Cadder v Her Majesty's Advocate* [2010] UKSC 43; 2011 SC (UKSC) 13.

[4] *Salduz v Turkey* (2008) 49 EHRR 421. The relevant Scottish legislation at the time of *Cadder* was ss. 14 and 15 of the Criminal Procedure (Scotland) Act 1995 but in form it was introduced under the Criminal Justice (Scotland) Act 1980.

Parliament as an emergency measure on 27 October, receiving the Royal Assent just two days later.[5] Mr Kenny MacAskill, the Cabinet Secretary for Justice in the Scottish National Party (SNP) Government, also announced that the High Court judge Lord Carloway was to be asked to carry out a further general review of Scottish criminal procedure with two main objectives in mind: compliance with the ECHR and ensuring a fair balance between the interests of prosecution and defence. It was immediately clear that one of the major questions which Lord Carloway would have to address was the nearly unique requirement of corroboration in Scots criminal law; that is, the need in a criminal trial to have two independent sources of evidence to establish any fact relevant to a criminal charge. When his Lordship reported finally in November 2011, the abolition of the requirement was indeed one of his central recommendations.[6]

Lord Advocate Elish Angiolini expressed her anxieties at the course of events while giving evidence to a Scottish Parliamentary committee on 8 February 2011, when she said:

> My concern is that because of the Supreme Court's approach there is a real danger that we will have not just harmonisation of our criminal law on procedure and evidence, but indeed a complete loss of identity for Scots law unless the Supreme Court process is genuinely rarely exercised and takes place in the context of a matter that is of substantial constitutional significance across the United Kingdom or where there is a very new piece of jurisprudence that is clearly ambiguous.[7]

What really stoked the blaze, however, was a further decision of the Supreme Court in another Scottish case, *Fraser v Her Majesty's Advocate*, published on 25 May 2011.[8] Once again, the Court overturned the High Court of Justiciary in holding that Fraser's trial had not met the requirements of the ECHR, since the prosecution had failed to disclose relevant evidence to the accused, and accordingly his murder conviction fell to be quashed. Mr MacAskill, still the Cabinet Secretary for Justice, responded with the comment that 'Scotland's distinct legal system, including our criminal law, has served our country well for centuries, ensuring justice for victims while also protecting the rights of those accused of a crime. We believe the UK Supreme Court should have no role in matters of Scots criminal law—a view supported by Scotland's leading legal figures'.[9] He also suggested that the Scottish Government might withhold the funding contribution it was required to make to the Supreme Court budget.[10] The First Minister, Alex

---

[5] For the Bill's passage see the Scottish Parliament website at <http://www.scottish.parliament.uk/ parliamentarybusiness/Bills/22586.aspx>.

[6] See The Carloway Review: Report and Recommendations, accessible at <http://www.scotland.gov. uk/About/CarlowayReview>.

[7] Official Report of the Scottish Parliament Scotland Bill Committee, 8 February 2011, accessible at <http://www.scottish.parliament.uk/parliamentarybusiness/28862.aspx?r=6197>.

[8] *Fraser v Her Majesty's Advocate* [2011] UKSC 24; 2011 SC (UKSC) 113.

[9] BBC News Online 28 May 2011, <http://www.bbc.co.uk/news/uk-scotland-scotland-politics-13583705>.

[10] See *The Herald*, 31 May 2011, accessible at <http://www.heraldscotland.com/news/crime-courts/ macaskill-threat-to-end-supreme-court-funding-macaskill-threat-to-end-supreme-court-funding. 13900094>.

Salmond, perhaps still flushed with the extraordinary achievement of an outright majority for his party in the Scottish Parliament elections barely a month earlier, went even further when he allowed himself to say in an interview with the *Holyrood* magazine (published on 13 June):

> [W]hat needs to be addressed is the underlying issue—the principle that Scotland has, for hundreds of years, been a distinct criminal jurisdiction, and the High Court of Justiciary should be the final arbiter of criminal cases in Scotland, as was always the case. Before devolution, the House of Lords had no jurisdiction whatever in matters of Scots criminal law. The increasing involvement of the UK Supreme Court in second-guessing Scotland's highest criminal court of appeal is totally unsatisfactory, and creates additional delay and complexity which cannot serve the interests of justice.[11]

As ever with political controversy, it is necessary to read a little bit between and behind the lines of these statements in order to appreciate what was really at stake. While the SNP have long argued against the appeals from Scotland in civil matters which have been allowed since not long after the 1707 Union, and had indeed commissioned an independent expert report on alternatives to that system which was published early in 2010,[12] that subject was of little concern to anyone but lawyers, especially given the very small number of such civil appeals in any event. It was the distinct and possibly toxic link between the criminal law and enforceable human rights for those convicted of crime which underlay the populist appeal in the First Minister's remarks, as this further quotation from them makes clear:

> All I would say to Lord Hope [one of the Scottish Justices in the Supreme Court, who had given the leading opinions in both *Cadder* and *Fraser*] is that I probably know a wee bit about the legal system and he probably knows a wee bit about politics. [P]olitics and the law intertwine, and the political consequences of Lord Hope's judgements are extreme and when the citizens of Scotland understandably vent their fury about the prospect of some of the vilest people on the planet getting lots of money off the public purse, they don't go chapping at Lord Hope's door, they ask their parliament what they are doing about it.[13]

The fact that these alleged problems could be laid at the door of a court in London and, lurking even further abroad, the ECHR and the European Court of Human Rights thus helped to reinforce the overall SNP agenda of creating a climate of opinion in Scotland that would see independence as a way of escaping from this and other unpopular constraints upon Scottish political and legal processes.

The controversy also helped to create more specific pressure in relation to the Scotland Bill which some months earlier had begun to wend its way through parliamentary processes at both Westminster and Holyrood. The Bill was a United Kingdom measure amending the Scottish devolution settlement in ways

---

[11] *Holyrood Magazine*, No. 257, 13 June 2011 ('The Eck's Factor').

[12] Neil Walker, *Final Appellate Jurisdiction in the Scottish Legal System* (Scottish Government, 2010), accessible at <http://www.scotland.gov.uk/Resource/Doc/299388/0093334.pdf>.

[13] *Holyrood Magazine*, No. 257, 13 June 2011 ('The Eck's Factor'). For non-Scottophones, 'chapping' = 'knocking'.

which both expand and re-limit the powers of the Scottish Parliament and the Scottish Government (as the Executive was to be officially renamed), but the consent of the Scottish Parliament was required to allow the Bill to go forward. There was accordingly a clear opportunity for reconsideration of the position of the Lord Advocate's membership of the Executive/Government, which had given rise to the jurisdiction now enjoyed by the Supreme Court in Scottish criminal law. The matter was under active consideration even before the *Cadder* decision, and the Lord Advocate's comments in the Scottish Parliament already quoted were made in the setting of that discussion. In the event the pressure bore some fruit in that the Scotland Act 2012 (as the Bill became) now provides that the acts of the Lord Advocate as the head of the public prosecution service should indeed cease to be seen as subject to the 'devolution issues' jurisdiction of the Supreme Court. The Act then in effect takes back what it seems to have given away, however, by creating a new right of appeal to the Supreme Court in criminal cases in relation to issues of compatibility with not only the ECHR but also European Union law.[14] The consequences for Scots criminal law remain to be seen. But, for the moment the furore around the subject seems to have died down.[15]

All this, however interesting in itself, may seem somewhat removed both from the title of this contribution and from the concerns of this collection. Criminal law is certainly not seen today as part of private law, and while it may be part of public law, it is not the sort of public law with which the other contributors to this volume normally engage to any degree. But the criticism of the Supreme Court and the ECHR does at least show how issues about a country's law and legal system may become caught up with wider politics of national identity and self-determination. The idea that a particular system can be subordinated to external laws and courts in which that system has little direct voice, democratic or otherwise, has the potential to trigger strong defensive reactions, not only amongst lawyers in the system such as the apolitical Elish Angiolini, but also, more aggressively, by local nationalist politicians seeing the perceived invasions of independence as a way of swinging popular support behind their cause. One of the reasons for thinking that Scotland still exists three centuries after its union with England and the formation of the United Kingdom is that a fully fledged legal system still applies in the territory known as Scotland, different in various ways from its English counterpart, and with a history that (this time like English law) stretches back to the Middle Ages. The so-called 'stateless nation', it might be said, does indeed still possess in its legal system one of the major features of a state, enhancing the realism of claims to regain those other elements of statehood that may have gone missing since 1707.[16]

---

[14] See Scotland Act 2012, s. 36, amending s. 57(3) of the Scotland Act 1998 and inserting a new s 288AA (Appeals to the Supreme Court: compatibility issues) in the Criminal Procedure (Scotland) Act 1995.

[15] There will be a review of the new arrangements after three years of operation: see Scotland Office press release dated 21 March 2012: <http://www.scotlandoffice.gov.uk/scotlandoffice/16728.html>.

[16] For the 'stateless nation' see David McCrone, *Understanding Scotland: The Sociology of a Stateless Nation* (London: Routledge, 1992). The assumption that generally nation = state is a debatable one.

I. TO 1707

Law as a badge of national identity and independence in Scotland goes back to at least the 12th century, when it was part of the kingdom's claim to be free of rule from England.[17] A remarkable feature of this, however, is that the claim was made, not only in the secular context of the relationship between the King of Scots and the King of England, but also in the ecclesiastical world where the Scottish Church, lacking any archbishopric, nevertheless sought to be free from the overarching jurisdictional claims made by Canterbury and York. From 1192 on, a series of papal bulls recognized the *ecclesia Scoticana* as a 'special daughter', subject only to the Pope himself, and as a consequence of that relationship drew the conclusion that disputes arising in Scotland to which the canon law applied should be decided only within the kingdom by Scots or by papal appointees, subject only to the ultimate right of appeal to the papal courts in Rome. The principle appears to have applied throughout the 13th and later centuries until the severance of papal jurisdiction at the Reformation in 1560.

Towards the end of the 13th century, the principle that Scottish cases should be decided in Scotland also emerged as politically significant in the run-up to the wars of independence from England which finally began in earnest in 1306. So the 1290 Treaty of Birgham, which anticipated a possible Anglo-Scottish union following the planned marriage of Margaret, the child queen of Scots, to the male heir of King Edward I of England, provided for the preservation of 'the rights, laws, liberties and customs of the realm of Scotland . . . throughout the said realm and its borders', and declared that

> . . . no-one of the realm of Scotland by reason of any contract entered into or any offence committed in that realm, or in any case, shall be obliged to answer for this outwith the same realm, contrary to the laws and customs of the same realm, as has been reasonably observed down to the present. . . .[18]

Following the failure of this treaty through the death of Queen Margaret, and the 1296 deposition of her successor (King John Balliol) by Edward I, one of the ways through which English sovereignty was then asserted over Scotland was by allowing Scottish appeals to be heard at Westminster, and indeed for Edward to begin to contemplate exercising authority to make changes to Scottish laws and customs as he had already done in Wales.[19] This undermining of Scottish sovereignty was clearly an important element in the outbreak of the wars of independence in 1296, even if it is also clear that at the time many Scots were more than happy to accept a new status quo. In 1320 an early draft of what became the Declaration of Arbroath referred to the 'ancestral laws' of the kingdom alongside freedom as the objectives of the Scottish struggle with the English,

[17] For what follows see Hector L. MacQueen, '*Regiam Majestatem*, Scots Law and National Identity' (1995) 74 Scottish Historical Review 1.

[18] For the translation of the text of the Treaty of Birgham here quoted see Geoffrey W. S. Barrow, 'A Kingdom in Crisis: Scotland and the Maid of Norway' (1990) 69 Scottish Historical Review 120, appendix.

[19] See MacQueen, '*Regiam Majestatem*', 4–5.

while in the text finally sent to the Pope it was said that Robert Bruce had become king of Scots by virtue of 'his right of succession according to our laws and customs which we will defend till death'.[20]

The theme of maintaining the separateness of Scots law and the exclusive jurisdiction of Scottish courts persisted throughout the next four centuries whenever peaceful Anglo-Scottish union came under discussion, and forms an interesting background to the provisions of the 1707 Union on the subject. So, for example, in 1363, proposals for a union of Scotland and England, based on the succession to the then childless king of Scots, David II, of a member of the English royal house, echoed the Treaty of Birgham in providing that such a king would 'maintain the laws, statutes and customs of the kingdom of Scotland as established under the good kings of Scotland of the past', while 'in no way' would he 'summon or constrain the people of Scotland to compear in England or elsewhere outwith where they ought'.[21] The proposals were, however, rejected by the Scots. Nearly 200 years later, in 1542, another attempt at a negotiated Anglo-Scottish union was made following the death of King James V, leaving only his six-day-old daughter Mary to succeed him; but, as John Ford has pointed out, the Scottish stance in these negotiations was explicitly based upon the continuation of a separate Scots law and court structure 'without any appeal, reclaiming or seeking any remedy of law against the court outside the realm of Scotland'.[22] Dr Ford goes on to observe:

> [T]his stance was maintained with impressive consistency in all the policy state-
> ments issued by the Scots during the next century and a half. The insistence that
> the separate laws and judicial system of Scotland be preserved was reiterated in
> broadly similar terms in the negotiations that followed the Jacobean union in 1604,
> the Cromwellian conquest in 1652, and the Caroline trade dispute in 1669....[23]

But, as Dr Ford then notes, when it came to the negotiation preceding the 1707 Union (which, of course, was, unlike all its predecessors, a success in that agreement was reached, implemented, and has endured, albeit with modification along the way virtually from the outset), this long-established stance on Scots law and its legal system was adjusted in significant ways which introduced to the language of the discourse the distinction between public and private law.

We will turn to the detail of these adjustments shortly. But before we do so, it is worth dwelling for a moment or two more on some other aspects of the relationship between law and national identity in pre-Union Scotland. One element of this was that the authority of secular law rested ultimately on the authority

---

[20] See James Fergusson, *The Declaration of Arbroath* (Edinburgh, 1970), 8–9, 33, 52 note, 77.

[21] Thomas Thomson and Cosmo Innes (eds), *Acts of the Parliaments of Scotland*, vol. 1 (Edinburgh, 1875), 493 (translated from the original French). See also Archibald A. M. Duncan, 'A Question about the Succession, 1364', in *Miscellany XII* (Edinburgh: Scottish History Society, 1994) 1–57.

[22] See generally John D. Ford, 'Four Models of Union' (2011) Juridical Review 45, at 46–51. The quotation, the language of which I have modernized, may be found in *Records of the Parliaments of Scotland* (henceforth RPS, accessible at <http://www.rps.ac.uk>), 1543/3/12.

[23] Ford, 'Four Models', 56. See further on the different negotiations mentioned John D. Ford, 'The Legal Provisions in the Acts of Union' (2007) 66 Cambridge Law Journal 106, at 109, and literature there cited.

of the king. It applied in the territory that the king ruled; the king made law in the kingdom, and there was law about where one king's territory marched with that of another, as on the Anglo-Scottish border.[24] It is also true, as suggested by the medieval sources already quoted, that a perception of law as the customs of the people of the kingdom was an important further dimension of the pre-modern link between law and national identity.[25] But the role of a people in law-making was never defined in such a way as to prevail over that of the king. It was he who made statutes, albeit with their consent and advice, and while these statutes might fall into desuetude, it was certainly possible for statute to abolish custom, at least where it was unreasonable in nature. And the radical suggestion in the Declaration of Arbroath that, as the people put the king in place, so they could also unseat him if he failed to rule justly, does not really gain much support from other Scottish legal sources before the 1707 Union.[26] Scots lawyers of the early modern period seem to have seen the courts as the guardians and declarers of custom, who in carrying out this function made more use of the learned laws and their own previous decisions than of any investigation of how people generally behaved.[27]

There was nothing particularly unusual in any of these Scottish ideas, in either a British or a wider European context. The late Rees Davies wrote of medieval Wales that law 'could be cultivated as a bastion of national independence against the outsider'.[28] So in the Anglo-Welsh Treaty of Aberconwy in 1277, for example, it was provided that disputes arising in Wales should be decided according to the laws of Wales, implicitly rejecting the now possible alternative that English law and English jurisdiction should apply instead.[29] In a converse application of the same principle, the English conquerors of Ireland and Wales insisted that English law applied to the English and those of English descent in those lands, while the native Irish and Welsh were confined to their own laws—the exceptions of Irishry and Welshry.[30] Welsh legal nationalism met its English counterpart in 1279, when Llywelyn the prince of Wales argued that he should continue to 'have his own Welsh law', despite his submission to the king of England and his courts;

---

[24] For details see MacQueen, '*Regiam Majestatem*', 5–6, 7–8, 9–13.

[25] See further on this and the following sentences John W. Cairns, T. David Fergus, and Hector L. MacQueen, 'Legal Humanism and the History of Scots Law', in John MacQueen (ed.), *Humanism in Renaissance Scotland* (Edinburgh: Edinburgh University Press 1990) 48–74 at 60–66.

[26] Prominent amongst the non-lawyers in the 16th century are John Mair and George Buchanan. See further Roger A. Mason (ed.), *A Dialogue on the Law of Kingship among the Scots: a critical edition and translation of George Buchanan's 'De Iure Regni apud Scotos Dialogus'* (Farnham: Ashgate, 2004).

[27] See generally John D. Ford, *Law and Opinion in Scotland during the Seventeenth Century* (Oxford: Hart Publishing, 2007).

[28] R. Rees Davies, 'Law and National Identity in Thirteenth-century Wales', in R. Rees Davies et al. (eds), *Welsh Society and Nationhood* (Cardiff, 1984), 51–69 at 57. See also R. Rees Davies, 'The Peoples of Britain and Ireland 1100–1400 III. Laws and Customs' (1996) 6 (6th series) *Transactions of the Royal Historical Society* 1–23.

[29] Davies, 'Law and National Identity', 59.

[30] Davies, 'Peoples of Britain', 3–6. See too the Irish case of 1297 in which Henry the Scot's action under English law was held competent because although born in Scotland, he was English (probably meaning that English was his mother tongue), and he and his predecessors had used English law: Geoffrey W. S. Barrow, *The Anglo-Norman Era in Scottish History* (Oxford: Clarendon Press, 1980), 119, 146.

to which it was replied that cases in the king's court were 'governed...in accordance with a single common law and...proceed in that same court in accordance with the same law and not by diverse and mutually contradictory laws in one and the same court'.[31] In her work on *Kingdoms and Communities in Western Europe, 900–1300*, Susan Reynolds has concluded: 'In medieval terms, it was the fact of being a kingdom...and of sharing a single law and government which promoted a sense of solidarity among its subjects and made them describe themselves as a people'.[32] John Kelly notes how the growing claims of the Papacy and the church to a form of universal rule after 1100 prompted almost in reaction the growth of more assertive secular states under their monarchs, leading ultimately to recognition of the mutual sovereignty of kings, in which 'the king is now seen as not merely sovereign vis-à-vis the other potentates within his kingdom, but sovereign also in the sense of being immune from the jurisdiction of all other kings'.[33] The Scottish insistence on the link between its own sovereignty and the independent jurisdiction of its own courts thus fits well into this developing European theme.

Of course the sovereign claims of kings had also to be reconciled with the universalist ones of the papacy and the church courts, but boundaries between these separate jurisdictions were already being drawn in the 13th century. At least in Scotland and England, they were largely determined by secular authority, with the limits of ecclesiastical jurisdiction being defined and enforced by way of royal prohibitions, for example, against the church courts taking cases about lay landholdings. In general terms, the jurisdictional division made between church and kingdom in Scotland persisted until the Reformation, and certainly in later medieval Scotland there is little sign of any continuing controversy over where these dividing lines were drawn. The major exception was with regard to the ultimate appeal to the papal *curia* in ecclesiastical cases, with several 15th-century statutes seeking to restrict resort to Rome.[34] But this seems to have been because the process was seen as a significant drain on the country's wealth rather than as an undermining of the law administered in Scotland. I have argued elsewhere that from the perspective of later medieval Scottish royal government, the coexisting ecclesiastical and secular jurisdictions were treated as an integrated system of which the king was ultimately in charge for the most part.[35] The eventual abolition of papal jurisdiction was effected in the end by parliamentary

---

[31] See Davies, 'Peoples of Britain', 1–2; Michael T. Clanchy, *England and its Rulers 1066–1307*, 3rd edn (Oxford: Blackwell Publishing, 2006), 303.

[32] Susan Reynolds, *Kingdoms and Communities in Western Europe, 900–1300*, 2nd edn (Oxford: Oxford University Press, 1997), 253. See also Alan Harding, *Medieval Law and the Foundations of the State* (Oxford: Oxford University Press, 2002).

[33] John M. Kelly, *A Short History of Western Legal Theory* (Oxford: Oxford University Press, 1992), 127.

[34] For statutes against 'barratry' see RPS 1428/3/10, 1471/5/4, 1484/3/41, 1488/10/49–50, A1493/5/3–10, A1496/6/3. For enforcement of the statutes see Hector MacQueen, 'The King's Council and Church Courts in Later Medieval Scotland', in Harry Dorndorp et al. (eds), *Ius Romanum, Ius Commune, Ius Hodiernum: Studies in Honour of Eltjo J H Schrage on the Occasion of his 65th Birthday* (Amsterdam & Aalen: Scientia Verlag, 2010), 277–87 at 281.

[35] See generally MacQueen, 'King's Council and Church Courts'.

legislation in Scotland:[36] the ultimate assertion of the secular authority to determine the courts and law to be applied within the territory under its sway.

One further issue merits comment. Even by the 15th century, English lawyers were accustomed to distinguishing the law they practised—the common law—from the civil law; that is, the law of the Holy Roman Empire and other Continental kingdoms such as France, which was based upon the Roman law of Justinian's *Digest, Codex,* and *Institutes.* Moreover, English lawyers did this with considerable pride in the common law as the better of the two systems.[37] In Scotland, by contrast with England, lawyers had been accustomed to drawing upon the civil law as taught in the medieval universities of Europe to shape, understand, and fill gaps in their more native sources.[38] When in 1603 King James VI of Scotland inherited the English Crown as well, and began to promote the idea of a union of the laws of his two kingdoms, many English lawyers expressed their fears that this might eventually amount to a civil law take-over, just as the Scots worried (with rather more justification) that the union of laws would mean the extension of English law into Scotland, with Scots law downgraded at best to the level of a local custom, and at worst extinguished altogether like Welsh law. Neither concern materialized as James' great project proved abortive in the face of practical difficulty as well as lawyers' hostility, but a perception that the two laws were different in some fundamental ways had settled in, and was not wholly offset by the discovery that historically there had once been common ground between the systems, in particular in relation to the feudal land law.[39]

The last issue apart, everything discussed so far looks more like public than private law in its concerns, in that they all relate pre-eminently to the emerging medieval and early modern state, its governance structures, and its powers over the inhabitants of its territory. In this picture, private law is largely incidental, inasmuch as disputes between the king's subjects are to be dealt with in the king's courts and under the king's laws, save where they fall under the jurisdiction of the church and the canon law. Little if any reference is made to a distinction between public and private law in Scottish legal sources before 1707, and there is no sign at all that the distinction was of any consequence in the link between

[36] RPS, A1560/8/4.

[37] See in particular Shelley Lockwood (ed.), *Sir John Fortescue On the Laws and Governance of England* (Cambridge: Cambridge University Press, 1997), 27 ('Hence there is no gainsaying nor legitimate doubt but that the customs of the English are not only good but the best'). Fortescue wrote this between 1468 and 1471.

[38] See further on this Gero Dolezalek, *Scotland under* Jus Commune (Edinburgh: Stair Society vols 55–57, 2010).

[39] For the foregoing see Brian P. Levack, *The Formation of the British State: England, Scotland, and the Union, 1603–1707* (Oxford: Oxford University Press, 1987); see further Hector L. MacQueen, 'Glanvill Resarcinate: Sir John Skene and *Regiam Majestatem*', in Alasdair MacDonald et al. (eds), *The Renaissance in Scotland: Studies in Literature, Religion, History and Culture Offered to John Durkan* (London, New York, and Köln: E J Brill, 1994), 385–403.

national identity and law in general.[40] Again, Scotland seems to reflect a European picture.[41]

2. THE 1707 UNION: PUBLIC AND PRIVATE RIGHTS

Only in Article XVIII of the Union Agreement of 1707 does the public/private distinction in law begin to manifest itself, with the idea that 'public right' is henceforth malleable to make it the same throughout the new United Kingdom, whereas 'private rights' are to be changed only where that is for the 'evident utility of the subjects within Scotland'.[42] There was also a vital contrast here with the traditional Scottish position in discussions of union with England where, as we have seen, the preservation of Scots law as it stood had always previously been a non-negotiable point. Now change to the law was envisaged, with public law apparently more susceptible to alteration than private law; indeed, the Article itself authorized immediate Anglicization in that 'the Laws concerning Regulation of Trade, Customs, and . . . Excises . . . [was to] be the same in Scotland, from and after the Union as in England'.

As Professor Cairns and Dr Ford independently and more or less simultaneously pointed out at the time of the Union's tercentenary, the concepts of public and private right deployed in Article XVIII emerged from the Scottish side of the negotiation process, and were clearly drawn from the Roman law distinction between public and private law.[43] The concept of evident utility likewise had a Roman law root. Professor Cairns summarizes the evidence thus:

---

[40] Although see Brian P. Levack, 'Law, Sovereignty and the Union', in Roger A. Mason (ed.), *Scots and Britons: Scottish Political Thought and the Union of 1603* (Cambridge: Cambridge University Press, 1994), 213–37, discussing the political thought of the lawyers Thomas Craig (1538–1608) and John Russell (died 1613). Stair briefly refers to a distinction between public and private rights: *Institutions of the Law of Scotland* (1st edn 1681; 2nd edn 1693), I, 1, 23.

[41] Jean Domat (1625–1696) appears to have been the first leading European jurist to make significant use of the public/private law distinction. There is no reference to any discussion of the distinction in Kelly, *Western Legal Theory*; Harold J. Berman, *Law and Revolution: The Formation of the Western Legal Tradition* (Cambridge, Mass.: Harvard University Press, 1983); Manlio Bellomo (trans. Lydia G. Cochrane), *The Common Legal Past of Europe 1000–1800* (Washington DC: Catholic University Press of America, 1995); Olivia Robinson, David Fergus, and William Gordon, *European Legal History*, 3rd edn (London: Butterworths, 2000); or Randall Lesaffer, *European Legal History* (Cambridge: Cambridge University Press, 2009). Even those legal historians who produce histories of private law in Europe seem not to define their subject-matter or trace the history of the concept itself in any precise way: see, eg, Franz Wieacker (trans Tony Weir), *A History of Private Law in Europe* (Oxford: Clarendon Press, 1995); Raoul C. van Caenegem, *An Historical Introduction to Private Law* (Cambridge: Cambridge University Press, 1990); James Gordley, *Foundations of Private Law: Property, Tort, Contract, Unjust Enrichment* (Oxford: Oxford University Press, 2006). An interesting discussion of private law in history is found in Charles Donahue, Jr, 'Private Law Without the State and During its Formation' (2008) 56 American Journal of Comparative Law 541.

[42] The Union Agreement is here used as a verbal formula to embrace the Treaty of Union and the Acts of Union by which each Parliament involved gave effect to the Treaty. The text of the Scottish Act of Parliament may be consulted in RPS, 1706/10/257.

[43] John W. Cairns, 'The Origins of the Edinburgh Law School: the Union of 1707 and the Regius Chair' (2007) 11 Edinburgh Law Review 300 at 315–16; Ford, 'Legal Provisions', 117.

Near the beginning of the *Digest*, an extract from Ulpian's *Institutes* (D 1.1.1.2) states: 'There are two branches of legal study: public and private law.' The standard modern translation continues: 'Public law [*publicum ius*] is that which respects the establishment of the Roman commonwealth, private [*privatum ius*] that which respects individuals' interests, some matters being of public others of private interest.' The Latin '*publicum ius*' and '*privatum ius*' could as readily be translated 'public right' and 'private right', as in the Article of Union. 'Interest' and 'interests' are translations of the Latin '*utilitatis*' and '*utilia*' . . . In the slightly later title of the *digest* 'On Enactments by Emperors', the following passage occurs, again taken from Ulpian, this time from his work on *Fideicommissa* (D 1.4.2): 'In determining matters anew, there ought to be some clear evident utility [*evidens utilitas*], so as to justify departing from a rule of law which has seemed fair from time immemorial.' Thus the text (the standard translation is adapted slightly) was to the effect that the statutory reforms should only be for the evident utility of the citizenry.[44]

That the distinction was drawn from Roman law did not mean that its effects were completely clear to contemporaries, however. As Dr Ford shows, it was disputed amongst the Scots whether or not criminal law fell within the scope of private law.[45] The doubt may not have been altogether removed by the passage of the Treason Act at Westminster in 1708, in effect making the previous English law also the law in Scotland, since this may have been necessary primarily because the Union had created a single Crown for the newly united kingdom; that is, the Act related to public law in a necessarily criminal aspect of the subject. Likewise the passage of a Copyright Act in 1709–10 to apply throughout the United Kingdom (the Statute of Anne) may well have been seen as an aspect of public rather than private law, since the rights concerned were similar to patents; that is, essentially grants from the Crown which, even although made to individuals, were primarily for public rather than private benefit.[46]

The effect of the public/private distinction drawn in the 1707 Union was to make public right much more a matter for the United Kingdom as a whole, while private right, or private law, remained as it had been before the Union, and although changeable by Parliament, only against the yardstick of 'evident utility'. The contrast here with public right certainly meant that the law of private rights was not simply to be made the same on each side of the former border as a necessary corollary of the union. When Article XVIII was debated in the Scottish Parliament in October 1706, 'evident utility' seems to have been understood as making change to private rights unlikely or difficult to achieve, even although the text of the Article left unclear how the hands of the new United Kingdom Parliament could be kept tied should there be a desire to test the scope of the concept in any way.[47] Thus, private law, whatever it might be, was associated

[44] Cairns, 'Origins', 315–16 (references omitted).

[45] Ford, 'Legal Provisions', 108.

[46] See Hector L. MacQueen, 'Intellectual Property and the Common Law in Scotland c1700–c1850', in Catherine W. Ng et al., *The Common Law of Intellectual Property: Essays in Honour of Professor David Vaver* (Oxford: Hart Publishing, 2010) 21–43 at 22–23.

[47] Cairns, 'Origins', 314.

with continuing Scottish distinctiveness inside the Union from the outset. The same thinking could of course be applied on the other side of the border to English private law; but it may have mattered more to the Scots, and there seems never to have been any perception on either side in the run-up to 1707 that English law needed any explicit protection from the consequences of Union. Why that was so, in contrast to the anxieties that had existed in 1603, has been very well explained by Dr Ford.[48]

Professor Cairns has also lucidly explained how Article XVIII linked to the creation of a chair of Public Law and the Law of Nature and Nations at Edinburgh University in 1707, and the idea of *ius publicum* which underlay that project, connected to natural law thought and the study of the conduct of government on grounds of utility and public interest. This too could be tied in with the 'evident utility' which alone would allow change in private law.[49] The concepts of public and private law were also taken up by post-Union writers on Scots law, whose focus was however the private rather than the public.[50] William Forbes' *Institutes of the Law of Scotland* (1722–1730) was divided into two volumes, the first according to its title page dealing with private law, the second with criminal law, which Forbes saw as part of public law.[51] Private law consisted of 'Matters respecting mainly the Interests and Differences of particular Persons among themselves'. Forbes structured his account of private law around what he called its 'Objects', described as persons, their estates, and how these were acquired, extinguished, burdened, transmitted, and passed on to others, and, finally, the determination of civil disputes on these matters; that is, in essence, the Roman institutional framework of persons, things, and actions. Perhaps most crucial, however, was that this was the law about relations between people and their property within Scotland. Forbes' unpublished and never completed *Great Body of the Law of Scotland* also had separate parts devoted to private law and criminal law; these are followed, however, by a third part headed 'Comprehending the Publick Law', covering not only the Crown, Parliament, Offices of State and taxation, but also matters of commerce, things serving public uses (for

---

[48] Ford, 'Legal Articles', 116–18.

[49] Cairns, 'Origins', 317–26. See also John W. Cairns, 'Natural Law, National Laws, Parliaments and Multiple Monarchies: 1707 and Beyond', in Knud Haakonssen and Henrik Horstbøll (eds), *Northern Antiquities and National Identities* (Copenhagen: Royal Danish Academy of Sciences and Letters, 2007), 88–112.

[50] In addition to the writers cited below, see Alexander Bayne, *Notes for the Use of Students of the Municipal Law of Scotland* (Edinburgh, 1731), Title I para 2: 'Distributive justice is the Object of the Publick Law, commutative of the Private'. Bayne was the first professor of Scots law in the University of Edinburgh. His book consists of notes loosely connected to his lecture textbook, Sir George Mackenzie's *Institutions of the Laws of Scotland* (first published in Edinburgh in 1684, last edition 1758), which however makes no reference to the public/private law distinction.

[51] A reprint of this work, with an introduction by the present writer, appeared at the end of 2012: William Forbes, *The Institutes of the Law of Scotland* (Edinburgh: Edinburgh Legal Education Trust, 2012). On Forbes see John W. Cairns, 'The Origins of the Glasgow Law School: the Professors of Civil Law, 1714–61', in Peter Birks (ed.), *The Life of the Law: Proceedings of the Tenth British Legal History Conference Oxford 1991* (London: The Hambledon Press, 1993), 151–94 at 155–83.

example, bridges and harbours), and, finally, the courts themselves, ecclesiastical and temporal, as well as 'the order of judicial proceedings'.[52]

Lord Bankton's mid-18th-century *Institute* (1751) referred directly to the Treaty of Union in dividing the law between private and public right; for him, too, criminal law was part of public law save in so far as a crime might also found an action of damages by the aggrieved party.[53] Still later in the 18th century John Erskine, Professor of Scots Law at Edinburgh University, saw 'trade and manufactures' along with criminal law and 'police' as falling in under the banner of public law, 'which hath more immediately in view the public weal, and the preservation and good order of society'; whereas private law was 'that which is chiefly intended for ascertaining the civil rights of individuals'.[54] Again, the essentially domestic character of private law as the law operating between persons in Scotland and governing their property there comes through clearly. But by the beginning of the 19th century, the public/private law distinction had dropped out of use as a way of organizing general accounts of Scots law: it is not found in the lectures of Baron David Hume, Erskine's successor but one in the Edinburgh chair between 1786 and 1822,[55] or in the *Principles* or *Commentaries* of Hume's immediate successor, George Joseph Bell, who occupied the position until 1838 and focused most on what he called mercantile jurisprudence.[56]

In contrast to Article XVIII's departure from previous intransigence on the possibility of changing Scots law in the context of an Anglo-Scottish union, Article XIX of the 1707 Union at least appeared to continue another old theme by expressly preserving 'in all time coming' the Scottish civil and criminal court system, and declaring:

> that no Causes in Scotland be cognoscible by the Courts of Chancery, Queens-Bench, Common-Pleas, or any other Court in Westminster-hall; and that the said Courts, or any other of the like Nature, after the Union, shall have no Power to cognosce, review, or alter the Acts or Sentences of the Judicatures within Scotland, or stop the Execution of the same.

So as with private law, the court system could become part of Scotland continuing within the Union, a badge of identity which none the less performed a real function in the polity, and so was (and is) something more than a mere symbolic survival from the past. For some contemporaries, as Dr Ford has pointed out, there was a

---

[52] Forbes' *Great Body of the Law of Scotland* is accessible as a manuscript in Glasgow University Library and available at <http://www.forbes.gla.ac.uk/>.

[53] Andrew McDouall, Lord Bankton, *An Institute of the Laws of Scotland* (Edinburgh, 1751), I, i, 54–58 (also available in a reprint as vols 41–43 in the Stair Society series, edited with an introduction by William M. Gordon). See further Andrew R. C. Simpson, 'Learning, Honour and Patronage: the Career of Andrew McDouall, Lord Bankton 1746–61', in Hector L. MacQueen (ed.), *Miscellany VI* (Edinburgh: Stair Society vol. 54, 2009), 121–219.

[54] John Erskine, *An Institute of the Law of Scotland* (Edinburgh, 1773), I, i, 29.

[55] G. Campbell H. Paton (ed.), *Baron David Hume's Lectures 1786–1822* (6 vols, Edinburgh: Stair Society, 1939–58).

[56] On Bell see now Kenneth G. C. Reid, 'From Text-Book to Book of Authority: The *Principles* of George Joseph Bell' (2011) 15 Edinburgh Law Review 6.

vital link between the exclusive jurisdiction of the Scottish courts and the immunity of private law under Article XVIII to change except on grounds of evident utility, since the judicial power to develop the law would leave little or no need for legislative intervention from Westminster.[57] Bankton saw the chief focus of his *Institute* as the law on private rights as 'cognoscible before the court of session'.[58] But by silence, most probably deliberate, Article XIX also left a chink through which innovation could slip to deprive the courts of some of their independence. Nothing was said on the question of appeals from the Scottish courts to the new United Kingdom Parliament, and within a very short time after the Union came into effect on 1 May 1707 the House of Lords assumed the appellate jurisdiction in civil matters which has continued down to the present day, albeit now in the form of appeals to the UK Supreme Court.[59] So here too the 1707 Union actually saw a shift in a traditional Scots negotiating stance, tempering the claim to a wholly separate court system which had for so long underpinned assertions of Scottish sovereignty. On the other hand, a criminal appeal to the House of Lords was ultimately rejected, so in this way the criminal courts and the criminal law remained independent in a way that their civil counterparts did not.[60]

The crucial point of all this is that after 1707 the courts, private law, and also criminal law became significant reminders that Scotland still retained a distinct identity within the United Kingdom. Each continued to operate in a largely self-contained way, albeit to varying degrees in each case. They were bolstered by the continuing existence of a distinct and largely self-regulating legal profession which itself further required a distinct system of legal education and training as well as its own books, case reports, and, in due course, journals and professional periodicals. The system was further serviced by wholly Scottish institutions such as the land and other public registers. Private law in particular lay at the core of ordinary legal practice and thus contributed an element—mostly practical, mundane, and everyday, but none the less important for that—to the reality of Scottish 'civic autonomy' and its 'banal nationalism'.[61] Whig writers and commentators might criticize the backward feudalism of Scots law and be interested in the Union with England as a means toward modernization,[62] but they still

---

[57] Ford, 'Legal Articles', 138.

[58] *Institute* I, i, 58.

[59] See generally A. John MacLean, 'The 1707 Union: Scots law and the House of Lords' (1983) 4 Journal of Legal History 50; Richard S. Tompson, 'James Greenshields and the House of Lords: a reappraisal', in William M. Gordon and T. David Fergus (eds), *Legal History in the Making* (London, 1991), 109–24; John D. Ford, 'Protestations to Parliament for Remeid of Law' (2009) 88 Scottish Historical Review 57; John Finlay, 'Scots Lawyers and House of Lords Appeals in Eighteenth-century Britain' (2011) 32 Journal of Legal History 249.

[60] A. John MacLean, 'The House of Lords and Appeals from the High Court of Justiciary, 1707–1887', (1985) Juridical Review 192.

[61] 'Civic autonomy' is a key idea in Lindsay Paterson's important study, *The Autonomy of Modern Scotland* (Edinburgh: Edinburgh University Press, 1994), while 'banal nationalism', a nationalism that is low-key because unthreatened, is the coinage of Michael Billig, *Banal Nationalism* (London: Sage, 1995).

[62] See Colin Kidd, *Union and Unionisms: Political Thought in Scotland 1500–2000* (Cambridge: Cambridge University Press, 2008), 178–90; see also the same author's *Subverting Scotland's Past* (Cambridge: Cambridge University Press, 1993).

tended to see the work needed as something for the Scots to do for themselves.[63] Lord Kames (1696–1782), one of the judges, certainly thought that much could be achieved through the exercise of the equitable powers of the Court of Session.[64] Even after the control of 'evident utility' had been forgotten and the Westminster Parliament began in the 19th century to legislate about Scots private law, for example on marriage and key areas supporting the private law of property and obligations, such as conveyancing, debt enforcement, and bankruptcy, it was done, not in a spirit of creating uniformity throughout the United Kingdom, but with Scotland-only enactments.[65] Legislative reform of the courts also began in the 19th century, but with the exception of the introduction of civil jury trials in certain classes of case in 1815, the changes were again more measures from within than outright Anglicization.[66]

Public law beyond the criminal law could not be seen as wholly un-Scottish; for example, local government continued to be Scottish rather than determined along British or English lines,[67] while the constitutional question of the relationship between church and state in Scotland would be a fundamental issue dividing Scottish society throughout the 19th and into the 20th century.[68] The emergence of a Secretary for Scotland as a UK Government post in 1885 (to become a Secretary of State in 1926) was also important recognition that the governance of Scotland could not be completely subsumed within an overall United Kingdom structure. But other great matters of state by and large fell to be played out elsewhere than in Scotland or the Scottish courts, and the big books on the subject were mostly written and published south of the border, only rarely considering the Scottish dimension or indeed the Union of 1707 unless to dismiss it or minimize its significance. Dicey's characterization of the Union as merely another statute which the Westminster Parliament could amend or repeal in the simple exercise of its own absolute sovereignty is the best-known example.[69] The structure of the curriculum in the Scottish law faculties may also have helped to

---

[63] See John W. Cairns, 'Scottish Law, Scottish Lawyers and the Status of the Union', in John Robertson (ed.), *A Union for Empire: the Union of 1707 in British Political Thought* (Cambridge: Cambridge University Press, 1995), 243–68; MacQueen, '*Regiam Majestatem*', 19–24.

[64] This is the theme of his major work, *Principles of Equity*, first published in 1760 and reworked by him in further editions published in 1767 and 1778. There were two further posthumous editions. See further Andreas Rahmatian, 'Introduction: Lord Kames and his *Principles of Equity*' in a facsimile reprint of the 3rd edn published by The Lawbook Exchange, Clark, New Jersey, USA, 2011.

[65] David M. Walker, *A Legal History of Scotland Volume VI: The Nineteenth Century* (London: Butterworths LexisNexis, 2001), chs 19, 20, and 30.

[66] See Nicholas T. Phillipson, *The Scottish Whigs and the Court of Session 1785–1830* (Edinburgh: Stair Society, vol. 37, 1990); David Parratt, *The Development and Use of Written Pleadings in Scots Civil Procedure* (Edinburgh: Stair Society, vol. 48, 2006).

[67] See Anne E. Whetstone, *Scottish County Government in the Eighteenth and Nineteenth Centuries* (Edinburgh: John Donald, 1981).

[68] Lord Rodger of Earlsferry, *The Courts, the Church and the Constitution: Aspects of the Disruption of 1843* (Edinburgh: Edinburgh University Press, 2008).

[69] Albert Venn Dicey, *Introduction to the Study of the Law of the Constitution* (1st edn, 1885; 10th edn, 1959), ch 1. See also Albert Venn Dicey and Robert S. Rait, *Thoughts on the Union between England and Scotland* (London: Macmillan & Co Ltd, 1920).

diminish perceptions of Scottishness in public law. The course taught as Scots Law covered private law topics and criminal law (where that was not a separate subject). Public Law, in the guise of Constitutional History, was a distinct course, with a remit clearly not limited to Scotland. The same might also have been said, it should be pointed out, of the course on Mercantile (that is, commercial) Law (although presumably the Scottishness of the course of Conveyancing went without anyone having to say so). The Edinburgh Chair of Public Law and the Law of Nature and Nations meanwhile became more associated with general jurisprudence and international law than with public law per se.[70]

The distinctiveness of substantive private law did however begin to come under challenge in some respects as the 19th century progressed.[71] Perhaps for this reason Scots lawyers did take a serious interest in the German historical school of jurisprudence studies most associated with the name of Friedrich-Karl von Savigny, who argued that there was a deep connection between a country's customary law and the spirit of its people. The Historical School in Germany divided, however, over whether the country's customary law was the Roman law or a more Germanic custom.[72] By the century's end in Scotland it was generally thought that the creative role of Roman law in the development of Scots law was a thing of the past, essentially a matter of legal history even if it had left a deep imprint on the substance of the law;[73] but equally the medieval customary law was being, or in the case of the feudal land law, should be, consigned to oblivion too.[74] When the courts or textbook writers were faced with new problems, especially in the law of contract or delict, their instinctive response was increasingly to turn to the solutions to be found in the contemporary decisions of the English courts and the writings of English authors rather than in Roman law or the law of other countries where Roman law had been received. The ability to access non-English materials with confidence had been lost with the near (but not quite complete) evaporation of the tradition which had seen young Scots on their way to qualification in the Faculty of Advocates spend time in legal studies at Continental universities.[75] There was also a movement in favour of harmonization of commercial law across the United Kingdom, based on arguments that differences of law hampered cross-border trade. This led to the application in

---

[70] Neil MacCormick, 'On Public Law and the Law of Nature and Nations', (2007) 11 Edinburgh Law Review 149 at 154–57.

[71] See generally Kenneth G. C. Reid and Reinhard Zimmermann (eds), *A History of Private Law in Scotland* 2 vols (Oxford: Oxford University Press, 2000).

[72] See John W. Cairns, 'The Influence of the German Historical School in Nineteenth-century Edinburgh', (1994) 20 *Syracuse Journal of International Law and Commerce* 191–203; Kidd, *Union and Unionisms*, 191–95.

[73] See, eg, Henry Goudy, *An Inaugural Lecture on the Fate of Roman Law North and South of the Tweed* (London, 1894); John Dove Wilson, 'The Reception of Roman Law in Scotland', (1897) 9 Juridical Review 361.

[74] MacQueen, 'Regiam Majestatem', 24–25; Kidd, *Union and Unionisms*, 197–98.

[75] Cf how in the second half of the 19th century Scots with an intellectual interest in law were attracted to Pandectist German law faculties: Alan Rodger, 'Scottish Advocates in the Nineteenth Century: the German Connection', (1994) 110 Law Quarterly Review 563.

Scotland of statutes such as the Sale of Goods Act 1893 which had been drafted initially as quasi-codifications of existing English law and were then lightly altered to bring the Scots on board without undue stress or strain.[76] Insofar as commercial law was part of private law (which might not have been wholly clear under the terms of the 1707 Union or in the way in which the university law curriculum had come to be structured), the result was significant Anglicization within the latter; in particular in property law, where the Sale of Goods Act preferred the English rules of transfer to the very different Scottish ones.

3. LEGAL NATIONALISM IN 20TH-CENTURY SCOTLAND

The rise in 20th-century Scotland of what has been dubbed 'legal nationalism' was at least in part a reaction to the trends in private and commercial law just discussed. But there were many other factors in play. One was no doubt the growth in political Scottish nationalism after the First World War,[77] although the only prominent legal nationalist to be also a political nationalist was Andrew Dewar Gibb (1888–1974), who held the Regius Chair of Law at Glasgow University from 1934 to 1958.[78] He wrote of the link between the nation and its law, 'consonant, despite all that has happened, with the spirit of the people'.[79] So far as we can tell, he seems to have been generally content with the substance of the law, but he was critical of the court structure and proposed various reforms, notably the greater use of the Sheriff Court.[80] Gibb's best-known book is a historically based assault on the appellate jurisdiction of the House of Lords in Scotland, published under the pungent title *Law from Over the Border* and ending with the comment that this was scarcely the court in which the law of Scotland might have been expounded and justice done between man and man since the Union: 'A priori that was unlikely and experience seems to have borne out the a priori view'.[81] Lindsay Farmer has however clearly demonstrated Gibb's

---

[76] Alan Rodger, 'The Codification of Commercial Law in Victorian Britain' (1993) 108 *Law Quarterly Review* 570–90. See also Kidd, *Union and Unionisms*, 195–98.

[77] For a detailed analysis of inter-war nationalist politics in Scotland, see Richard J. Finlay, *Independent and Free: Scottish Politics and the Origins of the Scottish National Party 1918–1945* (Edinburgh: John Donald, 1994).

[78] Ewen A. Cameron, 'Gibb, Andrew Dewar (1888–1974)', *Oxford Dictionary of National Biography*, Oxford University Press, October 2009; online edn, September 2010 <http://www.oxforddnb.com/view/article/58792>, accessed 26 February 2012. For an important critical assessment of Gibb see Lindsay Farmer, 'Under the Shadow of Parliament House: the Strange Case of Legal Nationalism', in Lindsay Farmer and Scott Veitch (eds), *The State of Scots Law: Law and Government after the Devolution Settlement* (Edinburgh: Butterworths, 2001), 151–64. Some of Gibb's more sympathetic qualities are apparent in Hector L. MacQueen, ' "A picture of what will be some day the law of the civilised nations": comparative law and the destiny of Scots law' in *Towards Europeanization of Private Law: Essays in Honour of Professor Jerzy Rajski* (Warsaw: C. H. Beck, 2007), 521–38, at 522–26.

[79] Andrew Dewar Gibb, *The Shadow on Parliament House: Has Scots Law a Future?* Porpoise Pamphlets No. 4 (Edinburgh, 1932), 9. Parliament House in Edinburgh has been the home of the Court of Session since the 17th century and was also the seat of the Scottish Parliament before 1707.

[80] Gibb, *Shadow on Parliament House*, 30–31.

[81] Andrew Dewar Gibb, *Law from Over the Border: A Short Account of a Strange Jurisdiction* (Edinburgh: W. Green & Son Ltd, 1950), 129. The book was dedicated 'in Friendship and Admiration' to Lord President Cooper, for whom see further at pp. 188–93.

sympathies for fascist, anti-semitic, and anti-Irish Catholic positions, and his support for nationalism and the maintenance of the traditional identity of Scots law as a way of resisting the growth of big government and public social welfare programmes. So, Farmer suggests, legal nationalism can 'be seen as a reaction to the growth of the role of government with the rise of the welfare state'. He adds with reference to Gibb's political views that 'as we seek a more coherent explanation for [legal nationalism's] emergence, we should not ignore the more ignoble roots of the tradition in the right-wing, racist, and elitist politics of the 1930s'.[82]

This pessimistic view must, however, be balanced, or so I have argued elsewhere, by the link between the thinking of those who have been dubbed legal nationalists, and the growth outside Scotland of the study of comparative law.[83] This rapidly developing academic field is increasingly focusing upon the ways in which, as a result of their histories, legal systems differed in their approach to, but not necessarily their solutions of, concrete problems. If solutions tended to be similar, might it be possible to unify law in support of finding ways in which the recently warring nations might live more peacefully together, at least in Europe? The comparative lawyers had in particular identified and were exploring in depth the vital divide between the empirical and pragmatic common law of England, developing on a case-by-case basis, and the highly systematic and increasingly codified civil law of the European Continent. How might this apparent gulf be bridged? On 16 February 1924, Henri Lévy-Ullmann, Professor of Comparative Civil Law at the Sorbonne, gave a lecture on Scots law at the General Assembly of the Society of Comparative Legislation in Paris.[84] Originally published in French, an English translation of the lecture by F. P. Walton appeared in the main Scottish academic law journal, the *Juridical Review*, in 1925.[85] In the lecture Lévy-Ullmann discussed the varied historical sources and development of Scots law, drawing attention in particular to Roman, feudal, and English influences. He summarized his overall view of the law as follows:

> [I]t is a law of Roman and feudal origin which has been adapted in the course of eight centuries by legislation and by judicial decisions to the needs of the Scottish people, and during the last century has, little by little, been combining with the English law by a slow operation of fusion . . . [The adaptation has been carried out] with extraordinary skill. In the whole field of private law the Scots have revealed themselves admirable makers and adapters of laws.[86]

Lévy-Ullmann concluded, in a passage destined to become famous (at least amongst Scots lawyers), that 'Scots law as it stands gives us a picture of what

---

[82] Farmer, 'Shadow of Parliament House', 162–63.

[83] See generally MacQueen, 'Picture'.

[84] On Lévy-Ullmann, see Bénédicte Fauvarque-Cosson, 'Comparative Law in France', in Matthias Reimann and Reinhard Zimmermann (eds), *Oxford Handbook of Comparative Law* (Oxford: Oxford University Press, 2007), 44–45.

[85] Henri Lévy-Ullmann (trans. Frederick P. Walton), 'The Law of Scotland', (1925) 37 Juridical Review 370. The original version of the article, entitled 'Le Droit écossais', was published in the 1924 volume of the *Bulletin de la Société de Législation comparée*.

[86] Lévy-Ullmann, 'Law of Scotland', 375, 384.

will be some day (perhaps at the end of this century) the law of the civilized nations, namely a combination between the Anglo-Saxon system and the continental system'.[87] Under the stimulus provided by the First World War and the foundation of the League of Nations, Lévy-Ullmann seems to have been the first to detect the potential of a mixed system as a model for international, or even global, unification of law.

The common law of England and, significantly, its history were the focus of Lévy-Ullmann's comparative researches,[88] and it was in the course of this that he discovered Scots law and its mixture of the two traditions previously thought to be so sharply distinct. Most probably his attention had been drawn to it by his translator Walton, who himself had worked in comparative law for many years, specializing in comparisons with French law, and who was one of the first to identify a group of systems (including Scotland) intermediate between the common and the civil laws.[89] Lévy-Ullmann's lecture had a remarkable and enduring impact on the Scots legal nationalists. An early and approving reference to his observations was made by Andrew Dewar Gibb in 1932.[90] The theme of Scots law as a mixed system worthy of comparative study in an international context was picked up by the Scottish House of Lords judge, Lord Macmillan (1873–1952), around the same time as Gibb's pamphlet. Macmillan, it may be noted parenthetically here, had been Lord Advocate to the first Labour Government in 1924, although this was a non-political appointment. His real political sympathies lay with the Unionist (that is, in modern terms, Conservative) Party for which, like Gibb before him, he had once been an unsuccessful Parliamentary candidate.[91] In August 1932 he gave an address on Scots law to the International Congress of Comparative Law at The Hague.[92] Although he made no direct reference to Lévy-Ullmann's paper, it is difficult to believe that it had no influence on his presentation. In particular, Macmillan can be seen as drawing on Lévy-Ullmann's notion of Scots lawyers picking up and adapting law from other sources. He cited the words of the late 17th-century Institutional Writer, Stair: 'no man can be a knowing lawyer in any nation who hath not well pondered and

---

[87] Lévy-Ullmann, 'Law of Scotland', 390.

[88] His major work on the subject, *Éléments d'introduction générale à l'étude des sciences juridiques: le système juridique de l'Angleterre. Tome premier, Le système traditionnel* (Paris, 1928), appeared in translation as *The English Legal Tradition: Its Sources and History* (London: Macmillan & Co Ltd, 1935), with brief references to Scots law at xxiii–iv, and 132–33.

[89] Walton also developed the idea of legal borrowing and transplantation between systems, rendering him sceptical of a close link between a nation's laws and the spirit of the people. See further MacQueen, 'Picture', 528–30; John W. Cairns, 'Development of Comparative Law in Great Britain', in Reimann and Zimmermann (eds), *Oxford Handbook of Comparative Law*, 131–73 at 144–46; Kidd, *Union and Unionisms*, 199.

[90] Gibb, *Shadow on Parliament House*, 38.

[91] See Robert Stevens, 'Macmillan, Hugh Pattison, Baron Macmillan (1873–1952)', *Oxford Dictionary of National Biography*, Oxford University Press, 2004 <http://www.oxforddnb.com/view/article/34800>, accessed 25 February 2012. On the Unionist Party see Kidd, *Union and Unionisms*, 10–23. The Union alluded to was the British-Irish Union of 1800, not the 1707 Union.

[92] 'Scots Law as a Subject of Comparative Study', reprinted in Lord Macmillan's collected papers, *Law and Other Things* (Cambridge: Cambridge University Press, 1937), 102–17.

digested in his mind the common law of the world'.[93] Macmillan further referred
to Bankton, who compared Scots with English law because:

> [S]ince the union of the two kingdoms, there is such intercourse between the
> subjects of South and North Britain, that it must be of great moment that the laws
> of both be generally understood and their agreement or diversity attended to; so
> that people, in their mutual correspondence, may regulate themselves accordingly;
> and the respective laws and usages may likewise receive some light from the
> comparison.[94]

Finally, Macmillan quoted another 18th-century Scots lawyer, Lord Kames, who
had commented of the best method of studying law, 'I know none more rational
than a careful and judicious comparison of the laws of different countries'.[95]

Macmillan acknowledged, however, that in modern times 'the law of Scotland
has failed to attract to any great extent the notice of students of comparative
jurisprudence, and while this omission may be regrettable it is scarcely surprising, for little has been done by Scottish legal writers themselves to promote
interest in it'.[96] In the years that followed, Macmillan himself began to take
further action. In 1934 he was one of the prime movers amongst a distinguished
group of lawyers and historians who published proposals for the formation of a
Scottish legal history society to be known as the Stair Society.[97] The proposal
quoted once more Lévy-Ullmann's famous passage about Scots law as a picture
of a future law of the world. In a scheme for a society dedicated to legal history,
this highlighting of the future may seem paradoxical, but the authors were clearly
of the mind that the principal reasons for interest in the history of Scots law were
the 'mixed' character of the Scottish legal system, and the importance of this for
comparative legal science as identified by Lévy-Ullmann. The proposal contains
the following passage about Scots law:

> It is also of unique interest among the legal systems of the world in that it affords the
> only instance of the combination in theory and practice of the Civil Law and the
> Common Law, the two great rivals for supremacy in the legal world. On the one hand,
> it has drawn its inspiration largely from the law of Rome, yet unlike the continental
> nations under the Civil Law it has no code: on the other hand, while it shares the
> respect for precedents distinctive of the Common Law, it has also been systematised in
> the works of authoritative institutional writers. As a practical compromise between
> code law and case law it is a characteristic product of the Scottish genius.[98]

---

[93] Stair, *Institutions of the Law of Scotland*, 1st edn (Edinburgh, 1681), I, i, proemium.

[94] Bankton, *Institute*, preface.

[95] Henry Home Lord Kames, *Historical Law Tracts*, 1st edn (Edinburgh, 1757), preface.

[96] Macmillan, 'Scots Law', 108. On the dearth of comparative law in the Scottish law schools before 1939,
see John C. Gardner, 'The Study of Comparative Law in Great Britain' (1932) 14 Journal of Comparative
Legislation and International Law 201.

[97] For the text of the proposal see (1934) 46 Juridical Review 197. For Macmillan's own account of the
development see his memoirs, *A Man of Law's Tale* (London: Macmillan & Co. Ltd, 1952) 214–16; also his
Law and Other Things, 130–32. See further Thomas H. Drysdale, 'The Stair Society: The Early Years', in
Hector L. MacQueen (ed.), *Miscellany V* (Edinburgh: Stair Society, vol. 52, 2006), 243–57 at 245–48.

[98] (1934) 46 *Juridical Review* at 197.

The Stair Society's promoters, it should be noted, here meant by 'Scottish genius', not a claim to a higher or superior intellectual quality or capacity, but rather a 'spirit' or 'characteristic disposition' of the system, as when one speaks of the 'genius of place'.

The same notion informed Macmillan's Rede Lecture, 'Two Ways of Thinking', delivered in Cambridge in May 1934.[99] The contrasting modes of thought were the theoretical and the practical, or the deductive and the inductive, and Macmillan illustrated this first with the distinction between the Civil Law and the Common Law and then, more specifically, by contrasting Scots and English law. The argument was finally extended into theology and philosophy, with Macmillan positing the existence of a 'mental cleavage' between Scotland and England, which he attributed to a 'deep-rooted racial difference'.[100] That angle was, perhaps fortunately, not elaborated in his lecture; instead he went on to say that, judging from results, the inductive English approach might be preferable, but that nonetheless the world needed both ways of thinking. Translating back into the terms of comparative law (as Macmillan did not), that might be taken to mean that ultimately mixed systems were better than 'pure' ones.

Another prominent lawyer involved in the Stair Society proposal in 1934 was Thomas Cooper KC MP (1892–1955), then Solicitor-General for Scotland and later a judge in the Scottish courts who became Lord President and Lord Justice General in 1947.[101] Even this brief summary of his career makes clear that legal history was not his only interest. Cooper was active politically, another Unionist who stood for Parliament in that interest in 1930 and was finally elected in 1935, although to become a member of the National Government as Solicitor General for Scotland, and, later, as Lord Advocate.[102] While Cooper was therefore on the right politically, he seems much more moderate in his position than his friend Andrew Dewar Gibb, and he was certainly not a political nationalist. A contemporary, while noting that Cooper 'took a peculiarly black view of modern economic conditions', also observed that 'In his radicalism, he was scarcely a typical Conservative politician and a generation earlier he would certainly have been an Asquithian Liberal'.[103] Like Gibb, Cooper saw 'a remarkable and increasing tendency by the Executive to encroach farther and farther

---

[99] Macmillan, *Law and Other Things*, 76–101.

[100] Macmillan, *Law and Other Things*, 89.

[101] See Lord Keith of Avonholm, 'Cooper, Thomas Mackay, Baron Cooper of Culross (1892–1955)', rev. *Oxford Dictionary of National Biography*, Oxford University Press, 2004 <http://www.oxforddnb.com/view/article/32554>, accessed 25 February 2012; Hector L. MacQueen, 'Legal Nationalism: The Case of Lord Cooper', in Norma M. Dawson (ed.), *Reflections on Law and History: Irish Legal History Society Discourses and Other Papers, 2000–2005* (Dublin: Four Courts Press, 2006), 83–98.

[102] For some context, see Ian G. C. Hutchinson, 'Scottish Unionism between the two world wars', in Catriona M. M. Macdonald (ed.), *Unionist Scotland 1800–1997* (Edinburgh: John Donald, 1998).

[103] Fiona Craddock (ed.), *The Journal of Sir Randall Philip, OBE, QC: Public and Private Life in Scotland 1947–57* (Edinburgh: Pentland Press, 1998), at 5, 6. Asquith's Liberal Government of 1908–16 introduced substantial social welfare reform and significantly curtailed the powers of the House of Lords as the upper legislative chamber of Parliament. It failed however to give women the vote.

upon the legislative and judicial functions of government',[104] and he could write about how 'private law is receding all along the line and public law is taking its place'.[105] But unlike Gibb, Cooper seems to have accepted the inevitability of the growth of the state in the social and economic conditions prevailing after 1918. Later on in his public career, in 1942, he headed the committee of inquiry which recommended the establishment by the state of the North of Scotland Hydro-Electric Board, to dam Highland rivers and utilize the water resources thus obtained to provide electricity and employment in the Highlands; the aim being, as the report expressed it, 'to give the Highlands and the Highlanders a future as well as a past'.[106] The overall question for Cooper was how to find and maintain a balance between government and the individual in the altered circumstances of the modern world. In this he thought that private law and the judicial system still had roles to play alongside, perhaps even against, public law, at least as it stood in his time.

At the heart of Cooper's concerns was the proliferation—or, as he put it, the 'perplexing variety and lack of system'[107]—of administrative tribunals discharging judicial and quasi-judicial functions in the new dispensation, as opposed to the courts. 'More and more matters affecting the private rights of the subject are being committed to the unexaminable discretion of the executive or the oracular pronouncements of ad hoc tribunals, before whom in some cases lawyers are actually forbidden to appear', he wrote.[108] Cooper also attacked as containing no more than 'a faint tincture of juristic principle', 'the vast tracts of so-called "law" the mastery of each of which is the lifework of a specialist—Income Tax, Social Insurance, Local Government and many others',[109] and spoke of being 'imprisoned in the network of modern departmental regulations [which] have no better title to be recognised as an integral part of our system of jurisprudence than the current issue of the railway timetable'.[110]

The overall theme was a familiar one, given focus for lawyers by the English Lord Chief Justice, Lord Hewart, in his book *The New Despotism*, published in 1929. But the interest of Cooper's contribution to the debate is its attack upon the use of administrative officials to perform judicial functions part-time. Two solutions lay to hand: one, the use instead of officials of the full-time, legally qualified Scottish Sheriff in the role of administrative judge ('on the score of efficiency the probabilities are all in favour of the experienced professional judge

---

[104] Lord Cooper of Culross, *Selected Papers 1922–1954* (Edinburgh: Oliver & Boyd, 1957), 26 (written 1929).

[105] Cooper, *Selected Papers*, 208.

[106] *Report of the Committee on Hydro-Electric Development in Scotland* [Lord Cooper, Chairman], Cmd 6406, 1942.

[107] Cooper, *Selected Papers*, 28 (written 1929).

[108] Cooper, *Selected Papers*, 155.

[109] Cooper, *Selected Papers*, 180. Cooper himself had as early as 1920 co-authored with Sir W. E. Whyte *The Law of Housing and Town Planning* (London: Hodge, 1920); so he wrote of what he had been in an earlier life.

[110] Cooper, *Selected Papers*, 174.

and against the casual amateur'[111]); the other, the development of a British *droit administratif*, comparable to the French system, by which the courts would regulate the conduct of tribunals and officials.[112]

Another revealing passage shows why he thought private law still mattered to the people of Scotland:

> [W]hen we speak of a legal system let us think rather of the body of principles and doctrines which determine personal status and relations, which regulate the acquisition and enjoyment of property and its transfer between the living or its transmission from the dead, which define and control contractual and other obligations, and which provide for the enforcement of rights and the remedying of wrongs. These are the matters which inevitably touch the lives of all citizens at many points from the cradle to the grave, and their regulation is a function of government with which no civilised community can dispense and on the due administration of which the well-being of every society depends.[113]

'The truth is,' wrote Cooper later in the same publication, striking a Savigny-esque note and also echoing Gibb, 'that law is the reflection of the spirit of a people, and so long as the Scots are conscious that they are a people, they must preserve their law'.[114] But whatever else his political conservatism may have entailed, Cooper was not a reactionary preserver of either the good old Scots law or the established ways of doing judicial business. When Lord Advocate, he successfully established machinery for the legislative reform of Scots law and saw to the implementation of its recommendations in Parliament.[115] The unreformed law of intestate succession was a major reproach in his eyes,[116] and like Gibb he wanted to change the way the courts worked the better to serve the litigant.[117] Like Macmillan, he was interested in comparative law, but more as a means of modernizing the law of Scotland than of using it as an example to the rest of the world. He was from 1936 a Council member of the Society of Comparative Legislation,[118] and after the Second World War encouraged the teaching of comparative law in the Scottish law faculties, again in support of the development of Scots law.[119]

Cooper also worked extensively on his legal history at this period, in particular the medieval history of Scots law.[120] This research reinforced arguments for the

---

[111] Cooper, *Selected Papers*, 36.

[112] Cooper, *Selected Papers*, 158–59, 266–75.

[113] Cooper, *Selected Papers*, 174.

[114] Cooper, *Selected Papers*, 199; see also 144 ('Nothing would more effectively contribute to the swift obliteration of the individuality of the Scottish people than the loss of the legal system under which we have lived since the dawn of history').

[115] MacQueen, 'Legal Nationalism', 93.

[116] Cooper, *Selected Papers*, 150, 189.

[117] MacQueen, 'Legal Nationalism', 92.

[118] For Cooper's membership of the Council of the Society of Comparative Legislation, see (1936) 18 Journal of Comparative Legislation & International Law 3rd series, vii (a reference for which I am grateful to John Cairns). On the Society, see Cairns, 'Development of Comparative Law', 153–55.

[119] Cooper, *Selected Papers*, 142–52, 159.

[120] Hector L. MacQueen, 'Legal Nationalism: Lord Cooper, Legal History and Comparative Law' (2005) 9 Edinburgh Law Review 395.

use of comparative law in modern times: 'the Scottish lawyer has been first and foremost a comparative lawyer since the thirteenth century',[121] while little in Scots law 'could justly be described as aboriginal and indigenous'.[122] This view may have derived originally from Lévy Ullmann's comments about the 'extraordinary skill' with which Scots lawyers had fused the diverse elements of their system, showing themselves to be 'admirable makers and adapters of laws'.[123] To look outside itself for inspiration was perhaps the hallmark—or genius—of Scots law. But, Cooper continued, it had to look in the right direction. Scots law's historical affinities were with Roman law and its modern offshoots. 'If Scots Law is not merely to survive but to thrive', he wrote, 'we must renew and deepen our contacts with these kindred legal systems, and draw from them the inspiration for perfecting Scots Law as an instrument for the service of our people in the days ahead'.[124] English law, on the other hand, would be an 'unwholesome' contact for Scots law, at least if allowed to operate in isolation; recent influence from that source was not the result of voluntary borrowing but of forced loans from Westminster, whether via the legislature or the House of Lords as the final appellate court.[125]

This represented a significant shift in position from Cooper. In 1936, writing for the first time about medieval law, he had said:

> There is here a rich and almost unexplored field for the investigator—the law of Scotland as it was before it became deeply permeated by the law of Rome, the Canon Law, and the law of the feus... There is indeed a sense in which Stair is open to the criticism which Dutch lawyers have directed against Grotius and Voet—that he enslaved his country to an alien system, or at least that he largely discarded or ignored its native rules, and sought to break the natural continuity of their development.[126]

Even at the time there was a striking contrast between Cooper's 'enslaving alien system' and how some other lawyers characterized the Roman element of Scots law. In 1937, for example, the scholarly Lord President of the Court of Session, Wilfrid Normand, wrote:

> [T]here are chapters in Scots Law today in which we may feel confident that a decision in harmony with the texts of the great Roman jurists will harmonize also with the genius of our law... We have in the tradition of Roman Law a vast and unexhausted treasure house of principle, highly rationalized and deeply humanistic, which we must not neglect if we are to maintain the identity of Scots Law in the necessary changes and modifications of the future. For unless our law continues to

---

[121] Cooper, *Selected Papers*, 159.

[122] Cooper, *Selected Papers*, at 143. But see 184, 185, and 195, for particular praise of marriage, land, and criminal law as the products of native and immemorial custom without the intrusion of alien influences.

[123] Lévy Ullmann, 'Law of Scotland', 375, 384.

[124] Cooper, *Selected Papers*, 145.

[125] Cooper, *Selected Papers*, 144, 180–82.

[126] T. M. Cooper, 'Regiam Majestatem and the Auld Lawes', in Hector McKechnie (ed.), *The Sources and Literature of Scots Law* (Edinburgh: Stair Society, vol. 1, 1936), 77.

grow in accordance with that tradition it will run a grave risk of becoming a debased imitation of the Law of England, stumbling and halting before every new problem where we have no English precedent to guide us. From that fate our law students and future practitioners can save us by a right appreciation of the Roman tradition in the Law of Scotland and by accepting it as an active principle of natural growth and development.[127]

Cooper had thus moved from what in the German Historical School might have been described as a Germanist to join Normand in a Romanist position in relation to the history of Scots law as well as its future development.

History also lay at the root of Cooper's best-known judicial contribution to public law, the opinion in the 'E II R' case in 1953, *MacCormick v Lord Advocate*, in which he declared that '[t]he principle of the unlimited sovereignty of Parliament is a distinctively English principle which has no counterpart in Scottish constitutional law'.[128] As has been pointed out elsewhere, Cooper had, during the Second World War, given judgments supporting the Diceyan view of the status of the Union Agreement,[129] but since then, he had been much involved in the travails of the History of Parliament project, as chairman of its Scottish Committee from 1948 to 1955. In 1951 the scheme became one for the history of the Westminster Parliament only, and it had been decided not to accept any break in that account at 1707.[130] This experience must surely lie behind the following passage in the *MacCormick* opinion:

> Considering that the Union legislation extinguished the Parliaments of Scotland and England and replaced them by a new Parliament, I have difficulty in seeing why it should have been supposed that the new Parliament of Great Britain must inherit all the peculiar characteristics of the English Parliament but none of the Scottish Parliament, as if all that happened in 1707 was that Scottish representatives were admitted to the Parliament of England. That is not what was done.[131]

So the *MacCormick* opinion does indeed manifest a form of legal nationalism in the public law arena.[132] But none of this seems to have led the life-long political Unionist Cooper to question further the legal significance of the Union, or whether it made, or should have made, any provision for the rights and freedoms of individuals within the state it had created; for example, by way of Article XVIII's reference to 'evident utility' as a condition of change to private law. Nor did he offer any attempt to explore Scottish sources for the principles which

---

[127] Foreword to James Spencer Muirhead, *Outline of Roman Law* (Edinburgh: W. Green & Son Ltd, 1937). See also James Mackintosh, *Roman Law in Modern Practice* (Edinburgh: W. Green & Son Ltd, 1934).

[128] 1953 SC 396, 411. But see Colin Kidd, 'Sovereignty and the Scottish Constitution before 1707' (2004) Juridical Review 225–36.

[129] Hector L. MacQueen, 'Two Toms and an Ideology for Scots Law: T. B. Smith and Lord Cooper of Culross', in Elspeth Reid and David L. Carey Miller (eds), *A Mixed Legal System in Transition: T B Smith and the Progress of Scots Law* (Edinburgh: Edinburgh University Press, 2005), 44–72 at 68.

[130] See Margaret D. Young, *The Parliaments of Scotland: Burgh and Shire Commissioners*, vol. 1 (Edinburgh: HMSO, 1992), preface, for a fuller account.

[131] *MacCormick v Lord Advocate* 1953 SC 396, 411.

[132] See further Gavin Little, 'A Flag in the Wind: *MacCormick v Lord Advocate*', in John P. Grant and Elaine E. Sutherland (eds), *Scots Law Tales* (Dundee: Dundee University Press, 2010), 23–44.

might govern the *droit administratif,* which he seems to have seen as essentially a British project.[133] And it may be that the Universal Declaration of Human Rights of 1948 and the European Convention on Human Rights of 1950 were in his eyes but instances of what he called in another discussion context (international codification of private law) 'the dead levels of an insipid internationalism imposed from without'.[134] He certainly made no mention of either text when writing in 1950 that 'so long as the democratic ideal survives, even as a pious fiction, there *must* be a residuum of protected individual rights and an impartial judicial authority to enforce and safeguard them'.[135]

A final point of interest in Cooper's later writings is a rejection of Lord Macmillan's preference for the inductive common law approach to problems, because of 'its reliance upon slowly developing tracts of judicial decisions evolved with infinite caution by generations of elderly and timorous judges conditioned by Victorian ideals'.[136] Civilian methods of legal thinking were the best guarantee 'if we are to avoid the ultimate disaster of witnessing our systems of law replaced by the opportunism of arbitrary dictatorships'.[137] That is, however, a rather curious remark given the very recent experiences of fascist dictatorship in civilian and codified Germany and Italy at the time Cooper was writing (1949); indeed Italy's latest Codice civile of 1942 was a product of the Mussolini regime. But other comments in Cooper's piece about the 'twilight of landownership and the afternoon of private property'[138] may suggest that what he had in mind was socialist 'dictatorship' rather closer to home, and a perceived need for clear statements of individual private rights such as might be better provided by a civil code than the courts. The desirability of codification (although only of civil and not of criminal law) was certainly another of his major themes in general.[139]

Cooper died in 1955 and, as I have suggested elsewhere, his legal nationalist standard was more or less self-consciously taken up by T. B. Smith (1915–1988), Professor of Scots Law at Aberdeen and later Professor of Civil, then Scots, Law at Edinburgh before he became finally a Scottish Law Commissioner and first General Editor of the Stair Memorial Encyclopaedia of the Laws of Scotland.[140] Smith's contribution has been very fully analysed by different hands in recent times, and there is accordingly less need to dwell here on the details of his legal nationalist writings.[141] Smith was a proud Scot who wore a kilt whenever he left

---

[133] See however Cooper, *Selected Papers,* 116–23, for a paper first published in 1946 and entitled 'The King *versus* The Court of Session', which discussed a 1599 assertion of judicial independence of the executive.

[134] Cooper, *Selected Papers,* 147.

[135] Cooper, *Selected Papers,* 216. The European Court of Human Rights did not come into existence until 1959.

[136] Cooper, *Selected Papers,* 208.

[137] Cooper, *Selected Papers,* 209.

[138] Cooper, *Selected Papers,* 208.

[139] MacQueen, 'Two Toms', 49–53 (see note 49 on opposition to codification of criminal law).

[140] See generally MacQueen, 'Two Toms'.

[141] See in particular the collection Reid and Carey Miller (eds), *Mixed Legal System,* and Kidd, *Union and Unionisms,* 201–209. On the latter see my review at (2010) 14 Edinburgh Law Review 151.

his native land, but outside the law his nationalism was cultural rather than political. His politics, whatever they may have been, did not emerge in public espousal of any particular party.[142] Like Cooper, his legal nationalism did not consist in the promotion of Scots law so much as in its salvation from Anglicization, or at any rate unthinking Anglicization. Smith followed Cooper, but with far more detail on the substance of the law, in arguing that Scots law had developed by way of borrowing from elsewhere, and that most of what was good about it derived ultimately from civilian sources and civilian legal thinking. In contrast, 'borrowings' from non-civilian England, whether by statute or through decisions of the courts, tended to sit at best uneasily within the Scottish system. Viewed objectively, the systematic civilian approach was preferable to the inductive common law.[143]

Smith, however, rejected Cooper's linkage between Scots law and the spirit of the people.[144] George Gretton has expressed Smith's position with customary clarity:

> There is, *as such*, nothing especially Scottish about the Civilian tradition. For Smith, the Civilian tradition within Scots law is not to be classed with shortbread and tartan. Had it not been for the special relationship with England, Scotland's Civilian tradition would have been no more specially 'Scottish' than, say, Portugal's Civilian tradition is specially 'Portuguese'.[145]

Professor Gretton has also rightly pointed out that Smith's focus in thinking about the civilian tradition in Scotland was on the core areas of private law—that is, contract, delict, and moveable property—and that his work largely neglected the fields of commercial law, land-ownership, and conveyancing. This, Professor Gretton suggests, probably reflected the divisions of the traditional Scottish LLB curriculum into the separate subjects of Scots Law, Mercantile Law, and Conveyancing.[146] But it is also worth pointing out that Smith did *not* neglect two other areas of law: public law and criminal law. Under the overall heading of 'Public Law', five chapters and nearly 200 pages of his remarkable *Short Commentary on the Law of Scotland* (1962) were devoted to a general account of the subjects, and there were numerous other contributions elsewhere about them. Both played a part in his legal nationalist agenda, albeit to a lesser degree than the

---

[142] I was once told (whether or not by Smith himself I cannot now recall) that T. B. (who lived in Morham, East Lothian) voted for John Mackintosh, who became MP for Berwick and East Lothian on the right of the Labour Party from 1966 until his early death aged 48 in 1978. Mackintosh supported devolution, and wrote *The Devolution of Power* (1966) and *The British Cabinet* (1968). After Mackintosh's death, Smith returned to his 'natural allegiance'—which was, however, not specified to me. I suspect classical Liberal rather than Tory.

[143] See, eg, Hector L. MacQueen, 'Glory with Gloag or the Stake with Stair? T B Smith and the Scots Law of Contract', in Reid and Carey Miller (eds), *Mixed Legal System*, 138–72.

[144] See MacQueen, 'Two Toms', 63–64.

[145] George L. Gretton, 'The Rational and the National: Thomas Broun Smith', in Reid and Carey Miller (eds), *Mixed Legal System*, 30–43 at 34–35.

[146] Gretton, 'Rational and National', 37–41.

core of private law (the overall heading for some 30 chapters and over 600 pages in the *Short Commentary*).

On public law, Smith's most visible contribution was to the debate prompted by *MacCormick v Lord Advocate*,[147] but he also argued that other aspects of Scottish constitutional law were not necessarily the same as those of English law, which had been taken too readily to apply throughout the United Kingdom. The public rights of the individual—personal liberty, freedom of expression, opinion, and religion, for example—were protected at common law in Scotland.[148] An analysis of the implications for the Scottish legal system of some form of devolution, published in 1970, has been substantially borne out by the actual form of devolution provided by the Scotland Act 1998.[149] Late in his career Smith also produced a short book called *Basic Rights and their Enforcement*, which deals with human rights and advocates the adoption of the European Convention on Human Rights as a judicially enforceable Bill of Rights in the United Kingdom.[150] Smith's writing on criminal law was more about procedure than the substance of the law, although the latter was by no means ignored. He saw criminal law as very much a native Scottish product, with early Roman law borrowings largely displaced by the decisions of the High Court of Justiciary and the writings of later jurists such as David Hume. There had been little legislation and the House of Lords had no appellate jurisdiction, so there had been no forced borrowings from England either.[151] Whether or not as a direct result, Scottish criminal justice was 'not only well suited to the needs of Scotland, but also inspire[d] liberal reforms in England'.[152] Smith thus did not anticipate the havoc that Convention rights would later wreak upon the Scottish criminal justice system.

4. CONCLUSIONS

The time has arrived to attempt to draw some conclusions from the material just surveyed. It is no surprise to find law, private as well as public, contributing to national identity. In particular, an independent law and legal system has been associated with the sovereignty of states for a very long time. Not only does it usually mean that the law is made and administered within the state in question, it may also entail the rejection of the laws of other states as utterly irrelevant. The medieval example provided by the refusal of the English courts to accept Welsh

---

[147] T. B. Smith, 'The Union of 1707 as Fundamental Law', (1957) Public Law 99, republished with addendum in T. B. Smith, *Studies Critical and Comparative* (Edinburgh: W. Green & Son Ltd, 1962), 1–27.

[148] See T. B. Smith, *British Justice: The Scottish Contribution* (Hamlyn Lectures Thirteenth Series, London: Stevens & Sons Ltd, 1961), 196–213; T. B. Smith, *A Short Commentary on the Law of Scotland* (Edinburgh: W. Green & Son Ltd, 1962), Pt Two (headed 'Public Law').

[149] T. B. Smith, 'Scottish Nationalism, Law and Self-government', in Neil MacCormick (ed), *The Scottish Debate* (Edinburgh: Scottish Academic Press, 1970) 34–51, discussed in MacQueen, 'Two Toms', 70–71.

[150] T. B. Smith, *Basic Rights and their Enforcement* (Bombay: N. M. Tripathi Private Ltd, 1979).

[151] Smith, *British Justice*, 95–140; Smith, *Short Commentary*, 116–238; Smith, *Studies Critical and Comparative*, 241–92.

[152] Smith, *British Justice*, 95.

law in the 13th century can be matched in modern times by US Supreme Court Justice Scalia's rejection of the relevance of foreign law to the interpretation of the US Constitution.[153] But for an equally long time the laws of sovereign states have coexisted with laws which carried an authority that crossed state boundaries. Canon law is the obvious example historically, while the vitality of Roman law in Europe a millennium and more after the fall of Rome should also be kept in mind. Today, European Union and European human rights law are the major instances of such supranational law. The existence and enforceability of these supranational laws within and over the domestic law of states will and do raise questions about the latter's identity and continuity. A new example is provided by the proposal for a European Union sales contract law which, even although it will not purport to displace its domestic equivalents, has provoked much hostility from lawyers in member states, often expressed in barely cloaked nationalist terms.[154]

In the United Kingdom since 1707 there has also been the problem of different legal systems within a single state, albeit one that was deliberately created in that form out of the partial amalgamation of two former states. The position of the smaller and therefore more vulnerable system has been a matter of concern to many active within it throughout the three centuries of the United Kingdom's existence, and more occasionally to those such as politicians whose interest has been largely dependent on the happenstance of events such as the fallout from the *Cadder* case. That concern has been expressed in nationalist terms more than once, including by those who would not have associated themselves with other forms of nationalist politics, at least those aimed at the reinstatement of an independent Scotland. But, while the expressions of concern have quite frequently linked Scots law in some way with the spirit of the Scottish people in a manner easy to mock or dislike, they cannot be accused of involving any complacency or conservatism about the state of the law or the legal system, or indeed of any desire to revert to some Utopian state of things thought to have existed at any time in the past. With the possible exception of Lord Macmillan,[155] all those on my 20th-century cast list were reformers and progressives; their arguments with those who disagreed with them were about the way forward rather than in favour of going back. They all saw the law as the servant of the people to whom it applied, and thought that it was in some way failing in that task.

---

[153] *Roper v Simmons* 543 US 551 (2005). This, however, came in a dissenting opinion.

[154] See Proposal for a Regulation of the European Parliament and of the Council on a Common European Sales Law, Brussels, 11.10.2011, COM (2011) 635 final. My comments here are prompted by some of the papers presented at a seminar on 'Private Law and Nationalism' held in the Faculty of Law at the University of Amsterdam on 3 February 2012. A key source for many speakers was the responses to European Commission consultations on contract law, available on the European Commission DG Justice Contract Law website <http://ec.europa.eu/justice/contract/>.

[155] Macmillan's performance as a Law Lord did not match his rhetoric outside court, and it is noteworthy that his most famous and radical speech, that in *Donoghue v Stevenson* 1932 SC (HL) 32, was, thanks to the persuasive powers of his colleague Lord Atkin, couched in much bolder terms than he had originally planned: see Alan Rodger, 'Lord Macmillan's Speech in *Donoghue v Stevenson*', (1992) 108 Law Quarterly Review 236.

The importance of private law in this discussion may appear surprising to some. Nils Jansen's recent observation that private law's own conceptual and intellectual structures lead to it standing somewhat apart from the general political process carries the implication that other branches of law are more engaged in that process, and hence more readily associated with the political debate of which nationalism is generally part.[156] With Ralf Michaels, Jansen has argued for the relative autonomy of private law through its claim to a normative rationality and a value system that does not depend upon governmental authority or its democratic establishment.[157] History supports the argument in that much of private law has developed historically from either Roman or canon law, and has thus been received into domestic law, even if there are then variations in how the law has since developed within any given jurisdiction. But on this argument private law is fundamentally not 'national' or, more neutrally, jurisdiction-specific, in its very nature. The claim can be supported with the observation that the stuff of private law does not depend in any way on there being a state or perhaps even some lesser form of authority. Whatever way their wider society may be organized, individuals are born, grow up, form affective relationships, have children, lay claim to possessions, make arrangements with others for immediate or future performance, harm or are harmed by others intentionally or otherwise, grow old and frail, and eventually die with or without possessions to be transferred on somehow to those who survive them. The state is not needed for these inevitable facts of the human condition to raise questions needing resolution, or indeed to provide answers to them.

What then does the example of Scotland tell us in this discussion? Along with the rest of the United Kingdom, it reminds us that private law can also be a sub-state phenomenon. It suggests that we cannot altogether ignore the national and the contingent in understanding the significance of private law. Further, while private law may indeed be able to go beyond the state and participate in the challenges of globalization, Europeanization, and privatization, it can also be seen by some as a form of defence for the individual against the continuing encroachments of state power. They may wish to give public law more of a private feel by arming the individual against the claims of the state. But the wider debate is also significant when we consider how much of Scots private law is still un-legislated law. Whether we see it as the product of court decisions, juristic writings, the custom of the people, or some mixture of these elements which in some sense is still going on, much of its content has actually depended on legal transplants from sources which lay beyond the sovereignty of either pre-Union Scotland or the United Kingdom.[158] T. B. Smith's argument, that it was not so much the

---

[156] Nils Jansen, *The Making of Legal Authority: Non-legislative Codifications in Historical and Comparative Perspective* (Oxford: Oxford University Press, 2010), 19.

[157] Nils Jansen and Ralf Michaels, 'Private Law and the State: Comparative Perceptions and Historical Observations', (2007) 71 Rabelszeitschrift 345; Ralf Michaels and Nils Jansen, 'Private Law Beyond the State? Europeanization, Globalization, Privatization', (2006) 54 American Journal of Comparative Law 843. And see further the special issue of the AJCL edited by Jansen and Michaels, and entitled 'Beyond the State? Rethinking Private Law': (2008) 56 American Journal of Comparative Law 527.

[158] On the comparative law idea of legal transplants, see Cairns, 'Comparative Law in Britain', 146 (Walton), 150 (R. W. Lee), 170–71 (Alan Watson).

Scottishness of the kind of law he promoted as its stronger qualities of reason and coherence by comparison with English law, also fits well with the Jansen/Michaels argument. Yet, much of English private law is also not the product of legislation or state activity (except insofar as the courts are part of the state). Those who practise and teach it usually stand reasonably convinced of its relative merits as a pragmatic response to real problems, contrasting significantly with other, more theoretical systems, even if not all would go so far as their 15th-century predecessors in claiming it to be the best possible law. Perceptions of difference will therefore continue to be important in the future development of private law, above all when a system feels subject to serious challenge from some alternative way of seeing or doing things, but also as an instinctive response to schemes for international unification or harmonization. Perhaps private law ought not to matter when it comes to claims of national identity; the reality is that it does.

THE EVOLUTION OF PUBLIC LAW?

10

Globalization and the Transcendence of the Public/Private Divide—What is Public Law under Conditions of Globalization?

Inger-Johanne Sand

I. INTRODUCTION—WHAT IS PUBLIC LAW IN GLOBAL AND RISK SOCIETY?

Public law as an institution and as a way of thinking in law has a long and highly differentiated history. In its present form, in modern democratic nation-states, public law is inherently a part of the tradition of the nation-state and its related concepts such as sovereignty, democracy, freedom, rights, constitutionalism, the principle of legality, and public government and administration. Public law is unavoidably also an ambiguous and paradoxical concept; it is law by the people, for the people. 'The people' are the subject and the object of public law, its author and addressee. Public law is part of the interdependent relationship between politics and law, and between democracy and individual rights. Public law can also be seen as the crucial regulatory and normative link between the 'force' of the state and the freedom and rights of its citizens. Public law endows rights and guarantees freedom, but also regulates the use of force and administrative power which can be used both for and against citizens. Modern public law requires authority, the voice and participation of the people, and contextual knowledge and reflexivity.

Public law is both the structure and a necessary dynamic of change and variation in society. It includes both the administrative and regulatory law of a variety of social and technical fields and the more exceptional uses of force. It has been the expression of 'the general will' and of the sovereign, but has over time been transformed to more pluralistic, democratic, diverse, open, and dynamic forms. It conveys social values, but also technocratic and bureaucratic forms. Public administration has become more varied and polycentric than before, both in its organizational forms and its substance. In relation to citizens, it has traditionally been the law of the nation-states but increasingly includes European (or other regional) law and public international law. Both on the domestic and the international levels, many public administrative agencies are more like expert bureaucracies than democratically controlled organizations. Public administration increasingly involves not only the rule of law and public regulatory law but also contract and competition law mechanisms thus transcending the public/private law boundary and becoming increasingly diverse in its modes of operation. Public law has thus expanded its scope to include an increasing number of social, knowledge-based, and technological areas and is at the same time blurring the boundaries between state and society.[1]

Over time public law has developed procedural and substantive principles which have been vital in securing the legitimacy of modern democratic and rule-of-law states. Legality, fundamental rights, rule-of-law procedures, transparency, reasonableness, various forms of justice, and judicial review are examples of principles expressed in modern public law.[2] Within these principles are contained both important values for the functioning of an open society but also contradictions, differences, and ambiguities related to the dualities of the rule of law and democracy, justice, efficiency, and the performance and limitations of power. The continuous evolution of public law is occurring within the dynamics of the ambiguities and differences of the principles of public law and at the same time challenging some of its main values.

The public law of modern states has evolved historically and expanded from rule-of-law and penal law orientations to ambitious administrative regulation of a wide range of important social issues. In the first phase of modernity, public law evolved to incorporate fundamental constitutional rights and the development of institutions, procedural legality, and criminal law. With industrialization and urbanization areas of substantive public and administrative law evolved, such as welfare law, labour law, economic regulatory law, and zoning and building law. From the 1960s and 1970s onwards, new challenges of modernity had evolved and new and more ambitious public regulatory law emerged such as more ambitious forms of welfare law, environmental protection, industrial protection, and gender equality, to name but a few. Public law had become a vital and active instrument of political and social reform and created new social structures and institutions. By the 1980s, more liberal economic regulation, with an emphasis on competition law but also spreading to many other fields, emerged, as well as more detailed regulations of specific issues and new technologies. Regulations ensuring free movement and competition law have created significant forms of interconnection and interdependencies between public and private law and the economy, and also between individual rights and regulatory regimes. A more liberal economic regime has been implemented through public law. Increasingly extensive and intensive uses of new technologies leading to what has been labelled 'the risk society' have also been regulated through public law notwithstanding significant uncertain and, at times, unpredictable consequences.[3] Public law is, then, increasingly regulating the future with significant uncertainty, and in tandem with continuously changing technologies.

---

[1] Helmut Willke, 'The tragedy of the state' (1986) Archiv für recht- und Sozialphilosophie 455.

[2] Ch 2, this book.

[3] Gunther Teubner, 'Reflexives Recht', (1982) vol. LXVIII no. 1 Archiv für Recht- und Sozialphilosophie 13 et seq; Duncan Kennedy, 'Three globalizations of law and legal thought: 1850–2000', in *The New Law and Legal Development*, David Trubek and Alvaro Santos (eds)

Various social, economic, technological, and political changes are currently affecting the preconditions and the operations of both governance and government in general, and of public law with significant effects on its procedures, principles, and substance. First of all, the number of *international organizations*, treaties, and dispute-settlement bodies and courts have increased significantly over the last fifty years, as well as the effects of law produced by these actors. A significant part of public law is now produced or at least initiated by international organizations and negotiations as public international law. The *peoples* behind public international law, and its interests, are heterogeneous in a very different way than the people of a nation-state. The quality and the forms of democratic procedures are different than those on a national level. In this way, the procedures and the context of the production of public law have changed significantly. Secondly, on the international level public law appears *fragmented and asymmetric*, regulated on a treaty-by-treaty basis, and is thus quite different from the more harmonized and balancing methods of domestic public law. Thirdly, public law has expanded to regulate an increasing number of areas, many of which are discursively dominated by *highly specialized knowledge and technologies*. Law tends to become parasitic on other codes and rationalities in ways which may affect legal rationality and principles. The regulation of highly specialized technologies also implies the evaluation of risk. Fourthly, legal areas and mechanisms which traditionally have been labelled as either public or private law, such as public regulation, rights, and contracts, have increasingly become more *interconnected and interdependent,* and thus less distinctive from each other. Rights have become an increasingly vital part of public regulation and are in many ways part of both public and private law. Public agencies use contracts, corporations, and competition. Private actors increasingly regulate their activities through a variety of norms and guidelines. NGOs have become an increasingly significant part of public life and public regulation.

The changes referred to earlier are influencing to a significant extent many of the characteristics of public law as it has emerged in modern democratic nation-states. Public law is currently emerging in a more polycontextural and pluralistic landscape than in the era dominated by the nation-state. It is the expression of several institutions, of national as well as international levels of government, and of various forms of interaction between public and private actors, reflecting the dispersion of sovereignty and the distribution of public tasks in society. There is thus a substantive differentiation in, and an expansion of, public law and the institutions involved, which impacts concepts such as 'the general will', 'the common good', and the balancing of various public interests and considerations. This, in turn, may affect the understanding of legitimacy. Furthermore, public law refers to an increasing number of substantively quite different regulatory discourses, many of them highly specialized and part of new technologies. This substantive expansion contributes to the further differentiation of public law. Public and private law principles and standards are also becoming increasingly

(Cambridge: Cambridge University Press, 2006); Helmuth Willke, *Die Ironie des Staates* (Frankfurt: Suhrkamp, 1992); Niklas Luhmann, *Risk: A Sociological Theory* (Berlin: de Gruyter, 1993).

interconnected. Contract law and individual rights are increasingly influential parts of public law, and are thus also changing both the configuration and principles of public law. Still, many of the procedural and substantive principles and values of modern public law remain. Another qualitative change concerns the globalization of social and economic dynamics, but with insufficient political, legal, and democratic procedures and institutions in place, and thus an uncertainty as to how 'the common good' is to be understood and interpreted. This chapter will explore some of these changes in the evolution and the understanding of public law illustrated by specific examples.

2. PUBLIC / PRIVATE LAW BOUNDARIES AND THE DIFFERENTIATION AND GLOBALIZATION OF SOCIETY

Public law retains a vital role in modern societies, but what it regulates, how, and by whom have all undergone significant change. The preconditions, function, and forms of public law have changed inter alia due to a number of factors. First of all there are processes of *functional and communicative differentiation* in society leading to an increasing social differentiation and specialization in the areas regulated by public law.[4] The high degrees of differentiation and specialization of the scientific and economic systems and their semantics have led to equivalent forms of specialization of the sub-systems and semantics of law. The specialization of economic and scientific communications will additionally tend to lead to resistance to political and legal forms of regulation. Law will create structural or organizational couplings with other function systems and their semantics, leading to the transferring of such semantics into law and combining them with legal concepts and regulatory forms. Public law will increasingly emerge as a variety of differentiated sectors or themes with their distinct logics and semantics, and less as an expression of a 'whole' society with unified consensus of the balancing between the different logics, values, and interests. This is further emphasized by the fragmented character of international law. The definition of the 'general will' will increasingly depend on processes and discourses within the different and specific sectors and their institutions previous to or as part of legal regulations, and will be less influenced by consensual and general discourses of the 'common good' of society. The increasing specialization within the different sectors or areas will tend towards sector-specific regulations and to more difficult processes of balancing between the different discourses and values. Dependence on sector-specific discourses and semantics will question the existence of a 'general' will.

Moreover, and connected to the preceding development, there has been a *general expansion of law* in most social areas. This expansion of law occurs on several levels of law: it includes public regulatory law, the use of contracts, trade

---

[4] Niklas Luhmann, *The Differentiation of Society* (New York: Columbia University Press, 1981); Niklas Luhmann, *Das Recht der Gesellschaft* (Frankfurt: Suhrkamp, 1993) chs 11–12; Niklas Luhmann, 'The Modern Sciences and Phenomenology', in *Theories of Distinction*, Michael Rasch (ed.) (Stanford: Stanford University Press, 2002).

law, and free movement of goods, services, persons, and capital, and human rights, which often are applied in connection with each other. The expansion of law may thus create more intensive couplings between the different forms of public law and private law, the transcendence of their boundaries, and more intensive forms of legalization. The expansion of law, and its regulation of new technologies, has also led to the legal regulation of areas which previously have been seen as private or personal, or as professionally regulated by technical standards and guidelines. Notable examples include the more detailed regulations of health services, the use of medical biotechnologies, in particular the use of reproductive techniques and prenatal tests, and child–parent relations, as well as social welfare benefits and services. The uses of new technologies have led to public regulation at the boundaries between public and private law or transcending the distinction altogether. The expansion of rights paradoxically often leads to more detailed public regulations in order to implement and secure the rights. One example is the right to non-discrimination which can be quite complex to define and adjudicate as it often sits on the balance between quite different public and private values, such as freedom of expression and various forms of social protection. The changes from a more macro- to a more micro- and market-oriented focus in economic public discourses has also led to an increasing interweaving between public and private economic dynamics. Free movement, rights, markets, and competition are primary institutions of a liberal economy, but are also intensively legally and publicly regulated with a market-oriented regulatory focus.[5]

Most social areas are regulated by public legislation and often controlled in different ways by public agencies. Public and private law thus increasingly *interact horizontally* across society. Many areas are regulated by both public law and private contracts and organized by both public agencies and private corporations. Public and private law *combine and interact in a variety of different ways*. They depend on and use each other. They combine but also compete. Institutional and legal couplings, such as privatization of public utilities, state-owned corporations, and competition law evolve in the interface between public and private law and their respective values. The same standards of economic efficiency often apply in both spheres.

Furthermore, there is *an expansion of law also on the inter- and transnational levels* with a corresponding institutional architecture, including courts, in areas which previously have been primarily regulated on the domestic and nation-state level.[6] International treaties increasingly regulate trade, competition, the environment, climate, labour, and human rights law with direct or indirect effects. International trade and competition law are regulatory regimes with significant effects, both

---

[5] See among the many texts on this: *Constitutionalism, Multilevel Trade, Governance and Social Regulation*, Christian Joerges and Ernst-Ulrich Petersmann (eds) (Oxford: Hart, 2006).

[6] Saskia Sassen, *Territories, Authorities, Rights* (Princeton: Princeton University Press, 2006); Andreas Fischer-Lescano, 'Globalverfassung: Verfassung der Weltgesellschaft' (2002) Archiv für Recht- und Sozialphilosophie; Gunther Teubner, *Constitutional Fragments. Societal Constitutionalism, and Globalization* (Oxford: Oxford University Press, 2012).

procedural and substantive, on public and administrative law at the international and domestic levels. There is a greater variety of political and legal institutions involved in the legislative, administrative, and adjudicative processes. The legal structures of the EU and WTO, in particular, with their preference for and focus on free movement and liberal trade and competition as legal and policy goals have had significant effects on other areas of domestic law and on the structure, goals, and principles of public law.[7] Economic and market-oriented law has become an increasingly vital part of public law. The internationalization of law has led to complex and interdependent multi-level institutional systems and has had significant effects on the structure and the institutions of public law.

Finally, *new forms of law* have evolved. *Self-regulation* and other more autonomous forms are increasingly applied and may be seen as lying on the boundary between public and private law or as qualitatively new legal forms.[8] Public legislation frequently delegates the implementation of law in some areas to self-regulatory mechanisms and more distanced forms of public control. Moreover, the expansion and differentiation of law has also led to various forms of *inclusion of citizens and non-public actors and organizations* in the various processes connected to public regulation. Forms of self-regulation, consumer rights, and patient rights are examples.

Some areas develop *organizations and institutions of their own* for the implementation of regulatory decision-making and control, as part of public agencies, privately organized, or organized by sector. In some cases international institutions or agencies are developed to standardize, harmonize, or regulate highly specialized areas. One well-known example is the Internet Corporation for Assigned Names and Numbers (ICANN), but other examples include UN-based agencies such as the Codex Alimentarius of the FAO/WHO, the UNHCR, and the WTO.[9] *Self-regulatory mechanisms* are used by both public institutions and private organizations. Regulatory and semantic resistance from highly specialized areas can be a well-known problem for public regulatory law. This problem has become more urgent in scope and intensity because the different areas have become increasingly specialized, and thus internally defined, communicatively as well as normatively. A vital problem is how to develop legal concepts, standards, and procedures which include a wider societal scope, also addressing the various negative side-effects and consequences of new technologies, including relevant ethical problems.

[7] Joseph H. H. Weiler (ed.), *The EU, the WTO, and the NAFTA: towards a common law of international trade* (Oxford: Oxford University Press, 2000); Christian Joerges and Ellen Vos (eds), *EU Committees: Social Regulation, Law and Politics* (Oxford: Hart, 1999); Anne-Marie Slaughter, *A New World Order* (Princeton: Princeton University Press, 2004).

[8] See examples in Christian Joerges, Inger-Johanne Sand, and Gunther Teubner (eds), *Transnational Governance and Constitutionalism* (Oxford: Hart, 2004); Gunther Teubner and Andreas Fischer-Lescano, 'Regime-Collisions: The Vain Search for Legal Unity in the Fragmentation of International Law' (2004) 25 Michigan Journal of International Law 999; Gunther Teubner, *Constitutional Fragments. Societal Constitutionalism, and Globalization*.

[9] See note 8.

The societal, institutional, and communicative changes referred to contribute to changes in *how we perceive of society* and of what society is, including how we perceive of the concepts of the public, the state, civil society, the interfaces between the public and private and between the state and civil society, and how we manage or choose to regulate society. Society and the 'public' have become functionally and communicatively differentiated with significant consequences for public law, for the definition of the common good, and the evolution of social practices and norms including legal norms. With the expansion of rights in general, and of human rights in particular, public and private law mechanisms and concepts have become increasingly interconnected and interdependent. The differentiation of the economy has created new interactions and interdependencies between public budgets and markets. New technologies and knowledge create new institutions in society and diversify how power is dispersed. Technologies and knowledge are public dynamics, but also intervene in people's private lives. They contribute significantly to the transcendence of the distinctions between public and private spheres. Public law is not only about controlling the power of the state, but also about controlling the power of a variety of new technologies, with highly structuring, enabling, and potentially coercive qualities.[10]

The globalization of many social, cultural, and economic dynamics will mean that many societal dynamics will evolve at the same time on several institutional and territorial levels which are intensely interconnected and interdependent.[11] On the different institutional and organizational levels, the social dynamics refer to different conceptions of society and different cultural and value preferences. The public law of such cross-boundary strata and frontier zones will have to deal with the multi-levelled social context of both legislation and adjudication, and with the pressure to harmonize even across different social contexts.[12] Public law emerges on domestic, regional, international, and transnational levels according to different procedures and different forms of democratic or other forms of decision-making. In some cases there will be institutional harmonization, in other cases differences will be upheld. Semantic and normative patterns which develop with high degrees of autonomy, such as in specialized technologies, may show resistance to open regulatory democratic processes. Forms of democracy practised on the level of the nation-state are clearly insufficient for many of the regulatory challenges of public law. Global or international institutions are, on the other hand, also insufficiently developed in democratic terms. The consequences of these changes for public law are diverse, still very much in progress and difficult to sufficiently describe and analyse at this stage. In the ensuing section I will analyse some examples and aspects of these changes.

---

[10] Gunther Teubner, 'Societal Constitutionalism', in *Transnational Governance and Constitutionalism.*

[11] Joseph H. H. Weiler, *The Constitution of Europe* (Cambridge: Cambridge University Press, 1999); Teubner and Fischer-Lescano, 'Regime-Collisions'; Slaughter, *A New World Order* ; Sassen, *Territories, Authorities, Rights.*

[12] Sassen, *Territories, Authorities, Rights.*

3. FOUR EXAMPLES OF NEW PUBLIC GLOBAL

AND INTERNATIONAL LAW

3.1 *International and European economic law as a differentiation of public/private law*

The free movement of goods, persons, services, and capital, and competition law of the EU is public regulatory law, and at the same time, and equally vitally, organizes the relations between private actors and guarantees rights. These regulations illustrate both the differentiation of public law and the close inter-action between public and private law. In the EC and EU treaties, economic regulations with the purposes of creating a common market among the member states and more efficient competition with heavier restrictions on state subsidies have been the primary regulatory goals. From the late 1970s this also coincided with a more general monetary, micro-economic, and market orientation in economic policies. Compared with the member-states' more general regulatory systems, the EU treaties and case law contained a more specific economic legislation. In EU law, economic and market-oriented goals have been more fully developed and given preferential treatment compared to other regulatory goals. The free movement of goods, persons, services, and capital, and com-petition law are seen as the most fundamental norms and equivalent principles of Community legislation and are its most fully developed areas of regulation. Social, environmental, and other regulations are treated as exceptions which require strict justification.[13] These regulatory patterns have been developed in order to ensure an effective implementation of free movement and competition. Exceptions are accepted when they are based on objective and non-discriminatory criteria, deemed necessary and proportionate in order to implement accepted public policy objectives, and are applied non-arbitrarily and according to proced-ures which are easily accessible and transparent.[14] Social and environmental protection are to be accorded a high level of protection, but they must not violate or infringe upon the economic regulatory goals. ECJ case law such as *Watts, Laval,* and *Viking,* among others, allows for a high level of protection of non-economic goals; however, the decisions illustrate how the economic goals of free movement receive the primary protection under EU law.[15] In *Laval,* the court accepted that the right to collective bargaining may be a fundamental right, but it can only be exercised subject to certain restrictions and must be reconciled with the requirements relating to rights protected under the EU treaty, such as the free movement of persons and services.[16]

The ECJ has developed highly specialized and precise semantics and patterns of argumentation concerning the interpretation of free movement and the

---

[13] Case C-341/05 *Laval un Partneri Ltd. v Svenska Byggnadsarbetareförbundet and Others* [2007] ECR I-11767 para 87, 101 flw.

[14] Case C-372/04 *The Queen, on the application of: Yvonne Watts v Bedford Primary Care Trust and Secretary of State for Health* [2006] ECR I-04325 para 116; *Laval* para 91 flw.

[15] Case C-438/05 *International Transport Workers' Federation and Finnish Seamen's Union v Viking Line ABP and OÜ Viking Line Eesti* [2007] ECR I-10779.

[16] *Laval* paras 91–96.

standards of non-discrimination in relation to other goals.[17] This is clearly within the remit of public law, but it differentiates public law by creating a particular regulatory scheme of economic law under the standards of free movement and competition law with an effective ban on state subsidies, including on public services. Free movement of goods, services, persons, and capital are seen as rights under the treaties to be fully protected. Other types of rights can also be seen as parts of the general principles of the EU treaties, but are protected in compliance with economic freedoms. EU public law is a particular legal regime with enumerated competences and not a fully comprehensive legal regime subject to the general will of the people with a general balancing of different regulatory goals. WTO economic law shares many of the general characteristics of regulatory specification and delimitation of EU law, but with differences in the specific forms for regulation and with a lack of harmonization. WTO law is a more economically specific legal regime than the EU. The environmental and health protections of the General Agreement on Tariffs and Trade (GATT) Art. XX and the Agreement on the Application of Sanitary and Phytosanitary Measures (SPS) are clearly insufficient as protective regulations in themselves.

The lessons so far from the legislation and the case law of the free movement of the EU and of the WTO is that it has been easier to develop the economically based free-movement regulations effectively, than to establish standards for the protection of the environment, health, and social rights. Effective markets and competition have so far been given preferential treatment. Environmental and health protection are subject to the demands of scientific evidence for hazards and for protective measures. Precaution is applied pursuant to the demands for scientific evidence. Sustainability and ethical considerations are still underdeveloped, legally speaking.[18]

3.2 New interfaces between public and private economic and administrative law

Also within the domestic public regulatory regimes of democratic nation-states there are many signs of an increased differentiation, specialization, and market-orientation of public law and economic regulations with an increased focus on the uses of markets, competition, and economic efficiency both in public regulations and in state agencies. Macro-oriented and planning law instruments have been replaced by competition, benchmarking, privatization, and deregulation. The latter instruments enable an increased autonomy and specialization of the economic ends both within themselves and in relation to other policy goals. The insistence on economic efficiency and the use of competition as regulatory mechanisms leads to clearer distinctions between economic and other policies

---

[17] Cf Case 24/68 *Commission v Italy* [1969] ECR 193; Case 8/74 *Procureur du Roi v Dassonville* [1974] ECR 837; Case 120/78 *Cassis de Dijon* [1979] ECR 649; Case C-267/91 and C-268/91 *Keck and Mithouard* [1993] ECR I-6097; Joseph H. H. Weiler, 'The Constitution of the Common Market Place: Text and Context in the Evolution of the Free Movement of Goods', in *The Evolution of EU Law*, Paul Craig and Gráinne de Búrca (eds) (Oxford: Oxford University Press, 1999); Christian Joerges, 'Free trade: the erosion of national and the birth of transnational governance' (2005) 13 European Review 93.

[18] Oren Perez, *Ecological Sensitivity and Global Legal Pluralism* (Oxford: Hart, 2004) chs 3–4.

and regulatory goals. Public agencies have also become more clearly separated into different types of agencies depending on whether their functions are policy-oriented, performing/producing, regulatory, or controlling.

In Norwegian public law, for example, there has been an immense increase in the use of contracts and other market- and competition-oriented regulatory mechanisms as part of public regulatory regimes.[19] Competition has become an increasingly vital standard and regulatory mechanism applied in public regulation and the further organization of the public sector. Examples include the requirement for a certain return rate on all public investments, even if they are for the general good, the use of public procurement, benchmarking, privatization, and the use of competition as an internal standard. When the OECD in 2003 reported on the status of Norwegian public administration, the main concern of the evaluation was to what degree and how the various public sectors applied 'competition', benchmarking, public procurement, etc.

State-owned corporations, wholly or partially owned, are used for public services, communications, energy production, and other policy areas, such as telecommunications and oil and gas production. Because of the more general history of the use of state corporations in Norway, particularly with regard to hydroelectricity and oil and gas production, Norway has a large number of state-owned corporations. They are run as autonomous corporations on market terms. The three largest corporations in Norway today are partially state owned, the two largest with a clear (state-) majority ownership, Telenor and Statoil. They were both first wholly state owned, and then listed on the NY Stock Exchange for partial private ownership, which inevitably means running them according to market rationality with the government acting as a professional commercial owner. Privatization and market participation also means a more visible exposure of commercial risks in public budgets. In addition to this, a part of the Norwegian state's ownership of Statoil has been placed in a separate corporation fully owned by the state, with the sole function of managing the ownership of Statoil. The Norwegian state's revenue from oil and gas production has for some years now been placed in a state-owned (sovereign wealth) fund, the Norwegian state's pension fund. It is the second largest sovereign wealth fund in the world, with a capitalization of approximately 3,000 million Norwegian krone (£320 million) (2011). The Santiago principles, or 'Generally Accepted Practices and Principles for Sovereign Wealth Funds' (GAPP), are applied by the fund. The annual use of the fund (by the state) is set at a standard rate of 4 per cent return on investment. Both the fund and the state's ownership in Statoil and Telenor underscore the close interaction and interdependence between public and private law and their respective principles and concerns. Both the petroleum and the telecommunication sectors are heavily regulated to ensure the security of production as well as the management of environmental and other hazards. These sectors are also examples of the very close and politically complex interactions between different

---

[19] Inger-Johanne Sand, 'Changes in the organization of public administration and in the relations between the public and the private sectors. Consequences of the evolution of Europeanisation, globalisation and risk society', ARENA working-paper no. 2/2002.

types of public and private corporations and institutions. They are examples of vital societal infrastructures which require different combinations of corporations and public agencies. Other examples are postal services, railways, energy production, water as public utility, airports, etc. Pension policies and funds are another area of complex interdependence between public and private institutions. Changes in the public sector and public law do not lead to its demise, but rather to its differentiation, specialization, and close interaction with private-sector actors. Instead of consensus and balancing between the different policy areas there is interaction and interdependence based on differentiation and autonomy.

3.3 The regulation of the internet—between public, commercial, and transnational law, and the rights of citizens

The internet is part of the public sphere and the 'new' civil society but can also probably best be characterized as a public/private hybrid. It includes masses of private exchanges, but in ways which cannot be guaranteed as private. New networks like Facebook are characterized by the same communications being in both the public and private spheres, thereby blurring the boundaries between them. It is international in how it functions, but depends on specific national installations. The internet and its various sub-organizations are networks, but arguably also new types of societal institutions. Public authorities use the internet for both internal and external communications purposes. The regulation of the internet escapes some of the most traditional forms of public regulatory law with their emphasis on control, by its technology dependence and cross-boundary character. It was started by US defense authorities and is not regulated by an international organization in a traditional sense. The user-based ICANN has become the de facto regulator of domain names internationally, albeit with different states having specific agencies which are appointed to manage domain names nationally.[20]

The internet is in its construction primarily technology-driven, but its development and use are influenced by commercial and non-commercial actors alike. New software and data programs developed by private companies such as Microsoft, Google, Facebook, and Amazon continuously change the ways the internet functions as well as developing new formats for its use. Thus, technological, civil society and commercial dynamics and actors interact closely, albeit in complex and in transparent ways, in the development of the internet, and in how it functions, technologically as well as socially. At the same time it is one of the most vital elements of public communicative infrastructure and the public domain. Consequently it is on the one hand vital for how the state public sector functions, and on the other, enabling an increasingly active non-state public sector.

---

[20] Jochen von Bernstorff, 'The Structural Limitations of Network Governance: ICANN as a Case in Point', in *Transnational Governance and Constitutionalism*.

Public law regulates certain aspects of the use of the internet, such as the regulation of e-commerce and trade, criminal law, and the protection of freedom of expression on the internet. Technology changes and commercial actors continuously create new challenges for the legal regulation of the internet in relation to the classic principles and methods of public law. The internet does, however, support claims for transparency. It has created a form of public sector and established new bridges between the public and the private spheres in modern society. It invades our private sphere both with and without our consent, with the potential to have an immense impact on our lives with consequences that are often not considered. The internet invites participation in situations which seem private, but which become, in fact, public. It invites use, with immense access to information on a global scale, but participation leaves traces. It is a continuously changing infrastructure, and we have still not developed a sufficient set of public law principles, guidelines, values, and considerations for its regulation, state or non-state. The combination of its accessibility, scope of information, transparency, and the vague boundaries between public and private, invites the risk of the potential for misuse or misconception of its use. It is a new non-state public sphere functioning under conditions of globalization, politically and commercially, and creating complex issues for public regulation, for example, in relation to privacy and ethics.

3.4 The regulation of bio- and genetic technologies—between science, markets, politics, law, and ethics

Another new regulatory challenge for public law and with effects of transcending the public/private distinction is the regulation of the new bio- and genetic technologies which have enabled more intensive and invasive forms of biological and genetic engineering which have great potential but also pose significant hazards and risks for health and the environment. With respect to genetic technologies, there are complex ethical implications and questions concerning human dignity involved. Such technologies are 'global facts' insofar as they are disseminated and used globally in many different societal contexts with quite diverse ethical and political views. They are consequently regulated differently in international and domestic regimes. On the one hand, new biotechnologies are in demand in order to improve food production and the treatment of disease. On the other hand the uses of genetically modified organisms (GMOs) in food and plant production may spread in uncontrolled ways, and have cross-boundary effects with potentially irreversible and damaging consequences for local varieties of biodiversity. Genetic knowledge may also create complex ethical dilemmas, and the immediate benefits are not always clear. The use of GMOs, medical biotechnologies, and genetic technologies affect a variety of interests and values, and may have extremely diverse, invasive, and uncertain consequences. Technologies are developed in research and commercial facilities. Their application may have positive effects on food production and the treatment of many diseases, but they may also have uncertain, irreversible, ethically dubious, and significant negative effects. Technologies are commercially exploited and thus relevant for trade, but are also objects of risk analysis and further research by the scientific community. The application of different technologies affects the interests and values of a broad constituency including consumers, patients, and farmers. This illustrates the diversity of interests involved in public law regulations and the diversity of relevant substantive considerations, values, and principles.

The dissemination of new biotechnologies is global. Their use is, however, unevenly distributed, and the views on their relevance politically and ethically diverse. The different economic, environmental, and health regulatory regimes which may affect the use of such technologies, collide in different and unpredictable ways. Regulation of the use of new biotechnologies is, however, to a large extent affected by economic regulation on free movement. The regulatory regimes which affect the use of biotechnologies are both international and domestic, and are frequently uncoordinated. On the international level the most effective public regulatory regimes with relevance also for the regulation of biotechnology are the WTO treaties, which include trade in food and medicines but without specific regulation for biotechnology products and health services. The Agreement on Sanitary and Phytosanitary Measures (SPS) regulates sanitary and phytosanitary protection as part of the trade treaty. Risk assessments are used to decide when such protection mechanisms are necessary.[21] Precautionary measures may be applied, but subject to a reasonable time frame for risk assessment and scientific indications for risk. The Agreement on Trade Related Aspects of Intellectual Property Rights (IPR) (TRIPS) regulates IPR and thus harmonizes regulations for patent rights, including medical patents.

There have been several cases before the WTO Disputè Settlement Bodies (DSB) concerning the use of new biotechnologies in food, in particular *AB report* WT/DS 26/98 EC—Hormones and *Panel report* WT/DS 291–293/2006 EC—Biotech. In both cases the panel or the Appellate Body found in favour of the states applying the technologies in question because they did not find sufficient reasons, in the form of scientific evidence for hazards, for the ban on the import of hormone-treated meat and biotech food into the EU.[22] Precautionary measures were limited to temporary measures, and ethical considerations per se are not part of the regulations, with the exception of *ordre public* considerations.[23] Under EU law the economic regulations are similar, but the EU goes further in substantive harmonizing regulations, with precautionary measures, concerning GMOs and aspects of medical biotechnology, such as Directive 2001/18/EC of the European Parliament and of the Council of 12 March 2001 on the deliberate release into the environment of genetically modified organisms (repealing Council Directive 90/220/EEC [2001] OJ L 106/1), and Directive 98/44/EC of the

---

[21] Joseph H. H. Weiler (ed.), *The EU, the WTO, and the NAFTA: towards a common law of international trade*; Thomas Cottier and Daniel Wüger, *Genetic engineering and the world trade system: World Trade Forum* (Oxford: Oxford University Press, 2008); Oren Perez, *Ecological sensitivity and global legal pluralism: rethinking the trade and environment debate*; Francis Fukuyama, *Our Posthuman Future: Consequences of the Biotechnology Revolution* (New York: Farrar, Straus and Giroux, 2002).

[22] Inger-Johanne Sand, 'The legal regulation of the environment and new technologies' (2001) 22(2) Zeitschrift für Rechtssoziologie 169.

[23] Cf Report from ILA Committee on Biotechnology, chair Thomas Cottier (Hague, 2010).

European Parliament and of the Council of 6 July 1998 on the legal protection of biotechnological inventions [1998] OJ L 213/13. The EU has argued for changes relating to measures taken pursuant to the precautionary principle so that longer periods of time can be used for further research in cases where there are indications of scientific evidence for hazards. This is exemplified in the two cases referred to above decided by the Panel and the Apellate Body of the WTO DSB. The cases resulted in extensive reports which should be seen as examples not only of trade law, but also of public international law. The main structural constraint for consideration of the issues is that of trade law, as follows from the WTO treaties, but the cases are a good illustration of just how entangled different legal and policy areas have become, and the problems created by the lack of sufficient international regulation under the WTO umbrella concerning health and environmental protection as well as the omission of ethical considerations from the regime. The examples illustrate the lack of general principles in public international law, and its dependence on the specific treaties. Another example of the implications of WTO law on the use of medical biotechnology is the effect of the TRIPS agreement and the harmonization of patent regulations on the production of medicines. Costly medicines may be too expensive for less-developed states. The production and the costs of HIV medicine is an example in point. The great need for such medicines in South Africa and Brazil led first to court cases and then concessions from the international pharmaceutical companies for the production of cheaper such medicines in Brazil for use in poorer and less developed states.[24]

There are however several international (soft law) declarations under the auspices of the United Nations Educational, Scientific and Cultural Organization (UNESCO) concerning the regulation of biotechnology and bioethics: the Universal Declaration on Bioethics and Human Rights (2005), and the Universal Declaration on the Human Genome and Human Rights (1997). They include bioethical principles but are not part of sanctionable regimes. With their emphasis on bioethics and on ethical considerations more widely, they illustrate a different type of public international law than the trade treaties. The regulation of medical biotechnology is primarily done on a national basis. In particular, the regulation of reproductive techniques and prenatal tests are culturally and ethically sensitive, and what is and is not allowed varies significantly even among states which share many cultural values and traditions. The Convention on Biological Diversity (CBD, UNEP, 1992) and subsequent Cartagena Protocol on Biosafety (UNEP, 2000) are more specifically and operatively formulated in terms of rights, and refer to international courts, including access to genetic resources on mutually agreed terms and prior informed consent, and access to and transfer of technology. Precaution, sustainability, and ethical considerations are insufficiently dealt with in these conventions even if protection of biodiversity, access to genetic resources, and sharing of technologies are their main goals.

---

[24] Gunther Teubner and Andreas Fischer-Lescano, 'Regime-Collisions: The Vain Search for Unity in the Fragmentation of Global Law'; Boaventura de Sousa Santos and César Rodríguez-Garavito (eds), *Law and Globalization from Below: Towards a Cosmopolitan Legality* (New York: Cambridge University Press, 2005).

The themes and examples referred to in this section illustrate on the one hand, how public international law is lacking in general principles and fragmented and diverse in its different disciplines and treaties, and on the other hand, how the same treaty themes are deeply entangled and interdependent in how they function. The examples also illustrate the immense diversity with regard to objects, considerations, and values of public law, and the unavoidable conflicts of law within the framework of public law.

4. CONCLUSIONS: WHAT IS PUBLIC LAW UNDER CONDITIONS OF GLOBALIZATION?

The substance, the principles, the procedures, and the institutions of public law mirror society, the practices and the regulation of power, and the relations between actors. Public law is an expression of power, and it regulates power. Public law has been a quintessential feature of the infrastructure of modern nation-states. It is difficult to conceive of states without public law. Both the processes of globalization and the increasing functional and communicative differentiation of politics, law, economics, science, and their many operative sub-systems, have led to significant changes and an increased diversity of the themes, procedures, concepts, and institutions of public law, and the concept of the public.[25] The wide variety of objects and themes of public regulation indicate an equivalent variety of public agencies, procedures, and principles. Society, and thus also the public sphere, has become increasingly communicatively and institutionally differentiated by the differentiation of politics, law, economics, science, and their many organizational sub-systems. It is therefore less clear whether and how 'the common good' can be defined. It has been said that public law has moved from disciplining a repressive state, to regulating a variety of new technologies.[26] Conflicts concern citizens and technological regimes as much as citizens and the state. Technologies are treated more as given realities, and not as political or accountable institutions. Inter- and transnational institutions have become part of political and legal decision-making, but they are not always democratic nor held accountable. They stand in a different relation to the citizens than the state. How political decisions are made, and how consensus and compromise are reached, are different on a global or international basis from that of the domestic level not only in terms of different politico-legal regimes, but also because they refer to a much more culturally heterogeneous foundation.

The consequences for public law of these changes concern many of its qualities. We need to ask *what is society*, and *what is the public in society*, under conditions of globalization. We need to look into what the functions of public law are, what its institutions are, how they can be legitimized, and how rule-of-law institutions can be upheld under more legally pluralistic and societally complex

---

[25] Niklas Luhmann, *The Differentiation of Society; Risk: A Sociological Theory.*

[26] Gunther Teubner, 'The King's Many Bodies' (1997) 31 Law and Society Review 763; Gunther Teubner, 'Societal Constitutionalism'.

situations. Three types of consequences can be pointed to here: first, globalization and various forms of multi-level governance will have *consequences for the forms and the procedures of democracy* in the creation of public law and thus also of its legitimacy. Decision-making on the international level will imply more indirect democratic participation. It may involve significant compromises. It may also mean a more specialized, and at times technocratic, sector-by-sector, institutional decision-making process. On the other hand, international treaties and organizations have the potential to include cross-boundary problems and dynamics in ways nation-states cannot, and thus have the potential to respond more realistically to a wider democratic polity in relation to current problems even if procedures are more indirect and complex.

Secondly, *the themes and problems of public law are changing* at both the domestic and the international levels to those of a more liberal economy and to the regulation of a variety of technologies. Several regulatory areas exemplify the changes, the transcendence of the public/private divide, and the institutional consequences involved. Public economic regulatory regimes are focused on creating fair conditions for competition, liberal markets, and free movement. A well-functioning market economy is seen as vital also for macro-economic purposes. In liberal market theories there are close connections between micro- and macro-economics. Liberal rights are seen as the basis for a functioning economy. Free-movement regulations and competition law, such as in the EU, are however in effect quite intricate and detailed regulatory regimes. Even liberal rights have to draw boundaries between them and various forms of social protection. Domestic public regulations in a liberal economy apply a variety of market-oriented mechanisms which are also exemplary of the transcendence of the public/private divide including public procurement, privatization of services, state-owned corporations, benchmarking, evaluation, certification, and accreditation. State-owned corporations and public pension funds are good examples of the fusion between corporate, private, and public economics, and of the links between public and private accountability, and between social and economic responsibility.[27] By way of illustration, the Norwegian Pension Fund (based on petroleum taxes and income) depends on oil and gas prices, the international stock market, and the public regulatory regimes of many states, but is also a vital public asset and operates according to public economic and legal standards. The internet has become the most vital communications infrastructure, and is public and private at the same time. Created by US defense authorities, it functions as a common utility defined by its technologies and uses. It is a technology network used by public and private actors. Its domain-name (and organizing) company is ICANN, a non-governmental organization, which cooperates with governmental advisory committees. Certain aspects of internet use are regulated by public authorities, but the impact of the internet must primarily be explained by its technology and the potential for use created by this. The regulation of the use of

---

[27] Inger-Johanne Sand, 'Changes in the organization of public administration and in the relations between the public and the private sectors. Consequences of the evolution of Europeanisation, globalisation and risk society'.

new bio- and genetic technologies is another example of a social issue and accompanying legal regulation transcending the traditional boundaries between public and private. Some of the main problems of current regulations concern complex risk assessment and ethical problems. The risk assessment relies heavily on specialized science. The ethical issues transcend public/private distinctions, discourses, and values. Both the internet and new biotechnologies are technologies with significant effects on society, also ethical, creating new institutions beyond the state and classic public law institutions. They require public law regulation. The autonomy of technologies does however pose challenges for legal interventions.[28]

Thirdly, *the regulatory challenges* are now global, technological, risk-oriented, ethical, and involve the transcendence of public/private law distinctions. New technologies, their global use and exploitation, an increased focus on human rights, and more intensive combinations of public and private law mechanisms have produced complex regulatory themes which have extended the boundaries of public law, and how we think about it. Public regulations are increasingly formulated in more heterogeneous social, cultural, and political contexts. The new regulatory themes and their global context have led to the emergence of new regulatory concepts, standards, and principles, or to a renewed focus on certain concepts. Substantive regulatory concepts are needed in order to formulate a baseline of human rights protection, environmental and health protection, and some forms of social protection. Several such concepts have been formulated, but they are still too vague, too indeterminate, and insufficiently developed. Some of these concepts include human dignity, precaution, health safety, sustainability, biodiversity, generational justice, and ethical standards. These are vital concepts, but they need to be more precisely defined and more robustly interpreted, particularly in relation to economic standards. At the same time public law is still essentially defined by the classical procedures and principles of modern democratic societies, such as the rule of law, objectivity, rationality, impartiality, transparency, and participation, in addition to democratic participation and legitimacy mentioned earlier. Additionally proportionality may be used to provide context to particular functional aims as well as define the relationship between various goals. Further reflection on the use and development of both the newer and the more classical concepts is a vital issue for further research in public international as well as domestic public law.

---

[28] Teubner and Fischer-Lescano, 'Regime-Collisions'; Gunther Teubner, Hans Lindahl, Emilios Christodoulidis and Chris Thornhill, 'Constitutionalising Polycontextuality' (2011) 20(2) Social and Legal Studies 209.

❧ 11 ❧

(The Failure of) Public Law and
the Deliberative Turn*

Oliver Gerstenberg

I. BACKGROUND DILEMMA: NEGATIVE (PRAGMATIC)
VERSUS ASPIRATIONAL CONSTITUTIONALISM

Contemporary constitutional theory has trapped itself in a false dilemma. There is today a widespread consensus that every constitution's abstract and open-textured provisions are subject to protracted, reasonable disagreement among interpreters, not only constitutional courts and legislatures and the ordinary courts, but also in the European context, between national constitutional courts, the Court of Justice of the European Union (CJEU), and the European Court of Human Rights (ECtHR).[1] Given this set of circumstances, then the increasingly central role of courts in national and supranational polities, through the mechanism of judicial review, is problematic. Two different conceptions of constitutions and the role of courts in their interpretation and enforcement are frequently advanced to deal with this problem.

The first proposes a 'return' to limiting judicial review to a purely negative constitutionalism; that is, that the only principles which should be contained in a constitution are those which can be reasonably subjected to judicial review. Constitutional guarantees against the conduct of government operations should be restrictive, negative defensive liberties of the individual against the state, which can easily be contained within legal rules. By contrast, a second view advocates viewing the constitution as an aspirational document, although significantly without a prominent role for courts in its interpretation and application. As such, the constitution should reflect and give expression to a set of publicly shared values as well as the hopes and aims of society as a whole. Part of this

* For comments, detailed suggestions, and discussion, from which this paper has greatly benefitted over various stages, I would like to thank Charles F. Sabel, Cormac Mac Amhlaigh, and Neil Walker. I would also like to thank Richard Bellamy for ongoing discussion concerning the ECtHR, the *Hirst* case, and forms of judicial review. For a discussion of closely related issues, cf Mark Tushnet's Comment on an article of mine, together with my response, on <http://www.iconnectblog.com/2012/11/article-review-response-mark-tushnet-and-oliver-gerstenberg-on-rights-adjudication/>.

[1] L. Garlicki, 'Cooperation of courts: The role of supranational jurisdictions in Europe' (2008) 6(3–4) International Journal of Constitutional Law 509, 512, who speaks of a 'triangle that has, at its three vertices, the various national ... constitutional courts, the ECJ, and the ECtHR'.

recognition is the explicit inclusion of positive rights within the constitution itself; rights, that is, which direct the state to protect individuals against threats to these values, not from government, but from private actors in private–horizontal (civil society) relationships. However, these rights are realized away from the courts, in the sphere of politics.

The aim of this chapter is to suggest, against the backdrop of ever-growing court scepticism, the possibility of a third, proceduralist, view to the two positions outlined above. It argues that the 'de-nationalized', constitutional rights regime in Europe is moving beyond minimalist–negative constitutionalism, and increasingly towards the terrain of ambitious positive rights, but it does so by enlisting (rather than undermining) national diversity and subsidiarity in a recursive, experimentalist process. Moreover, it argues that this development is a good thing, and that this recursive process shows the possibility of a 'deliberative turn' in public law scholarship. This proceduralist 'deliberative turn' preserves an important role for courts both under conditions of deep and reasonable disagreement about rights as well as with respect to the aspirational view of constitutionalism, arguing that the European context of a multidimensional system of rights protection provides an illuminating illustration of this ideal. The core of a proceduralist view is the idea of a *recursive process*, in which understandings of principles and paradigmatic instances of their application mutually shape and transform one another. Thus, the role of courts in this proceduralist model, including the ECtHR or the CJEU, lies in mobilizing other actors, namely national courts, through the formulation of a broad framework of principles. This forces national courts to reconsider their longstanding jurisprudence or 'automatic'—legal and factual—default assumptions in the light of those framework principles. As 'outsider-courts', the ECtHR and the CJEU can trigger innovation and raise the standard of justification states must meet by giving a voice to hitherto marginalized groups and their concerns. But, crucially, those framework-principles are themselves subject to revision and reconsideration as the experience of dealing with the diverse national contexts of discovery and application accumulates.

The chapter will proceed as follows: first, it will explore the dichotomy between negative and aspirational constitutionalism in order to situate the proceduralist move in the context of debate. It will then, by way of implication, suggest that the proceduralist turn provides us with a useful response to various forms of scepticism about Euro-constitutionalism beyond the state. It will subsequently explore various strategies in which 'outsider courts' can play a benign, proceduralizing role vis-à-vis national law.

2. IS THERE A FAILURE OF (PUBLIC) LAW?

The starting point for our discussion regarding the problems with current practices of public law, and in particular the institution of judicial review and the role of courts in constitutional interpretation, is Max Weber's observations on the 'materialization' of law; that is, judicial recourse to social values of justice and fairness, as a challenge to legal formalism. As Weber noted:[2]

> New demands for a 'social law' to be based upon such emotionally colored ethical postulates as 'justice' or 'human dignity,' and directed against the very dominance of a mere business morality, have arisen with the emergence of the modern class problem . . . By these demands, legal formalism itself has been challenged. Such a concept as economic duress, or the attempt to treat as immoral, and thus as invalid, a contract because of a gross disproportion between promise and consideration, are derived from norms which, from the legal standpoint, are entirely amorphous and which are neither juristic nor conventional nor traditional in character but ethical and which claim as their legitimation substantive justice rather than formal legality.

This threat to legality is compounded by the 'status ideologies of the lawyers themselves' and the 'demand for "judicial creativeness" at least where the statute is silent'.[3] Four different responses to this problem of judicial policy-making and legislation can be identified. The first prioritizes the autonomy of a self-regulating private economic law of mutual coordination in the place of public law and views a particular role for the judiciary within this self-regulating practice. The other three responses to the overweening role of the judiciary in contemporary public law reject the view that all legality should be tethered to the market, but they all, in different ways, grapple with the concerns about the transformation of constitutional courts—in Kelsenian language—from 'negative legislators' into 'positive legislators', to the detriment both of democracy and of the integrity of ordinary law.

2.1 Ordoliberalism: private (economic) law versus public law

Ordoliberalism is legal thought which sees the role of law as maintaining and preserving the economic sphere from political interference, and it lent particular theoretical support to the European project, now the EU and the ECHR, on the grounds of a belief in rather a neat division of labour. It saw the role of a new and autonomous European economic law as implementing and protecting a system of open markets and undistorted competition at the supranational level from political interference, while at the same time allowing member states to retain competence in the area of social regulation compatible with open markets.[4]

The lodestar of these developments was the 'liberal principle' that the contracting states should not allow the political to contaminate the economic; the idea, as Wilhelm Röpke put it, 'of the widest possible separation of the two

---

[2] M. Weber, *Economy and Society: An Outline of Interpretive Sociology*, G. Roth and C. Wittich (eds) (Berkeley: University of California Press, 1978) 886.

[3] Weber, *Economy and Society*, 886.

[4] As Mestmäcker wrote, 'it is the task of the Community to guarantee and implement a policy of open markets and undistorted competition, while the Member States retain legislative and executive powers that are compatible with open markets'. E. J. Mestmäcker, 'On the Legitimacy of European Law' 58 RABELSZ 615 at 633 (1994).

spheres of government and economy ... of Imperium and Dominum ...'.[5] By observing 'this principle of separation', indeed, by radicalizing 'the largest possible "depoliticization" of the economic sphere', it would become possible, Röpke argued, 'to reduce to a minimum the economic significance of the coexistence of sovereign states with their different legal orders ... systems of administration and separate citizenships'.[6] As a consequence, the 'economic process [could be] transferred from the sphere of administration, public law, penal courts, in short, of the "State", to the sphere of the market, of private law, of property, in short of the "society"'.

This notion resonated with Hayek's early views in the 1940s which anticipated a 'new form of international government under which certain strictly defined powers are transferred to an international authority, while in all other respects the individual countries remain responsible for their internal affairs',[7] the role of which was to preserve 'international order or lasting peace'[8] in the absence of 'any common ideals of distributive justice'.[9]

From the viewpoint of judicial review, the courts were simply to uphold the economic law of open and free markets against interference by states. This would be achieved, in part, by endowing private actors with negative rights which could be enforced against states attempting to interfere in the economy or create restrictions or obstacles to free and open markets.

2.2 Constitutional positivism

The second response to the 'materialization' of the law and the potential activism of judges was the constitutional positivism of Austrian jurist, Hans Kelsen. Kelsen is widely credited with being the inventor of a European-style, centralized model of judicial review with a constitutional court specifically made responsible for reviewing the constitutionality of government acts.[10] The contrast with this model, as Kelsen himself emphasized,[11] was that of the US system, which had a 'diffused' system of review where 'any judge of any court, in any case, at any

---

[5] W. Röpke, 'Economic Order and International Law' in *Recueil des courses* (The Hague: Martinus Nijhoff Publishers, 1954), 207–70, 224.

[6] W. Röpke, 'Economic Order and International Law'. cf. fn. 5.

[7] F. A. Hayek, *The Road to Serfdom* (London: Routledge, 1944) 239.

[8] Hayek, *The Road to Serfdom*, 226.

[9] Hayek, *The Road to Serfdom*, 228. And 'The need is for an international political authority which, without power to direct the different people what they must do, must be able to restrain them from action which will damage others. The powers ... are ... essentially the powers of the ultra-liberal "laissez-faire" state'. Later, in F. A. Hayek, *Law, Legislation, and Liberty: Volume 1, Rules and Order* (Chicago: The University of Chicago Press,1973), he explained: 'The constitution is essentially a superstructure erected over a pre-existing system of law to organize the enforcement of that law ... [and] to support these preexisting rules'. That pre-existing system of law is private economic law—the rules of free movement of economic factors and of free contractual exchange—as the pure form of law.

[10] A. Stone Sweet, 'Why Europe Rejected American Judicial Review' (2003) 101 Michigan Law Review 2744.

[11] H. Kelsen, 'Judicial Review of Legislation. A Comparative Study of the Austrian and the American Constitution' (1942) 4 The Journal of Politics 183.

time, at the behest of any litigating party, has the power to declare a law unconstitutional'.[12] Two features were central to Kelsen's model of courts structures; firstly, the concentration of all the constitutional review powers within a single body, the constitutional court at the apex of the legal system, and secondly, the positioning of this court outside and independent from the ordinary appellate system of courts.

Kelsen's centralized model differs from the ordoliberal view of the role of courts through its insistence that the rule of law not be limited to maintaining the boundaries of a competitive market. Indeed, the appeal of the Kelsenian model of a detached constitutional court lies in its capacity to increase the constitution's democratic responsiveness to changing social values. The constitution can become a tool to challenge the 'authority of the traditional civil law courts and the psychology of their judges'.[13] Indeed, constitutional law could provide a normative vantage point from which to challenge the view that 'constitutional law passes, administrative law persists',[14] or the view that '*Staatsrecht vergeht, Privatrecht besteht*'—public (state) law passes, private law persists.[15]

However, significantly Kelsen himself excluded individual rights from the domain of a *justiciable* constitution. He considered the judicial review of politics—the annulment of statutes by the constitutional court—to be itself an inherently and irredeemably *political* activity. A justiciable constitution must not, he insisted, contain any open-ended provisions in need of interpretation, such as constitutional rights or abstract concepts such as justice, liberty, equality, and morality, and he warned of the dangers to democracy and the rule of law resulting from writing or reading 'supra-positive'[16] norms and open-textured, justice-related concepts into a constitution. The danger lay in transforming constitutional courts from 'negative legislators' into 'positive legislators'; that is, a role where the element of the unconstrained, free creation (*freie Schöpfung*) of the content of law would prevail over the element of mere law-application, where constitutional constraint would prevail.[17] The salutary firewall between 'positive' and 'negative' legislators would collapse.[18]

---

[12] A. Stone-Sweet, 'Why Europe Rejected American Judicial Review', 2770.

[13] L. Garlicki, 'Cooperation of courts: The role of supranational jurisdictions in Europe', 45.

[14] O. Mayer, *Deutsches Verwaltungsrecht*, vol. 1, 3rd edn (München: Duncker & Humblot, 1924, 1969 reprint).

[15] Cf Hayek, *Law, Legislation and Liberty*, Vol 1, 135 and 178 (fn), referring to Hans Huber, but also to J. E. M. Portalis, *Discours préliminaire du premier projet de code civil* (1801) in Conference du Code Civil (Paris, 1805), col. I, p. xiv: 'L'experience prouve que les hommes changes plus facilement le domination que de lois' [sic].

[16] H. Kelsen, 'Wesen and Entwicklung der Staatsgerichtsbarkeit', *VVDStL* (1929) 30, 52.

[17] Kelsen, 'Wesen and Entwicklung der Staatsgerichtsbarkeit', 55 f.

[18] '[I]f—as is sometimes the case—the constitution itself contains references to such principles by invoking ideals of "justice," "freedom," "equality," "morality" etc. without any specification of their meaning... The delegation of justice, freedom, equality, morality etc.... means nothing else but the empowerment of the legislature as well as of the [judicial and administrative organs] who apply and execute the law to use the resulting leeway according to their own free discretion... any arbitrary content could be seen as justifiable... But with respect to constitutional adjudication... these principles can play an extremely dangerous role... What the majority of judges [of a constitutional court] considers

As such, it puts democracy centre stage and centralized judicial review in a single constitutional court (thus enabling the emancipation of constitutional law from ordinary law), but it also—for reasons related to Weberian value scepticism—provided a bulwark against the emergence of a judge-made constitution.

2.3 The 'liberaler Rechtsstaat'

A third response to the materialization of the law was particularly prevalent in post-war Germany as the new Basic law was put into practice. During this period the Kelsensian idea of the separation of jurisdictions began to fade and the idea of a judge-made constitution took off. The German Basic Law, for instance, stipulated in Article I III that the Bill of Rights 'shall bind the legislature, the executive, and the judiciary as directly enforceable law'. Writing in the 1950s, Ernst Forsthoff argued that there was a stark choice to be made between a 'parliamentary-legislative state' and a 'jurisdictional state', where the constitutional court would rule supreme.[19] In order to allow the legislature to take centre stage and avoid government by judiciary, Forsthoff argued that a justiciable constitution had to be restricted to adjudicating on negative liberties, and the judiciary should only adopt formalist canons of interpretation, such as textualism, original intent, and systematic context.[20] The consequences of the constitutionalization of specific areas of law through judicial review would be a shift from the *Gesetzesstaat* to the self-programming autocracies of *Richterstaat* and *Verwaltungsstaat*; a state, that is, where constitutional courts arrogate to themselves the monopoly on government functions including both the power to legislate and apply legislation.

In doing so, Forsthoff identified a significant problem; that of a constitutional court going beyond the traditional realm of constitutional law, invading other branches of law. A result of the 'constitutionalization' of specific branches of the law would be the subjection of the normative content of each of those branches not only to ordinary law, issued by the legislature, but to judge-made constitutional law.

Hence, Forsthoff rejected Rudolf Smend's proposal to overcome the problem of constitutionalization in 1928 in the context of Weimar and then in an influential article in January 1933,[21] where he conceived of the constitution as a system of values rather than a body of rules. These values expressed the shared civic-republican aspirations of the *citizens* and elements of 'substantive integration',

---

as just, can be the exact opposite of what the majority of the people consider as just [with the consequence of] a highly inappropriate shift of power from the parliament to an instance outside the parliament; an instance which can become exponent of political forces entirely different from those, which find expression within the parliament'. Kelsen, 'Wesen, and Entwicklung der Staatsgerichtsbarkeit', *VVDStL*, 70 (Oliver Gerstenberg, trans.).

[19]   E. Forsthoff, *Rechtsstaat im Wandel, Verfassungsrechtliche Abhandlungen*, 2nd edn, 1954–1973 (1976) 173.

[20]   E. Forsthoff, *Rechtsstaat im Wandel*.

[21]   Bürger und Bourgeois im deutschen Staatsrecht: Rede gehalten bei der Reichsgründungsfeier der Friedrich-Wilhelms-Universität Berlin am 18 Januar 1933, Preussische Druckerei- und Verlags-Aktiengesellschaft, 1933.

rather than rules applied by the courts and addressed to the *bourgeoisie*. Although not justiciable, their institutional role and the efficacy of the values would inspire and guide the exercise of the discretion of all state institutions.

By contrast, Forsthoff argued that the Basic Law was strictly technical, statutory law and did not contain open-ended commitments. The 'liberal logics', as he put it, of the formal and freedom-oriented *Rechtstaat* were spelled out in the public, abstract, and general norms that could be applied as rules, and there was a structural correspondence between the rules of the liberal *Rechtstaat* and the market-based capitalist economy.[22] 'The constitution', Forsthoff concluded, 'cannot be social law [*Sozialgesetz*]';[23] for it is 'the task of the legislator to concretize a constitutional norm to such an extent that its execution is possible by way of enforcement of the statutory legal norm'.[24]

2.4 Post-Rawlsian positive 'aspirational' constitutionalism

The fourth response to this problem of the materialization of the law is particularly influenced by the work of John Rawls. This position addresses squarely the issue of deep and good-faith disagreement about constitutional provisions, not least constitutional rights. It asks how the coercive power of the state may be justified to those who disagree with its exercise due to the fact that, on the one hand, in a just society laws must be justifiable to each and every individual subject to them, but also, because of the 'burdens of judgment', we cannot all agree on which laws are to be supported and adopted. The answer to this conundrum of liberal legality on the Rawlsian model lies in a *proceduralist move*, where individuals with persistently differing (but often reasonable) understandings of justice and fairness may nonetheless be parties to an overlapping consensus within an institutional framework of democratic legitimacy. This framework should be used to decide how disagreements over substance are to be dealt with. If individuals agree to this framework-procedure, then they have in some relevant sense agreed to the laws which the procedure produces, and hence laws will be, *pro tanto*, justified.[25]

Rawls himself provided a generous notion of 'background justice', of the requirements of justice any modern political society must meet which include not only the requirements of equality of economic and other opportunity in a formal, legal sense, but also a 'fair' equality of opportunity, as well as a requirement to make the situation of the economically worst-off as favourable as

---

[22] Forsthoff, *Rechtsstaat im Wandel*, 174, referring to M. Weber.

[23] Forsthoff, *Rechtsstaat im Wandel*, 180.

[24] Forsthoff, *Rechtsstaat im Wandel*, 180.

[25] Cf: 'Without tying ourselves to naïve claims about a clean separabilty of substance from procedure, it seems we can sometimes reasonably hope that parties caught in profound disagreement about matters of great importance to them—those being what we call the "substance" of their debate—can nevertheless be brought to agree on an institutional framework (call it "procedure") to be used in deciding how those matters are to be dealt with'. F. Michelman, *Poverty in Liberalism: A Comment on the Constitutional Essentials* (2012) at 14, available at <http://www.papers.ssrn.com/sol3/papers.cfm?abstract_id=2133457>.

possible while respecting the equal basic liberties of everyone (the difference principle).[26] Underlying this conception of background justice was the view that individual choices, expressed and coordinated within the private law of contract, will result in substantial inequalities in actual outcomes among individuals, in addition to, and reinforcing, the inequalities in *ex ante* life prospects.[27] The question then arises as to how to secure this background justice in terms of institutional design, and in particular whether socio-economic rights are justiciable and whether they should be enforced by courts. Significantly, Rawls himself did not include fair equality of opportunity among the (justiciable) constitutional essentials, which define the framework of democratic legitimacy.[28] The constitutional essentials only comprise the defensive basic liberties, such as basic liberal rights of conscience, free expression, etc. The reason for this exclusion was Rawls' view that socio-economic rights are far more complex, numerous, contestable, and debatable than the defensive liberties, and hence not justiciable.

Post-Rawlsian constitutionalism thus reserves the full integrity of constitutional public law values at the normative level against a backdrop of growing court scepticism at the institutional level.

3. EUROPEAN CONSTITUTIONALISM ENTERS THE SCENE

The four responses to the question of the legitimacy of judicial review and the role of courts in interpreting and applying the constitution as a response to the problems reflected in Weber's materialization of the law were developed, with the partial exception of ordoliberalism, within the context of the state and state institutions. However, these problems are arguably exacerbated with respect to the post-state arena, and in particular the dense governance structures prevailing in Europe, particularly through the EU and ECHR. If judicial review is undemocratic at the state level, then it is particularly problematic at the post-state level where courts and judges are not even members of the political community whose laws are being adjudicated.

The main concern within Euro-constitutionalism is the 'phenomenon of parallel constitutional protection (multidimensionality)';[29] that is, the plurality of partly overlapping, partly conflicting, non-hierarchical rights-protecting legal

---

[26] J. Rawls, *A Theory of Justice* (Cambridge, Mass: Harvard University Press, 1971) 302.

[27] As T. Nagel explains, there is an intrinsic connection between the requirement of 'procedural background justice' and the idea of a collective responsibility of society as a whole: '[t]he moral key to Rawls' more expansive position [in comparison to economic liberalism] is in the idea that, because of the essential role of the state, the law, and the conventions of property in making possible the extraordinary productivity and accumulations of a modern economy, we bear collective responsibility for the general shape of what results from the sum of individual choices within that framework'. In T. Nagel, 'Rawls and Liberalism' in S. Freeman (ed.), *The Cambridge Companion to Rawls* (Cambridge: Cambridge University Press, 2003), 80.

[28] J. Rawls, *Political Liberalism* (New York: Columbia University Press, 1993) 229–30, explaining that we can expect more agreement about 'whether the principles for the basic rights and liberties are realized' than 'whether the aims of the principles covering social and economic inequalities are realized'.

[29] Garlicki, *Cooperation of courts: The role of supranational jurisdictions in Europe*, 511.

orders including domestic legal orders, EU law, the ECHR, and general public international law. The responsibility for the adequate protection of individual rights is no longer the exclusive task of national law, but is shared within that new constitutional architecture beyond the state. Yet this raises familiar concerns regarding the effect of this multidimensionality on national law. For example, Dieter Grimm fears the relativization of national constitutions by international courts such as the ECtHR, which 'do not stay within the traditional framework of international law'.[30] He fears the narrowing of the 'field of application'[31] of national law through the effectiveness and primacy of EU law in national courts. This results in the EU's court, the CJEU, aggregating for itself the powers of national constitutional courts. He concludes that any notions of constitutionalism and constitutionalization at the supranational level are misleading 'insofar as they nourish the hope that the loss national constitutions suffer from international-ization and globalization could be compensated for on the supranational level'.[32]

In a similar vein, the leading proponent for a revival of *droit publique*, Martin Loughlin, provides a thoroughly pessimistic outlook for post-state constitutional-ism. For Loughlin, the export of constitutionalism beyond the state context is fraught with danger. In particular this danger is exacerbated by the fact that any such post-state constitutional discourse would be unduly *'strained'* if founded on the constitutional ideal of popular authorization. The result, argues Loughlin, is 'constitutionalization' rather than constitutionalism, a 'free-standing process of rationalist constitutional design' which can operate without the fiction of popular authorization. However, he counsels that without some appeal to a 'people' as a long-stop function, an 'authoritarian constitutionalism' would emerge, a new 'imperial network' which 'will seek to secure the legitimacy of its global rule'.[33]

These concerns closely resonate with Fritz Scharpf's diagnosis of a growing constitutional asymmetry within the European architecture. Judicialization and judge-made law has had, according to Scharpf's defeatist account, 'a liberalizing and deregulatory impact on the socioeconomic regimes of EU Member States', thus confirming the 'liberal transformation which Hayek had expected'.[34] The political project of European integration was to be realized by an economic program effectuated through the rule of law. On the one hand, the emphasis on 'integration through law' had, of course, to do with political stagnation at various historical stages of the integration project and could be understood as an audacious but also a prudentially wise choice, insofar as transnational legality helped, as Weiler has pointed out, prevent free-riding and provided stability and continuity to any acquis even in periods of political instability and wavering commitment.[35] Yet, on the other hand, the reliance on law also, by way of an

---

[30] D. Grimm, 'The Constitution in the Process of Denationalization' (2005) 12(4) Constellations 447, 457.

[31] Grimm, 'The Constitution in the Process of Denationalization', 457.

[32] Grimm, 'The Constitution in the Process of Denationalization', 457.

[33] M. Loughlin, 'In Defence of Staatslehre' (2009) 48 *Der Staat* 1–27, 26.

[34] F. W. Scharpf, 'The Asymmetry of European Integration: or why the EU cannot be a "Social Market Economy"', KFG Working Paper No 6 (2009), abstract, 6. 2009.

[35] Weiler, *The Constitution of Europe* (Cambridge: Cambridge University Press, 1999), ch 2.

unintended consequence, fatefully led, according to Scharpf's bleak diagnosis, to a constitutional asymmetry or bias overall towards individualist economic liberalism to the detriment of civic-republican, public law values embedded in national law, leaving it without defence against encroachment. As such, 'national [constitutional] courts cannot be expected to constrain the impact of a [CJEU] case law that dynamically extends the domain of protected individualism at the expense of political capacities for collective self-determination'.[36]

4. THE TREND TOWARDS A PROCEDURALIZATION OF PUBLIC LAW

'Europe' is and remains interesting, precisely because its complex and multidimensional legal architecture illustrates such a proceduralist turn and experimentalist arrangement.

Considering the EU context in particular, Francis Jacobs, one-time Advocate General of the CJEU, observes that the European rule of law 'cannot coexist with traditional conceptions of sovereignty'.[37] Rejecting a merely formal conception of the rule of law, Jacobs points to the ongoing emergence and crystallization of a more substantive European-wide conception of the rule of law as an embodiment and expression of 'certain values which seem, at least in Europe, widely accepted as essential to modern social and political life'.[38] *Sovereignty* shifts from the national parliamentary legislator to the fundamental legal values themselves and the multi-level architecture of complex enforcement. As such: 'principles of national law may have a positive influence on the development of EU law; conversely, EC law may have a beneficial influence on the development of national law'.[39]

As a consequence of these mutual interactions, these values have been supported by the impact of EU law and the ECHR.[40] This is particularly the case, Jacobs argues, with respect to its far-reaching jurisprudence on the principle of equal treatment. In developing the law on equal treatment, the CJEU has often raised the standards of justification to the benefit of weaker parties, and it has done so by encouraging experimentation at the level of national law with regard to the implementation of the principle of equal treatment.

Another response to the charges of the hegemony and uniformity of post-state constitutionalism is offered by Neil Walker, in the context of Neil MacCormick's influential work on legal pluralism and particularly the question of how the 'publicness' of public law in the face of the pluralism of legal orders in the

---

[36] F. Scharpf, 'Perpetual momentum: directed and unconstrained?' (2012) 19(1) Journal of European Public Policy 127, 136. A related critique is made by Richard Bellamy in this context. Relying on an egalitarian and civic-republican conception of 'political constitutionalism', Bellamy argues that the 'people's law' will transmogrify into a 'lawyers' law' through denationalization. Stripped of its democratic context, this law would be insufficiently 'open to social and political pressures towards equality of access and membership'.

[37] F. Jacobs, *The Sovereignty of Law: The European Way* (New York: Cambridge University Press, 2007) 8.

[38] Jacobs, *The Sovereignty of Law*, 8.

[39] Jacobs, *The Sovereignty of Law*, 17.

[40] Jacobs, *The Sovereignty of Law*, 62–63.

European context can be redeemed.[41] Taking seriously, the insight that 'the plurality of legal orders within the European legal space is not yet to demonstrate their pluralism',[42] Walker is interested in identifying a 'kind of inter-systemic "non-Law" of universalisability of justification'[43] that combines recognition of legal-systemic pluralism with the idea of mutual constitutional justification. Walker is sympathetic to MacCormick's view that '"the settled positive charac-ter" of any particular unit of law remain[s] stubbornly "jurisdiction-relative"'[44] and therefore 'systemic', and therefore expresses a deep concern about what he fears is a formidable 'procrustean dilemma' of either abandoning unity or abandoning plurality. On the one hand, to the extent that we lean towards pluralism, we may not be able to 'add anything, theoretically, to our understand-ing of how, if at all, law sounds and connects beyond the boundaries of a particular legal order'.[45] But on the other hand, to the extent that we lean towards a view of 'how law functions *qua* law beyond the boundaries of the legal order', we could not do so 'without turning plurality back into a new kind of systemic unity that necessarily denies the distinctiveness and interdependence of the parts . . . and [without] so destroy[ing] the distinctive integrity of the parts',[46] thereby succumbing to the charges of post-state constitutionalism outlined in the previous section.

Walker's way out of this dilemma lies in an analogy to moral theory—in the idea of a reciprocal application of a 'Kantian categorical imperative' between and among the plural legal *systems*—just as we would or should as *persons*, acting from a moral point of view, and 'being prepared to think through . . . the broader consequences [of actions] for all relevant others if all relevant others were to act like us'.[47] Emerging from '[t]his kind of thinking' is an idea of comity or 'community of exchange', 'something less than positive law but more than purely strategic interaction'.[48] As Walker explains and summarizes his view:

> [w]here the positive law of any system runs out, and the terms of trade have to be worked out between the overlapping systems, then the relevant "law" here may simply be the autonomous requirement on all parties to think of their actions and decisions in law-like terms. This involves no obligation that they comply with the same substantive universals . . . Instead, the sources of these substantive universals remain the overlapping legal systems themselves.[49]

---

[41] N. Walker, 'Reconciling MacCormick: Constitutional Pluralism and the Unity of Practical Reason' (2011) 24 Ratio Juris 369.

[42] Walker, 'Reconciling MacCormick', 376.

[43] Walker, 'Reconciling MacCormick', 383.

[44] Walker, 'Reconciling MacCormick', 375. He also cautions against views developed by O. Gerstenberg and C. F. Sabel, 'Directly-Deliberative Polyarchy: An Institutional Ideal for Europe?' in C. Joerges and R. Dehousse (eds), *Good Governance in the European Union* (Oxford: Oxford University Press, 2002).

[45] Walker, 'Reconciling MacCormick', 376.

[46] Walker, 'Reconciling MacCormick', 376.

[47] Walker, 'Reconciling MacCormick', 381.

[48] Walker, 'Reconciling MacCormick', 382.

[49] Walker, 'Reconciling MacCormick', 382.

Walker's careful formulations bristle with possibility. In order to illustrate the 'productive dynamic', which he asks us to imagine, he points to the 'iterative relations of the EU with external normative orders', such as with the UN Security Council and its sanctions regime for terrorist suspects. Referring to the notorious *Kadi* judgment,[50] he argues that while there is no 'agreed meta-law' between the legal orders reconciling anti-terrorism policy (the UN policy on the freezing of financial assets of people suspected of terrorism) with fundamental rights guaranteed by the EU (for example, the right to be heard and to effective judicial protection, allowing a suspect to challenge the listing and to clear his name), a productive dynamic becomes nonetheless possible and can gather steam, if—and as long as—each legal system involved (the EU, the UN) is prepared to engage in universal reasoning and in justifying its stance to all relevant parties.

Hence, Walker restricts the possibility of shared common ground between conflicting legal orders to 'non-Law', to a 'non-legal sphere of common practical reasoning',[51] but one may wonder whether this restriction to 'non-Law' is plausible. Is it true that the only form or sphere of inter-systemic objectivity is, or must remain, non-legal? Restricting the possibility for common ground between and among the plural legal orders to 'non-Law' dismisses the idea of the productive dynamic being jurisgenerative. The restriction seems reminiscent of a source-based positivist conception of law that risks overstating jurisdiction-relativity (one which substitutes 'systems' for states/societies/peoples as the relevant positive social fact) and understates the important role played by the general principles of law, which form the intersection between and among the plural legal orders and recognition of which is content-dependent, as Jacobs has argued. Certainly, the 'sources' of these fundamental principles remain the plural legal orders themselves, from which they originate, insofar as, for example, the CJEU derives those principles not only from the national legal orders, but also from the ECHR, from other international documents, and from the EU Charter of Fundamental Rights. But these fundamental—legal—principles (consider, for example, the principle prohibiting age discrimination) nonetheless constitute a principled *legal* link[52] among the various plural legal orders. This link still provides the various legal orders with sufficient leeway as to the forms and methods of how to contextualize or render concrete those principles in practice. Hence, Walker's concerns about an imperial 'meta-law', which remains insensitive to the 'integrity of the parts', may seem unwarranted, at least, when stated at this level of generality. Indeed, in other writings he emphasizes the 'continuing relevance of ideas of constitutionalism and public law' and suggests the possibility of 'a postnational iteration of constitutionalism and public law', so there is, nuances aside, a lot of common ground with the proceduralist agenda suggested here.

---

[50] Joined Cases C-402/05 P and C-415/05 *Yassin Abdullah Kadi and Al Barakaat International Foundation v Council of the European Union and Commission of the European Communities* [2008] ECR I-6351.

[51] Walker, 'Reconciling MacCormick', 383.

[52] C. F. Sabel and O. Gerstenberg, 'Constitutionalising an Overlapping Consensus: The ECJ and the Emergence of a Coordinate Constitutional order' (2010) 16(5) European law Journal 511.

The proceduralist turn advocated here can point towards a (legal) solution for the tension between negative and aspirational constitutionalism as well as assuage the concerns of European constitutional sceptics. Indeed, *contra* the European sceptics, 'Europe' is and remains an interesting canvas on which to develop this proceduralist model precisely because its complex and multidimensional legal architecture calls for experimental approaches to public law and adjudication. Whereas the two regional organisms—the Council of Europe and the EU—have taken over a significant portion of the competences of nation-states and elaborated their own autonomous legal orders, they have increased the standard of justification states must meet. Both legal orders serve to render more explicit fundamental legal principles which operate as a yardstick of justification. So, by forcing justification, intervention on the basis of an emergent understanding of principle does not have the character of an imposition of answers that forecloses future debate. Rather, intervention into national law is forcing reconsideration of, and often casting aside, existing—often stereotypical and automatic—assumptions within national law and politics in the light of an emergent and deeper understanding of principle. The multidimensionality of constitutional rights protection thus is less a threat to the integrity of national law but instead, a self-conscious project with the aim of continuously 'widening the horizon' of relevant reasons and, *mutatis mutandis*, of 'widening the audience' through inclusion of hitherto marginalized groups and individuals. Of course, there may be slippage but where the experimentalist process works and where an understanding of fundamental *legal* principles (as opposed to the non-legal solutions of Walker's practical reason) gradually crystallize over time, there may result a justificatory ascent, an updating of national legal systems, and a strengthening of the rule of law. Crucially, then, the experimentalist legal process is recursive; on the one hand, moral judgment is required—experimentalist courts do not just sit on the fences of major social disputes—but that judgment is itself structured by and transformed through the interplay of the national and European legal orders. The adjustment and simultaneous updating both at the national and the European levels, which 'outsider courts' can provoke and facilitate, can be seen as illustrations of the 'deliberative turn' in public law. To illustrate this procedural model, two examples, one from EU law and the other from ECHR law, will suffice.

4.1 EU law, freedom of religion, and refugee status

The CJEU's Grand Chamber decision in *Germany v Y & Z*,[53] involved the meaning of religious freedom under Art. 10(1) of the Charter of Fundamental Rights, and also the proper interpretation of the Council Directive 2004/83/EC which sets European-wide minimum standards for the qualification and status of third-country nationals or stateless persons as refugees. According to Arts. 2(c) and 9(1)(a) of the Directive, recognition as a refugee presupposes 'a well-founded fear of being persecuted', and the acts of persecution must 'be sufficiently serious

---

[53] Joined Cases C-71/11 and C-99/11 *Federal Republic of Germany v Y and Z* (not yet published).

by their nature'. The Directive refers to the Geneva Convention Relating to the Status of Refugees (1951) as its cornerstone. The right to religious freedom is enshrined in Art. 10(1) of the EU Charter, which directly corresponds to the right guaranteed by Art. 9 (1) ECHR. Both these documents stipulate that:

> Everyone has the right to freedom of thought, conscience and religion; this right includes freedom to change his religion or belief and freedom, either alone or in community with others and in public or private, to manifest his religion or belief, in worship, teaching, practice and observance.

The applicants—Y and Z—had entered Germany and applied for asylum and protection as refugees. They were both members of the Muslim *Ahmadiyya* community, which is an Islamic reform movement. They claimed that because of their membership of that community, and as a result of their religious beliefs, which—as required by those beliefs—they also practised in public, they had been persecuted, physically mistreated, and imprisoned in their country of origin, Pakistan. The Pakistani Criminal Code provides that members of the *Ahmadiyya* religious community may face imprisonment or even death. The German Bundesamt rejected Y's and Z's applications for asylum, declaring them liable to deportation on the grounds of insufficient evidence for the contention that both applicants had left their country of origin because of a well-founded fear of persecution.

The referring German Federal Administrative Supreme Court (*Bundesverwaltungsgericht*) wanted to know whether Germany could refuse granting asylum on the grounds that, first, according to a long-standing legal doctrine in Germany, predating the transposition of the directive into national law, only a very narrowly defined so-called 'core area' of religious freedom was deemed worthy of protection: the *'forum internum'*, meaning the private—but not the public— exercise of religious freedom. The German court clearly was of the view that the restrictions on Ahmadis in Pakistan—which concern the practice of their faith in public—do not constitute interference with those 'core areas'. Moreover, there was, according to the German authorities, nothing whatsoever in the findings of the lower (fact-finding) courts on how Y and Z practise their faith in Germany to establish that Y and Z cannot *refrain* from certain activities *which do not form part of those 'core areas' of religious practice*. Thus, the question before the ECJ was whether Germany could refuse the granting of asylum at least on the grounds that the applicants could legitimately be expected to avoid persecution in their home country by abstaining from religious practice in public.

The Grand Chamber of the CJEU answered this question in the negative. Explicitly referring to the ECHR, the CJEU observed that '[f]reedom of religion is one of the foundations of a democratic society and is a basic human right'.[54] However, not any interference with religious freedom could constitute an act of persecution triggering the right to asylum under the directive. Rather, there had to be a 'severe violation' of religious freedom having a significant effect on the

---

[54] Joined Cases C-71/11 and C-99/11 *Federal Republic of Germany v Y and Z* (not yet published), para 57.

person concerned. Hence, the Directive had to be interpreted in the light of the principle.

In elaborating the meaning of the concept of a severe violation, the Grand Chamber rejected the German doctrine of a 'core area' of religious freedom as entirely irrelevant, and also rejected with it the German distinction between a private religious practice (allegedly more worthy of protection)—the *forum internum*—and public religious activities (allegedly less worthy of protection)—the *forum externum*.[55]

Hence, what *really matters*, when it comes to determining whether a given interference with religious freedom (Art. 10(1) of the Charter) can constitute a 'sufficiently serious' form of persecution according to Art. 9(1) of the Directive, is the severity and the nature of the repression itself—the risk of being prosecuted or subjected to inhuman or degrading treatment because of religious faith, not the private or public nature of its exercise. The national authorities must take all the personal contextual circumstances into account. And, importantly, those circumstances must also include a person's 'subjective circumstances', such as whether the observance of a certain religious practice in public is of particular importance to the person concerned in order to preserve his or her religious identity.

Moreover, the Grand Chamber also insisted, in its response to the Federal Administrative Court's second question, that EU law does not expect the person concerned to avoid exposure to persecution in his home country by abstaining from religious practice in public. Instead, where the person concerned 'will follow a religious practice which will expose him to a real risk of persecution, he should be granted refugee status ... The fact that he could avoid that risk by abstaining from certain religious practices is, in principle, irrelevant'.[56]

What this example illustrates, it is argued, is that a supranational court, the CJEU, can play a benign role vis-à-vis vulnerable, often despised, individuals who seek protection, by mobilizing the national courts and by directing them to take into account the importance of a fundamental principle within the pursuit of domestic legal and policy concerns. There is an independent moral judgment—national law clearly fell short of the principle and was off the mark. EU judicial intervention can thus reopen the arrested development of national law by throwing into question formalistic domestic legal concepts, such as the idea of a private 'core area' of religious freedom. In this sense, the CJEU plays a proceduralizing role with regard to principle. This result is even more remarkable as the CJEU—an economic court—plays this role in the domain of freedom of religion, a crucial freedom also under national constitutional law. The CJEU

---

[55] Joined Cases C-71/11 and C-99/11 *Federal Republic of Germany v Y and Z* (not yet published), para 65: 'It follows that acts which, on account of their intrinsic severity as well as the severity of their consequences for the person concerned, may be regarded as constituting persecution must be identified, not on the basis of the particular aspect of religious freedom that is being interfered with but on the basis of the nature of the repression inflicted on the individual and its consequences'.

[56] Joined Cases C-71/11 and C-99/11 *Federal Republic of Germany v Y and Z* (not yet published), para 79.

gives the principle of religious freedom a morally generous reading, as entailing the state's positive obligation to protect, in recognition of the principled import- ance of religious freedom in a democratic society. In this way, the CJEU strengthens the rule of law. The CJEU, if you will, sets up a 'regime', within which domestic actors themselves can find an answer ('application'), in light of the circumstances and national understanding of separation of powers, but unequivocally constrained by an EU-wide framework principle.

4.2 The right to family life and the treatment of prisoners under the ECHR

Recent ECtHR rulings have given rise to intense controversy and national resistance, and perhaps, on the court's side, a sense of *illusions perdues*. Crisis has put the question of method squarely on the table. On the one hand, since the procedural rules of the ECHR require the exhaustion of all domestic remedies, there will always already be a national constitutional or highest supreme court (*Fachgericht*) decision, deserving deference. On the other hand, the ECtHR must protect the correct interpretation of the Convention. It is committed to a consti- tutional practice of evolving, dynamic interpretation in the (as the ECHR's Preamble says) 'further realization' of human rights and fundamental freedoms.[57] The tension between both dimensions—the attention to the importance of principle, on the one hand, and subsidiarity, on the other—animates and guides the search for proceduralist solutions. Consider the following two sets of illustra- tions. In both, the Court opens up 'closed (legal) regimes', concerning families and prisons, forcing modernization in ways initially not anticipated from within national law and politics.

4.2.1 Right to family life

In 2004, in a child custody dispute, the ECtHR found that decisions of the German authorities rendered in 2001—in particular, the denial of the natural father's right of access to his child—had violated Article 8 ECHR. In its much- discussed *Görgülü* decision,[58] the German Bundesverfassungsgericht (BVG) con- firmed, in principle, the authority of the ECtHR judgments. Domestic courts are, in principle, under an obligation to give full effect to the judgments of the ECtHR, given the 'constitutional significance' of the guarantees of the Conven- tion. Moreover, the BVG's ruling expanded the constitutional complaint proced- ure. A complainant may now challenge indirectly the violation of a Convention right before the BVG by arguing that, in the interpretation of a fundamental right, the jurisprudence of the ECtHR relevant to the coinciding Convention right has been disregarded. But the BVG also noted that it would settle any conflict between the Basic Law and the ECHR in terms of the Basic Law.

---

[57] J.-P. Costa, 'On the Legitimacy of the European Court of Human Rights' Judgment' (2011) 7 European Constitutional Law Review 173, 178 f.

[58] *Görgülü*, Bundesverfassungsgericht [BVerfG] [Federal Constitutional Court] 14 October 2004, 111 BVerFGE 307.

In particular, in the area of private law, where the ECHR applies horizontally and where the national courts:[59]

> have to structure multipolar fundamental rights situations, it is always important that various subjective legal positions are sensitively weighed against each other, and if there is a change . . . in the actual or legal circumstances, this weighing may lead to a different result. There may therefore be constitutional problems if one of the subjects of fundamental rights in conflict with another obtains an [ECtHR] judgment in his or her favour . . . and German courts schematically apply this decision to the private-law relationship, with the result that the holder of fundamental rights who has "lost" in this case and was possibly not involved in the proceedings at the [ECtHR] would no longer be able to take an effective part in the proceedings as a party.

As such, what this case illustrates is that domestic courts remain indispensable and seem better equipped to resolve multi-polar private law conflicts, given the ECtHR's lack of full information. Yet those cautions notwithstanding, the ECtHR retains an important *proceduralizing* role.

In several striking follow-up cases, such as *Zaunegger*,[60] *Anayo*,[61] and *Schneider*,[62] the ECtHR developed background principles of child custody law, '[h]aving regard to the realities of family life in the 21st century',[63] by rejecting various context-indifferent stereotypical assumptions, entrenched in national private law and concerning 'existing family relationships', and by requiring national courts to openly strike a balance between the competing interests involved.

The legal assumption in *Anayo* was a rule under the German Civil Code (*Bürgerliches Gesetzbuch*) according to which the *existing relationship* between a legal father and the child had to automatically take precedence over the relationship between biological father and child; the biological father's right to access was considered to be conditional upon the biological father having borne 'actual responsibility' for the child in the past or present; that is, on an existing 'social and family relationship' with the child, regardless of the child's best interest and context. As a consequence of that legal presumption, any legal right to access could be removed by the mother's and legal father's blocking any access to the child in the first place. The reasons why the biological father had not previously established a 'social and family relationship' with the child concerned had been irrelevant for the domestic courts' findings. In response, the Grand Chamber

---

[59] The court continued: 'German courts must give precedence to interpretation in accordance with the Convention. The situation is different only if observing the decision of the [ECtHR], for example, because the facts on which it is based have changed, clearly violates statute law to the contrary or German constitutional provisions . . . [or] the fundamental rights of third parties. "Take into account" means taking notice of the Convention provision as interpreted by the [ECtHR] and applying it to the case, provided the application does not violate prior-ranking law, in particular constitutional law', paras 50, 62.

[60] *Zaunegger v Germany* Application 22028/04, 3 December 2009.

[61] *Anayo v Germany* Application 20578/07, 21 December 2010.

[62] *Schneider v Germany* Application 17080/07), 15 September 2011.

[63] *Schneider*, para 100.

required the domestic authorities to strike a 'fair balance' between the competing rights under Art. 8 ECHR not only of the two parents and the child, but of several individuals concerned (the mother, the legal father, the biological father, the married couple's biological children, and the children who emanated from the relationship of the mother with the biological father).

The facts in *Schneider* were particularly intriguing. The mother of the child concerned acknowledged that the applicant might be the child's father, but that her husband may also be the father, a fact that was not established by the domestic courts. Moreover, the mother took the view that contacts between the applicant and the child would jeopardize the child's welfare and that of her family. It was uncontroversial that under German law the applicant's acknowledgment of paternity was not valid as the legal father's paternity prevailed under the provisions of the German Civil Code; nor had the applicant, according to the Civil Code, any right to contest the legal father's paternity, as the child was living with him. Those provisions were aimed at pursuing the best interests of a married couple and their children. The ECtHR emphasized that German law had the effect of leaving the applicant without any remedy at all. Not only were separate paternity proceedings bound to fail under the regime set up by the BGB (the applicant having no right to contest the paternity of the legal father, as the latter was living with the child), but those proceedings (would have to be) aimed at obtaining the status of the child's legal parent, thereby terminating another's legal paternity. The court argued that they 'must therefore be considered to have a fundamentally different and far-reaching objective than the establishment of biological paternity for the specific purposes of having contact with the child concerned and information about that child's development'.[64]

4.2.2 Prisoners' Rights

In 2009, the ECtHR considered a German law, which was upheld by the BVG, on the imposition and unlimited duration of preventive detention—which allowed further detention of convicted criminals beyond their prison sentence in the interest of public security—to be a violation of the Convention.[65]

Following a change in the domestic German criminal law in 1998, the duration of a convicted person's first period of preventive detention could be extended retrospectively from a maximum period of ten years to an unlimited period of time. The amended Criminal Code put no special measures in place directed at persons subject to preventative detention and aimed at reducing the danger they represent, and thus at limiting the duration of their detention to what is strictly necessary in order to prevent them from committing further offences, and the suspension of preventative detention on probation was subject to a court's finding that there was no danger that the detainee will commit further serious offences—a condition difficult, if not impossible, to fulfil. The applicant, who had served his prison sentence and also had, after completion of that prison sentence, spent ten years in preventative detention, in 2001 lodged a complaint before the

---

[64] *Schneider*, para 102.

[65] *M v Germany* Application 9359/04, 17 December 2009.

BVG against his continued, unlimited preventive detention beyond the ten-year period, made possible by the amendment of the Criminal Code. He argued that the amended Criminal Code violated the prohibition under the German Basic Law of retrospective punishment and entailed life-long imprisonment without any prospect of release. But in its 84-page judgment of 2004, the BVG refused to consider the impugned provisions of the German Criminal Code as unconstitutional, arguing (among other things) that the prohibition of retrospective punishment did not extend to measures of corrections and prevention, even when they were directly connected with the qualifying offence.

The ECtHR based its ruling on Art. 5(1) ECHR, which guarantees the right to liberty with certain restrictions, including the lawful detention of a person 'after conviction by a competent court',[66] and on Art. 7 ECHR (*nullum crimen, nulla poena sine lege*). In response to the BVG's judgment, the ECtHR ruled that:

> [T]he word 'after' in [Art. 5(1)(a)] does not simply mean that the 'detention' must follow the 'conviction' in point of time. There must be sufficient causal connection between the conviction and the deprivation of liberty at issue ... However, with the passage of time, the causal link between the initial conviction and a further deprivation of liberty gradually becomes less strong and might eventually be broken if a position were reached in which a decision not to release was based on grounds that were inconsistent with the objectives of the initial decision (by a sentencing court) or on an assessment that was unreasonable in terms of those objectives.[67]

The ECtHR concluded that the contested provisions of the German Criminal Code constituted an additional penalty which was imposed on the applicant retrospectively, under a law enacted after the applicant had committed his offence.

Subsequently, in 2011, in its *Preventive Detention* ruling,[68] the BVG—against the backdrop of extensive academic and public controversy in Germany—reversed its previous case law in response to the ECtHR's ruling. The BVG annulled the contested provisions of the Criminal Code, now arguing that prison sentences and preventive detention served fundamentally different objectives and therefore a marked distance between both had to be kept, *as a matter of German law*. A retrospective imposition of preventative detention constituted an infringement of the rule of law principle enshrined in the German Basic Law. To prevent encroachments on the right to liberty under the Basic Law, preventative detention is subject to a strict review or proportionality. In particular, the BVG confirmed its stance in *Görgülü* that 'the text of the Convention and the case-law of the European Court of Human Rights serve as interpretation aids for the determination of the contents and scope of the fundamental rights and of

---

[66] Article 5(1)(a) ECHR.

[67] *M v Germany*, para 88 and confirmed in *Mork v Germany* Applications 31047/04 and 43386/08), 9 June 2011, para 48 ff.

[68] BVerfG, 2 BvR 2365/09 of 4 May 2011.

rule-of-law principles enshrined in the Basic Law'.[69] Moreover, the BVG reversed its previous decision on detention orders, notwithstanding the final and binding effect of its previous 2004 ruling arguing that the ECtHR's decisions introduce changes relevant for the interpretation of the Basic Law, and which supersede the previous decisions of the BVG. It continued:

> The openness of the Basic Law to international law [*Völkerrechtsfreundlichkeit*] expresses an understanding of sovereignty that not only does not oppose international and supranational integration, it presupposes and expects it. Against this background, the 'final word' of the German Constitution is not an obstacle to an international and European dialogue of courts but rather its normative foundation.[70]

Subsequently, in 2011, in its ruling *Mork v Germany*, the ECtHR acknowledged the BVG's conversion.[71]

In this way, the ECtHR was a catalyst for the development of (domestic German) law by stating a framework principle reminding the BVG of the fundamentally different objectives of punishment and preventive detention. By specifying and emphasizing the importance of the 'fundamental principles' governing preventive detentions, the ECtHR forced the BVG to reconsider its previous case law and to update its domestic legal doctrine in the light of European principle. The ECtHR did not 'colonize' national law—national courts remain at liberty to revise and to present the required changes of national law as a matter of what national constitutional law itself requires.[72]

Of course the proceduralist model is not infallible and it is not difficult to think of potential failures, such as where dialogue may degenerate into a stand-off or to (more or less) polite evasion. One example of such potential deterioration of the dialogic relationship is the sequence of decisions concerning prisoners' right to

---

[69] BVerfG, 2 BvR 2365/09 of 4 May 2011.

[70] BVerfG, 2 BvR 2365/09 of 4.5.2011, at 89: 'Die Völkerrechtsfreundlichkeit des Grundgesetzes ist damit Ausdruck eines Souveränitätsverständnisses, das einer Einbindung in inter- und supranationale Zusammenhänge sowie deren Weiterentwicklung nicht nur nicht entgegensteht, sondern diese voraussetzt und erwartet. Vor diesem Hintergrund steht auch das "letzte Wort" der deutschen Verfassung einem internationalen und europäischen Dialog der Gerichte nicht entgegen, sondern ist dessen normative Grundlage'.

[71] 'In its judgment, the Federal Constitutional Court stressed that the fact that the Constitution stood above the Convention in the domestic hierarchy of norms was not an obstacle to an international and European dialogue between the courts, but was, on the contrary, its normative basis in view of the fact that the Constitution was to be interpreted in a manner that was open to public international law (*völkerrechtsfreundliche Auslegung*). In its reasoning, the Federal Constitutional Court relied on the interpretation of Article 5 and Article 7 of the Convention made by this Court in its judgment in the case of *M v Germany* [cited earlier]... The Court takes note... of the reversal of the [BVG's] case-law concerning preventive detention... It welcomes the Federal Constitutional Court's approach of interpreting the provisions of the Basic Law also in the light of the Convention and this Court's case-law, which demonstrates the court's continuing commitment to the protection of fundamental rights not only on national, but also European level'. *Mork v Germany*, paras 31 and 54.

[72] Although whether the German response in practice amounts to more than a face-saving exercise remains to be seen and a lot of domestic resistance against the ECtHR's role remains, in particular among the ordinary courts. I would like to thank ECtHR judge Professor András Sajo for discussion of this point at a recent conference in London.

vote, and in particular, the sustained resistance by the British government to implementing changes in the law in this area.[73] In particular, the ECtHR's ruling in *Hirst v UK* was based on the following three considerations: first, when sentencing, the criminal courts in England and Wales had made no reference to disenfranchisement and there was no apparent direct link between the facts of any individual case and the removal of the right to vote; secondly, the fact that the UK legislation in the area was a 'blunt instrument',[74] which stripped of their Convention right to vote a significant category of persons in an indiscriminate manner; and, thirdly, there was found to be no evidence of there being 'any substantive debate by members of the legislature on the continued justification in light of modern-day penal policy and of current human rights standards for maintaining such a general restriction on the right of prisoners to vote', and of the Parliament ever seeking 'to weigh the competing interests or to assess the proportionality of a blanket ban on the right of a convicted prisoner to vote'.[75]

The British Government, in response, considered that the Grand Chamber's findings in *Hirst* 'were wrong and that the Court should revisit its decision'.[76] In particular, it disagreed that a system that stripped all convicted prisoners of the right to vote for as long as they were serving their sentence was a 'blunt instrument', because 'there was no doubt that the impugned measure pursued a legitimate aim, namely, enhancing civic responsibility and respect for the rule of law and encouraging citizen-like conduct', and 'because only those individuals guilty of offences serious enough to warrant imprisonment were deprived of the right to vote, the correlation between the offence committed and the aim pursued was established'.[77]

However, in the subsequent case of *Scoppola v Italy*, the ECtHR replied that

> It does not appear . . . that anything has occurred or changed at the European and Convention levels since the *Hirst (No 2)* judgment that might lend support to the suggestion that the principles set forth in that case should be re-examined. On the contrary, analysis of the relevant international and European documents . . . and comparative-law information . . . reveals the opposite trend, if anything—towards fewer restrictions on convicted prisoners' voting rights.[78]

Yet, on the facts of the case, in *Scoppola*, the ECtHR, rather than reaffirming its landmark decision in *Hirst*, retreated from it and concluded that the Italian

---

[73] Cf R. Bellamy, 'The Democratic Legitimacy of International Human Rights Conventions: Political Constitutionalism and the Hirst Case', on file with author.

[74] Moreover it was found to 'impose a blanket restriction on all convicted prisoners in prison'; to apply 'automatically to such prisoners, irrespective of the length of their sentence and irrespective of the nature or gravity of their offence and their individual circumstances'; and with the consequence that '[s]uch a general, automatic and indiscriminate restriction on a vitally important Convention right must be seen as falling outside any acceptable margin of appreciation, however wide that margin might be'. *Hirst v UK (No 2)* (2004) 38 EHRR 40 para 82.

[75] *Hirst*, para 80.

[76] *Scoppola v Italy* Application 126/05 22 May 2012, para 78.

[77] *Scoppola v Italy*. For further background on these cases, cf R. Bellamy [ms 2012].

[78] *Scoppola*, para 95.

system did not have the general, automatic, and indiscriminate character that led it, in the *Hirst (No 2)* case, to find a violation. As the dissenting Judge Björgvinsson explained, in both cases the applicants faced a similar situation; both were serving life-long prison sentences, one for manslaughter (Hirst), the other for murder. Although the national laws on which the forfeiture of voting rights was based differed in some respects, the concrete effect was for both prisoners the same; the automatic forfeiture of their right to vote as a result of a life sentence. UK law provided that a convicted person, during the time of his detention, is legally incapable of voting in any parliamentary or local election. Prisoners automatically regain their right to vote on release from prison. Italian law, by contrast, provided that persons sentenced to penalties entailing a ban from public office may not vote. As a consequence, persons sentenced to less than three years in prison continued to enjoy the right to vote. Those sentenced to three to five years forfeit their right to vote for five years, and prisoners sentenced to five years or more were deprived of their right to vote for life. Thus, the main difference between the two was that Italian law deprived of voting rights only those who were sentenced to three years or more in prison, while UK law deprived all prisoners for the duration of their sentence. Italian law could for this reason be seen to be more lenient than UK law, but it was also stricter in the sense that it deprived prisoners of their right to vote beyond the duration of their prison sentence and, for a large group of prisoners, for life. As Björgvinsson concludes in his dissenting opinion:

> In sum, I find the distinction made in this judgment between these two cases as a ground for justifying different conclusions to be unsatisfactory. The present judgment offers a very narrow interpretation of the *Hirst* judgment and in fact a retreat from the main arguments advanced therein. Regrettably the judgment in the present case has now stripped the *Hirst* judgment of all its bite as a landmark precedent for the protection of prisoners' voting rights in Europe.

As such, then, the prisoner voting saga shows how failures can emerge where principles are not maintained and the supranational court abdicates its role as the catalyst for national legal development in the face of resistance from national authorities. The prospect of failure raises the vexed question of whether proceduralism and the deliberative turn in public law can produce and regenerate their own foundations and conditions of success. Common ground might just dwindle and whither away in a multidimensional system. Centrifugal tendencies might prevail along the lines of Böckenförde's theorem where the modern, democratic, and secular state lives on foundations which it cannot properly guarantee.[79]

---

[79] '*Der freiheitliche, säkularisierte Staat lebt von Voraussetzungen, die er selbst nicht garantieren kann. Das ist das große Wagnis, das er, um der Freiheit willen, eingegangen ist. Als freiheitlicher Staat kann er einerseits nur bestehen, wenn sich die Freiheit, die er seinen Bürgern gewährt, von innen her, aus der moralischen Substanz des einzelnen und der Homogenität der Gesellschaft, reguliert. Andererseits kann er diese inneren Regulierungskräfte nicht von sich aus, das heißt, mit den Mitteln des Rechtszwanges und autoritativen Gebots zu garantieren versuchen, ohne seine Freiheitlichkeit aufzugeben und—auf säkularisierter Ebene—in jenen Totalitätsanspruch zurückzufallen, aus dem er in den konfessionellen Bürgerkriegen herausgeführt hat.* E.-W. Böckenförde, *Staat, Gesellschaft, Freiheit* (Frankfurt am Main: Suhrkamp, 1976) 60.

However, a more optimistic view is that the ongoing interplay between sufficiently abstract constitutional concepts and principles on the one hand, and some shared agreement on paradigmatic instances of law on the other, may allow conversation to continue rather than break down. On this latter view, which this chapter defends—that convergence is possible but never self-executing—the problems of multidimensional constitutionalism are continuous with the legal pluralism within national legal orders themselves—along the line of the Quinean *apperçu* that problems of radical translation begin at home. What the European multidimensional system of rights protection brings to the fore—and what may be its proper rationale, on the account presented here—is the idea of constitutionalism as a form of mutual learning. But whereas aspirationalists appeal to a shared ethos and to non-law, the proceduralist account emphasizes the institutional framework itself for the exploration of difference and disagreement and for mutual scrutiny and review.

5. CONCLUSION

Democratic constitutionalism then need not be inimical to judicial review beyond the state, if judicial review is understood along more 'intelligent' lines, as requiring deliberation and experimentation. A more experimentalist view of adjudication (and of 'law-application' generally), then, might assuage concerns about 'relativization' (Grimm), 'authoritarian constitutionalism' (Loughlin), or 'constitutional asymmetry' (Scharpf), or the emergence of a 'legal constitutionalism' corrosive of—if not altogether corrupting—democracy's egalitarian internal morality (Bellamy). Proceduralism might point towards new ground beyond the stark dilemma between negative constitutionalism (minimalism) and constitutional aspirationalism. Just as principles embedded in national law exert a transformative upward pressure on EU law and on the ECHR, forcing reconsideration, so do, conversely, EU law and the ECHR have a benign, constitutionally transformative, and reconsideration-forcing influence on the development of the national rule of law. The European multidimensional system provides an institutional framework within which understanding of principles and paradigmatic instances of their application mutually shape and transform one another in a process of reflective (dis-)equilibrium. In other words, it forces you to reconsider—to make explicit the reasons for why you can, or can't help asylum seekers, legal biological parents, or even prisoners, who feature in the often novel, sometimes moving, case law. The emergent law's polyarchy thus unleashes a productive dynamic, which helps to disrupt routine assumptions, forces sensitivity to context, enables learning, and opens up the law—both private, public, and constitutional—to changing social values.

12

The Post-national Horizon of Constitutionalism and Public Law: Paradigm Extension or Paradigm Exhaustion?

Neil Walker

I. TWO NEOLOGISMS

A great deal of conceptual contestation, and no less confusion, attends the busy contemporary debate over the prospects and desirability of constitutionalism beyond the state, or what is sometimes called post-national constitutionalism. The idea of 'public law', or of a more general association of 'law' with 'publicness', is sometimes offered as a crucial move in this debate. It is presented as a way of staking out of the semantic high-ground, the key to resolving differences of perspective.[1] But since, as we shall see, the meaning and scope of a post-national 'public law' is also unclear and conflicted, this move reveals no magic formula and can offer no decisive resolution of the higher profile contestation about the credentials of constitutionalism beyond the state.[2]

This should not surprise us. Both key terms—post-national constitutionalism and post-national public law—are neologisms. They are relatively recently emergent formulations coined in recognition of an ever denser web of transnational legal relations, which is one important dimension of the contemporary pattern of globalization.[3] Both terms, and the themes they address, are products of the

---

[1] See, for example, B. Kingsbury, 'The Concept of "Law" in Global Administrative Law' (2009) 20 European Journal of International Law 23; 'International Law as Inter-Public Law' in H. S. Richardson and M. S. Williams (eds) *Moral Universalism and Pluralism* (New York: NYU Press, 2009) 67–104; N. Krisch, *Beyond Constitutionalism?* (Oxford: Oxford University Press, 2010); A. Von Bogdandy, P. Dann and M. Goldmann, 'Developing the Publicness of Public International Law: Towards a legal framework for Global Governance Activities' (2008) 9 German Law Journal 1375; J. Waldron, 'Can There be a Democratic Jurisprudence?' in *New York University Public law and Legal Theory Working Papers* (2008) 35, available at <http://papers.ssrn.com/sol3/papers.cfm?abstract_id=1280923>.

[2] My claim is not that the debate about transnational constitutionalism has a higher profile than the debate about transnational public law in the sense of being regarded as more important or attracting more intense debate *within* legal scholarship. That is a moot point, and undoubtedly the academic debate on law's 'publicness' has attracted increasing attention in recent years. See, eg, C. Michelon, G. Clunie, C. McCorkindale, and H. Psarras (eds) *The Public in Law* (Aldershot: Ashgate, 2012). My argument is a more basic one; that at the level of wider public awareness and participation, the constitutional debate retains the greater resonance, particularly in Europe in the context and in the aftermath of the debate over a written Constitution for the European Union; see notes 52–55, following.

[3] See, eg, P. Zumbansen, 'Comparative, global and transnational constitutionalism: The emergence of a transnational legal-pluralist order' (2012) 1 Global Constitutionalism 16.

disruption of the state-centred 'order of orders'[4] of the high modern age, and of the open-ended search for a new language of legal authority adequate to a shifting global, political, and economic configuration. Both terms, therefore, have a speculative quality, at best a tentative hold on the legal imagination.[5] They have arisen out of a shifting legal landscape and address still unsettled features of that landscape. So we should not expect one term to guarantee the stable grounding that the other cannot provide for itself.

Nevertheless, there is merit in pursuing discussion of these two concepts on the same page. For, importantly, ideas of post-national constitutionalism and post-national public law or legal publicness, while displaying significant differences of focus and emphasis, begin from the same broad approach to the problem of legal authority in a globalizing age. They start from the premise that it is both desirable and possible to adapt a historically state-concentrated discourse of authority to the increasingly dense post-state regulatory environment. They both suppose, more particularly, that the kind of law which for long was the exclusive or predominant domain of the state, and whose very authority is intimately associated with that of the state—whether 'constitutional' or 'public' law—ought to be and is capable of being drawn upon and applied to new non-state-based contexts of regulation.

Situating post-national constitutionalism and post-national public law within the one framework of inquiry, therefore, as the present chapter seeks to do, can help us to clarify and address much of what is at stake in the broader debate about law's transnational resonance. As a threshold concern, this inclusive framework allows us to specify and illuminate the division between those *who see the legal forms and vocabulary of statehood as a mobile resource, and as an indispensable part of any answer to the question of the authority of the expanding domain of law beyond the state,*[6] and those who do not. In other words—and those I have taken for my title—are the paradigms of public law and of constitutionalism confined to and exhausted by the state-based point of reference, or is there scope for and value in their post-national extension? In pursuit of a developed answer to that question, our framework then allows us to identify the main options that are available in any such adaptation of a state-concentrated discourse to a post-national environment, permits us to tease out the strengths and weakness of these options, and invites us to explore the important points of agreement and contention between them. In conclusion, it will be argued that the possibilities and the difficulties of reconciling these various adaptations, far from demonstrating the intrinsic inappropriateness or inadvisability, on balance, of taking ideas of constitutionalism and public law beyond the state, indicate quite the opposite. For what we are faced with is in fact strongly reminiscent of the mix of mutual support and tension between different dimensions of constitutionalism and public law that has long obtained in the state setting.

---

[4] N. Walker 'Beyond Boundary Disputes and Basic Grids: Mapping the Global Disorder of Normative Orders' (2008) 6 International Journal of Constitutional Law 373.

[5] Walker, 'Beyond Boundary Disputes'. See also N. Walker, *Intimations of Global Law* (Nijmegen: Wolf Legal, forthcoming).

[6] See, eg, Ch 14.

But before embarking on this course of inquiry, we need to provide some further clarification of our focal terms. The comparison between post-national constitutionalism and post-national public law is facilitated by the fact that, in addition to their *substantive* common ground—their sharing of the same combination of endorsement of the statist legacy and post-state aspirational horizon, they also display the same basic range of *forms* of reference. Each root term, 'constitutionalism' and 'public law', is used both in the manner of an *external* account, to indicate the materials of an established genre of practical reason, and to articulate an open-ended set of claims *internal* to the established genre, including both 'jurisdictional' claims about the applicability of the genre to different contexts and action-generating claims drawing upon the resources of the genre in deciding practical questions. Each term, it follows, embraces both a (quasi) descriptive[7] dimension, as viewed from a detached standpoint, as well as diagnostic and prescriptive dimensions, as assumed from an engaged standpoint.

Firstly, at the level of external description, we refer, using the 'c' word or the 'p' word, to the inventory of existing legal forms, institutions, and discourses that are conventionally understood as 'constitutional' or 'public'. So, in this descriptive mode, we use the terms constitutional law and public law to record and report upon the vast array of structures, from written constitutions to the various organs of government, and of processes, from democratic legislation to judicial review, that fall within the relevant established canon of positive law. Secondly, at the diagnostic level, we invoke our key terms to refer to the range of situations, including but not necessarily limited to those that already exhibit the relevant legal forms, institutions, and discourses, which we deem to be appropriately understood and evaluated in 'constitutional' or 'public' terms. So we conceive, in this diagnostic mode, of situations or circumstances as of 'constitutional' import, not only because the conventional legal materials may be much in evidence, but also where we deem deeper standards of fit to be met; where, for instance, the relevant situations or circumstances presuppose or conduce to the establishment of fundamental legal authority or engage basic rights. Similarly, we conceive of situations and circumstances as appropriate vehicles for or venues of 'public law' not only because the relevant doctrinal forms are already in place, but also where, for example, particular populations self-understood or recognized as 'publics' are addressed, supposedly 'public' functions or interests are engaged, or certain collective characteristics of the production and supply of benefits obtain, as in the classical economic conception of 'public goods'.[8] Thirdly, at the prescriptive level, we use the language of 'constitutionalism' or invoke the 'public' quality of law to call upon a set of standards and values of legal provision—again including

---

[7] Of course, reporting on social 'facts' is always more than mere description. No social phenomena are self-describing and no account of social phenomena is uninfluenced by the perspective and priorities of the account-giver. Even the most detached account of relatively stable and institutionally embedded social phenomena such as legal rules, therefore, involves an element of selection and interpretation. Hence, the qualifier 'quasi'.

[8] Which counts public goods as those displaying the twin attributes of non-excludability and non-rivalness of consumption. See, eg, J. M. Buchanan, 'Public Goods in Theory and Practice: A Note on the Minasian-Samuelson Discussion' (1967) 10 Journal of Law and Economics 193.

but not necessarily limited to those standards and values already contained in existing legal forms, institutions, and discourses. The various standards and values involved operate at different levels of abstraction; from highly general ideas such as dignity, equality, and liberty, through broadly institutionalized goods, such as the rule of law, separation of powers, or parliamentary government, to more specific standards and mechanisms of general pertinence across government (for example, standards of 'good administration' or of probity in public office) or between government and citizens (for example, catalogues of individual 'freedom' and forms of judicial and other redress).[9]

We will have more to say about the different dimensions of constitutional and public law in the sections following. However, one broad conclusion can be anticipated. For constitutional and public law, in their strongly overlapping but distinct ways, the relationship between the three dimensions, relayed along a mutually reinforcing circuit, accounts for a strong bias towards a state-embedded conception of law. Both our diagnosis of the appropriateness of contexts to treatment in constitutional or public law terms and our sense of the relevant standards and values of treatment are heavily influenced by the vast, cumulative datum of established state institutions and practice. Reciprocally, the standing—and our understanding—of existing state institutions and practice *as* paradigmatically 'constitutional' or 'public' is corroborated by our continuously reinforced sense of what count as appropriate 'constitutional' or 'public' contexts, values, and standards. What remains to be seen is what, if any, scope there is for either constitutionalism or public law to break out of this confirmatory circle of state-centredness.

2. FOUR PERSPECTIVES ON POST-NATIONAL LAW

We can distinguish four main positions around which to organize our discussion. These are located along a continuum between scepticism and affirmation of the relevance of public law and constitutionalism to the transnational context. First, and addressing our threshold concern about the very possibility and desirability of transposing a state-concentrated and state-embedded discourse, there are those who deny the prospects of robust forms of constitutionalism extending beyond the state and who also, typically for closely connected reasons, dismiss the prospects of robust forms of public law and publicness extending beyond the state. We can call this stance, in which there is a close causal and conceptual link between publicness, constitutionalism, and statehood, one of *double scepticism* of legal transnationalism. Beyond that wholesale rejection of the prospects of the transnational relocation of robust forms of state-centred law, there are two more selectively sceptical positions. Second, then, there are those who are sceptical about the prospects of robust forms of constitutionalism beyond the state but not about the prospects of robust forms of public law beyond the state. We can call

---

[9] For one particularly rich discussion of the range, variety, and diverse levels of constitutional goods, see A. Brudner, *Constitutional Goods* (Oxford: Oxford University Press, 2004).

this position one of *transnational constitutional scepticism*. Third, as an alternative form of selective scepticism, there are those who, conversely, are sceptical about robust forms of transnational public law, but not about robust forms of constitutionalism beyond the state. We can call this position one of *transnational public law scepticism*. And finally, at the opposite end of the continuum, there are those who, with differing emphases, are sceptical neither about robust forms of constitutionalism beyond the state nor about transnational public law. We can, in shorthand, call this range of positions one of *double affirmation* of the translation of paradigmatically state-based forms of legality to the transnational domain.

We must, at the outset, say something about the significance of the adjective 'robust' in the classifications used earlier. The point is a simple but important one. For reasons we develop in our exploration of *double scepticism*, no-one, however broadly resistant to the general transferability of notion of constitutionalism and public law to the post-national context, would disallow that these notions retain *some* resonance beyond the state. That, indeed, is why we use the language of scepticism rather than outright *denial* in characterizing various positions. As we shall see,[10] the reasons why even strong sceptics are bound to concede something to the post-national position are relevant to our overall conclusions, since they point to features of our key concepts that are significant in considering their future prospects. Our immediate priority, however, is to sharpen our analytical tools by insisting that a clear line can and should, nevertheless, be drawn between the affirmation of 'robust' and 'non-robust' post-national forms. By robust forms we mean to include only those forms, first, that indicate *significant* features of the transnational legal landscape, as opposed to marginal phenomena or exotic instances; and, second, that are or claim to be relatively self-standing and so *autonomous* from the national roots of constitutional and public law.

3. DOUBLE SCEPTICISM

3.1 *Two versions of double scepticism*

The double sceptics of transnational constitutionalism and transnational public law range across two positions—or, rather, a continuum of possibilities framed by two positions. What these positions have in common is that they treat ideas of 'constitution' and of 'public law' alike as so deeply embedded within, and so closely intertwined with, the modern state, and as so closely implicated in its development, that it becomes difficult if not impossible to conceive of how they might prosper once detached from that context. For these positions the confirmatory circle of state-centredness is indeed a closed one.

One such position is *culturalist* in nature. It holds the idea of a constitution and of public law to be hollow, or at least deficient, in the absence of certain key cultural productions, including the idea of a democratically self-constituting and self-constituted 'people'—a self-realizing 'public'—possessing comprehensive powers of self-determination and self-legislation; in so doing introducing, as a

---

[10] Section 3.2 following.

second sense of 'publicness', an internal distinction between a capacious and integrated sphere of 'public' and thus politically negotiable affairs of government, and a domain of private and thus legal-rights-protected interests. It is claimed, in other words, that our built environment of legal and political forms and institutions is ultimately contingent upon certain prior or emergent socio-cultural facts concerning identity, solidarity, and allegiance, without which any self-styled constitutional project and any framework of public law dedicated to a particular 'public', and its publicly self-acknowledged affairs and institutions, are fated to amount to either a dead letter or a much more modest accomplishment.[11] Both constitutionalism, typically in the form of a foundational event and document, and public law more generally, as the resilient yet adaptable normative framework and principles of government, are in this view, first products of, and only second, subsidiary causes and reinforcing guarantees of a certain socio-cultural formation. As only the modern state has known such a socio-cultural formation, and since even if the modern state is no longer so robust in these terms it still constitutes a standing impediment to the development of similar socio-cultural formations at non-state sites, there can be no tangible prospect of a full constitutionalism and a full development of public law beyond the state.

A second double-sceptic position runs even deeper than the culturalist argument and puts a state-centred conception of constitutionalism and public law more clearly to the fore. This approach, closely associated in the UK context with the work of Martin Loughlin, has a profoundly *epistemic* quality. It focuses on the very idea of the modern state, and of the legal and political imaginary associated with the idea of the modern state as embracing 'a scheme of intelligibility . . . a comprehensive way of seeing, understanding and acting in the world'[12] that is simultaneously jurisgenerative and politico-generative in quality. It involves a framing or constitutive sense of 'public law'—of *ius publicum* or *droit politique*—that is necessarily prior and prerequisite to a full, modern articulation of the idea of the 'constitution' and 'public law' conceived of as positive law. The key insight here, and what distinguishes it from the culturalist position, is that the concept of the modern state, understood as a particular type of pre-positive but nevertheless jural relationship between territory, ruling authority, and people, is cause rather than consequence. It is not the mere expression and fruit of a prior cultural achievement—an accomplishment of national affinity and solidarity supplying the 'battery of power'[13] necessary to run the constitutional machine effectively. More than that, the category of the modern state involves a way of knowing and a way of being that embrace the idea of a self-constituting and self-regulating collective subject with no mandate or justification beyond the compact or consent of its individual agents; and in the absence of the self-assertion and self-comprehension of such an abstract constituent subject the very idea of a constituted polity is simply unimaginable.

---

[11] See eg, D. Grimm, 'The Constitution in the Process of Denationalization' (2005) 12 Constellations 447.

[12] See, eg, M. Loughlin, 'In Defence of *Staatslehre*' (2009) 48 Der Staat 1.

[13] M. Canovan, *Nationhood and Political Theory* (Edward Elgar: Cheltenham, 1996) 80.

For all their differences, the two positions—culturalist and epistemic—have certain important features in common. In both cases the message is strongly conveyed that the modern idea and practice of constitutionalism and public law could not have developed in the first place except in the context and through the medium of the nation and the state, which are themselves in one vision (epistemic), but not the other (cultural), already juridical categories. Importantly, both approaches conceive of legal authority in similar ways. Both involve a *pedigree* conception of the authority of constitutionalism and of public law, as somehow derived from and dependent upon a particular socio-political lineage. In addition, both involve an emphasis on the affirmative dimension of that authority—its manifestation as governing capacity or *gubernaculum*—as vital and prior, although also, as a feature of the reduction of that capacity to positive law, a strain of self-discipline and self-limitation in recognition of the underlying rights and interests of the individuals who make up the collective subject of government.[14] That is to say, it is the putatively democratic or meta-democratic source, whether the cultural substratum of the people or the epistemic framing of publicness, that is fundamental and indispensable in bequeathing legitimacy to the positive forms of constitutional law and public law more generally, and so in securing the institutional edifice of an expansive and integrated but self-containing system of government, which is the equally fundamental and indispensable expression of public power. And while this way of conceiving of legal authority may not, as matter of logical necessity, entirely rule out the possibility of a new pedigree and a similarly intense governing capacity—and so of a comparable constitutionalism and public law—emerging in other contexts and through a body other than the state, it certainly stacks the odds against such a development and places a heavy burden on the defenders of post-state constitutionalism to explain just how this might be possible.

The strength of the sceptical case is enhanced by one further feature that culturalist and epistemic versions share. In both approaches constitutionalism and publicness are closely connected and strongly complementary themes. The constitution is either both the consequence of a prior sense of the 'public' as a putative political community, and the source of a further normative distinction between the 'public' and the 'private' conceived of as domains of activity and interest of that political community, as in the culturalist vision, or it is the deep frame through which both of these aspects of 'publicness' are assumed, as in the epistemic vision. In either case, then, each term—constitutionalism and publicness—tends to reinforce the other in foregrounding the nation-state.

It follows from their emphatic state-centredness that proponents of the double sceptical view of constitutionalism and public law tend towards what Mattias Kumm calls the 'nostalgic' approach to global legal development.[15] For all the force of their arguments that the intertwined ideas and ideals of constitutionalism and public law cannot be unbundled from the state without significant cost, the

---

[14] See, eg, Loughlin, note 12. See also Loughlin, *The Idea of Public Law* (Oxford: Oxford University Press, 2003) ch 7; *Foundations of Public Law* (Oxford: Oxford University Press, 2010) ch 12.

[15] M. Kumm, 'The best of times and the worst of times' in P. Dobner and M. Loughlin (eds), *The Twilight of Constitutionalism* (Oxford: Oxford University Press, 2010) 202–19.

danger of this approach, as always with nostalgia, is of a kind of imaginative cul-de-sac. When considering the resources of constitutionalism and public law in a globalizing age, their default becomes one of optimism towards the past and pessimism in the face of the future. Their options, given their dismissal of any plausible prospect of the comprehensive adaptation of the state-suffused registers of constitutionalism and public law in a post-national environment, narrow to a wishful rewinding of the modernist legacy to its Westphalian pomp, a defensive consolidation of the reduced remit of a state-centred law, or a fatalistic acceptance of the redundancy of a paradigm in the face of inexorable post-national trends.[16]

3.2 Concessions to post-nationalism

Yet, we should be careful how far we push this analysis. As already intimated, even the most pronouncedly sceptical position would not deny some significance to constitutionalism or public law beyond the state.

If we consider, first, post-national constitutional law, we can point to two distinct strands of residual recognition from a sceptical standpoint. On the one hand, the constitutional label, here understood as a basic and non-exclusive brand, may be presented as a familiar descriptor of the foundational regulatory framework of many forms of social organization other than states that we find situated either within or across states. Legally, these might range from highly informal normative arrangements, as with the constitutive rules of many of the intermediate associations of national and transnational civil society—from NGOs and charities to political parties and sporting associations—to much more formal structures such as the United Nations Charter or other framework treaties of international organizations. The consequence, and sometimes—as in a prominent British politician's famous comparison of the abortive EU Constitutional Treaty of 2004 to the constitution of a Golf Club—the explicit aim[17] of this concession, is to dilute and devalue the currency of constitutional language. The suggestion is that many entities can be described as constitutional in a thin normative sense without possessing the thick social imaginary or cultural roots associated with the modern state. What is merely the topsoil of positive rules in the deeply sedimented structure of the state may, therefore, be the sole or primary bonding agent in many lesser collective projects that neither possess

---

[16] See, eg, Grimm, 'The Constitution in the Process of Denationalization'. Not all double sceptics strike a pessimistic tone; only those (many) who believe something is lost in the non-translatability of the resources of constitutionalism and public law to the post-national setting. There are two other possibilities. First, the resources of constitutionalism and public law, while still deemed appropriate to the nation-state context, may be viewed as entirely inappropriate to the market context of postnational relations, for which another form of law, far from being 'second-best', is considered more suitable. See, eg, U. Haltern 'Pathos and Patina: The Failure and Promise of Constitutionalism in the European Imagination' (2003) 9 European Law Journal 14. Secondly, the resources of constitutionalism and public law may be viewed as of limited and declining value even in the nation state context, a conclusion reinforced by the changing nature and less dominant role of the state in an age of increasing transnational power and authority. See, eg, K. H. Ladeur 'We the European People—Relache?' (2008) 14 European Law Journal 147. See also Teubner, n 42 following, Sabel and Zeitlin, note 50 following.

[17] See, eg, M. Kumm, 'Beyond Golf Clubs and the Judicialization of Politics: Why Europe has a Constitution Properly So Called' (2006) 54 American Journal of Comparative Law 505.

nor demand the breadth or depth of common sympathy or commitment of the state. But where the normative framework does stand alone in this way, so the argument runs, what we have is merely a kind of constitutionalism-lite; or, to put it another way, a 'constitution without constitutionalism'[18]—a regulatory super-structure which neither feeds nor is fed by a strong socio-cultural base.

In the second place, the sceptic might concede the post-national relevance of constitutionalism if registered or conceived of as a constraint upon government authority rather than as the prior establishment of that authority. The typical motivation here, as befits the sceptical temper, is one of suspicion of post-national authority. Constitutionalism is understood negatively. It embraces the limiting dimension of 'constituted' authority—the legal reduction and restriction of gov-ernmental power.[19] This involves an actual or projected set of measures intended to limit or monitor the flow of power towards a new post-national entity and so away from the state, which is thereby preserved as the proper source and site of constitutional law conceived of affirmatively—as the basic capacity to govern. Again, the EU Constitutional Treaty provides a case in point. When, in the heat of debate, avowedly Eurosceptical sources such as *The Economist* magazine were won over to the idea of a European Union Constitution, it was because such a document, by dint of new or enhanced mechanisms such as a charter of rights and a competence catalogue, was seen as way of conditioning and reining in rather than embedding and augmenting supranational capacity.[20]

What these two cases reveal, on closer inspection, is a link between the diverse roots of the constitutional idea, with its expansive range of descriptive, diagnos-tic, and prescriptive references, and its flexible response to new circumstances. On the one hand, both in descriptive and diagnostic vein, the sense of *a* consti-tution as a canonical document or set of documents containing a discrete body of positive law—upon which one strand of the sceptical concession to post-national constitutional law depends—has long existed alongside the sense of *the* consti-tution as referring to the deep and interlayered structure of established power within the polity. As far back as the classical Roman state, the idea of constitution has incorporated this double sense,[21] ambiguously poised between reference to the process or immediate product of legal 'constituting', and reference to what we recognize as firmly established—as already 'constituted'.[22] The thin positive and the thick non-positive versions of constitutionalism today track this etymo-logical duality.

---

[18] J. Weiler, *The Constitution of Europe* (Cambridge: Cambridge University Press, 1999) 298.

[19] See Section 2.

[20] See *The Economist*, 15 December 2001.

[21] In imperial times the decrees of the emperor, which collectively defined the extent of state action, were known as *constitutiones*; see G. Maddox, 'A Note on the Meaning of "Constitution"' (1982) 76 American Political Science Review 805; D. Grimm 'Types of Constitution' in M. Rosenfeld and A. Sajo (eds), *The Oxford Handbook of Comparative Constitutional Law* (Oxford: Oxford University Press, 2012) 98–132.

[22] According to one author, the idea of constitution, by embracing such contrasting emphases, 'seems to cut across the essentialist-nonessentialist distinction', D. Lutz, *Principles of Constitutional Design* (Cambridge: Cambridge University Press, 2006) 188.

On the other hand, and in both descriptive and prescriptive vein, there is just as venerable and just as resilient a distinction between constitutional law as *gubernaculum* and constitutional law as *jurisidictio,* with the one referring to the establishment of governmental capacity and the other to the forms—actual or ideal—of its restraint.[23] The invocation of constitutionalism as a bridle upon new forms of post-national power refers back, once again, to just one half of a continuing distinction.

If we now turn to the ways in which post-national public law is acknowledged in minor key from a sceptical perspective, a similar pattern emerges. On the one hand, markedly more so than in transnational constitutionalism, which, considered *as* law, tends to remain merely aspirational, or implicit, or limited to sub-legal regulatory contexts, there are many solid traces of publicness in transnational legal doctrine. In any external account, therefore, these will be unavoidably and so uncontroversially described as such. For example, a number of key concepts in both EU law and the law of the European Convention on Human Rights (ECHR)—the continent's two most prominent transnational legal orders—invoke the idea of publicness. These include public morality, public policy, public health, public security, public safety, and public order.[24] In the one case, EU law, the relevant terms qualify the unconstrained transnational circulation of the factors of production, while in the other, the ECHR, they qualify the transnational protection of rights and freedoms. And while the superficial thrust of these and similar concepts may be *against* transnationalism, with the 'public' point of reference for the interest or good in question often being the public of a specific state, or at least the public located in the territory of a specific state, that by no means tells us the whole story. Sometimes the interest or good of a wider transnational public constituency is clearly contemplated[25] and in all cases the concepts themselves are defined by reference to broad state-indifferent and state-transcendent standards, subject to the authoritative interpretation and enforcement of the transnationally located and empowered judicial and administrative organs of the EU and ECHR.

Let us now switch focus from first-order *doctrine* to the second-order *disciplinary* classification of legal material,[26] a category which, in its double connotation of the 'passive' collation of doctrinal materials and their 'active' arrangement, straddles the distinction between detached and engaged, and between descriptive, diagnostic, and prescriptive. Here we can report, first, a further uncontroversial, if modest, core of common understanding of public law's transnational

---

[23] See, eg, C. H. McIlwain, *Constitutionalism Ancient and Modern,* 2nd edn (Ithaca: Cornell University Press, 1958).

[24] See variously, Treaty on the Functioning of the European Union, Arts. 36, 45, and, 52; European Convention on Human Rights, Arts. 8–11.

[25] For example, as regards restrictions on free movement between states within the EU on grounds of public health, given the form taken by the threat in question those controls designed to prevent the spread of diseases with epidemic potential are clearly aimed at safeguarding the European 'public' in general and not just particular national or territorial publics; see Directive 2004/38/EC on Citizens' free movement rights, Art. 29.

[26] I develop this distinction at length in 'On the Necessarily Public Quality of Law' in C. Michelon et al. (eds), *The Public in Law,* 9–34.

resonance. Today, the idea of a state-internal discipline of 'public law' which is concerned with demarcating those areas in which the state and its emanations and analogues are in direct relation with individuals and other legal persons, or in which different organs or agencies of the state are in relationship with one another, retains validity as an organizing and educating frame, as one of the essential maps through which we contemplate and comprehend the legal world. Equally, no-one would deny the continuing place of the disciplinary domain of *'public* international law' in any recognizable map of the legal world. It remains the key classificatory term to distinguish the corpus of law that subsists between states from the corpus of choice-of-law rules concerning the appropriately applicable internal state law in situations where there is more than one candidate, with the latter category going under the label of *'private* international law'.[27]

For sceptics, of course, the publicness of public international law has been, and remains, a derived or delegated characteristic, and so, on account of its lack of autonomy, of only marginal contribution to the fund of post-national law. It is a branch of law qualifying as public precisely because it is authorized by and between the primary locations of 'publicness', namely, the states. However, beyond this uncontroversial core meaning, the disciplinary label that the sceptics are prepared to endorse has long been the subject of a more expansive reading. Here, at the cutting diagnostic and prescriptive edge of disciplinary classification, the publicness of public international law has always been understood, in the alternative, in global terms—as a separately sourced *ius gentium*.[28] And even for sceptics, importantly, there are some features of the doctrinal field framed by public international law, such as general principles or *ius cogens*, which it is difficult to make sense of without conceding something to a vision which claims validity and authority other than as the delegated product of state consent.[29]

We will have more to say about more expansive disciplinary renderings of post-national public law below.[30] The immediate point to pursue is that our sense of the publicness of law, at least as much as that of constitutionalism, is widely ramified, with diverse historical roots and resonances across pre-modern and modern ages. Although perennially concerned with the framing, either of the self-recognizing subjects, or of the resilient contexts of collective action and interaction that reach beyond the confines of family or other special affinity, the idea of the public in law has had many and diverse particular orientations.[31]

---

[27] On the origins of the distinction between public and private international law, see H. Muir Watt, 'Private International Law Beyond the Schism' (2011) 2 Transnational Legal Theory 347.

[28] See, eg, J. Waldron, 'Foreign Law and the Modern *Ius Gentium*' (2005) 119 Harvard Law Review 129; N. Walker, 'Out of Place and Out of Time: Law's Fading Co-ordinates' (2010) 14 Edinburgh Law Review 13.

[29] See, eg, E. de Wet, 'The International Constitutional Order' (2006) 55 International and Comparative Law Quarterly 51.

[30] See Section 4.1.

[31] Raymond Geuss captures this diversity well: 'there is no such thing as *the* public/private distinction, or, at any rate, it is a deep mistake to think that there is a single substantive distinction here that can be made to do any real philosophical or political work'; *Public Goods, Private Goods* (Princeton: Princeton University Press, 2003) 106. Instead, he claims, it is a division that has grown over pre-modern and

Sometimes our sense of legal publicness concerns the openness or expansiveness of modes of access to or control over property, space, or information; sometimes it concerns the realm of matters that concern everyone as opposed to purely personal or group concerns (that is, *res publicae)*; and sometimes the emphasis is on the limits rather than the extent of the public domain—on the 'liberal' demarcation of a protected area of private activity and autonomous choice.[32] Depending on the context and background, doctrinal questions may vary, the public/private boundary may be drawn at a different diagnostic point, and the prescriptive consequences of the classificatory choice may diverge.

Publicness in law, then, even from a sceptical vantage point, is perhaps more accurately described as a disseminating rather than as a disappearing category. And in that dissemination, and especially as it crosses the 'barrier' between state and non-state, we see evidence, at the margins, of legal doctrine and thought evolving in a reflexive manner. Legal concepts of publicness, whether first-order doctrinal practice or second-order disciplinary framing, do not come to be applied to non-state contexts randomly, but rather through an iterative and progressive process of conscious adaptation, or tacit affirmation of resemblance, to the state-based heritage. Even for those most sceptical of transnational legal publicness, therefore, the propensity for non-robust strains of legal publicness to pass from state to transnational must be recognized as an inevitable feature of the evolution of law's discursive register in an age of the development of new transnational circuits of economic and cultural power.

4. SELECTIVE SCEPTICISM

So far, in emphasizing both the underlying state bias of constitutionalism and public law and the undeniability of a post-national supplement, we have concentrated on what our two key notions have in common. In the present section, as we come to consider more discriminating forms of scepticism, the focus will switch to the ways in which they differ.

4.1 Transnational constitutional scepticism

Let us turn, first, to the transnational constitutional sceptics. Unlike the double sceptics, they believe in a robust conception of public law beyond the state, while remaining sceptical about transnational constitutionalism. This position is perhaps most closely associated with the work of the Global Administrative Law project,[33] but includes other similar transnational visions of public law.[34] The

---

modern times, bringing together '[d]isparate components—conceptual fragments, theories, folk reactions, crude distinctions that are useful in highly specific practical contexts, tacit value assumptions— from different sources and belonging to different spheres' at 10.

[32] Geuss, *Public Goods, Private Goods*, chs 2–4.

[33] The literature is huge. For the formative text, see B. Kingsbury, R. B. Stewart, and N. Krisch, 'The Emergence of Global Administrative Law' (2005) 68 Law and Contemporary Problems 15.

[34] See, eg, Von Bogdandy et al., 'Developing the Publicness of Public International Law'; D. Dyzenhaus (ed.), *The Unity of Public Law* (Oxford: Hart, 2004). See also Ch 13 this book.

focus is on the proliferating regimes of transnational regulation that exercise authority of the kind traditionally associated with the public authority of the state, but where the link with the original authority of the state has been radically attenuated or lost. These new regimes range widely in form and substance, including the globally extended administrative and regulatory activities of UN bodies such as the World Health Organization and the Financial Action Task Force; informal transnational financial networks such as the Basle Committee of heads of central banks; bottom-up coordinated administration between national regulators with overlapping objectives in matters such as nuclear safety and biodiversity conservation; hybrid public/private transnational representative bodies such as the Internet Corporation for Assigned Names and Numbers; and purely privately initiated but broadly publicly endorsed bodies such as the International Standardisation Organization, concerned with product harmonization, or international sport's World Anti-Doping Agency.[35]

In the development of this orientation we observe the drawing of a key distinction—one which, as we shall see, implicitly informs much position-taking in the post-national debate. For in the perspective of global administrative law, the emphasis tends to be on 'throughput' or process, and 'output' or substantive outcomes, over 'input' and pedigree. On the one hand, this kind of approach curtails the prospects of the familiar constitutional form being reproduced at the transnational level—at least the deep form associated with a 'foundational constitutionalism'[36] grounded in the constitutive pact of the self-identifying people. On the other hand, a significant level of continuity is claimed with the state public law tradition in terms of basic ideals and operating system. According to one prominent scholar of global administrative law, for example, the manifold sites of transnational administrative justice operating in the absence of—or attenuated from—state constitutional roots, should be framed and guided by general principles of legality, rationality, and proportionality, together with respect for the rule of law and basic protection of human rights.[37] Over time, it is claimed, these normative ideals, all of which are concerned not with the original pedigree or the generation of political power, but with the tasks of 'channeling, managing, shaping and constraining political power'[38] during or 'after the fact' of its emergence in the countless crevices of transnational authority, tend to circulate more widely and more readily. Gradually, 'as the layers of common normative practice thicken, they come to be argued for and adopted through a mixture of comparative study and a sense that they are (or are becoming) obligatory'.[39]

The accent, therefore, is on how newly 'publicized' forms of authority can compensate for the kind of originary constituent power that we associate with

---

[35] See Kingsbury et al., 'The Emergence of Global Administrative Law'.

[36] See N. Krisch, *Beyond Constitutionalism: The Pluralist Structure of Postnational Law* (Oxford: Oxford University Press, 2010).

[37] See Kingsbury, 'The Concept of "Law" in Global Administrative Law', and 'International Law as Inter-Public Law'.

[38] Kingsbury, 'The Concept of "Law"', 32.

[39] Kingsbury, 'The Concept of "Law"', 30.

the state constitutional tradition and which is difficult if not impossible to replicate in the post-national context. On this reading, the public quality of legal authority is defined first and foremost in contradistinction to a purely private conception, where only the personal or narrow sectional interests of particular individuals or populations count, and where law is merely instrumental to these interests. Instead, the affirmation of the 'public' quality of law involves the insistence that the collective interest of 'the whole society'[40] somehow be served. That collective interest may be identified and acted upon by reference to general criteria of 'good governance', whose overall objectivity and situational appropriateness is guaranteed by a combination of strong process standards of transparency, reason-giving, and accountability, and a complex dynamic of social learning and reinforcement and of mutual responsibility across the myriad sites of transnational regulation.

It is worth stressing, however, that this kind of approach engages only part of our understanding of law's 'public' quality. As was mentioned earlier, 'publicness' registers at two levels in our imagination of modern law. It applies both to the particular collective 'public' as the source or reference point of law, and to the domain of 'public' matters and interests which are to be treated as topics of general concern through law. The first sense of public is particular and nominal, while the second is general and adjectival, and it is only the second sense that tends to be emphasized by the transnational constitutional sceptics.[41] They do so armed with the double conviction that a general political ethic of 'public' reason and concern can seek to fill the absence of a constitutive 'public'—can simulate the kind of commitment to individual-respecting pursuit of the common good that any such voluntary collective would be bound to endorse—and that, in any case, there is little or no scope in the transnational domain to remedy that absence.

4.2 Transnational public law scepticism

Conversely, those who are sceptics of transnational public law but affirmers of transnational constitutionalism tend to be more interested in new origins and 'input'—in the distinctiveness of the motivating source—than in the form of the throughput or the content of the output. The focus here is on the *familiarly* 'constitutive' nature of the regulation of increasingly differentiated social fields, themselves *unfamiliar* in terms of and irreducible to the general public/private divide. Gunther Teubner, a leading exponent of the theory of 'societal constitutionalism', has developed one of the most refined—not to say rarified—versions of this approach.[42]

---

[40] Waldron, 'Can There be a Democratic Jurisprudence?', 39.

[41] Krisch, *Beyond Constitutionalism*, is a notable exception. His critique of state-centred foundational constitutionalism does not prevent him from promoting an idea of 'public autonomy', which, significantly influenced by Habermas, is as concerned with the constitutive conditions of publicness in postnational sectors as it is with the means by which and the standards according to which it is sustained (89–105).

[42] See in particular, Teubner, *Constitutional Fragments: Societal Constitutionalism and Globalization* (Oxford: Oxford University Press, 2012).

For all his use of constitutional language, Teubner is at pains to distinguish his approach from the conventional wisdom of foundational constitutionalism. The idea of the constitution as a documentary initiative through which pre-political collective potential, or constituent power, is transformed into full-blown legal and political community is one he finds misleading and underspecified even at the level of the state, and all the more inadequate in the highly fragmented transnational sphere where the 'general ubiquity'[43] of state action knows no parallel. The collective subjects of transnational regimes are more specialist and their remit is more restricted. The idea of a cosmopolitan 'people' or 'public' forming the basis of an encompassing normatively-ordered political society, therefore, holds little relevance—even as founding myth still less as an empirical substrate. Not only are the 'public policy' sectors familiar from the integrated state polity divided into so many transnational regimes, but different societal sub-systems which extend beyond the traditional purview of public policy (for example, in the organization of the economy, or of education or sport, or of the arts or the sciences) operate according to codes which employ the normative incentives of law in variable and more or less central ways.[44]

Yet, Teubner would maintain that the idea of transnational constitutionalism, quite differently conceived from the state-based original, nevertheless remains important as a way of accounting for a highly differentiated societal formation and understanding the legitimacy requirements of the new global configuration. Drawing on the insights of systems theory, rather than discard the idea of constituent power, he reinterprets it as '*a communicative potential,* a type of social energy'[45]—a way of characterizing the collective '"constitutional subject" [as] not simply a semantic artifact ... but rather a pulsating process at the interface of consciousness and communication'.[46] Teubner, in short, wants to treat societal constitutionalism as a fluid form of sectoral *self*-constitution. In so doing he distinguishes between the widely replicated and increasingly intensified function of sectoral differentiation and specialization, which he sees as a key feature of the general dynamic of transnational society, and the particular self-generating process followed and form taken, which varies significantly not only from the original statist paradigm but also between different global sub-sectors. The many 'capillary constitutions'[47] of transnational society, to which more or less formal legal documents—from framework treaties to industry codes—contribute to a variable extent, supply in their very different contexts both a symbology of collective self-understanding and self-projection, and an operating code or social technology for the framing of collective action.

In a key set of insights, Teubner argues that, in their discrete specialization and functional concentration, the sub-spheres of transnational society escape our received modern distinction between a generically public and a generically private sphere, and so cannot be assessed and evaluated in accordance with

---

[43] Teubner, *Constitutional Fragments*, 132.

[44] Teubner, *Constitutional Fragments*, ch 4.

[45] Teubner, *Constitutional Fragments*, 62.

[46] Teubner, *Constitutional Fragments*, 63.

[47] Teubner, *Constitutional Fragments*, 83.

conventional standards of a holistic public interest and public good. Instead, we should understand and judge their constitutional adequacy in terms of their success in achieving a balance between the autonomy and self-limitation of different functional sectors *inter se* in a highly fragmented global order—with autonomy, as a modern ideal which respects freedom and equality, retained and inherited from the state tradition.[48] In this view, the key 'constitutive' puzzle faced by the key stakeholders of relatively autonomous global subsectors and by those many who are indirectly affected by their activities—namely, how to balance the freedom of those most concerned with and affected by a given practice to govern that given practice, against the need to limit its expansion into other spheres and to curb its tendency to encroach on the autonomy of other sectors of social practice and their key stakeholders—can nevertheless still be rendered in constitutionally recognizable terms. For, arguably, this balancing requirement is the moral equivalent under a globally differentiated order of the constitutive design puzzle of the high modern order; namely, how to safeguard the 'internal sovereignty' of 'the people' while ensuring that their 'external sovereignty' does not compromise the internal sovereignty of others.[49]

This approach, many of its findings endorsed by those who do not share Teubner's attachment to systems theory,[50] provides the reverse image of transnational constitutional scepticism. Granted, just as law's 'publicness', through historical and continuing usage, is a fertile enough signifier to include input as well as throughput and output dimensions, so, conversely, constitutional law, as we have seen, is a sufficiently versatile category to include not just the constitution but also the regulation and restraint of political authority; that is, not just the exercise of constituent power and its transformation into *gubernaculum,* but also *jurisidictio.* So while the point of departure may be different, each term ultimately extends across the same territory, and, indeed, has done so—with different emphases at different times and places—throughout the modern age, in which it has served as a state-centred discourse.[51] Yet just as constitution-sceptic projects such as global administrative law tend to engage only that part of law's public quality which does not deal with 'constitutive' matters,[52] so, conversely,

---

[48] See, eg, G. Teubner, 'Constitutionalising Polycontextuality' (2011) 20 Social and Legal Studies 209.

[49] Teubner, 'Constitutionalising Polycontextuality', 209. See also Krisch, *Beyond Constitutionalism,* espousing very similar views about the need to 'balance inclusiveness and particularity' (101) in autonomous sectors, while eschewing the language of constitutionalism (see also note 41 earlier).

[50] See Krisch, *Beyond Constitutionalism;* see also the work of Charles Sabel and his collaborators, eg, C. F. Sabel and J. Zeitlin 'The New Architecture of Experimentalist Governance in the EU' (2008) 14 European Law Journal, 271; from a more culturally informed conception of difference, see J. Tully, *Strange Multiplicity: Constitutionalism in an Age of Diversity* (Cambridge: Cambridge Unuversity Press, 1995); and from a more international law-focused perspective, see A. Peters, 'Membership in the Global Constitutional Community' in J. Klabbers, A. Peters, and G. Ulfstein (eds), *The Constitutionalization of International Law* (Oxford: Oxford University Press, 2009) 153–263, 201–203.

[51] On these shifts of emphasis, see N. Walker, 'Constitutionalism and the Incompleteness of Democracy: An Iterative Relationship' in (2010) 39(3) Rechtsfilosofie & rechtstheorie 206, 206–13.

[52] But see Krisch, *Beyond Constitutionalism.* We should not, however, be surprised by such exceptions. As becomes more generally evident in our discussion of double affirmation in Section 5 following, the deep and resilient distinction between particular and general, input and throughput/output, is only loosely reflected in the discriminating choice of the language of constitutionalism or publicness. As noted in

public law-sceptical projects such as societal or sectoral constitutionalism engage only that dimension of constitutionalism that *does* deal with such matters. In other words, whereas transnational constitutional scepticism typically eschews the nominal and particular in favour of the adjectival and the general, transnational public law scepticism tends to do precisely the opposite. It concentrates on the many particulars of a fragmented constitutional landscape, as well as the relations between these particulars, at the expense of any conception of internal standards which are common across domains.

An only selective *scepticism*, therefore, as in the two cases just discussed, is, equally, an only selective *affirmation* of the transferability of a state-centred legal rubric to the transnational domain. Selectivity, of course, does not imply arbitrariness. Each approach has its reasoned elaboration. Transnational constitutional scepticism is born of a sense that the prospects of a post-national constituent power are remote, while it is possible to replicate other parts of the public law portfolio. Transnational public law scepticism is born of a sense that generic publicness lacks traction in the fragmented transnational world, yet that it remain possible, *mutatis mutandis,* to identify the formative influences and take seriously the constitutive credentials of these fragments. But, of course, neither side can be correct in their selective critique without undermining the other, and by dint of their disagreement, they threaten to return us to the double sceptical position. Are there any other alternatives which allow the affirmative dimension of one or both positions to be salvaged?

5. DOUBLE AFFIRMATION

If we turn, finally, to the double affirmers of transnational constitutionalism and transnational public law, they seek to provide a positive answer to our last question. Again we can identify two distinct positions. Unlike the selective sceptics, these positions do not start from the premise that the promise of the state-centred approach can only be *partially* redeemed at the transnational level. Rather, while they continue to focus on the mobility of one aspect of the legacy of the state, they view this as the key aspect, and, therefore as capable of securing a full(er) reiteration of the virtues of the state-centred approach transnationally. Yet, these approaches remain inherently one-sided. Just as is the case between the transnational public law sceptics and the transnational constitutional sceptics, in their development and defence we can observe a continuing tension between an input or pedigree conception of authority and a throughput or output conception.

5.1 Post-national constituent power

In the first place, there are those who have argued for the applicability of a version of constitutionalism bearing a significant family resemblance to state-based foundational constitutionalism to post-state entities such as the EU. The

---

Section 3.2, the terms are just too broad and varied in their historical signification to become narrowly compartmentalized and consistently applied in contemporary post-national use. See also note 74 following.

idea here—one I have endorsed[53]—is that even in the 'post-constituent'[54] remoteness of a mature transnational regulation system which first emerged as a merely intergovernmental compact, it is possible, through a documentary constitutional settlement presented as a self-standing political pact, to homologate or nurture a sense of a meta-democratically validated transnational political community with a wide-ranging political agenda and a distinct sense of the public good. On this view, the vital coordinates of a robustly autonomous legal supranationalism—namely the transnational demos, transnational public sphere, and transnational public law—need not be contradicted by or precluded by an extant sense of political community and framework of constitutional and public law at the national level.[55]

Of course, such a view remains vulnerable to failure of initiative, as in the EU case, or, even if the initiative were to be successful, to the possible failure of its long-term post-initiative gambit to reinforce the socio-political contours of political community that it presupposes.[56] It also remains vulnerable, on a broader front, to the charge that this kind of popularly endorsed constitutional initiative is, in any case, quite inappropriate to most contexts of transnational regulation, and that the alternative 'constitutive' and self-regulatory foundations of the sectoral 'post-public' regimes cited by the champions of societal constitutionalism in these other and increasingly typical contexts of transnational regulation provide at best a poor substitute in terms of 'democratic' pedigree.[57]

One riposte to this criticism, recalling the general charge of undue pessimism levelled at the double sceptics, is that we should not underestimate the potential for the democratic regeneration of international organizations, even if this does not take the capital 'C' Constitutional form attempted in the EU. In recent years there has, for instance, been a revival in ideas of transnational parliamentarianism, building on existing examples in institutions such as the Assembly of the Council of Europe, the MERCOSUR Parliament, the Pan-African Parliament of the African Union, and the ASEAN Inter-Parliamentary Assembly.[58] Yet, with the exception of certain radical but only marginally supported schemes for a global popular assembly,[59] and of others which seek to build on a strongly international

---

[53] See, eg, N. Walker, 'The European Union's Unresolved Constitution' in Rosenfeld and Sajo (eds), *The Oxford Handbook of Comparative Constitutional Law*, 1185–208.

[54] See N. Walker, 'Post-constituent Constitutionalism? The Case of the EU' in Loughlin and Walker (eds), *The Paradox of Constitutionalism* (Oxford: Oxford University Press, 2007) 247–68.

[55] Habermas is a key reference point here. See, eg, his 'Why Europe Needs A Constitution' (2001) 11 New Left Review 5; 'The Crisis of the European Union in the Light of a Constitutionalization of International Law' (2012) 23 European Journal of International Law 335.

[56] See, eg, A Moravcsik, 'What Can we Learn from the Collapse of the European Constitutional Project?' (2006) 47 Politische Vierteljahresschrift 2.

[57] See, eg, D. Grimm, 'The Achievement of Constitutionalism and its Prospects in a Changed World' in P. Dobner and M. Loughlin (eds), *The Twilight of Constitutionalism?* (Oxford: Oxford University Press, 2010) 3–22.

[58] See, eg, A. Von Bogdandy, 'The European Lesson for International Democracy: The Significance of Articles 9–12 EU Treaty for International Organizations' (2012) 23 European Journal of International Law 315.

[59] See, eg, R. Falk and A. Strauss, 'On The Creation of a Global People's Assembly: Legitimacy and the Power of Popular Sovereignty' (2000) 36 Stanford Journal of International Law 1.

communitarian reading of the post-war founding of the United Nations,[60] such models tend to renounce or marginalize any ambition to found such democracy in a constitutive transnational 'people'. Rather, the emphasis tends to be on how democracy can be reconfigured in ways which stress more or less direct forms of representation, and upon proxy values such as transparency and deliberation.[61]

What is most revealing about this strain of thinking, and the reservations it incorporates or provokes, is that transnational foundational constitutionalism is challenged not just because of its false or misplaced empirical credentials. What we find is not only a questioning of the plausibility of a transnational popular sovereignty, or a fear that, to the extent that it is plausible, this would result in an unwelcome hollowing out of national democracy—attitudes which we find variably distributed amongst both the double sceptics and the transnational constitutional sceptics. In addition, although sometimes obscured by these more prominent objections, even many of those who appear relatively optimistic about transnational democratic potential and well-disposed towards its fulfilment, nevertheless seem to be anxious about asking for too much of a good thing. Rather than bemoan or apologize for the cultural limits to transnational democratic growth, they tend to emphasize the importance of other forces—expertise, impartiality, policy long-sightedness, and other values—individual and minority rights, associational autonomy, as supplementary and even moderating influences in the transnational constitutional domain.[62] What this suggests, importantly, is that inasmuch as the double affirmation of the transnational relevance of constitutionalism and public law is claimed to rest predominantly upon the constitutive side of the equation—on the authorizing legitimacy and energizing effect of new sites of constituent power and their attendant public spheres—there is a reluctance to treat this as an unalloyed good.

5.2 Cosmopolitan public law

An alternative doubly affirmative vision is of a continuous and 'cosmopolitan'[63] constitutionalism and public law. For Mattias Kumm—a thoughtful and influential exponent of this view—the modernist past, understood *senso largo*, remains the key to the future. The philosophical core and basic 'political imaginary'[64] of constitutionalism and public law—terms which, tellingly, he treats as entirely compatible, indeed as virtually interchangeable, in the post-national domain[65]—has not altered

---

[60] See, eg, B. Fassbender, 'The United Nations Charter as the Constitution of the International Community' (1998) 36 Columbia Journal of International Law 529.

[61] See, eg, Von Bogdandy, 'The European Lesson for International Democracy', 326 *et seq*.

[62] Von Bogdandy, 'The European Lesson for International Democracy', 326 *et seq*. See also G. De Burca, 'Developing Democracy Beyond the State' (2008) 46 Columbia Journal of Transnational Law 221.

[63] See, eg, M. Kumm, 'The Cosmopolitan Turn in Constitutionalism: On the Relationship between Constitutionalism in and beyond the State' in J. L. Dunoff and J. P. Trachtman (eds), *Ruling the World?* (Cambridge: Cambridge University Press, 2009) 258–325. For a similar cosmopolitan perspective, see A. Stone Sweet, 'A Cosmopolitan Legal Order: Constitutional Pluralism and Rights Adjudication in Europe' (2012) 1 Global Constitutionalism 53.

[64] See C. Taylor, *Modern Social Imaginaries* (Durham: Duke University Press, 2003).

[65] See M. Kumm, 'How Does European Law Fit into the World of Public Law?' in J. Neyer and A. Wiener (eds), *Political Theory of the European Union* (Oxford: Oxford University Press, 2011) 111–38.

since the advent of modern constitutionalism through the medium of the maturing state system of late 18th-century Europe and America. Crucially, what is constitutionally basic for him is not a matter of institutional architecture, still less of the conception of pedigree that informs that architecture, but of the underlying normative principles and the imagining of society that nurtures these normative principles. These normative principles flow from the basic modernist constructivist ambition with which we are already familiar from the perspective of the state-centred double sceptics.[66] This involves a vision, distinct from the coercive, personal, or metaphysically valorized power systems of the Middle Ages, of persons self-conceived as free and equal individuals acting collectively to deliberate, develop, and implement their own conception of the common interest or public good. From these origins, according to Kumm, we can derive a set of universal constitutional and public law commitments to principles of legality, subsidiarity, adequate participation and accountability, public reason, and rights-protection.[67]

Against this larger canvas, it is argued, the detail of the traditional state-centred public law system assumes a more modest significance than is often appreciated within constitutional thought. It is exposed as but one institutional blueprint for giving effect to the underlying principles, rather than an exclusive, dominant, or even optimal template for constitutional government. Instead, under conditions of intensifying globalization the basically cosmopolitan texture of *any* constitutionalism committed to universal principles becomes more apparent, and the state is now but one constitutional player on a wider stage. As free and equal persons operating under certain constraints of interest, information, geography, and affinity, we continue to respect particular contexts of decision-making and public interest formation, and the principles of subsidiarity, participation, and accountability recognize this. However, as free and equal persons we are also categorically committed to acknowledgment of the freedom and equality of all others, and so to the universal nature of our political condition. In this way, we can reconcile our attachment to particular polities and sites of authority with a belief in an overarching normative framework which informs the terms of our various particular manifestations of public authority. In the final analysis, the global division of the world into particular polities remains inevitable, but the particular form that such a division takes is not so; rather, it is contingent upon shifts in the underlying circuits of social and economic power. What is more, the universal nature of the claim implies that the particular pedigree—including the immediate democratic deficiencies of that pedigree—is less important than commitment to the very ideals and principles which both underpin democratic pedigree and would provide its 'natural' complement.

For all its suggestiveness, the Kumm thesis is open to a range of criticisms that mirrors the challenge to the idea of post-national constituent power. On the one hand, there is an empirical critique. Even if we are attracted to its vision, is the cosmopolitan approach not vulnerable to the charge of utopianism, or of

---

[66] Section 3.2.

[67] Kumm, 'How Does European Law Fit into the World of Public Law?'.

complacency? If understood primarily in aspirational terms, is there not a chasm between the cosmopolitan's principles and the actual state of global politics and economics, a pattern marked by the combination of fugitive power—of collectively unauthorized and unaccountable concentrations of transnational interests, and an increasingly obtuse and incoherent network of legal authority? Against this, Kumm counters that cosmopolitanism, far from describing a distant ideal, is actually the 'best' interpretation of much historical and existing constitutional practice both in and beyond the state. Yet, while he is adept at showing how certain legal sites do demonstrate a sophisticated appreciation of the demands of cosmopolitan public reason, it is notable that these tend to be judicial sites, and tend to be situated in the European stronghold of mature post-national governance.[68] There remains a danger of complacency in this assessment, a failure to explain how public reason can systematically prevail over private interest in contexts where the conditions of public will formation, and the epistemic and authoritative weight associated with such will formation, are often conspicuous by their remoteness or absence.

On the other hand, there is a normative critique, which connects to and reinforces elements of the empirical critique. In theory as well as in practice, does the universalism and singularity of Kumm's vision—the idea that the general principles of constitutionalism and public law are applicable to all circumstances and can always be interwoven to form one cloth—not threaten to subordinate the nominal and particular dimensions of constitutionalism and publicness unduly to the adjectival and general? Certainly, the emphasis on subsidiarity and participation shows that Kumm is far from blind to the need to recognize the authority of collective voice. But does cosmopolitanism's uniform algebra—its insistence on situating the voice of any particular public within a universal formula of good global governance—not unduly 'cabin' and curtail the idea of constituent power? In a nutshell, does his confidence in cosmopolitanism's objective ability to discern and balance the principles of good governance not risk the very 'triumphalism'[69] which he himself so rightly diagnoses as the equally unpalatable alternative to the double sceptic's constitutional nostalgia? Is this, in the final analysis, not just one more hegemonic move on behalf of a holistic constitutional vision, one that illegitimately downplays democratic pedigree?

6. CONCLUSION

The retention of both constitutionalism and public law as central terms in the global legal prospectus speaks to the promise and the challenge, the hopes and the fears, associated with a certain way of thinking about the world of law and politics. Beyond the state-centredness of double scepticism, what the various conceptions of the transnational considered above suggest, and what is made most explicit in Kumm's cosmopolitanism, is that in considering the continuing relevance of ideas of constitutionalism and public law, we should draw a distinction between the architecture of a state-centred order, and the deeper legal and

---

[68] Kumm, ns 63 and 65.   [69] Kumm, see note 15.

political imaginary of the modern age. The state-centred architecture has certainly supplied the most developed articulation of that underlying perspective, but we should not assume that just because the former may be eroding, the latter should not or cannot be sustained. Continued investment in the 'c' word and the 'p' word in the post-national context reflects that belief. Yet, because both terms, as we have seen,[70] operate across various levels of abstraction and can refer as much to concrete doctrine or design as to underlying orientation, their retention also starkly poses the question—and exposes the difficulties—of finding and constructing a new and suitable architecture for a post-national modernity.

Yet, it is important to insist that the onus of responding to a shifting global power mosaic does not rest only with the post-national sympathizers. Even for the double sceptics, as we have seen, our key terms cannot but retain some currency in the post-national domain, whether as doctrinal innovation or descriptors of informal normativity, or as resources of disciplinary construction, and so of legal imagination more generally.[71] What this underlines is that the resilience of our key concepts is not just about certain future possibilities to which only some subscribe, but about the insistent weight of our legacy and the inescapability of present circumstances, which all are bound to recognize. The legal world cannot be rethought and remade _ab initio_ and holistically, but only armed with the doctrinal and conceptual resources we already have at our disposal and only by first addressing the particular circumstances in which we are already and inevitably implicated. Even for those who are pessimistic about their adequacy to any long-term vision of a post-national world, therefore, extant notions of constitutionalism and public law remain vital, and so must be treated as at least minimally pliant resources in the short-term in the unavoidable matter of reflecting upon and responding incrementally to discrete shifts in our jurisgenerative circumstances. What is more, as there _never_ can be a legal _tabula rasa_—as the contemplation of legal change always does and always will start with the here and now, and so with what is already in place—short-term response and long-term vision, in any world view, are ultimately inextricable and necessarily mutually informative. This does not mean, of course, that the double sceptics are bound to become subscribers to robust post-national conceptions of constitutionalism or public law by default. But it does mean that they cannot avoid the long-term questions which lead some to offer such general post-national conceptions, or escape the fact that short-term and particular responses and solutions already and inevitably implicate the long-term and the general.

Where, beyond the deep reservations of double scepticism, the debate over the future of constitutionalism and public law _does_ become fully engaged, it tends to reduce to a tension between pedigree and process or content-centred definitions of law's public nature. This we can already observe negatively, in the nostalgia of the double sceptics with their strong emphasis on pedigree. But it is also vividly present in the competing visions of the transnational public law sceptics and the transnational constitutionals sceptics, as well as in the tensions between different forms of double affirmation of transnational constitutionalism and public law.

---

[70] See Sections 1 and 3.2.   [71] See Section 3.2.

In conclusion, we can offer two thoughts about this stubborn fault-line, reflections which may themselves on first impression seem to stand in uneasy juxtaposition. On the one hand, the tension between input and output, subjective and objective, is one that is bound to recur and to renew itself across different post-national contexts. On the other hand, the obstinate centrality of the tensions and the divisions this provokes should not lead us to think that we are asking the wrong questions. In particular, it should not be taken as proof that the discourses of constitutionalism and public law are, after all, inappropriate to the post-national domain. Quite the opposite. Far from displaying the exhaustion of state-incubated legal paradigms despite their best efforts at extension, the unease of post-national legal thought in fact merely reminds us of a familiar set of concerns. It does no more than reflect the deep and resilient ambivalence of the modernist heritage of individual autonomy and equality as concerned simultaneously to valorize the collective expression of that autonomy and equality and to protect its individual expression from collective encroachment.[72] This, as is evident from the formulations of the double sceptics, has been as much a defining antinomy of the state-centred age and its legal expression as it is of our emergent post-national horizon. Long-standing opposition in the state context between collective and individual, voice and rights, supremacy of legislation and finality of adjudication, constituent power and constituted authority, and between the two resonances of constitutionalism, particular and universal,[73] speak to precisely the same foregrounding of two orientations which provide necessary mutual support and supplementation while also being locked in mutual contest.[74] Each is both a condition of and a corrective to the other. What supplies vital balance also—inexorably—breeds conflicting interplay. Just as in the state context, the contribution of the post-national iteration of constitutionalism and public law to the long course of modernity depends upon a continued appreciation that this is a relationship which, however altered its background circumstances, can know and should know no final resolution.[75]

---

[72] See Walker, 'Constitutionalism and the Incompleteness of Democracy', 223–33.

[73] Walker, 'Constitutionalism and the Incompleteness of Democracy', 206–23.

[74] Indeed, to muddy the terminological waters still further, in some times and places the same key tension does not name publicness as such, but has instead been presented as one of constitutionalism versus democracy. On this view, far from emphasizing foundations and *gubernaculum*, constitutionalism is understood solely as *jurisidictio*. See Walker, 'Constitutionalism and the Incompleteness of Democracy', 206–13, 223–33. This reinforces the argument about the linguistic openness of our key terms; see note 52 earlier.

[75] See Walker, 'Constitutionalism and the Incompleteness of Democracy'. And for a similar approach, see G. Palombella, 'The Rule of Law and its Core' in G. Palombella and N. Walker (eds), *Relocating the Rule of Law* (Oxford: Hart, 2009) 17–42. My own approach also owes something to Habermas's analysis of the symbiosis of public and private autonomy as the key to the justification of the political settlement of modernity, but differs in emphasizing the 'incompleteness' of their reconciliation. See, eg, J. Habermas, 'Constitutional Democracy: A Paradoxical Union of Contradictory Principles?' (2001) 29 Political Theory 766. For a more recent development of a Habermasian position that is highly sensitive to the diverse forms of contemporary law, see R. Forst, *A Right to Justification: Elements of a Constructivist Theory of Justice* (New York, Columbia University Press, 2011, J. Flynn (trans.)). For a critique of my own position from a Habermasian perspective, see S. Rummens, 'The Co-originality of Law and Democracy in the Moral Horizon of Modernity' (2010) 39(3) Rechtsfilosofie & rechtstheorie 256, and for my response, see N. Walker, 'Constitutionalism and the Incompleteness of Democracy; A Reply to Four Critics' (2010) 39(3) Rechtsfilosofie & rechtstheorie 276 ff.

❧ 13 ❧

The Global Governance of Public Law

Megan Donaldson and Benedict Kingsbury

Whether the growing importance and density of global regulatory governance is helping usher in an epoch that is 'After Public Law'—the provocative if elliptical title of the present book—or is instead helping shape an innovative future for the transforming field of public law, is the theme addressed in this chapter. We examine a difficult but interesting case, the World Bank's detailed and highly prescriptive *Handbook for Evaluating Infrastructure Regulatory Systems*.[1] We address two dimensions of public law implicated by the *Handbook*. First, the *Handbook* exemplifies the increasingly significant phenomenon of global institutions seeking to alter the apparatus and doctrines of national public law. Second, the *Handbook* and evaluations of national systems made pursuant to it are typical of the challenges posed, for conceptions of public law and legitimacy, by the governance activities of global or other extra-national institutions: which (if any) of their activities should be subject to public law principles and controls, how and under what conditions might this be accomplished, and what might be the effects?[2]

The *Handbook* is characteristic of a growing body of advisory literature, generated by or under the auspices of regional or global institutions, which draws on forms and vocabularies having an affinity to (public) law as well as to managerial governance, and makes substantive interventions in national public law and public institutional design, while informed primarily by economic theory on regulation rather than public law itself. While much has been said about interventions in national public law aimed at promoting democratization, greater protection of human rights, anti-corruption, anti-terrorism capacity, and other prominent agendas, the *Handbook* and related prescriptions reflect the major but less-noticed impacts on national public law resulting from externally influenced approaches to regulation of infrastructure, competition, intellectual property, trade, data-gathering, public procurement, and a host of other areas of economic, social, and environmental regulation. Where global institutions are able to exert real influence on the detailed design and operation of national regulatory institutions, and the precepts of public law in which these are embedded, through the supply of expertise or funding, pressure or legitimation, global institutional

---

[1] Ashley C. Brown, Jon Stern, and Bernard Tenenbaum with Defne Gencer, *Handbook for Evaluating Infrastructure Regulatory Systems* (World Bank: Washington DC, 2006).

[2] This chapter draws with permission on arguments developed more extensively in an article by Megan Donaldson and Benedict Kingsbury in (2013) 13 Chicago Journal of International Law.

action of this kind can itself be a form of governance.[3] The *Handbook* thus provides a fertile and useful case through which to explore the reach and complexity of global governance of national public law, particularly as it is brought to bear on developing countries, and in an area of policy crucial for human life and well-being. By focusing on the implications for public law of even relatively technocratic aspects of global governance, and on the particular dynamics that arise in the developing world, we hope to offer a counterpoint to recent literature on global public law and global constitutionalism, much of which is highly abstract and informed by experiences in Europe.

The *Handbook* was developed against the backdrop of disappointment (certainly among neo-liberal reformers) with the performance of newly established infrastructure regulators, and growing recognition of the difficulties associated with establishing such regulators in many developing countries. From the 1990s the World Bank shifted from predominantly 'bricks and mortar' projects to add emphasis on developing the national regulatory environment necessary to attract foreign investment to infrastructure sectors.[4] However, some regulators did not develop the capacities and independence the World Bank thought they needed; consumers and citizens were, in some cases, violently opposed to commercialization and privatization projects; and total investment in infrastructure fell.[5] The Bank's 2003 Infrastructure Action Plan called for a major overhaul of the Bank's infrastructure lending, and the *Handbook* had its origins in one element of the Action Plan: the development of standardized 'diagnostic' assessments of investment, institutional, and policy frameworks in the infrastructure sectors of different countries.[6] The *Handbook* itself was authored by four regulatory specialists, two holding primarily academic positions but with long experience as consultants or advisers on regulatory matters to various countries and agencies, including the World Bank, and two individuals then holding posts within the Bank. The *Handbook* now features in the World Bank's 'PPP in Infrastructure Resource Center',[7] and in the 'Body of Knowledge' on infrastructure regulation.[8] It has been used to carry out evaluations leading to regulatory reform in Jamaica,[9]

---

[3] On the particularities of regulatory reform and design in the developing world, see Navroz K. Dubash and Bronwen Morgan (eds), *The Rise of the Regulatory State of the Global South* (Oxford: Oxford University Press, 2013).

[4] See World Bank, 'Infrastructure Action Plan' (2003) 2.

[5] *Handbook*, 13–14; see also Jon Stern, 'The Evaluation of Regulatory Agencies', in Robert Baldwin, Martin Cave, and Martin Lodge (eds), *The Oxford Handbook of Regulation* (Oxford: Oxford University Press, 2010) 223–58.

[6] *Handbook*, 14 fn 5. Although examples and analysis in the *Handbook* are drawn primarily from the electricity sector, the authors suggest that most of the *Handbook* is applicable to the regulation of other infrastructure as well, 23.

[7] See <http://ppp.worldbank.org/public-private-partnership/sector/energy/laws-regulations> (last accessed 30 January 2013).

[8] Developed by the Public Utility Research Center at the University of Florida, in collaboration with institutions including the World Bank. See <http://regulationbodyofknowledge.org/regulatory-process/references/> (last accessed 30 January 2013).

[9] Stern, 'Evaluation of Regulatory Agencies'.

and is cited in the policy and academic literature on regulatory design and evaluation.[10]

The *Handbook* is a highly sophisticated book-length 'road map' for evaluation of both governance in, and performance of, existing regulatory systems.[11] Digesting the specific experiences and ideas of international development agencies and consultants, the *Handbook* sets out a comprehensive vision, sometimes explicit and sometimes implicit, of the nature, purpose, and design of national regulation itself, and of the proper arrangement of the polity and economy, in sectors such as electricity, water, and telecommunications. It endorses a model of independent regulatory agencies overseeing privatized, or at least commercialized, service provision.[12] While the *Handbook* deals with the design and evaluation of regulatory systems in countries in which there is limited capacity and willingness to move to independent regulatory agencies, and sets out 'solutions' to forge 'transitional' regulatory systems in these cases, it still reflects a strong expectation that 'transitional' systems should ultimately adopt the accepted best practice.[13]

The *Handbook's* vision of regulation is systematized as three 'meta-principles' which must be satisfied by any regulatory system if it is to be sustainable, then a list of 'principles', and more concrete 'standards' that implement these 'meta-principles' for the independent regulator model. In this hierarchy of 'meta-principles', 'principles', and 'standards', the *Handbook* deftly invokes abstract concepts such as 'transparency' and 'accountability' that draw on languages of legality, rule of law, and public law, as well as discourses of 'good governance'.

The *Handbook* is also explicitly designed as a tool for diffusion of the regulatory policy it embraces, outlining techniques by which experts can increase the influence of their recommendations within states. We do not survey the ways in which the *Handbook* has been used in practice—which might diverge from what its authors or the Bank intended—but the *Handbook* can nevertheless be analysed as a blueprint for particular activities. Most obviously, it sets out detailed methodologies for three kinds of evaluation (short, mid-level, and in-depth), going into increasing detail about actual practices of regulation, and about the merits or otherwise of substantive decisions made. Evaluations are likely to be a condition of, or part of the process of project design for, a loan from a multilateral development bank (MDB) or aid agency, and evaluators are typically World Bank staff, counterparts in other similar institutions, consultants, or experts from policy research institutes.[14] The *Handbook* embraces the central role played by experts in

---

[10]   See, eg, Darryl S. L. Jarvis and Benjamin K. Sovacool, 'Conceptualizing and evaluating best practices in electricity and water regulatory governance' (2011) 36 Energy 4340–52.

[11]   *Handbook*, xii.

[12]   The *Handbook* concentrates on economic regulation (rather than regulation concerning, for example, health and safety), and asserts that commercialized entities are much more responsive to regulation of this kind than are public entities shielded from market pressures, 21. Commercialization, in turn, is said to require a significant degree of private corporate involvement, particularly in the developing world, 90; 21–22.

[13]   *Handbook*, 81.

[14]   *Handbook*, 168–69. For 'in-depth' investigations the *Handbook* recommends a team of three, including an international expert 'experienced in both regulatory and sectoral matters in both his or her own

certain fields as vectors of policy and as ongoing advisers.[15] Evaluators are encouraged to be persuasive advocates of the approved regulatory model, presenting 'stepping-stones that can move a country from a starting point of no formal regulatory system to a best-practice regulatory system',[16] and drawing on techniques of benchmarking and comparison. Quantitative rankings or 'indicators' are used to simplify information about complex social phenomena,[17] manage the diversity of regulatory contexts across jurisdictions, and spur competitive inclinations that promote reform. Once an evaluation is complete, for example, the *Handbook* suggests that evaluators 'present, at least initially, the "big picture" in a single overall governance ranking', as '[a] policymaker is much more likely to pay attention if he sees a single number that shows that his country's electricity regulatory commission ranks five out of six in his region rather than numerous tables filled with raw data that are hard to grasp'.[18]

In Section 1 of this chapter, we examine the global governance of national regulation and public law as manifested in the *Handbook's* vision of regulation. We argue that its hierarchy of meta-principles, principles, and standards resembles, at least in superficial respects, the structure of a legal system or body of law (Section 1.1), and is expressed in a language that resonates with traditions of (public) law and legality, as well as other discourses of governance (Section 1.2). We suggest that these features of the *Handbook* work to reinforce the persuasiveness of the content, and that the choice of language may have effects in knitting together different regimes of governance, and fostering the diffusion of policies and ideas between them. Within this framework, the *Handbook's* prescriptions address the deep structure of national public law, by reinforcing a particular theory of the nature and roles of the state, and intervene in the detailed content of national public law (Section 1.3).[19]

In Section 2, we address a different form of public law: the nature and possible roles of (incipient) global public law in channelling and constraining the kinds of exercise of governance powers instantiated by the preparation and promulgation of the *Handbook* and its use in evaluations. We do not here address the many bodies of substantive public international law which may bear on national regulatory processes and indirectly on regulatory prescriptions of international organizations. Our focus is on the procedural dimensions. We consider first the reach and significance of global administrative law as it has developed within global institutions, and second an approach which would treat the promulgation

---

country, as well as in other countries and cultures [and ideally having] advanced academic credentials in relevant disciplines (for example, law, economics, engineering, and/or accounting)', a local expert that has similar credentials and is well connected and respected in the domestic regulatory system, and a local lawyer: *Handbook*, 304–305.

[15] See, eg, *Handbook*, 106–108, 217, 228–29.

[16] *Handbook*, 79.

[17] Kevin E. Davis, Benedict Kingsbury, and Sally Engle Merry, 'Indicators as a Technology of Global Governance' (2012) 46 Law and Society Review 71–104. See, eg, *Handbook*, 83–88.

[18] *Handbook*, 32.

[19] For further discussion of transnational influences on national law, see Gregory Shaffer (ed.), *Transnational Legal Ordering and State Change* (Cambridge: Cambridge University Press, 2013).

and implementation of the *Handbook* as exercises of 'international public authority'. However, we highlight several ways in which in the ideas and framing of these approaches limit their capacity to deal comprehensively with the challenging issues posed by the *Handbook* and related activities.

Finally, in Section 3, we argue that the *Handbook's* prescriptions, and the regulation of activities such as promulgation of the *Handbook* and conduct of evaluations in accordance with it, can probably be made, with creative lawyering backed by a political project, to represent part of the future of public law rather than its supersession. This depends of course not only on paths charted in the future, but also on stipulating a meaning of 'public law'. In this chapter we take 'public law' to include not only what is conventionally described as national public law (the law constituting and controlling the exercise of governmental power) and public international law, but also—at least potentially—a body of law transcending governmental and intergovernmental relationships that could from some standpoints be described as 'public'. We do not, however, specify this 'public' quality in any detail.[20] Rather than defending any one conception or definition of public law, we emphasize the ways in which some aspects of the readily recognizable languages of public law and legality—primarily those concerned with procedural norms rather than rights or self-government—are increasingly imbricated in newer languages of governance. This imbrication affects the nature and pathways of global influences on national public law. It may also affect doctrinal framings and institutional specificities in the development and practice, *vel non*, of global public law.

I. GLOBAL GOVERNANCE OF NATIONAL PUBLIC LAW

1.1 *Meta-principles, principles, standards: the* Handbook's *law-like form*

The *Handbook* sets out a very elaborate benchmark for regulatory systems. At the peak of the whole edifice are three 'meta-principles' of 'credibility', 'legitimacy', and 'transparency', which (according to the *Handbook*) any regulatory regime, transitional or otherwise, must satisfy if it is to function.[21] The *Handbook* goes on to spell out ten 'principles' necessary to implement the meta-principles in the context of an independent regulator model: independence, accountability, transparency and public participation, predictability, clarity of roles, completeness and clarity in rules, proportionality,[22] provision to the regulator of the powers required to carry out its mandate, appropriate institutional characteristics,[23]

---

[20] For discussion, see Benedict Kingsbury, 'International Law as Inter-Public Law', in Henry Richardson and Melissa Williams (eds), *Moral Universalism and Pluralism* (New York: New York University Press, 2009) 167–204; Ming-Sung Kuo, 'Inter-public legality or post-public legitimacy? Global governance and the curious case of global administrative law as a new paradigm of law' (2012) 10 International Journal of Constitutional Law 1050–75; Gianluigi Palombella, 'Global Legislation and Its Discontents' (2012), <http://papers.ssrn.com/sol3/papers.cfm?abstract_id=2067427> (last accessed 30 January 2013).

[21] *Handbook*, 59.

[22] ie, recourse to minimum regulatory intervention necessary to attain particular goals for the sector.

[23] eg, appropriate education and training opportunities for commissioners and staff.

and integrity. The 'principles' are in turn accompanied by numerous 'standards', constituting 'a checklist of specific actions that would be needed to implement the 3 meta-principles and 10 general principles . . . provid[ing] the bridge to go . . . from the "theoretical" to the "practical" '.[24] The standards are organized under headings which correspond to the 'principles' in some instances, but do not correspond with them in others. For example, the first three standards, headed 'legal framework', 'legal powers', and 'property and contract rights', transcend the confines of any one principle.

Taken together, the standards provide a detailed and far-reaching scheme, full compliance with which may necessitate significant changes to applicable laws and institutional arrangements in many developing—and indeed, developed—countries. In some other texts of global and regional institutions, the juxtaposition of abstract principles with more specific material provides flexibility for local choices or, where there is contestation within the global institution about the measures to be taken, preserves the ability of global institutions to set out a relatively ambitious program of reform while accommodating dissent on particular points.[25] Some element of tailoring to local circumstances may be present in the *Handbook*; for example, the standards provide different mechanisms to ensure transparency depending on whether the multi-member regulatory commission makes decisions by voting, or by negotiation and consensus.[26] The *Handbook* also refers to 'transitional regulatory systems', which are not expected to meet all the standards set out as best practice. However, the meta-principles, principles, and standards still serve as a benchmark for assessing progress in transitional regulatory systems,[27] and even transitional regimes are expected to evolve to the best practice model over time. Moreover, the *Handbook* does not suggest that the 'standards' proposed may be replaced by divergent local approaches capable of fulfilling the same 'principles'. The main force of the hierarchical organization of the benchmarks thus lies not in the openings it provides for local variation but in the way it works to enforce the coherence and persuasiveness of the recommendations overall. The edifice of 'meta-principles', 'principles', and 'standards' gives comprehensive and systematic content to abstractions such as 'legitimacy'. Conversely, these abstractions, posited as universal and framed in a language that itself carries a normative charge (discussed further in Section 1.2), validate the specific prescriptions by connecting them up to a broader vision of the political economy of infrastructure.

One aspect of the rhetorical force of the interconnected meta-principles, principles, and standards may be their resemblance—in the hierarchical form,

---

[24] *Handbook*, 185.

[25] See, eg, Susan Block-Lieb and Terence Halliday, 'Harmonization and Modernization in UNCITRAL's Legislative Guide on Insolvency Law' (2007) 42 Texas International Law Journal 475–514, 507–12 (discussing the 'new legal technology' of the 'legislative guide'). On the increasing use by global and regional organizations of 'legal technologies' of this kind, see Terence C. Halliday, Susan Block-Lieb, and Bruce G. Carruthers, 'Rhetorical legitimation: global scripts as strategic devices of international organizations' (2010) 8 Socio-Economic Review 77–112.

[26] *Handbook*, 233–34.

[27] *Handbook*, 92.

and the varying specificity of requirements—to the structure of bodies of law and of legal systems. These patterns of precise directions in the service of more general 'principles' have some affinity with both the systemic quality, and the oscillation between the general and the particular, common to positive law and modes of legal reasoning. This formal resemblance, however, is somewhat belied by the content. Higher-order 'principles' in law tend both to retain some residual meaning not exhausted by more specific provisions, and to have some autonomous normative or purposive content that renders them susceptible to reinterpretation over time. While the 'meta-principles' have the abstraction common to 'principles' as higher order legal norms, the wider context of the *Handbook* makes clear that these are not analogous to constitutional provisions, capable of reinterpretation through normative argument about what 'legitimacy' as such demands, or about how to blend deontological and utilitarian considerations. Rather, the meta-principles reflect almost purely functionalist assumptions of what is required to attract private investment and maintain support for this arrangement, or at least its toleration, by the public,[28] which is in turn connected to a theory that only this investment can provide the infrastructure vitally necessary for development. The 'principles' are then interpreted in light of this preordained structure.[29]

1.2 *The* Handbook's *language of law and governance*

Individual terms that loom large in the *Handbook's* 'meta-principles' and 'principles' ('accountability', 'transparency', and so forth) have resonance in (Anglo-American) administrative law, and in increasingly influential languages of governance which are themselves shaped in part by public law traditions, but informed also by criteria of bureaucratic and economic efficiency.

The *Handbook's* prescriptions for reform can be understood as making operational criteria of 'good governance' of the kind embraced and diffused in recent years by the World Bank and other international institutions. Those responsible for producing the Bank's 'Worldwide Governance Indicators' have acknowledged the multiplicity and diversity of definitions of 'governance', and in particular a divergence regarding the importance of democratic accountability to citizens, but have nevertheless concluded that there is some degree of consensus on 'the importance of a capable state operating under the rule of law'.[30] The functionalist, neo-liberal orientation of the 'governance' measured by

---

[28] *Handbook*, 1, 13.

[29] Of course, it may not be the case that investors *are* most reassured by exactly the measures set out in the *Handbook*; confidence in the security of investments might also flow from close relationships with senior officials, for example, or close relationships between the host state and the investors' home state governments, or possibilities for issue linkage in other areas (the latter two may be particularly relevant, at least once disputes have arisen, where investors are themselves state-owned).

[30] Daniel Kaufmann and Aart Kraay, 'Governance Indicators: Where Are We, Where Should We Be Going?', World Bank Policy Research Working Paper No 4370 (2007) 6. For further iterations of the indicators' composition, see Daniel Kaufmann, Aart Kraay, and Massimo Mastruzzi, 'The Worldwide Governance Indicators: Methodology and Analytical Issues', World Bank Policy Research Working Paper No 5430 (2010).

Bank indicators is relatively clear, but many aspects of this agenda, particularly the rule of law, the functioning of regulatory institutions, and the control and oversight of public officials, have also been central to public law.

Moreover, setting the *Handbook's* 'principles', themselves no doubt loosely informed by these ideas about good governance, alongside articulations by legal theorists of the values or characteristics of public law,[31] or the properties of law as a whole,[32] is revealing. In some cases, the principles mentioned in the *Handbook* find more or less direct counterparts in these other discourses. 'Accountability' and 'public participation', for example, also appear in Taggart's list of public law values, and the 'principle' of 'transparency' bears a relation to the value of 'openness'. In other cases, the 'principles' have counterparts at the level of concept, if not vocabulary. 'Predictability', for example, corresponds to a number of Fuller's attributes of a legal system: that rules be published, intelligible, possible to comply with, prospective, not subject to constant change, and followed by the officials enforcing them. Principles of clarity of roles, and completeness and clarity in rules, also correspond to some of Fuller's attributes (published rules, free from contradiction), and perhaps to a public law value of 'rationality'.

The fact that many of the terms that appear in the *Handbook's* meta-principles and principles have these linguistic or conceptual affinities with traditions of public law within the state, and by association with ideals of democracy and self-government with which public law has historically been connected, no doubt gives the terms some normative appeal. The *Handbook*, though, does not connect the principles, or the detailed administrative law reform proposals in the standards, back to foundational political structures and ideals; rather, it takes an instrumental view of both the role of the state and of law as a whole.

Accordingly, one way of reading the *Handbook* is that it co-opts a normatively charged language to lend an aura of legitimacy and consensus to much narrower, and politically contestable, ends. This reading of the *Handbook* would echo concerns that the vocabulary and values of public law are masking the dominance of an 'administrative rationality' antithetical to legality.[33] Rather than functioning to pass one thing (technocratic governance) off as another (rule of law or something like it), we suggest that the *Handbook's* flexible, hybrid discourse of governance brings the two into relation. Arguably, the *Handbook* is framed in this language—rather than, say, a purely economic vocabulary—precisely because, while normatively charged, this language is not reducible to a single established set of substantive commitments. The vocabulary in which the 'principles' are

---

[31] Among the many articulations of 'public law values', Taggart's distillation provides a helpful example: openness, fairness, participation, impartiality, accountability, honesty, rationality: Michael Taggart, 'The Province of Administrative Law Determined', in Taggart (ed.), *The Province of Administrative Law* (Oxford: Hart Publishing, 1997) 1–20, 3.

[32] For example, Fuller's desiderata for a legal system include the existence of general rules, and their publication, prospectivity, clarity, compatibility, possibility of compliance, constancy, and congruence with officials' actions: Lon L. Fuller, *The Morality of Law* (rev. edn) (New Haven: Yale University Press, 1969).

[33] See, eg, Alexander Somek, 'Administration without Sovereignty', in Petra Dobner and Martin Loughlin (eds), *The Twilight of Constitutionalism?* (Oxford: Oxford University Press, 2010) 267–87.

expressed is a new *lingua franca*, incorporating terms taken from different discourses.[34] Lawyers, government officials, experts, non-government organizations, and corporations may all find the language familiar; although they might understand its contents in radically different ways, they can deploy it to speak intelligibly to one another, and it may both appeal to, and be taken up by, similarly socialized elites in countries or organizations with otherwise inimical values or political structures.

The very indeterminacy of the language may both make possible the persistence of very different understandings of its content, by concealing the magnitude of differences in substantive understanding, and provide a platform for diffusion and cross-fertilization of ideas about this content between actors who appear to have committed to similar programs. For example, the *Handbook* accepts the likely pluralism of views on concepts such as 'fairness', and opens the path for patterns of borrowing and transposition as the various actors deal with each other:

> To be acceptable, the process by which [regulatory] decisions are made must be consistent with local notions of fairness and justice. The other perspective that needs to be satisfied is that of the investors, many of whom are likely to be foreign, in the case of developing countries. Just as residents of the country need to be satisfied that the process is fair, so too do international investors who may have different views of fairness than local residents.[35]

The political consequences of this process of diffusion remain open to some extent. Given the relative positions of investors and groups within host states that may be able to influence the process of regulatory decision-making, there is room for scepticism about the likely shape of the consensus on 'fairness' that might emerge from the process envisaged in the *Handbook*. On the other hand, rhetorical and conceptual limits to this language, and to terms such as 'fairness', rule out some artifices of reconstruction and overextension. Precisely because it has an abstract and normative dimension, the language of governance may, in some situations, have the result of opening avenues for contestation that could develop into some more democratic and emancipatory system; in other cases, the invocation and deployment of this language may drain its normative significance and political potential. Much depends on the individuals and institutions engaged in the debate.

1.3 *The* Handbook's *theory of the (regulatory) state and intervention in public law*

The *Handbook* reflects and reinforces an implicit model of the (regulatory) state,[36] with significant implications for the scope and operation of public law and the role of the government in achieving social ends, and the *Handbook's* standards prescribe extensive reforms to systems of national public law.

---

[34] See, on the deliberate adoption of 'universal' vocabularies as a strategy for building consensus and avoiding the impression that particular national approaches dominate global deliberations, Block-Lieb and Halliday, 'Harmonization and Modernization' 498–500.

[35] *Handbook*, 30.

[36] Giandomenico Majone, 'From the Positive to the Regulatory State: Causes and Consequences of Changes in the Mode of Governance' (1997) 17 Journal of Public Policy 139–67.

In the model set out in the *Handbook*, the state draws back from any direct role in managing or providing access to infrastructure such as electricity and water, and even from any direct role as a regulator. At the same time, however, the state is called upon to undertake a wide range of functions to create or preserve the conditions necessary for other actors—both corporations and 'independent' regulators—to operate. Particularly where there is a need for major adjustments in pricing, the government must support the regulator in pursuing often controversial measures.[37] More generally, '[t]he police power of the state will be needed to enforce laws against theft of service'.[38] The state must also furnish a range of other 'prerequisites', including legislative bodies capable of enacting adequate laws, a functioning dispute resolution process, and a 'reasonable overall quality of country governance'.[39]

Despite conceding this distinct role for the state, however, the *Handbook* envisages relations between actors, including the state and state institutions, in a bilateral or contractual paradigm, rather than any paradigm of the state as instantiating a higher-order public interest, collective identity, or community of shared fate. Of the 'meta-principles', 'credibility' refers to *investors'* confidence that the regulator will honour commitments, 'legitimacy' is defined as *consumers'* confidence that the regulator will protect them from monopoly power, and 'transparency' is 'implied' by the other two: '[t]he regulatory system must operate transparently so that investors and consumers "know the terms of the deal."'[40] The *Handbook* states that together, these meta-principles confer 'legitimacy' on a regulatory system, helping foster a 'demand' for sustainable regulation and thus allowing the regulatory system to take root.[41] The meta-principles are structured in the form of a bargain: something for both sides (investors and *consumers*, rather than the government or citizens as a whole), together with the background conditions required for both parties to have confidence that they are getting what is due. While recognizing the need for the regulatory system to be embedded in the society as a whole, the *Handbook* places the government in the background, providing the institutions to support the bargain. This approach is consistent with the *Handbook's* general preference for market-based approaches to delivery of public services, but it may also reflect a principled position that the state is required to take this background role precisely because it *is* a party to a bargain (the relevant concession contract, asset lease, or other arrangements, rather than the regulatory pact between investors and consumers), and thus cannot at the same time be the deciding judge of performance under these contracts or arrangements. This instantiation of the liberal principle that no party can be a judge in its own cause (*nemo iudex in causa sua*) would be consistent with the relegation of the state to the status of any other (interest-driven) actor.

The reforms fostered by the *Handbook* extend beyond the design of the regulator itself, into the architecture of the judicial system and the existing body of administrative law. Principle 9, for example, which stipulates that the

---

[37] *Handbook*, 89–90. [38] *Handbook*, 90. [39] *Handbook*, 92–93.
[40] *Handbook*, 55. [41] *Handbook*, 56.

regulator must have 'appropriate institutional characteristics' to carry out its mandate, encompasses 'Commissioners who are appropriately insulated from short-term political repercussions', bureaucratic requirements (concerning compensation, education, training, adequate budgets, and the ability to retain outside consultants, and so forth), but also a very specific system of judicial review:

> All regulatory decisions should be subject to final appeal to a single, impartial or independent, legally designated court or tribunal with the following requirements. The specified appeal forum should possess regulatory expertise. The regulatory decision should, with very limited exception, remain in force while the appeal is pending. And the appeal body should affirm regulatory decisions unless the following is true:
> • The regulators acted beyond their legal authority.
> • The regulators failed to follow appropriate procedural requirements.
> • The regulators acted arbitrarily or unreasonably.
> • The regulators acted against the plain weight of the evidence before the court.[42]

As Principle 9 demonstrates, the *Handbook* aims at potentially far-reaching interventions in the public law of states being evaluated, but sees these transformations in instrumental terms, mingling them with more mundane recommendations directed to efficient administration, and implying that matters like the standard of review applicable to regulatory decisions, and the funding arrangements enjoyed by the regulator, are of the same order. Unsurprisingly, given the functionalist orientation of the *Handbook* and its quest to identify generally applicable recommendations, the view of law and legal process that emerges from it is a thin, instrumental, and static one. The focus is on the capacity of law to organize processes and structure incentives, rather than on deeper and more political dimensions of law: its connection to self-government and political representation, its role in expressing particular values, its connection to particular modes of discourse (legislative debate or judicial reason-giving), or even its dynamic and systemic qualities.

The *Handbook* recognizes differences in the relative status of legal instruments, and favours promulgation of statutes (rather than executive decrees) as the means of establishing regulators and governing regulatory processes. However, the fact that legislation is 'more representative of political will', more transparent, and more likely to be the subject of public debate, is important because these features make changes to the regime, once it is established, more difficult.[43] There is no suggestion that it matters, other than perhaps for practical reasons relating to the likelihood of passage, whether a statute was drafted in a consultative manner, rather than formulated by the executive on the advice of global consultants (indeed, the *Handbook* recommends including a local lawyer on the project team, so that if the government accepts particular recommendations, the consultants can provide advice on specific language required to implement the recommendations, thus avoiding 'the delay of a second and separate legal analysis').[44]

---

[42] *Handbook*, 62–63.   [43] *Handbook*, 186.   [44] *Handbook*, 34.

A similar pattern of recognizing particular normative accounts of what the legal and political process should be, but then taking them into account only insofar as they are likely to translate into practical opposition to the desired scheme, is evident in the discussion of how to handle dispute resolution in 'transitional' regulatory systems. Where courts are slow or corrupt, thorough-going judicial reform will be necessary in the long run, but a short-term solution is also required to get the regulatory system functioning. It is acknowledged that options such as alternative dispute resolution and private arbitration, which could be provided for in the contract, are not appropriate for regulatoty disputes, involving as they do the interests of 'non-parties' such as consumers, and issues of public policy.[45] Aside from these 'theoretical constraints on bypassing judicial or legally created appellate tribunals', there are 'practical, realpolitik reasons' not to do so: enforcing arbitral decisions is difficult; resort to these alternative dispute resolution mechanisms can cause 'public resentment that "outsiders" are deciding critical infrastructure matters in a country other than their own', and there are 'basic legal and constitutional questions about using private means to enforce or overrule the otherwise lawful decisions of duly constituted agencies of the state'.[46] The proposed approach is to allow disputes to be adjudicated by the courts but, where possible, to create specialized tribunals to handle these disputes, or at least allow for optional or mandatory recourse to a panel of experts that could provide non-binding advice. Using specialized tribunals and, to a lesser extent, expert advisers, would 'increas[e] the probability that decisions would be made in a consistent manner with a coherent and discernible pattern'.[47] The emphasis is on outcomes and particularly their role in stabilizing and rendering predictable the regulatory regime.

The preference for specialized tribunals dealing only with regulatory disputes in infrastructure sectors is one reflection of the disaggregated way in which the *Handbook* deals with the legal order. Given the complexity of these issues and the need for a uniform checklist, the *Handbook* cannot dwell on local legal particular-ities except as a barrier to be overcome. There is little sense of the integration of norms into a coherent system, either vertically or horizontally. Constitutional principle appears in the *Handbook* primarily as a constraint on regulatory design, and the only substantive aspect of law that is considered in much detail is respect for property rights.[48] Similarly, it is not clear how the austere criteria and demanding standard of review recommended for regulatory disputes are intended to relate—if at all—to the standard of review used in other contexts (or even by regulators in non-infrastructure sectors), or how the legal regime applicable to infrastructure regulation knits together with different areas of public and private law implicated in the recommendations (which might encompass some or all of administrative law, laws of evidence, civil procedure, corporate law, employment law, and so forth). The overall picture is one of a legal enclave applicable to a subset of regulators and only tenuously related to the surrounding fabric of norms and institutions.

---

[45] *Handbook*, 105.   [46] *Handbook*, 105–106.   [47] *Handbook*, 106.   [48] *Handbook*, 197–200.

2. A PUBLIC LAW OF GLOBAL GOVERNANCE?

The *Handbook* and other initiatives in the regulatory area are among a wide assortment of global legal regimes which assume, or seek to realize, particular features of domestic public law. Interventions in the areas of democratization and rule of law aim at fundamental reorganizations of domestic political and legal systems, while international and regional human rights law has its own vision of domestic public law as a system for the recognition and vindication of rights.[49] The kinds of activity manifest in, and made possible by, the *Handbook*, while only one part of the larger picture of global interventions in national public law, are nevertheless indicative of important features of contemporary governance: the plethora of different institutional sites, the involvement of both state and non-state actors, the influence of epistemic communities working in and through different institutions, and the profound consequences that these complex and diffuse interactions can have for communities in particular countries.

Although the *Handbook* is designed for use by any state, it is most likely to be deployed, and evaluations most likely to be carried out, in states with resource or capacity constraints which cause them to turn to MDBs or foreign aid as a source of funds for infrastructure. In many (although not all) such states, systems of public law may be very limited even in formal terms, and there may be serious obstacles to citizens or civil society groups using existing laws to vindicate rights or intervene in processes of policy reform, or making their voices heard in the political system. While the contents of the *Handbook* reflect a judgment in good faith by experts with many years of experience in infrastructure reform that the model of independent regulators and commercialized or privatized provision represents the best hope for sustainable and effective infrastructure (and the sorts of surgical, functional interventions in existing public law advocated by the *Handbook* represent the best means of establishing this model), the choice of how to fund and operate infrastructure has irreducibly political dimensions. The combination of essentially contestable political and economic ideals, pressure on governments in need of funds, and often limited public law to guarantee participation or consultation with groups outside the executive is likely to leave sectoral experts, whether drafters of the *Handbook* or members of evaluation teams, with a great deal of influence. State governments may make the ultimate decision whether to accept or reject reforms, and legislation will usually need to be passed to effect reforms, requiring at least some political support, but the extent to which this process reflects broader support in the society affected may be highly questionable, especially when the government presents reforms as a single package.

Despite the likely influence of the institutions and individuals involved in the evaluation of national regulation, their close engagement with the public law of the states being evaluated, and their recourse to a language drawing on the

---

[49] Human rights may have specific implications for the regulation of infrastructure in sectors that play particularly important roles in the realization of rights, and in particular may require that privatization or regulatory reform protects vulnerable populations. On the ways in which human rights translate to particular demands for regulation, see Bronwen Morgan, *Water on Tap: Rights and Regulation in the Transnational Governance of Urban Water Services* (Cambridge: Cambridge University Press, 2011).

vocabulary of public law, these institutions and individuals are not, at least in orthodox doctrinal terms, themselves bound in to any comprehensive system of public law. The World Bank, for example, is a formal inter-state organization, and exists within and is subject to, a body of public international law (arguably including human rights law, although the Bank has resisted any suggestion that it is directly bound by such law). Individual evaluators are presumably acting within overlapping, institution-specific contracts and policies, and local laws applying to individuals, as well as in fidelity to professional standards and perhaps a personal commitment to improving infrastructure regulation and furthering development. However, these regimes deal only incidentally with the influence that advice has on national policy, and are not addressed to some of the central concerns of public law. In particular, they do not impose relationships of responsibility or accountability to those affected by evaluators' actions or decisions (either the political choices embodied in them, or the extent to which the actions or decisions were in fact correct on whatever functional or technical blueprint is adopted).

One response to the burgeoning practices of governance occurring beyond the political and legal apparatus of individual states has been to argue that the interventions of global institutions in fact *are*, or *should be*, subject to some structure of public law. We here consider two variants of this response: global administrative law, and approaches focused on international public authority.

2.1 Global administrative law

Global administrative law potentially subjects extra-national governance to procedural constraints, in particular greater transparency, participation, reasoned decision-making, and formal review, in order to make it more accountable to those affected by it.[50] Some elements of these procedural checks already exist. They are often specific to individual institutions or regimes, and may not be enforceable in any judicial tribunal. Further systematization will depend on the ways in which existing mechanisms can be disseminated through other institutions and integrated with more basic and generally applicable legal principles, and on the development of judicial or other fora in which they may be enforced.[51]

The World Bank—the institution with which the *Handbook* is most closely connected—has adopted a range of what might be identified as global administrative law mechanisms, including a revised 'access to information' policy, an Inspection Panel inquiring into compliance with internal policies, and 'safeguards' policies requiring public consultation on certain projects. These institutional developments provide some possibilities for the contestation of broad approaches evident in, for example, the *Handbook*, and their translation into specific programs and projects. Interested groups may be able to track evolving

---

[50] Benedict Kingsbury, Nico Krisch, and Richard B. Stewart, 'The Emergence of Global Administrative Law' (2005) 68 Law and Contemporary Problems 15–64.

[51] See, eg, Sabino Cassese, 'A Global Due Process of Law?', in Gordon Anthony et al. (eds), *Values in Global Administrative Law* (Oxford: Hart, 2011) 17–60, 52–53.

thinking on regulatory issues, or follow reports on how similar projects have fared elsewhere, through documents released automatically, or by invoking the access to information policy to request further documents. Where evaluations and associated policy recommendations are used to underpin projects in particular countries, the Inspection Panel may be invoked where the level and nature of public consultation has fallen short of what is required by the Bank's internal policies.

However, there are limits to the potential of mechanisms such as these to ensure that expert institutions and evaluators are accountable for the technical quality and consequences of the reforms they promote, and that those reforms in fact reflect the wishes, needs, and priorities of citizens rather than the agenda of ruling elites. In the context of the *Handbook*, we identify three main limitations.

First, global administrative law is dependent on institutions. Some degree of formalization of the exercise of power is required in order to subject this exercise to procedural constraints. Much of the power exercised in and through documents such as the *Handbook*, and the evaluations for which it provides, works through expertise and the dominance of particular visions of the economy and polity. These are crystallized through formal practices such as evaluation, preparation of reports, decisions on project lending, and drafting of legislation. Global administrative law mechanisms or principles might be applied at these points, perhaps by insisting, for example, that the evaluation include consultation with particular marginalized communities, or that the process by which the Bank or other funders persuade the government of necessary reforms be more transparent, or at least involve the legislature or community groups in some meaningful way, rather than remaining within the executive. However, rights to access, or participate in, these formal and institutional practices may not effect any real opening up of the epistemic landscape, and may even reinforce the dominance of current approaches.

Second, global administrative law focuses on the processes through which decisions should be made, rather than on the 'constitutional' question of which bodies should be making the decisions, and on what basis they claim the authority to do so (matters that are more or less settled in a formal sense by democratic traditions and constitutional law in the domestic context, however precarious or distorted these constraints may be in practice). Of course, the procedural and 'constitutional' are not easily separated. Even procedural norms such as participation and accountability may indirectly orient thinking on foundational questions of authority (for example, applying such procedural norms to processes like evaluation in the *Handbook* might foster a more deferential or deliberative engagement with existing local law and practice). As global administrative law evolves, and is subject to challenge in more formalized domains or in the courts, it will increasingly confront questions of institutional authority, constituency, and representation.[52] For the moment, however, global administrative law as it applies

---

[52] As foreshadowed in Nico Krisch, 'Global Administrative Law and the Constitutional Ambition', in Dobner and Loughlin (eds), *The Twilight of Constitutionalism?* (Oxford: Oxford University Press, 2010) 245–66.

to global institutions and actors remains rather insulated from these matters and, insofar as the global administrative law approach suggests that decisions taken by a whole range of bodies might be legitimated by procedural means, tends to be in some tension with substantive demands that decisions be made in some institutions rather than others. Where existing global governance structures valorize expertise as a basis for authority, global administrative law may merely serve to ensure wider access to, and participation in, the wielding of this expertise, rather than challenging the privileging of economic, legal, or accounting expertise in the first place. The interest of those challenging the direction of reform is likely to lie in advocating for a different worldview altogether. While institutional features such as access to information policies may assist them in gathering the information they need to build a campaign, the main thrust of advocacy is likely to lie beyond, and in fact in opposition to, existing governance structures.

Of course, if exercises such as the preparation of the *Handbook* and the conduct of evaluations escape any ready analysis, much less institutional scrutiny or recourse, in public law terms, this is not necessarily attributable only to their extra-national character. The decentralized, epistemic power in evidence in publications such as the *Handbook*, together with the involvement of private actors (in the form of individual experts and evaluators) may not be markedly different from purely nationally driven reform scenarios, in which governments, even those not seeking funding from the MDBs, are influenced to some extent by policy advice, modelling, projections, and research from consulting firms, academics, think-tanks, and the like (and, less salubriously, from lobbyists and interested parties themselves) in addition to the views of their own bureaucrats. It is not clear that there is much of a basis in even the highly systematized and developed public law of advanced democracies (implicitly taken as a model by much of the advisory literature) for challenging the political or social assumptions underlying expert advice or holding consultants or advisers responsible if they later turn out to have been wrong (save for contractual provisions for formal advisory relationships, or criminal law or professional misconduct provisions in cases of corruption or gross incompetence). In theory, citizens in a state in which the government has adopted reforms based on the expert advice of a consulting firm may not be in that different a position from citizens in a state in which the government has adopted reforms based on the intervention of an international institution, MDB, or team of international experts. This does not mean that national public law provides no resources for situations of this kind, simply that the role of expertise in governance presents a dilemma for broader participation and deliberation which is felt in many different sites, global and local.

Third, the capacity of global administrative law to respond to the challenges posed by instruments such as the *Handbook* may be limited by the kinship between global administrative law and the de-localized language of governance evident in such instruments. We have suggested that the *Handbook* manifests, and makes use of, a confluence of the vocabularies of public law and governance. The central principles of global administrative law are framed in a similar hybrid language—in part because global administrative law too must be at least intelligible within different traditions of public law, and capable of being invoked in a wide range of different institutional contexts, public and private. However, as with the language of the *Handbook*, its very malleability also leaves it open to redefinition and gradual evolution that will inevitably be shaped by distributions of power.[53] Given the current constellation of governance institutions, and the structures of power within states, there is likely to be considerable pressure for substantive understandings of international public law or global administrative law principles that favour dominant interests,[54] or those able to advocate on their terms, and the convergence in overarching vocabulary might make it difficult to challenge this.

2.2 *International public authority*

Whereas global administrative law may emerge in a range of different contexts and institutions, including entities not formally 'public' or exercising power delegated by states or other recognizably public entities, the legal scholarship on 'international public authority' has pursued an *ex ante* categorization of institutions and instruments as exercising international public authority and therefore subject to a corpus of public law, including human rights law.[55] Von Bogdandy, Dann, and Goldmann argue for a framework in which 'authority' is held to be exercised not only when an institution issues binding legal commands, but whenever an institution has the capacity to condition a legal subject ('conditioning' including, for example, situations in which an act 'builds up pressure for another legal subject to follow its impetus', or an institution 'carves out the cognitive environment of the issue ... in a manner that marginalizes alternative perspectives', as long as the communicative power involved reaches a certain threshold).[56] The subject of this conditioning may be an individual, private association, enterprise, state, or public institution, although the ultimate normative concern is one of individual freedom and political self-determination.[57] The 'international public' character of

---

[53] This is not to say that the dominant understandings remain static. Techniques of governance that serve to increase the weight and influence of global prescriptions in national regulatory policy-making also sustain a process of learning on the part of global actors. The *Handbook* is evidently the fruit of much reflection on the particular circumstances of developing countries, and draws on developing country experiences to fashion recommendations for transitional regimes, and 'solutions' to common problems faced.

[54] See, eg, B. S. Chimni, 'Co-Option and Resistance: Two Faces of Global Administrative Law' (2005) 37 N.Y.U. Journal of International Law & Politics 799–827.

[55] On this approach, see, eg, Armin von Bogdandy, Philipp Dann, and Matthias Goldmann, 'Developing the Publicness of Public International Law: Towards a Legal Framework for Global Governance Activities' (2008) 9 German Law Journal 1375–1400; Armin von Bogdandy and Matthias Goldmann, 'Taming and Framing Indicators: A Legal Reconstruction of the OECD's Programme for International Student Assessment (PISA)' in Kevin Davis, Angelina Fisher, Benedict Kingsbury, and Sally Engle Merry (eds), *Governance by Indicators: Global Power Through Quantification and Rankings* (Oxford: Oxford University Press, 2012) 52–85.

[56] Von Bogdandy, Dann, and Goldmann, 'Developing the Publicness of Public International Law' 1376, 1382; Von Bogdandy and Goldmann, 'Taming and Framing Indicators' 66.

[57] Von Bogdandy, Dann, and Goldmann, 'Developing the Publicness of Public International Law' 1376, 1383.

authority derives from its legal basis: the fact that it is exercised on the basis of (even informal) acts of public authorities like states and international institutions.

In the case of reform of domestic regulatory systems, the effect on the behaviour of individuals is attenuated: the actual effect on individuals' access to infrastructure or their ability to participate in regulatory reform processes is mediated by the choices of evaluators regarding what to recommend, and the decisions of the government about what recommendations to act on, and how to implement them. These governmental decisions may also diverge from what evaluators would advise, although the decisions will often be taken under pressure where the evaluation is a condition of funding or aid, given that the whole thrust of the evaluation process is to deliver ready-made reforms, including even the constitutional and statutory changes. The authority at stake in the issuing of the *Handbook* and in preparation of evaluations in accordance with it is thus more akin to 'conditioning' than outright determination (the judgment of when epistemic influence can be said to have occurred at a sufficient threshold to 'condition' behaviour is, however, a fine one).[58] The difficulty of determining whether the drafting of the *Handbook* and the undertaking of evaluations are exercises of 'international' and 'public' authority illustrates the challenges of applying an essentially hierarchical and formalist classification to the messy circumstances of governance. The preparation of a text such as the *Handbook* is one of a myriad of acts undertaken by and under the auspices of interstate organizations, although it is unlikely to have any specific authorization from state representatives. From the standpoint of this scholarship, the *use* of the *Handbook* in particular circumstances and the conduct of evaluations by teams of specialists (at least insofar as they occur at the behest of particular donor states) may actually be clearer instances of 'international public authority' than the drafting of the *Handbook* in the first place.

If defined as an exercise of international public authority, the preparation of a prescriptive manual like the *Handbook* and the conduct of evaluations would be subject to a public law framework, including both procedural dimensions similar to those emphasized in global administrative law, and some substantive component of fundamental rights.[59] Von Bogdandy and Goldmann have suggested that it is possible to identify in relatively abstract terms a range of 'instruments' of governance, each of which may be subject to distinct public law-inspired

---

[58] Moreover, in the realm of epistemic authority, it is perhaps unusual that one actor alone 'carves out the cognitive environment' within which policies come to be conceived and debated. The picture is more often one of gradual shifts in a discourse involving multiple entities or individuals, and often influenced by a whole range of historic, economic, and social dimensions.

[59] See, eg, Armin von Bogdandy and Matthias Goldmann, 'Sovereign Debt Restructurings as Exercises of International Public Authority: Towards a Decentralized Sovereign Insolvency Law' (25 May 2012). The rights dimension might be articulated in various ways. At a minimum, global institutions, and processes undertaken under their auspices, might be required to accommodate, rather than undermine, existing rights obligations of parties affected by the evaluation, including constitutional and international law obligations of states the regulatory systems of which are under evaluation. In some cases this may be a significant constraint on the approach taken by evaluators to both access to infrastructure (in light of rights to, for example, health, food, and water), and to the process of regulatory reform (in light of rights to, for example, political participation and equality).

frameworks.[60] The production of the *Handbook* and of country evaluations are arguably manifestations of what they classify as the instrument of 'national performance assessments'.[61] On their view, the terms of such assessments should be laid out in advance (to ensure that political questions do not become subject to purely bureaucratic and technocratic resolution), and should involve debate and consultation with all groups concerned. Results of assessments should accord with scientific principles, be justified, and be open to criticism, perhaps in some institutionalized forum. Although it is debatable whether criteria of this kind can be applied directly to a program such as that set out in the *Handbook*, which (like probably the majority of advisory tools) was generated within a global institution rather than as a result of any deliberate decision by states' representatives, these points suggest that, at least on the 'international public authority' account, modes of governance and intervention exemplified by the *Handbook* would have to change significantly before they attained the 'legitimacy' for which that account of public law provides.

The international public authority approach is open to some of the same critiques as those made against global administrative law. The fact that many advisory exercises of the type exemplified by the *Handbook* are not pre-ordained by states in accordance with a reasonably detailed mandate, but rather evolve from institutions' internal practice, and are shaped by experts, relates to the point made earlier about global administrative law being limited in its capacity to disrupt epistemic power. Both are reflections of the difficulty, for public law in general, of coming to terms with the growing role of expertise in political rule. As with global administrative law, conceptualizing the governance activities of global institutions and those acting under their auspices in terms of international public authority does not yield a strong account of the proper *allocation* of power between actors. A notion of 'international public authority' simply implies that certain acts authorized by 'public' entities must be subject to a body of public law; but where private actors (experts, consultants) are able to exercise significant epistemic power beyond, or through, any formal institutional framework, and where *ex ante* mandates from states or public authorities for the expert work are impracticable, much activity of real political salience may simply not be reached.

3. GLOBAL GOVERNANCE—AFTER PUBLIC LAW?

As the *Handbook* indicates, even highly specific and technical modes of global governance now involve an intimate engagement with aspects of the public law

---

[60] Matthias Goldmann, 'Inside Relative Normativity: From Sources to Standard Instruments for the Exercise of International Public Authority' (2008) 9 German Law Journal 1865–1908.

[61] Defined as involving 'the revelation of empirical information with a claim to objectivity by international institutions that evaluate the outcomes of domestic policy, produced for the purposes of the latter and coupled with a light enforcement mechanism for future domestic policy that relies on the incentives created by iterative evaluations, public disclosure, country rankings, and/or specific policy recommendations': 'Taming and Framing Indicators' 75 (emphasis omitted). However, *Handbook* evaluations, although recommended for general, periodic use, are most likely to be conducted on states seeking funding for infrastructure support on a one-off basis rather than in regular assessments applicable to a number of states.

of states, particularly developing states. In the case of the *Handbook*, this extends to promotion of an implicit theory of the state with serious implications for the deep structure of public law, and to the making of detailed recommendations for reform of administrative law. The *Handbook's* prescriptions are structured in a form reminiscent of a system of law, in its hierarchy of meta-principles, principles, and standards. They draw on a language familiar from theories of law and legality, and carrying within it the values of public law, but it is a language also of late neo-liberal governance applicable to a wide range of institutions and bodies within and beyond the state. The prevalence of this language might itself, we suggest, be an instrument of diffusion of policy, or a means of connecting different institutions and regimes together on the basis of ostensibly shared visions of how to operate. However, the language may disguise significant divergences on questions of substance; and it may be deployed to serve many different ends.

Although global administrative law, or an international public authority approach, could be said to provide some basis for challenging the exercise of power reflected in, and fostered by, the *Handbook*, each of these approaches is also open to broader critiques about the mutability of the language of public law—not only the way in which it has merged with a more managerial or technocratic vocabulary, but its transposition to global and transnational contexts.[62] The growing prevalence of this de-localized language both in global initiatives to propel national reform (such as the *Handbook*), and in attempts to subject these initiatives to procedural constraints, may be at once pernicious and promising. On the one hand, there are clearly important questions about the content given to this language in particular sites, and its political implications. On the other, the prevalence of the language might be interpreted as reflecting the powerful grip of public law—or at least some of its outward forms—on the imagination, within global institutions, of the exercise and legitimation of power.

Running through these various developments are questions about comparison and comparative methodology, and the relation of the general or universal to the particular. The *Handbook* stands for a particular style of this work: a sophisticated tool, informed by a generation of experience with regulators in a range of developing countries, drawing on languages of governance and law together, and designed to both promote one model of regulation and generate recommendations tailored to the circumstances of particular countries regarding how to move towards this model. Approaches to a public law of global governance, whether the global administrative law that emerges in institutions through processes of borrowing and refinement, or the more doctrinally inspired international public authority (or other approaches, such as 'global constitutionalism', not discussed here), similarly involve comparative work, whether explicit or

---

[62] Questions of the latter kind have played out in debates regarding whether it is necessary, possible, or desirable to invoke 'constitutionalism' or 'constitutionalization' beyond the state, or to speak of a 'global administrative law'. See the papers collected in *The Twilight of Constitutionalism?* and, for analysis of what is required for the 'translation' of constitutionalism to the supranational context, Neil Walker, 'Postnational constitutionalism and the problem of translation' in J. H. H. Weiler and Marlene Wind (eds), *European Constitutionalism Beyond the State* (Cambridge: Cambridge University Press, 2003) 27–54, 36–38.

not: understanding the global and transnational as in some way analogous to the national, and intelligible in the political and legal terms that originated in the nation-state.[63]

Comparative study of national public law may be helpful in many ways to the study of global governance.[64] However, the distillation of abstract principles of public law for global bodies by headcount from different national systems, while useful in certain specific juridical contexts,[65] is unlikely to produce a 'global public law' that is resilient to the critiques already made of global administrative law and international public authority. Indeed, the great circumspection in international law toward the use of 'general principles of law' as a source of substantive rules is indicative of reasons to doubt that comparative analyses can produce a lengthy catalogue of strong rules of decision on substantive law that will be widely accepted for regulating the practice of global institutions.

Comparative law in fact could be most useful in directing attention back to specificities and variations between national systems and modes of rule which can be lost in the adoption of a single language or imagination of governance. One response to the merging of public law and managerialism has been to insist on the distinction between what is proper to public law, and what has lately been attached to it. Carol Harlow's careful disentangling of what she sees as classic 'principles of administrative law' (fairness, legality, consistency, rationality, impartiality) from both a thin account of the rule of law, promoted by economic liberals, and from 'values' (such as participation, openness, accountability) that are formulated largely beyond legal doctrine, and which she understands as deriving mainly from the 'good governance' agenda, or from the due process rights set out in human rights instruments and jurisprudence, is one example of such an endeavour.[66] It is crucial to be aware of the distinct intellectual and historical lineages of the vocabularies in which ideals of public law and adminis-tration are articulated, and of the different political visions and values on which these vocabularies draw. However, given widespread practices of privatization and 'new governance' within states, it is difficult to delimit and protect a particular sense for (public) law that would hold it entirely apart from other vocabularies, and other modes of control (such as 'governance' or 'manage-rialism') without substantive discussion of the content of the law in question.[67]

---

[63] For a more formal argument on comparative methodology, working from the national to the global, see Aleksandar Momirov and Andria Naudé Fourie, 'Vertical Comparative Law Methods: Tools for Conceptualising the International Rule of Law' (2009) 2 Erasmus Law Review 291–309.

[64] A valuable contribution is Susan Rose-Ackerman and Peter L. Lindseth (eds), *Comparative Administrative Law* (Cheltenham: Edward Elgar, 2010).

[65] See, eg, Stephan W. Schill (ed.), *International Investment Law and Comparative Public Law* (Oxford: Oxford University Press, 2010).

[66] Carol Harlow, 'Global Administrative Law: The Quest for Principles and Values' (2006) 17 European Journal of International Law 187–214. See also Harlow, 'Accountability as a Value in Global Governance and for Global Administrative Law' in Gordon Anthony et al. (eds), *Values in Global Administrative Law* (Oxford: Hart Publishing, 2011) 173–92.

[67] Even the most eloquent defenders of the view that procedural requirements such as Fuller's will make it more difficult for legal systems to function in undesirable or illiberal ways concede that the matter falls

Similarly, one possibility for those who might want to contest the broad approach taken in the *Handbook*, or the specific reforms that evaluators suggest in a particular state, is to seek to act in and through the individual, local contexts in which reforms are being applied. As reform programs are developed, local institutions may also provide forums, and specific local laws may provide substantive arguments, for challenging the framing of these programs. The *Handbook* implicitly accepts that there may be considerable friction between the local legal order and the sorts of statutory provisions that the *Handbook* recommends, so local legal provisions (for example, constitutional provisions relating to control of natural resources and preserving a role for state or public ownership) and local courts may furnish avenues for resistance or at least attempts to amend the program of reforms to be followed. Moreover, specific understandings of such terms as 'participation' and 'transparency', grounded in national public law, may provide both an important counterpoint to the de-localized and thus more malleable language used in the *Handbook*.

The *Handbook* as an instrument of prescription and evaluation—and the challenging problems for public lawyers of addressing the institutional dynamics and governance of its production and implementation and contestation—exemplify a blend of functionalist managerialism and attenuated normativity which some may argue lies 'after' public law. In our view, however, this swirl of ideas and practices reaching within and beyond the state can better be seen—and must be seen—as part of the future of public law. The *Handbook* itself bears witness to the functional need for public law, at least of a particular kind, to order the terrain for global actors, and to the energy with which global institutions and globalized experts address themselves to (re)constructing national public law. The specificities of national public law provide an important avenue for contestation of these global efforts (and in turn, perhaps, constitute one source of ideas, although probably not rules, for an emerging global public law). We have, however, suggested that the language and concepts of public law are increasingly intertwined with more diffuse and de-localized discourses, giving rise to a sort of *lingua franca* of governance which, while ubiquitous, conceals conceptual and political divergence. This suggests that the most fruitful engagement with a putative global public law, particularly global administrative law, is one that recognizes its current fluidity, seeing it not as a source of a particular formula for legitimacy or checklist of requirements, but as a field in which these requirements and their foundations are being articulated and contested.

---

to be resolved, at least in part, on historical and sociological grounds: David Dyzenhaus, 'The Legitimacy of the Rule of Law', in Dyzenhaus, Murray Hunt, and Grant Huscroft (eds), *A Simple Common Lawyer: Essays in Honour of Michael Taggart* (Oxford: Hart Publishing, 2009) 33–54, 49. At least in well-resourced states with a high level of organizational capacity, the legal system may function in a way that is entirely compliant with Fullerian desiderata, maintaining the full trust and confidence of foreign investors, but with profoundly illiberal consequences: see, eg, Tom Ginsburg, 'Administrative Law and the Judicial Control of Agents in Authoritarian Regimes' in Ginsburg and Tamir Moustafa (eds), *Rule by Law: The Politics of Courts in Authoritarian Regimes* (Cambridge: Cambridge University Press, 2008) 58–72.

❧ 14 ❧

The (re-)Constitution of the Public in a Global Arena

Gianluigi Palombella

I. INTRODUCTION

Our received views about the public and law are deeply associated with the modern notion of the state. From this state-centric perspective, there is hardly any 'public' outside its domain. In truth, public law relates, as with the case of Roman law, to communities and not fragmentary or individual interests. Modern understandings of the 'public in law' rely on its differentiation from private law, increasingly focusing on the authority exercised by the state over its citizens in a vertical relationship.[1]

In the modern state-centred tradition, a full narrative of public law entails the *political* nature and *pre-positive* roots of the public as vital factors of the beliefs and practices that generate the very essence of government.[2] But it is worth noticing that this *political* structuring of the public and public law, taken alone, captures only part of its complexity.

Rather, a different tradition in modern legal philosophical thought relies on the *juridical* generators of the public (Bentham and Kant are representative of this trend); and in truth, I think, the public in modernity is best captured as *doubly* constituted; that is, reflecting an interplay between its *legal* and *political* dimensions. This mixed or dualistic perspective better captures its multifaceted nature rather than some *reductio ad unum*.

Moreover, this two-dimensional nature is only fully comprehensible within the context of the state. In this light, the supposed fading of the state may end up undermining the 'public' in law. This obsolescence of the public is usually attributed to globalization, with its emergent pluralist, self-referential forms of legality that transgress the boundaries of a dated *jus publicum* as well as its conceptions of legitimate authority and questions the disciplinary distinction between public and private law.[3]

---

[1] This reflects the two-step process in modern philosophy involving, first of all, the institution of civil society (in contrast with a 'state of nature') and then the institution of the state (other than civil society itself). See generally, N. Bobbio, *Stato, governo, società* (Torino: Einaudi, 1980); M. Horwitz, 'The History of the Public/Private Distinction' (1982) 130 U. Pa. L. Rev. 1423; J. Habermas, *The Structural Transformation of the Public Sphere: An Inquiry into a Category of Bourgeois Society*, Th. Burger (trans.) (Cambridge, Mass: MIT Press, 1992).

[2] It is the line that goes from Bodin to Rousseau, from Hegel to Schmitt.

[3] Significant is 'Beyond the State: Rethinking Private Law', Special Symposium Issue (2008) 56 American Journal of Comparative Law.

In fact, that transformation of law and society, which is the subject of an extraordinary amount of scholarly attention,[4] depends upon the de-centring of the state, and on the fading and decoupling of the mutuality between the dual (legal and political) logics of the public. We also see a shift in language where 'governance', 'administration', and 'accountability', replace the once-pivotal notions of government, politics, and democracy, or the emergence of hybrid neologisms such as 'democratic governance'. These developments are only in part a reappraisal of older questions (for example, the controversies between political and legal constitutionalism, institutional or normativist theories of law, legal positivism, and natural law doctrines, and so forth). Whereas this reappraisal can shed some light on the contemporary developments regarding the public, such a *déjà vu* would be misleading; previous disputes revolved around the dominance of the state. The epistemic unity and uniqueness of *this* expression of the public is being challenged.

Insofar as we can see the attraction of a *dualistic* approach to defining the public, the 'decoupling' and imbalance of the legal and political aspects, occasioned by global transformations, are felt as a loss, dissolving the complex and original unity of the 'public' itself.

Nonetheless, the question of the *public* nature of law, as the vehicle that conveys legitimacy and authority, is still crucial, even to normative orders in search of theoretical 'recognition' and endorsement such as those flourishing in the global arena. Even the legality of normative sources in a post-state sphere is deemed to be contingent upon their 'public' nature.[5] As such, the 'public' is considered to be not (only) a branch of the law but the custodian and the generator of legality itself, its deep root.

Taking these factors into account, this chapter proposes a further argument by assuming that the reverse is true; that is, it will highlight the *legal* dimension in the modern understandings of the public, where the 'birth' of law is a necessary condition for the very constitution of publicness, and is therefore logically prior to the very constitution of 'publicness'.

In doing so, the argument will rely on a historical and conceptual narrative of the public as well as illustrating the utility of emphasizing how, along with the political matrix, the (Kantian) constitution of the 'legal category' (that is, the *autonomy of law*), is seen as the *precondition* of the public and a necessary *generator* of it.

These two elements are relevant to the question of the theory and prospects of the public and law 'beyond the state' where the public-as-*political* is absent, but *legality* is seemingly present (and recurrently evoked). As I shall argue, whereas reliance on the potential of law in the post-state environment can be appropriate, nonetheless the sheer creation of legality alone might be seen as insufficient to constitute a fully fledged public domain. Supranational legality is incrementally construed by unprecedented normative authorities, rules, regulations, and judicial bodies which challenge the conventional connection between the public and

---

[4] I offered my own insight, in *The Rule of Law in Global Governance: Its construction, function and import*, in 'The Straus Institute for Advanced Studies on Law and Justice' WP 05/2010.

[5] Cf B. Kingsbury, 'International Law as Inter-Public Law' in *Moral Universalism and Pluralism*, Henry S. Richardson and Melissa S. Williams (eds) (New York: New York University Press, 2009).

the state and in particular, with the substantive scope of a *political* community. Indeed, the flourishing of new normative entities in a global context is a distinctive phenomenon where the appeal to law is devoid of connections with the realms of social life. It thrives despite lacking support from those political determinants that state communities enjoy. Thus, even if a sui generic global public law asserts itself with increasing success, it lacks a vital ingredient and is therefore inchoate or incomplete.

The solution to this weakness of a global public law is still necessarily tentative. This weakness is not overcome by designing some constitutional and allegedly universal values that authorities and regulators beyond the state should be bound to respect. Even though we accept such a design, the problem of the (above recalled) 'incompleteness' of a global public legality would not be solved. Rather, the chapter will argue, the viability of supranational law as the institution of the 'public' will depend on whether its *balanced* integration is possible with those legal orders (corresponding with societies in territorial settings) that from time to time grant global normativity the necessary implementation and effectiveness in their own domain. The achievement of a *complete* dimension of publicness in global public law is impossible without connecting the legal measures issued by 'global authorities' with the political generators of normative power that are inherent in the concrete structures of 'real' communities of people. In the new 'global' context, such a reconnection hints at a *synthetic* or constructed notion of the public, tailored on a case-by-case basis, guaranteed by the rule of law, and applied to the *relations* between the different levels of orders and different levels of organization, supranational, regional, national, global, and local: some of which are sociopolitically embedded whereas others are not, but serve coordination in the pursuit of regulatory objectives or the protection of universal standards (such as human rights).

In what follows, after recalling the notion of the public law as 'political' (Section 1), I shall outline the 'legal' nature of the public, accounting for its essential (Kantian) profile, which can be called a 'public through law' (Section 2). Thereafter, I shall address the fate of their separation in the global setting (as it appears from the point of view of international relations and of global law) and the problem of 'suspended public' law (Section 3). Once these different scenarios of the public are outlined, I shall consider the problems and ways of their *re-coupling* through the perspective of the globe as a *multiversum* of legalities (Sections 4–6).[6]

2. THE 'PUBLIC AS POLITICAL LAW' APPROACH AND ITS LIMITS

There is a public law that does not match a doctrinal partition of existing *positive* law within a legal order. As Martin Loughlin has reminded us,[7] public law has a

---

[6] Albeit the route taken in this chapter recognizes the merits of pluralist, global constitutionalist, or administrative law theories, it purports to mend the partial and deracinated nature of the *public* that results from them. Thus, it has a different purpose and articulation.

[7] M. Loughlin, *The Idea of Public Law* (Oxford: Oxford University Press, 2003). See also Chapter 2, this book.

much deeper nature; it can be historically reconstructed in an essentially *political* sense, emerging as a transformation of the fundamental law (once deemed prior to the king and his rule: law that makes the king) into a secularized source of the authority and legitimacy of governmental ordering. In the modern era, the denaturalization of medieval sources of legitimate authority introduced new features: the autonomy of the 'political' sphere and the instrumental reflexivity of law as means of people's self-government. Insofar as this law makes the 'body politic', it is not law made by the government, but is rather the constitutive principles underpinning the right ordering of the state. The notion of law reflects the historical, both material and normative, constitution of reality, one which entails diverse factors, including cultural connotations along with the ethics of the land and deeply rooted beliefs that John Austin, the father of legal positivism, would relegate to sheer 'positive morality'. However, for Loughlin,[8] and through a tradition of thought that spans Bodin, Rousseau, and Hegel, this law is instead embedded in political right or *droit politique*. This is what Rousseau defined as 'the political laws, which constitute the form of Government'.[9] *Droit politique* entails 'rules, principles, canons, maxims, usages, and manners' which shape an 'autonomous world of the public sphere' where two opposite claims of individual autonomy and public authority[10] are reconciled for prudential purposes. Moreover, this law is not a restraint on power but is essential to the generation of power as 'political'.[11]

The distinctiveness of this construction lies in the fact that it is not addressed through an abstract, transcendental, formal apparatus of rational morality but is rooted in tradition and custom. In this sense, we can say, the constitution of state sovereignty is, if anything, a true manifestation of the '*Ding an sich*', as represented in the development of the Hegelian 'Objective Spirit'.[12]

Does this approach provide a complete overview of the public as it exists in modernity? Does it provide the theoretical tools that are necessary *vis à vis* the problems posed by globalization? Notwithstanding the strength and epistemic value of the *political* view of the public, there are further issues at stake. The 'political law' approach has its merits and its limits in representing the nature and evolution of the public. The Rousseauian solution to the problem of founding governmental authority and safeguarding individual liberty—through his conception of democracy—is in fact 'territorially based' and strongly dependent on the republican ethos of a community. Its basic premise is a renovated culture of the individual as a citizen; that is, fully shaped and forged according to the axiomatic correctness or infallibility of the '*volonté general*'. Equally, thinking of the 'public' in a Hegelian sense is premised on the historical experience of the state as a true 'universality', where individuals and the community appear as a

---

[8] Most recently, M. Loughlin, *Foundations of Public Law* (Oxford: Oxford University Press, 2010).

[9] J.-J. Rousseau, *The Social Contract and other later political writings*, V. Gurevitch edition (Cambridge: Cambridge University Press, 1997) 81.

[10] Loughlin, *Foundations*, 10–11.

[11] This means, for Loughlin, that kind of power which is inherent in the public sphere because it is founded on the consent of the people.

[12] G. W. F. Hegel, *Philosophy of Right*, T. M. Knox (trans.) (Oxford: Oxford University Press, 1952).

necessarily rational unity. The achievement and progress represented by the *state* and the 'general will' constitute, on this reading, the ideal of the public in law.

In the form of 'political right', law follows the political history of a people and their 'public'. *This* idea of public law, of itself, shares the fate of notions such as nation, territory, demos, and state that, despite their enduring importance, are losing their centrality in a globalized world.

Moreover, the 'political right' approach to public law not only generates difficulties in the extended post-state space, but also raises issues regarding its epistemic sufficiency *within* the state itself. The public is given definition through as concrete factors as ethics, territoriality, and culture. Nonetheless, it is poorly and less clearly conceptualized from a legal perspective; the normative service of *law* and its relative autonomy *vis à vis* the power structures that it sustains are paid scarce attention in this approach. The (counterfactual) potential of law wanes given the conflation between the factual and the normative, the rational, and the 'real'.

As such, ultimately, the 'political' holds the key to the whole. However, the insistence on this 'existential' nature of the public deprives us of legal safeguards for criticism and dissent, and paves the way for an 'ethics of the soil', a 'tyranny of values', and related bitter experiences which they have generated in the past century. In such cases, law did not play its modern role of resolving the puzzle— and maintaining an equilibrium—between private and public autonomy. Rather, it was a purely instrumental tool at the whim of the sovereign power, whose action could always appeal to legally unconstrained political necessity.

This criticism relates to a normative weakness. It does not reject either the fact of *pre*-positive political law as empowering and providing a foundation for government, or that positive law can be an instrument of governmental power. It does claim, however, that alongside 'political right', *positive* law can have (and historically has had) a role, a foundational role, in public law. This function of positive law provides a potential counterweight to the political (as we shall see in the next sections), generally to prevent powerful rulers from achieving *legally* all sorts of 'political' goals.

From the perspective of law as *political right*, the Schmittian 'state of exception'—where law and its guarantees are ignored—is seen as the true expression of the underlying nature of the public, that is why public law is what it is. Thus, the 'state of exception' is not conceived of as a suspended (or undecided) state, a 'zone of indifference' between law and politics; rather, it is said to reveal the essential and foundational source of the legitimization of the state. By way of example, the 1803 decision in *Marbury v Madison* 5 US 137 (1803) (US judicial review of legislation on the basis of constitutional standards) has been seen as the *transformation of the constitution* from a deep repository of *pre*-positive, political self-understanding of power, into a legal device of higher (positive) law. From the perspective of the political view of public law, this change in a constitution from a *pre*-positive substratum to a *legalized* institution is not welcome because it threatens the survival of public law as 'political right'.[13]

---

[13] Loughlin seems to view this transformation as a kind of dispersal of the complex resource of the political right, see *Foundations*, 293 ff.

On the contrary, and against that narrative, it must be recognized that it is precisely this 'transformation' which makes the constitution accessible to all, judges and citizens, and ceases to be the exclusive preserve and sheer source of inspiration of legislatures. This 'legalization of the constitution' can be seen as instituting a normative, legal tension that constrains the ultimate power. The (dormant Schmittian) sovereign cannot simply appeal to some obscure foundations of its legitimacy, but must follow legally framed paths, that can be procedurally and substantively monitored. The creation of a *legal* interposition (as the counterpart to the Schmittian 'authority interposition') opens up a different path, because it creates *spaces* of *divergence* between power (as contingent as it is) and law. When procedures, guarantees, and rights can be invoked universally as a higher law and cannot be simply suppressed by reference to the deeper soul of a nation, they are *legally posited* outside the remit of the most powerful (as constitutions attempt to do, affording a higher law protection even *vis-à-vis* the otherwise legitimate exercise of sovereignty pursuant to the principle of democracy). Legal positivization, then, can be said to articulate the puzzle between autonomy and authority, as well as between 'private' and 'public'.

Accordingly, and without necessarily rejecting the distinctive role of the law's *pre*-positive enduring sociopolitical determinants, public in law can be 'enlightened' by taking the view that it is centred upon the 'normative point' of law itself, of the 'legal' in its positive sense. The 'public' can be grasped not only through the ontological/political dimensions that human practice contributes to the law, but also by making sense of what law itself provides to the 'public', to its structure, and teleology.

As will be shown in the following sections, the constitution of the public can be considered as protecting what John Rawls called the two moral powers; namely, the capacity to set and pursue a conception of the good, which is a sovereign choice, and what is beyond the remit of such a choice; that is, the sense of justice.[14] The latter is essential to the fairness of social cooperation, and has been conventionally understood in connection with the institution of law. From this angle, the tension characterizing the 'ought' in law is equally essential to the constitution of the 'public'.

3. THE 'LEGAL' APPROACH: PUBLIC THROUGH LAW, OR THE CONCEPTION OF LAW AS AN AUTONOMOUS CATEGORY

A different approach to the public can build on the distinctive function of legality. The public character of law is evident in a number of ways. It is explicitly present in positivist writings, like those of Jeremy Bentham, who admits of law as providing the 'public'; that is, a common point of view beyond the parties, beyond individual judgment (albeit sound judgments, as utility-based judgments can be). Law allows for generalized and publicly followed, or mutually recognized,

---

[14] J. Rawls, *Justice as Fairness: A Restatement*, E. Kelly (ed.) (Cambridge, Mass: Harvard University Press, 2001), 6–7.

standpoints, that are available to all, and prescribes the general conditions of their validity. Bentham contrasts his view with a conception of law as customary rules of interaction among isolated individuals, or as he calls them, 'monades'.[15] As with Kant, for Bentham, law does not require the abandonment of the 'right to private judgment'. Nonetheless, by providing generally accessible criteria, it aims at ensuring social coordination by facing disagreements that stem both from individual interests and from ideal or principled divergences over collective issues.[16]

As Bentham argued, positive morality is insufficient for the public. It is difficult to think of the public as organized through moral beliefs. Any requisites of 'publicness' would be impossible to imagine outside the role provided by law. It is not simply that law overlaps with morality, but that morality requires the law in order to achieve its aims.

As Tony Honoré pointed out, in similar terms, morality cannot dispense with law. Its self-sufficiency is overestimated, insofar as there are many irreconcilable conflicts and moral intuitions as well as problems of distributive justice arising in social life which need to be spelled out in concrete situations. However, they must be 'filled' with law and framed by legal systems, if they are to be resolved.[17] Law acts as 'a determinant of justice'.[18] Thus, although the 'separation' of morality (from law) preserves critical moral thinking *vis-à-vis* the law, a viable morality—based on the need to coexist and cooperate with others—must have 'a legal component'.[19] Undoubtedly, this requires institutions and an authority that claims legal supremacy over the community which is the case both for states and, to a lesser extent, for the international legal order.

Kant provides a straightforward view of law as a *generator* of publicness which combines the creation of legal parameters with the problem of justice. In his view, unless man,

[W]ants to renounce any concepts of right, the first thing it has to resolve upon is the principle that it must leave the state of nature, in which each follows its own judgment, unite itself with all others (with which it cannot avoid interacting),

---

[15] J. Bentham, 'Of Laws in General', in J. H. Burns and H. L. A. Hart (eds), *The Collected Works of Jeremy Bentham* (London: The Athlone Press, 1970), 192.

[16] G. Postema, 'Bentham on the Public Character of Law' (1989) 1 Utilitas 41, addresses the problem of the public character of law in Bentham, as a coordinative service of law, finally concluding that the very weakness of Bentham's position is not in connecting law and coordination, but in underestimating the role that law plays after a legal solution has been reached: 'To focus only on the law's ability to put some questions beyond further debate obscures the role the law plays structuring the debate which continues. Legal arrangements, far from calming the political waters in the way Bentham's theory predicts, often attract and even invite disagreement and contention' (Postema, 'Bentham on the Public Character of Law', 60). Postema rightly points out that it must be taken into account that legal arrangements are often legitimated by attracting principled discussion, they can be constantly an object of contention, and significantly, they matter to us as a political question (Postema, 'Bentham on the Public Character of Law', 61).

[17] Tony Honoré, 'The Dependence of Morality on Law' (1993) 13 Oxford Journal of Legal Studies 1. Honoré also notes, correctly, that among those problems there are some created by law itself, that would not arise independently of the institutions of law (eg tax paying).

[18] Honoré, 16.   [19] Honoré, 2.

subject itself to a public lawful external coercion, and so enter into a condition in which what is to be recognized as belonging to it is determined *by law*.[20]

This reference to law is conceived by Kant as the *creation* of the public, and it amounts, in short, to a 'bootstrap conception' of the public, or the idea of public *through law*. To explain these points, let us follow Kant's reasoning.

Law and justice are resorted to conceptually in order to avoid the (state of nature) condition in which the abuse of personal liberty and external control is *unobjectionable*. Even if the state of nature need not be unjust, it is devoid of justice, so that men 'do one another no wrong when they feud among themselves'.[21] Nonetheless, 'in general they do wrong in the highest degree by willing to be and to remain in a condition that is not rightful, that is, in which no one is assured of what is his against violence'.[22] For that reason, man 'ought above all else to enter a civil condition', and accordingly 'each may impel the other by force to leave this state and enter into a rightful condition'.[23] The imperative *to exit the state of nature* is also the basic moral imperative related to the conservation of the only natural right, the right to liberty. What Kant requires for a civil state, that is, a rightful condition to be 'produced', is a 'sum of laws', or better a 'system of laws' that must be called 'public right'. This logical necessity, relating to external legislation as a means for the avoidance of violence and submission to the unilateral will of another person, applies to individuals as much as to peoples and nations (*jus gentium* and *jus cosmpoliticum*) simultaneously.[24]

Thus, there is a fundamental reason for law to be established; that is, the necessarily public nature of *justice,* that cannot be predicated from unilateral, self-referential positions, but relates to the equal liberty of all and independence of each from the will of the other. So, this is the route through which the law inheres necessarily in the public.

It should be emphasized, however, that such a route concerns *the right*, not the good or happiness. It is important to understand the argument concerning the positivity of law. It overcomes shortcomings of unilateral views over what is 'right', and controls the inevitably relational coexistence among peers. Divergences between conceptions soon become a source of injustice, and thus cannot be left to a spontaneous and provisional convergence, the customary event among 'monades' mentioned by Bentham. The *positivity* of law serves the interests of justice because it prevents unilateral domination: it constitutes the 'public' insofar as it forecloses its privatization, that is, its appropriation by a dominant private will. It rules out the possibility that relations among persons are decided through the subordination of one of the parties to conceptions of what is right by others.

---

[20] I. Kant, 'Metaphysical First Principles of the Doctrine of Right', in *The Metaphysics of Morals* [1797] Mary Gregor (trans.) (Cambridge: Cambridge University Press, 1996) (repr. 2003) 33, § 44, 90.

[21] Kant, 'Metaphysical First Principles', § 42, 86.

[22] Kant, 'Metaphysical First Principles', § 42, 86.

[23] Kant, 'Metaphysical First Principles', § 42, 86.

[24] Kant, 'Metaphysical First Principles', § 43, 89.

The institution of law, however, is intended to preserve justice in relations among individuals by preventing the imposition of one view of the good. Ideas of the good in an individual's life cannot be dictated through the 'public'.[25] While the individual pursuit of happiness is inherent to the Kantian philosophy of law, it can only be achieved by ensuring liberty among citizens. As long as individuals conform to what we owe to one another, according to a universal legislation of liberty, the question of the 'public' is both created, and ultimately controlled by, issues of justice (concerning the mutual respect of individual spheres of liberty), not by issues of ethics (concerning the choice of what is good for our prospect of happiness).

Similarly, law accordingly does not require anything other than mere compliance with legislation.[26] It does not require us to act to limit our freedom 'just for the sake of this obligation'.[27] As Kant writes, 'when the aim is not to teach virtue but only to set forth what is right, one may not and should not represent the law of right as itself an incentive to action'.[28] Accordingly, public legal institutions make coercion possible by preventing its exercise by private persons and making it consistent with equal freedom. Were self- (private) enforcement of our rights possible, the will and views of the more powerful would be unilaterally imposed on the sphere of right of the less powerful. This is the foundation of the Kantian ideal of the rule of law which ensures that private preferences do not prevail over justice. Thus, the appearance of law, the creation of 'public law', does not result from *pre*-positive political factors, as is the case with the 'political law' approach to the public, discussed in the previous section. In this different tradition of thought, the very birth of law comes from the exit from the 'state of nature' which involves the simultaneous creation of the public, of a civil state, and the protection of justice and liberty.[29]

---

[25] Moral legislation requires the universal recognition of human beings as coexisting under innate equal liberty. Therefore, 'No one can coerce me to be happy in his way (as he thinks of the welfare of other human beings); instead, each may seek his happiness in the way that seems good to him, provided he does not infringe upon that freedom of others to strive for a like end which can coexist with the freedom of everyone in accordance with a possible universal law (ie does not infringe upon this right of another)' (I. Kant, 'On the Common Saying: "That may be correct in theory, but it is of no use in practice"' [1793] in I. Kant, *Practical Philosophy*, M. J. Gregor (trans.) (Cambridge: Cambridge University Press, 1996) 291).

[26] I assume that consistent to this external character of the required compliance is the liberty-based justification of coercion: 'if a certain use of freedom is itself a hindrance to freedom in accordance with universal laws (ie, wrong), coercion that is opposed to this (as a hindering of a hindrance to freedom) is consistent with freedom in accordance with universal laws, that is, it is right. Hence there is connected with Right by the principle of contradiction an authorization to coerce someone who infringes upon it.' I. Kant, 'Metaphysical First Principles of the Doctrine of Right', 'Introduction to the Doctrine of Right', § D, in *The Metaphysics of Morals*, 25.

[27] Kant, 'Metaphysical First Principles', § C, 25. *En passant*, although it is a moral reason to justify our exit from the state of nature, it does not follow that we are obliged to comply with the law out of moral acceptance, ie for moral reasons.

[28] Kant, 'Metaphysical First Principles', § C, 24–25.

[29] Admittedly, this also has consequences over the compatible ideas of the common good. A social system must be envisaged that can grant independence, private liberties, and the necessary basis for property and freedom of contract. The objective of justice is what the public nature of law is about, that is, the prevention of one sidedness, the violation of liberty, and the creation of dependence. That is the moral reason why people can be compelled to leave the state of nature or comply with justice. They would otherwise be submitting others to their own whim. The *systematic* aspect implies that private

In this light, the normative quality and the conceivability of the public is essentially 'legal', and depends on the appearance of law as an autonomous and distinctive structure[30] of justice among individuals (Kant) and coordination (Bentham). The formation of the civil state is not a political imperative, in Rousseau's sense (and the political law conception outlined in the previous section) but is *legal* and is backed by moral justification. This conceptual distinction results from the fact that law is seen as a transcendental ideal, as the condition of coexistence through liberty, *before* any ethical objective (a specific vision of well-being) can be actually pursued. There is a necessary distinction, and a necessary connection, between justice and ethical/political choices. The tension between their mutually autonomous claims must be supported by institutional devices aimed at the preservation of the rule of law, that is, by preventing the possibility that the only content of the law is that expressed by dominant or majoritarian conceptions of the good.

This archetype of 'public through law' affords an open reminder of the *right* that cannot be encroached upon by the realization of an ethical *good*. The structural connection between public and law in the Kantian sense implies that if law's basis is not simply contingent on political elaboration of the good, it cannot either be based on the whim of the sovereign. From this perspective, the constitution of the public, even in Kantian terms, reflects the liberal roots of the 'rule of law ideal' as it can be traced back to the medieval rationale of the equilibrium between *jurisdictio* and *gubernaculum*.[31] In institutional terms, public institutions must prevent the unilateral appropriation of all available law by the sovereign as a tool at his disposal. Accordingly, the constitution of the public *through* law also impinges on the exercise of power, and its peculiar shaping of the common good. Although Kant excluded any right of rebellion, the Kantian legislator is still checked by dictates of reason, the conditions of universal legislation, and he has to conceive of law as though the people were legislating themselves for themselves. In this way, the sovereign cannot act in a way that would encroach upon justice (*jurisdictio*) and individual liberty. Both justice and liberty are the rationale of the 'imperative of public law' (as Kant calls it), and the sovereign has no power to rule them out.[32]

So far, I have sketched the two strands of the public, one cast by the substantive potential of the *political*, and the other by the Kantian illustration of *law* as an autonomous generator of publicness. In a stylized way, the two strands articulate diverse components of public order, by focusing on different dimensions. Taken *together* they illuminate the essence of the public as we understand it in the context of the state. In the changed circumstances of our transformed legal and

---

contractual intercourses without distributive justice would be ineffective and insufficient. This consolidates and reshapes private agreements under the common frame of the public in law.

[30] Umberto Cerroni has referred to the Kantian theory as the birth of the 'legal category' in one of the most outstanding books on Kant's legal philosophy: cf U. Cerroni, *Kant e la nascita della categoria giuridica* (Milano: Giuffrè, 1961).

[31] I proposed a reconstructed notion of the rule of law in 'The Rule of Law as an Institutional Ideal' in L. Morlino and G. Palombella (eds), *Rule of Law and Democracy* (Leiden: Brill, 2010).

[32] See Morlino and Palombella (eds), *Rule of Law and Democracy*, where I addressed this point at length.

political universe with a global reach, it is necessary to understand what survives of this dual dimension beyond the state.

4. 'PENELOPE'S PUBLIC': THE SUSPENDED STATUS OF THE GLOBE

In seeking the rationale of the public in the unchartered global setting there are many obstacles to overcome. First of all, however, the 'status of the globe' requires definition which will be done according to the viewpoints of two perspectives which have analysed the global sphere in depth: that of international relations theory and global administrative law.

Generally speaking, the 'global' is conceived of according to the position attributed to the idea of state sovereignty. International relations tends to position itself on the threshold between the realist dogma of anarchy, self-defence, self-interest, on the one hand, and the relentless weaving of institutions and norms on the other. The focus on the *limen* results from the contrasting reality of international relations, where the very construction of a unified, global public remains an ongoing but unfinished business, like Penelope's web in Greek mythology.

The emergence (and retreat) of the 'public' beyond the state is ambiguous, particularly from the perspective of international relations studies. From this perspective it is not produced by the ordering role of international *law*, whose positive validity is still being constantly questioned. International relations scholars aim to reflect a 'real' state of affairs,[33] and their conclusions—their accounts of the world beyond the state—are always in the centre between the two poles, evoked in the words of Hedley Bull, of a minimal international system and an 'international society', where,

> a group of states, conscious of certain common interests and common values, form a society in the sense that they conceive themselves to be bound by a common set of rules in their relations with one another, and share in the working of common institutions.[34]

This sentiment is also evident in Stephen Krasner's characterization of sovereignty as 'organized hypocrisy'. States exhibit 'patterns of behaviour' that do not coincide with 'professed norms'.[35]

Of course, from the *realist* perspective in international relations there is no alternative to a Hobbesian ontology based on the fixed, naturalized, self-interest of states, and ironically it is not even possible to follow the Hobbesian imperative, which is, *to abandon such a state of nature* ('exeundum e statu naturae'). On the other hand, 'constructivist' approaches tend towards the opposite pole, by suggesting a paradigm shift; they refuse the naturalized stereotype of the character of states arguing that *identities* are inter-subjectively shaped (for better or for

---

[33] See the seminal re-elaboration of the 'realistic' theory by Kenneth Waltz, structuring the international system as intrinsically anarchical, power-prone, and focused on the 'self-interested' behaviour of states: K. Waltz, *Theory of International Politics* (New York: McGraw-Hill, 1979) esp. 79–128.

[34] H. Bull, *The Anarchical Society* (New York: Columbia University Press, 1977) 13.

[35] S. D. Krasner, *Sovereignty: Organized Hypocrisy* (Princeton: Princeton University Press, 1999).

worse);[36] 'anarchy is what States make of it'[37] as Alexander Wendt famously observed. There is no doubt that this second approach paves the way for the construction of the public in the global arena, the incremental shaping, beyond international anarchy, of an environment potentially ordered by institutions and organized through law.

The insights from the international relations (IR) dimension should not be ignored when considering the global setting from the point of view of law and *legal studies*, be they international, administrative, or constitutional. IR theories offer a picture of a never-ending process of the construction of the public (in the sense of a civil state, instituted through normative authorities beyond the parties). The tentative move beyond the 'middle ground' (between state of nature and a governed environment) is nonetheless always at work, especially in the recurrent promotion and recognition of 'multilateralism'[38] which emphasizes the fact that norms can matter.[39] Inquiries about the role of legal norms in global relations— not by chance—have been part of the prospective agenda of liberal theories.[40] And by enhancing the role of normative *networks,* the epistemic value of a state-centered approach decreases, while institutions, networks, and multilevel inter-courses show the effect of 'disaggregating the States',[41] as part of the incremental weaving of the conditions for a global public beyond the state.

Before taking a closer look at the normative transformations on the globe, it is important to recognize the epistemic value of characterizing the constitution of the public in the global setting as Penelope's web; it is neither the structured state environment (the 'public' which we have been familiar with) nor an unavailable 'dry dock' (the state of nature) for our ship.[42] The constitution of the public, as in

---

[36] A. Wendt, 'Anarchy is What States Make of It: The Social Construction of Power Politics' (1992) 46, 2 International Organization, 391. See also Gerard J. Ruggie, 'What makes the World hang together? Neo-utilitarianism and the Social Constructivist Challenge', in G. J. Ruggie, *Constructing the World Polity: Essays in International Institutionalization* (London: Routledge, 1998) 1–39. See also A. Wendt, 'Collective Identity Formation and the International State' (1994) 88(2) American Political Science Review 384. In general, A. Caffarena, 'Il costruttivismo', in G. J. Ikenberry and V. E. Parsi (eds), *Teorie e metodi delle relazioni internazionali* (Bologna: Il Mulino, 2001) 71–93 (71 ff.).

[37] See A. Wendt, 'Anarchy is What States Make of It', note 36.

[38] J. A. Caporaso, 'International Relations Theory and Multilateralism: The Search for Foundations' (1992) 46(3) International Organization 603, writes: 'Multilateralism is a belief that activities ought to be organized on a universal (or at least many-sided) basis for a "relevant" group'.

[39] And less with anarchy, of course. Undoubtedly, anarchy means unilateralism: tellingly Robert Kagan notes, in his *Of Paradise and Power: America and Europe in the New World Order,* (New York: Knopf, 2003) 36, that it serves best the interests of the most powerful state, who better profits from lack of social or legal ordering.

[40] This is one of the main contributions from liberal theories in international relations. See A.-M. Slaughter, A. Tulumello, and St. Wood, 'International Law and International Relations Theory: A New Generation of Interdisciplinary Scholarship' (1998) 92 American Journal of International Law, 373, 378; and A.-M. Slaughter, 'International Law and International Relations Theory: A Dual Agenda' (1993) 87 American Journal of International Law 226 with reference to the 'Liberal Paradigm'.

[41] Slaughter, *A New World Order* (Princeton: Princeton University Press, 2005) 12 ff, esp. 131–65 (in the sense that they are cross-cutting states, and are able to network similarly concerned parts—institutions, administrative bodies, political entities, etc.—of diverse states).

[42] This draws on Neurath's metaphor: the sailor's struggle with repairing the ship, while navigating the open sea, that is, with no chance to bring it to a dry dock: 'We are like sailors who have to rebuild their

the Kantian design, means the abandonment of an environment devoid of ordering collective authorities and rules of justice. This holds true for the global setting as well. Given the sui-genericity of the extra- or inter-state domain, changes and institution-building endeavors are relevant to what can be perceived as resembling the emergence of the 'public'. Their pull toward multilateralism, regime creation, basic justice, judicial confrontation, and specialized global administrative regulations, inevitably poses a challenge to unilateralism and arbitrariness. Not so much because it makes them impossible but, on the contrary, because it makes them *conceivable*. These transformations can function therefore as epistemic institutions *vis-à-vis* arbitrariness and unilateralism which are difficult to conceive of in the absence of an institutional frame which 'creates' the category (that is, the yardstick against which something turns to be arbitrary or unilateral). Although arbitrariness and one-sidedness are usually thought to be features of a lawless state, in this case they are unimaginable. In a state-of-nature-like environment, as Kant would have had it, they cannot even emerge, precisely because they do not rest on some structure of naked power nor on an understanding of the world where no common frames for ordered coexistence is established.

The representations of the post-state environment from 'governance' as well as 'legal' perspectives, are based squarely on multilateral phenomena that constitute the currency of the constructive endeavor of an international 'public'. The growing and unstoppable proliferation of specific arrangements and transnational networks of common action, the formation of global legal regimes, can be seen as a rule-making and rule-driven phenomenon. Consideration of the features of the global space reveals the frames and grids of an emergent public which are expected to result from a law-centred process, that is from the *institutive* capacity of law (recalling a public-through-law scheme), and *not* from the construction of a global *state* or from the amplification of state-dependent/-derivative structures.

An *institutional* enterprise avails itself of rules. As MacCormick has shown in his theory of law, it includes institutive or identity defining norms, consequential and terminative rules.[43] Having focused on the whole of an 'institution', the question of temporal priority between practices and rules could be seen as a rather abstract one. But even MacCormick started by considering Searle's well-known distinction between regulative and constitutive rules where 'regulative rules regulate antecedently or independently existing forms of behaviour', and constitutive rules 'do not merely regulate, they create or define new forms of behaviour'.[44]

This distinction can help us understand certain features that converge in the idiosyncratic reality of the global, neither a 'state of nature' nor a modern state

---

ship on the open sea, without ever being able to dismantle it in dry dock and reconstruct it from the best components' (Otto Neurath, 'Protokollsätze', *Erkenntnis* (1932–3), reproduced as 'Protocol Statements', in Otto Neurath, *Philosophical Papers 1913–1946*, trans. R. S. Cohen and M. Neurath (eds) (Dordrecht: Reidel, 1983) 92).

[43] N. MacCormick, 'Law as Institutional Fact', in N. MacCormick and O. Weinberger, *An Institutional Theory of Law* (Dordrecht: Kluwer, 1986) 52–53.

[44] J. Searle, *Speech Acts* (Cambridge: Cambridge University Press, 1969) 33–34.

society, and beyond either's time and place.[45] 'Spontaneous' practices[46] have been identified as characteristic of the transnational setting. Nonetheless, they have been flanked increasingly by the *construction* of supranational regimes, whether state, private, or hybrid: a kind of Promethean endeavor rather than the effects of spill-over between domains or the unintended outcome of a *lex-mercatoria*.[47] Most of the cycle of spontaneous-institutionalized governance and government processes place interlocutors in a network of a mixed nature.[48] Those processes entail degrees of complexity, depending on their distance from and between the two extreme poles of a built-in practice of transnational law and the 'creation' of transnational, international, or supranational *regimes* (often centered upon organizations, regulatory and administrative bodies, and judicial entities). The *institutionalization* of domains of governance is increasing.[49] This is relevant to the emergence of a global dimension of public law, as different from the proliferation of transnational arrangements on the basis of inherently private intercourses (in the sense that Bentham defined agreement between 'monades', see Section 2).

As with MacCormick's depiction of institutional facts, such an institutionalization helps us make sense of the *legal* dimension as an effort to both overcome a 'provisional state', and to frame in normative terms the standards of the practices. In this way, the combined contribution of two different narratives can be discerned; one starts from the experience of common, private, spontaneous practices that slowly evolve as a precondition for the emergence of ad hoc rules of law, the other looks at the constitution of some institutional sets of rules—or a regime—as the precondition for newly forged practices where law grounds the 'broadening' of perspectives beyond individual views,[50] that is, *institutes* the dimension of the 'public'.

The second strand is emphasized here in order to shed light on the normative dimension of institution and regime building which has coordinating, multilaterally oriented functions and does not simply record or reflect, say, the

---

[45] See the elaboration on this point by N. Walker, 'Out of Place and Out of Time: Law's Fading Co-ordinates' (2010) 14 Edinburgh Law Review 13.

[46] Cf the contributions of Gunther Teubner, among which, 'Global Private Regimes: Neo-spontaneous Law and Dual Constitution of Autonomous Sectors?' in K. Ladeur (ed.), *Public Governance in an Age of Globalisation* (Aldershot: Ashgate, 2004); G. Teubner, 'Constitutionalising Polycontexturality', 2010, available at <http://www.jura.uni-frankfurt.de/1_Personal/em_profs/teubner/dokumente/ConstitutionalisingPolycontexturality_eng.pdfin>.

[47] The two aspects are interwoven, whether concurring or competing. Practices of economic actors, NGOs, social movements, epistemic communities of lawyers, judges, arbitrators, field experts, play a constructive and domain defining role, while being essential components of whatever processes in the global scenarios.

[48] See, eg Chapter 10.

[49] A good example is in the regional ambit of the European Union: the formalization in the Lisbon Treaty of the Open Method of Coordination, and the now long-standing governance structures like comitology and agencies.

[50] *En passant*, one can see the mirroring of two essential narratives of law, the first is a Humean narrative, the second is the function of law in Bentham's terms. Among others, on this distinction, as related to the two thinkers, G. Postema, 'Bentham on the Public character of Law' (see note 16) at 58.

experienced common practices of self-referential competitors in the market place.[51] But all these transformations also build *on the constitutive strength of legality* which creates the possibility of a *global public law* based on the fact that some jurisgenerative capacity is exercised with ordering consequences.

Of course, the global setting is organizing its transformations and emergence by a qualitative shift beyond state-focused narratives. Not all of this endeavor, then, resembles the features of the institutional structures of the state. Furthermore, their significance is based on the fact that they spread specialized knowledge which enhances the need for administrative decision-making through functional fields and sectors both within and beyond the state. Thus, 'the rise of information and of knowledge as the main resource and frame of reference for decision-making' defines functional borders, that is, generates multilayered relationships both within and beyond the state at the transnational level.[52] Accordingly, with respect to the social dimensions of the practices, collective interactions are expected to develop which not only are independent of national borders and established states, but cross-cut demos-like allegiance in transnational forms.[53] This could be viewed as a 'deliberative representative' space,[54] and at least in respect of the European Union, might afford deliberative experimental forms.[55] On this view, the *functional* division is called upon to replace *territorial* separation.[56] But, especially insofar as *global* regimes are concerned, it is clear that the inherent political quality, whether through the full control of states, or the will of the 'governed' or 'affected', disappears quickly.[57] They proceed on politically ambiguous formations, self-disseminating through specialization and clusters, they do not appeal to the precondition of democracy, and work by sidelining for the sake of viability the resilience of less treatable questions (like traditional democratic participation, self-legislative, or democratic devices). I shall return later to this essential scarcity of political fabric. However, it is precisely this nature of global governance which consequentially prompted concerns relating to accountability and responsiveness and the search for legal devices for transparency, control, revision, the

---

[51] Again, what Bentham would have equated with the customary interaction among 'monades', one that, though, in his view was still too far from resembling the service of law (J. Bentham, *Of Laws In General*, see note 15).

[52] K.-H. Ladeur, *The Emergence of Global Administrative Law and Transnational Regulation*, IILJ Working Paper 2011/1.

[53] They gather stakeholders, interested groups, public or private regulators, experts, judges, arbitrators, economic actors, as much as fluid social movements, NGOs, advocates, or pressure groups. On their role in constructing the global space and stabilizing normative expectations, see Robert Kehoane, *Social Norms and Agency in Global Politics*, Straus Institute WP, 07/2010.

[54] J. S. Dryzek and S. Niemeyer, 'Discursive Representation' (2008) 102(4) American Political Science Review 481.

[55] C. F. Sabel and J. Zeitlin (eds), *Experimentalist Governance in the European Union; Towards a New Architecture* (Oxford: Oxford University Press, 2010).

[56] Although, in the specific domain of the EU, it is more properly seen as a *hybrid* system, where governmental—or governing—and governance structures play complementary roles. P. Kjaer, *Between Governing and Governance* (Oxford: Hart, 2010).

[57] Among others, full acknowledgement of this in N. Krisch, *Beyond Constitutionalism: The Pluralist Structure of Postnational Law* (Oxford, Oxford University Press, 2010).

protection of affected interests, and procedural controls on decision-making which are evidenced in the rise of a 'global administrative law'.[58]

These are attempts at crossing the line between disorder and order, between private or unilateral and 'public', multilateral. The World Trade Organisation, the European Union, the United Nation Convention for the Law of the Sea, the European Convention on Human Rights, the Codex Alimentarius Commission, the International Standard Organization (and the impressive number of equivalent entities of diverse nature and status) all draw our attention away from the traditional realist view of international political relations and beyond the frame of the restricted 'public' of states.

From this perspective then, it cannot suffice to assume that global governance should consider international public authority as 'any authority exercised on the basis of a competence instituted by a common international act of public authorities, mostly states, to further a goal which they define, and are authorized to define, as a public interest'.[59] This definition entails the traditional view of the public, tracing it back to sources otherwise defined as, in themselves and already, 'public' in nature, like states, provided that they forge common interests. The generation of public at the global level is therefore still seen as a *derivative* and state-centred process.

However, the proliferation of global regimes gaining substantive governmental autonomy detached from the actual persistence of states' will and the frequent lack of state involvement in their activities, make such a contention (that the validity of their activities and norm-production is based on the state as the only recognized 'public') rather artificial. Transnational networking, the incremental attempt to build bridging meta-rules or principles of legality within and between organizations[60] show that theoretical work on global governance is more reliant on the promise of the *form of law*, than on the *form of state* as the controlling factor. In other words, the issue might well be reversed, so that instead of appealing to the public as a precondition of legality, *it is the claim to legality that appears to support the potential generation of the public.*

This explains how the global administrative *law* project relates to global governance. However, its theoretical underpinning is worth recalling. Benedict Kingsbury characterizes global regimes as *legal* regulators, and assumes that their

---

[58] Among the many works, see its application at WTO, in R. Stewart and M. Ratton Sanchez Badin, 'The World Trade Organization and Global Administrative Law' in Christian Joerges and Ernst-Ulrich Petersmann (eds), *Constitutionalism, multilevel trade governance and social regulation* (Oxford: Hart, forthcoming).

[59] Armin von Bogdandy, Philipp Dann, and Matthias Goldmann, *Developing the Publicness of Public International Law: Towards a Legal Framework for Global Governance Activities*, IILJ Colloquium Working Papers, 2009, 11. The authors are well aware of the need to integrate such a starting point, though, and envisage an eclectic approach, one that will have to combine 'constitutional, administrative and international institutional law approaches to global governance (and, thus, international institutions)' since they all 'share the aim of understanding, framing and taming the exercise of international public authority in the post-national constellation', 24–25.

[60] See G. Della Cananea, *Al di là dei confini statuali: Principi generali del diritto pubblico globale* (Bologna: Il Mulino, 2010) and S. Cassese, *Il diritto globale* (Torino: Einaudi, 2009) or S. Cassese, *The Globalization of Law*, 2006, at <http://www.iilj.org/GAL/documents/CasseseGlobalPaper.pdf>.

norms can be considered as law, provided that they satisfy some basic requisites as *criteria of legality;* first, social sources ('liberalized' since they embrace states or non-states entities as jurisgenerative); second, legality of rule production is made to depend as well on further requirements of 'publicness' (that is, rationality, proportionality, the rule of law, the principle of legality, and basic human rights deference).[61] This latter requirement which is externally imposed, curbs the self-legitimating drive of global regimes, borrowing from the way the public is conceptually envisaged in state-related contexts, domestic or international. Here the connection between legality and publicness is drawn by making legality depend on the requirements of publicness.

In the light of all this, I would submit that this dependence of legality *on* publicness can be turned on its head. The proposed requisites of publicness are in fact extrapolated from other existing contexts of *legality*. Indeed, its individual components, when seen as a whole, that is, requirements of publicness, *depend on law.* They cannot form a complex that stands as a whole anywhere else but inside (and through) law itself, indeed they belong to the domain of law. And in truth, they are best seen (*à la* Kant) as part of the construction of the 'right' through law, they are part of the process of the creation of the *public through law.* It is thus clearly our *commitment to a vision of legality* that grounds the institution of the public at the global level, not vice-versa (notwithstanding the attempt to depict some self-standing idea of 'publicness' as subsequently transposed into a criterion and premise for shaping our notion of legality).

5. PUBLIC DECOUPLED AND THE TWO TIERS
OF MULTILEVEL LEGALITIES

Whereas the legal perspective of the global public presents a particular challenge, the construction of the public in the widest environment cannot get rid of the fact that unlike the domestic setting, the 'global' level of legality, if any, always operates by impinging upon other legalities, primarily those of states, thereby requiring their cooperation, and that of political, judicial, and administrative entities. The European Union is a case in point, which 'does not do, it causes others to do'.[62]

If one takes this perspective, the very authority of global legality cannot stand alone and the consequential construction of the corresponding 'public' can only depend on the interaction and interface between *legalities,* between different legal orders. The *public through law* perspective in this context is *interfacial* and *incomplete* until such interaction takes place. If there is a global administrative law, for example, it does not exist by itself. As I shall explain soon, the components of other legalities are necessary to close the circle. This should not be confused with a lack of external binding force, the essence of 'real' law. Rather, this illustrates

---

[61] Such requisites of publicness are thus made part of the rules of recognition (through a kind of inclusive positivism). See B. Kingsbury, 'The Concept of "Law" in Global Administrative Law' (2009) 20(1) European Journal of International Law 23, at 25.

[62] See the point in S. Cassese, *Democrazia e Unione Europea,* 2002, 11 at <http://www.storiacostituzionale.it/doc/Cassese.pdf> (last visited May 2011).

the *composite nature of global legality*, one that must be conceived as in need of 'completion'.

Even considering the network of global regimes under the requirements of an updated concept of law such as the one suggested by the project of global administrative law, such a legality will always constitute an *other* from the perspective of existing state or regional legal orders, and given its structure (the shifts of power from state to global regulatory substantively autonomous govern-ance) it also does not fit into the category of international law, *stricto sensu*. Even if taken as a legality in and of itself, global regulatory law cannot determine the conditions of validity of *other* legal orders.[63] This is notwithstanding their close relationship and the operation of global regulatory law penetrating and affecting objects, fields, practices, peoples, and individuals in both local and global spaces.

Accordingly, there is a double dimension to global regulatory law. First of all, global legality, in the sense of regimes in global administrative law, where discrete rules of recognition are in progress, and further common principles—bridges—are slowly being devised and practised, firstly through judicial acts.[64] From this standpoint, the plurality of multilevel institutions and legal orders has to fall within its scope and authority (as its implementation-effectiveness chain). Contrary to this, in the second dimension, the same competing reality of the different legal orders emerges with a different sense: here they stand *per se,* are autonomous and independent, according to their own criteria of recognition. Overlooking this dual dimensionality can undermine attempts to develop global law, whether constitutionalist or administrative.[65]

The two dimensions intersect and both make prescriptive claims with respect to issues of interpretation, compliance, and implementation, or in the event of litigation, with respect to arbitration, adjudication, and the like. From the standpoint of global legality this intersection provides, however, the opportunity to 'complete' the 'composite' of the legal public.

Indeed, such *relations* take place between a *deracinated* global law and legal orders bearing different degrees of political and social embeddedness. The global regime's legality is of course a legal-technical artifice aimed at coping with complexity, and its formal isolation from the life of a real affected 'public' in real polities results in its *operational* dependence upon them. Its legality is always to be *completed*. The global legality level, therefore, can be seen at the same time as still *unsaturated*.[66]

---

[63] More at length in my *The Rule of Law in Global Governance: Its construction, function and import,* see note 4.

[64] S. Cassese, *I Tribunali di Babele* (Roma: Donzelli, 2009) and Brown, *A Common law of International adjudication* (Oxford: Oxford University Press, 2007).

[65] Theoretical constructions revolve mainly around one of the two dimensions: in the first dimension, either by drawing the architectures of full global primacy through legal schemes (substantive or formal), or by attenuating it in light of enhancing internal contestation or constitutional pluralism; in the second dimension, by supporting the discrete nature of legal orders, pluralism, and socio-political irreplaceable embeddedness.

[66] I used this notion earlier, in my 'Politics and Rights: The Future of the EU from a European Perspective' (2005) 18(3) Ratio Juris 400.

The second aspect of global legality's incompleteness is that of the political, one that regards the sources, 'players' or actors, means, and addressees which provide the 'flesh' in the domain of practice, and whose involvement draws attention to political concerns. As such, the quest for the *political* component of public law, one that can only look at those factors and actors, will be unsuccessful without them.

On this basis, the further 'regulative' aspects, the massive amount of regulatory norms for, say, standard-setting, trade liberalization, or with higher moral impact, human rights, environmental protection, global security, and climate financing, are too detached from constituencies, addressees, and affected life-worlds, insofar as they cannot even claim a 'located' space.[67] Notwithstanding their normative pretensions, they must, ironically, rely on the independent existence of real *polities* and penetrate them despite being distant from their social and political allegiances.

It is here that the global legal public emerges as an arrangement which needs to be completed; that is, one that can only work by way of being joined by sub-global legalities whose veils it pierces. Thus, the globally suspended *status quo* is the expression of an unsaturated legality, decoupled from the political components of the public *and at the same time* of the two-step profile of legality. The *public through law* in the global setting, therefore, remains 'suspended' with respect to its completion, until it is reconnected to the affected and/or governed, whether through 'deliberative' governance structures or through mediation with state law, or through the interplay between functional–territorial, horizontal–vertical, governance–governments hybrids.

In this setting, the Kantian imperative of public law works as a *transcendental scheme as well as* a criterion of coexistence, which is *necessary* but made *to be 'applied'*, in the sense of Kantian (intellectual) formal categories. The 'bootstrapping' of legality, beyond the state environment, points to a provisional scheme of 'publicness', whose self-driven logic lacks its coupling with the *political* generators of law. It needs to be filled by social, and therefore ethical and political, processes. It only creates conditions of justice among diverse 'goals', the ideas of the good, elaborated within the domains of discrete legalities (including the fabric of self referential goal-functional regimes), rationalities that inevitably, even if not always visibly, interfere with each other. Otherwise, it remains an idea of order with no corresponding social fabric, an abstract hypothesis of rule. In other words, it would still be an 'empty' public.

We therefore return to the question concerning the *dual* constitution of the public, its legal and political nature and how to redefine it in the context of plural legalities, how to mend the detachment of the legal and the political that are, as things stand, located on different planes of order.

Let us summarize the argument. In the Kantian scheme of the public, the birth of law is connected to its preoccupation with interference in the pursuit of liberty and independence. Coordination is clearly an important aspect, but behind it there is also a *moral* justificatory rationale for being under the law, for its very

---

[67] Another example for this criticism: Ming-Sung Kuo, 'The Concept of "Law" in Global Administrative Law: A Reply to Benedict Kingsbury' (2009) 20(4) European Journal of International Law 997.

existence[68] (that is, justice). The positivity of law is required, it is imperative to the constitution of the public.

The (global) public-through-law model does not include the 'political right', the 'counterpart' to which it is coupled in the domain of the modern state. But given the ensuing interweaving legalities, a double result should be pursued. First, the *activation of the justice-related function of the public through law*, as governing fairness and independence in the relations among mutually recognized orders; secondly, at the same time the incremental and discrete *re-coupling of that legal layer with the political generators* of the public as the latter are contributed by sub-global legalities, socially and politically embedded, which interact with the supra-state norm producers. The result is consistent with the notion of the global public through law, as described above; that is, as a prearranged *unsaturated* legality constantly tending towards its completion.

6. AN OVERVIEW OF THE PROBLEM OF 'EXTERNAL JURIDIFICATION'

The decoupling of the legal and political in the public is caused by the absence or the evaporation at the global level of the *social* fabric which hosts the public in a polity. Our concern *vis-à-vis* deracinated global regulatory law stems from its being the transmission belt of specialized regimes' imperatives of efficiency, irrespective of the needs and claims of societal orders that they affect. Such 'external' imperatives are capable of disturbing domestic equilibrium, overriding social concerns, replacing interpretations of rights, overwriting basic needs and the 'internal' meanings of regulated polities. Thus, the issue can be labelled as the phenomenon of the 'external juridification'.

The reconstitution of the public in global intercourses should reflect the search for a *balanced* relation between different levels of order. This has to be our concern as regards global regulatory law, and has emerged recurrently in many judicial cases. The EU itself has offered a number of examples to this regard.[69] In

---

[68] Postema (above note 16) considers coordination essential part of Bentham's law-as-public, defends it from the charge of being unrelated to matters of principle, and eventually recalls that law does not simply fix disagreements in a once and for all move, but plays its role in allowing for further argument, improvements, and change (what Bentham was not ready to accept).

[69] Cases like *Volkswagen, Laval, Viking, and Rüffert* (ECJ, decision of 23 October 2007: Case C-112/05 *Commission v Federal Republic of Germany* [2007] ECR I-08995; Case C-341/05, *Laval un Partneri Ltd v Svenska Byggnadsarbetareförbundet and Others* [2007] ECR I-11767; Case C-438/05 *International Transport Workers' Federation and Finnish Seamen's Union v Viking Line ABP and OÜ Viking Line Eesti* [2007] ECR I-10779; Case C-346/06, *Dirk Rüffert v Land Niedersachsen* [2008] ECR I-1989) have provoked questions regarding the acceptability—from both the EU and the Member States points of view—of a (pan-European) homogeneous socio-economic model replacing diversity in internal national assets and settings, eg by undermining an idiosyncratic and deeply cherished 'social market' capitalism model, as in *Volkswagen*, or redefining the content, exercise and scope of a fundamental right (as the right to strike, that in *Viking*, resulted in a conflict with Member States' constitutional traditions). In general, see C. Joerges and F. Rodl, *Social Market Economy as Europe's Social Model?*, EUI WP Law 2004/08. On *Volkswagen*, see eg, P. Zumbansen, D. Saam, 'The ECJ, Volkswagen and European Corporate Law: Reshaping the European Varieties of Capitalism', (2007) 8(11) German Law Journal 1028.

this connection, that is, the logic of interaction between orders, for example, Fritz Scharpf maintained that the straightforward supremacy of European law, as developed by the European Court of Justice (ECJ), has had 'the effect of transforming the hierarchical relation between European and national law into a hierarchical relation between liberal and republican constitutional principles'.[70] But beyond the internal tensions within the institutional domain of the European Union, other examples include the ways through which the ECtHR undertakes the protection of the rights enshrined in the Convention (which triggers possible conflicts *vis-à-vis* domestic order; for example, the understanding of freedom from religion in cases like that of the Crucifix, *Lautsi*, first decision 2009.)[71] Conversely, as an instance of the friction between supranational regulators *inter se*, one can think of the 'filtering' attitude taken by the ECJ through the EU denial of the direct effect of WTO rules;[72] or the refusal to subject its own primary norms to global security imperatives contained in Security Council resolutions.[73]

There is a theoretical pattern for approaching the confrontation between mutually external normativities and the possible imbalance between them. It was provided through the debate (in the 1980s) on the issue of the external *juridification* of 'authentic' social fabric at the state level. Jürgen Habermas addressed the shortcomings of welfare interventionist policies which introduced new conditions for legalized opportunities and entitlements into previously free domains of social life. The pattern thus relates to the internal social meanings of a polity and social fabric which are endangered by the imperatives of external orders.[74] This is precisely what is at stake when global regimes interfere with the internal 'meanings' embedded in the life of settled polities, by rewriting rights or subverting internal choices with regard, for instance, to education or labour.[75]

---

[70] F. Scharpf, 'Legitimacy in the Multi-level European Politiy', in P. Dobner and M. Loughlin (eds), *The Twilight of Constitutionalism?* (Oxford: Oxford University Press, 2010), 112. Scharpf refers to a problem of legitimacy: 'the liberal undermining' of 'republican legitimacy', 111. For a series of authors, such legitimacy in turn rests on a political, republican, conception of the constitution, as lastly recalled by M. Loughlin, 'What is constitutionalisation?', 47–69, and see also D. Grimm, 'The Achievement of Constitutionalism and its prospects in a changed world', 3–22.

[71] *Lautsi v Italy*, no. 30814/06 (Section 2) (fr)—(3.11.09).

[72] Claudio Dordi (ed), *The absence of direct effect of WTO in the EC and in other countries* (Turin: Giappichelli, 2010).

[73] Such as in the *Kadi* case. ECJ, 3 September 2008, Joined Cases C-402/05 P and C-415/05 P *Yassin Abdullah Kadi and Al Barakaat International Foundation v Council of the European Union and Commission of the European Communities* [2008] ECR I-6351. Of course, it is not in question the prima facie claim to primacy that regional or global rule-producers detain due to their incomparably (eg beyond states' particularism) comprehensive standpoints. But, it is questioned whether such primacy in general can become unconditional and content-independent.

[74] Jürgen Habermas, 'Law as Medium and Law as Institution' [trans. from *Theorie des kommunicativen Handelns* (Frankfurt: Suhrkamp, 1981) bd. II, 522–47 and *The Theory of Communicative Action* (Beacon Press, 1985)], in *Dilemmas of Law in the Welfare State*, Gunther Teubner (ed.) (Berlin: Walter de Gruyter, 1986) 209–11. As Habermas noted, law had to enter deeply in the detailed daily, personal, and social sphere once left outside of legal control, in order to accompany an assisted individual life from birth to death, 203–20.

[75] Tellingly, that was to raise legitimacy problems with reference to those 'autonomous' relations that for Habermas naturally avail themselves of communicative interactions (like in the realms of school law, social security, cultural reproduction, fields of moral sensitivity which extend to legal areas, such as criminal law, constitutional law, bioethical concerns), spheres that are in need of consensus-based law,

When referring to the project of creating a balanced global public, one could echo the concern voiced by Habermas in relation to the interventionist policies of the state in the 1980s. As Habermas argued, the

> [P]oint is to protect areas of life that are functionally dependent on social integration through values, norms and consensus formation, and to protect them from falling prey to the system imperatives of economic and administrative subsystems that grow with dynamics of their own. And finally to defend them from becoming converted, through the steering medium of the law, to a principle of socialization which is for them dysfunctional.[76]

In other words, what he called the risk of 'colonization' of the 'life world' which also occurs when global regimes make particular demands irrespective of the claims and needs of social actors, addressees, and constituencies that populate non-global levels of order.[77]

Outside the state domain, this *caveat* translates into the quest for an interactive equilibrium between the demands of legal orders, especially when external imperatives affect existing socially constituted domains. This is *a fortiori* the case in respect of areas of law that are particularly sensitive and deeply embedded in the idiosyncratic character, or identity, of the people.

It should not be a surprise, therefore, that it is precisely this reasoning which emerged in a rather different context, with regard to the EU, in the German Constitutional Court's 'Urteil' on the Lisbon Treaty. It reaffirms that EU competences should be exercised with caution, 'particularly in central political areas of the space of personal development and the shaping of living conditions by social policy. In these areas, it is particularly necessary to draw the limit where the co-ordination of cross-border situations is factually required'.[78] Accordingly, the Court stated that such sensitive areas include 'substantive and formal criminal law', fiscal decisions (especially those related to 'social policy considerations'), the 'shaping of living conditions in a social state', and all those 'decisions of particular cultural importance, for example on family law, the school and education system and on dealing with religious communities'.[79]

As such, top-down juridification and the resistance of states to global coordination, are in a constant search of equilibrium. The construction of the 'public' in

---

supported by *substantive* (it is not merely procedural) legitimacy. What was considered *systemic* integration—through policies obeying functional imperatives and implementing regulatory measures—jeopardizes the realms of the life world, by reinterpreting their relations through the lens of external rationalities. But, only the life world retains a 'reservoir' of meaning. Habermas, 'Law as Medium and Law as Institution', 206.

[76] Habermas, 'Law as Medium and Law as Institution', 220.

[77] According to Habermas the question whether an external legal imperative offers a 'guarantee' or a 'withdrawal' of freedom, can only be responded to 'from the viewpoint of the lifeworld', Habermas, 'Law as Medium and Law as Institution', 214.

[78] BVerfG, 2 BvE 2/08 vom 30.6.2009, Absatz-Nr. (1—421), <http://www.bverfg.de/entscheidungen/es20090630_2bve000208en.html>, see §§ 251–52, and ff.

[79] BVerfG, 2 BvE 2/08 vom 30.6.2009, Absatz-Nr. (1—421), <http://www.bverfg.de/entscheidungen/es20090630_2bve000208en.html>, see §§ 251–52, and ff.

the global sphere will depend on this latter aspect for the dual nature of the public to be reassembled.

7. CONCLUSION

Global law(s) attempts to weave the *public (only) through law,* and establish conditions of convergence and coordination. Nonetheless, the value of the appeal to law deserves recognition in so far as it can provide a forum for balancing the relations between legalities, and disqualify unjustified unilateral behaviour or *arbitrary* resistance.[80]

The global scenario, however, has to recompose the *duality* of the public and rescue its political salience. The lesson which emerges from the *public through law* model does not relate to the self-sufficiency of disembodied law, but to the design of otherwise absent guarantees. Its contribution is its appeal to framing conditions of fair coexistence. At the same time, it denounces its ever-incomplete nature that can only be completed in the substantive interplay with normative orders which bear constitutional 'thickness' and political voice.

The models for the re-coupling of the public in law are varied, but they must make it possible to confront, communicate, and justify the mutual claims of different legal orders. Their viability depends also on the weaving of relational patterns of confrontation among orders, many of which have been framed by judicial bodies, constitutional courts, or the ECJ, the ECtHR, and the like.[81] Analysing the implementation of rights in the ECHR, Judge Lech Garlicki has characterized this communication among courts, both horizontally and vertically, as a 'triangle of co-operation', to be cherished: 'there is always a potential for collisions, and then the triangle of co-operation may degenerate into a "Bermuda triangle" in which individual rights and liberties might simply disappear'.[82]

The rationale of diverse patterns of dialogue or confrontation can be explained as involving a double move: on the one hand they work, in fact, in the interface of

---

[80] Even the global administrative law project of submitting rule-makers' activities to procedural principles, transparency, ability to be revised, and deference to basic human rights, can advance both the pursuit of fairness and mutual recognition. But, for global administrative law the focus is primarily on shaping the global administrative law *in itself,* and forging the general principles that global regimes should follow in discharging their tasks. The reconstitution of the *dual public* concerns also a different plane, though, regarding the relations between regimes, and between global law and different levels of (legal) orders.

[81] In the variety of such methodologies, relevant examples, largely emphasized in European Union law scholarship, were offered by the Italian Constitutional Court 'counter-limits' doctrine or by the 'Solange' doctrine of the German Constitutional court. Others are found in the case law of the ECtHR, like the criteria of *equivalent protection,* or the *margin of appreciation.* As to the state of the art on the relations among jurisdictions, and the emerged patterns, Y. Shany, *Regulating Jurisdictional Interactions between National and International Courts* (Oxford: Oxford University Press, 2007).

[82] Lech Garlicki, 'Co-operation of courts: The role of supranational jurisdictions in Europe' (2008) 6 International Journal of Constitutional Law 512. However, examples of ongoing refinements and dialogued assessments also come from the practice of the ECtHR, for instance, in the instructive saga of Polish rent-control cases concerning property rights under rent-control legislation, that involved an ongoing process of moves and dialogues among the polish Constitutional Court, the ECtHR, and the Parliament; see Garlicki, 'Co-operation of courts', 514 ff.

the re-coupling of the legal and sociopolitical generators of the public, because they address the balance between the politically authorized, 'lower', discrete, legal orders and the more detached global law. On the other hand, they can only do so abiding by legal requirements in a wider 'public' arena, where legal reasons are invoked that purport to reach beyond the confines of each particular legal order. This presupposes the transcendental idea of, and a resort to, Kantian universals of coexistence. Thus, assuming that justice *between legalities* should matter is a necessary and promising perspective.

This can only happen, however, if the rule of law is seen as a common, relational, not merely parochial or internal, value.[83] The possibility of a global legal public depends on the fairness and co-operation, and not the elimination, of diverse legalities. Given the complex nature of the contemporary world, the challenge of re-coupling the 'public' is crucial and it can only be faced by starting with the basic duty of abandoning the kind of (ideally 'natural') state where injustice is still *not objectionable*.

---

[83] On this point, see my 'The Rule of Law beyond the State: Promises, Failures, Theory' (2009) 7(3) International Journal of Constitutional Law 2009, 442.

Index*

* Compiled by Alex Latham.